TRIUMPH OF THE SOUTH

Modern Economic and Social History Series

General Editor: Derek H. Aldcroft

Titles in this series include:

Governance, Growth and Global Leadership
The Role of the State in Technological Progress, 1750–2000
Espen Moe

Rethinking Nineteenth-Century Liberalism
Richard Cobden Bicentenary Essays
Edited by Anthony Howe and Simon Morgan

Alfred Herbert Ltd and the British Machine Tool Industry, 1887-1983
Roger Lloyd-Jones and M.J. Lewis

Taste, Trade and Technology
The Development of the International Meat Industry since 1840
Richard Perren

The Popularization of Malthus in Early Nineteenth-Century England
Martineau, Cobbett and the Pauper Press
James P. Huzel

Europe's Third World
The European Periphery in the Interwar Years
Derek H. Aldcroft

Industrial Reorganization and Government Policy in Interwar Britain
Julian Greaves

The Hidden Cost of Economic Development
The Biological Standard of Living in Antebellum Pennsylvania
Timothy Cuff

Demons of Domesticity
Women and the English Gas Industry, 1889–1939
Anne Clendinning

Britain and the Economic Problem of the Cold War
The Political Economy and the Economic Impact of the British Defence Effort, 1945-1955
Till Geiger

Triumph of the South

A Regional Economic History of Early Twentieth Century Britain

PETER SCOTT
University of Reading, UK

Routledge
Taylor & Francis Group
LONDON AND NEW YORK

First published 2007 by Ashgate Publishing

Reissued 2018 by Routledge
2 Park Square, Milton Park, Abingdon, Oxon OX14 4RN
605 Third Avenue, New York, NY 10017

First issued in paperback 2021

Routledge is an imprint of the Taylor & Francis Group, an informa business

A Library of Congress record exists under LC control number: 2006005223

ISBN 13: 978-0-815-39862-2 (hbk)
ISBN 13: 978-1-351-14404-9 (ebk)
ISBN 13: 978-1-138-35851-5 (pbk)

DOI: 10.4324/9781351144049

Contents

List of tables and figures

Tables

Figures

Modern Economic and Social History Series
General editor's preface

Economic and social history has been a flourishing subject of scholarly study during recent decades. Not only has the volume of literature increased enormously but the range of interest in time, space and subject matter has broadened considerably so that today there are many sub-branches of the subject which have developed considerable status in their own right.

One of the aims of this series is to encourage the publication of scholarly monographs on any aspect of modern economic and social history. The geographical coverage is world-wide and contributions on the non-British themes will be especially welcome. While emphasis will be placed on works embodying original research, it is also intended that the series should provide the opportunity to publish studies of a more general thematic nature which offer a reappraisal or critical analysis of major issues of debate.

Derek H. Aldcroft
University of Leicester

Preface

This study has a long lineage. My interest in regional development began during the latter stages of my Ph.D. research on the evolution of the British commercial property sector. My supervisor, Charles Feinstein, gave me tremendous encouragement and help regarding both the thesis and this 'post-doctoral' project. Following completion of my thesis I was fortunate to be able to commence research on interwar industrial development on a full-time basis for one year, thanks to a Junior Research Fellowship at Pembroke College, Oxford. The Department of Economics, University of Portsmouth, where I lectured in economic history from 1993–2001, were also generous in providing me with time and resources to continue my research and my current employer, the Department of Management, University of Reading, has been similarly generous. I would particularly like to thank my colleagues at the University of Reading's Centre for International Business History, for their continuing encouragement and support.

A Nuffield Foundation Social Science Small Grants Scheme award allowed Peter Walsh and myself to complete our research on new plant formation in interwar Britain, discussed in Chapters 6–8, while research funded by ESRC awards – on technical change in the British coal industry and on interwar suburban housing – also inform the analysis at various points. Particular thanks are due to the Arts and Humanities Research Council, for granting me a Research Leave Scheme Award to finally complete this book.

I am indebted to many people for help with this project over the years. Some of the themes were first explored in journal articles and I am grateful to the editors, people who read and commented on early drafts, and several anonymous referees, for their very valuable advice. Peter Walsh and Marian Bartlett provided me with important help regarding the analysis of interwar industrial development patterns. My research with Tim Rooth on early overseas multinationals in Britain also provided valuable information on the factors influencing interwar corporate location decisions. Fabian Panthaki, Peter Cook, and Jon Press provided generous help regarding technical aspects of preparing the text and illustrations.

Archival and other staff at the Age Concern Reminiscence Centre; Bank of England Archive; Bexley Local Studies and Archive Centre; British Library of Political and Economic Science Archives; Coventry Record Office; the Croydon and Watford reference libraries, Gunnersbury Park Museum Archives, John Laing plc; Letchworth Museum; London Metropolitan Archives; Modern Records Centre, Warwick; National Archives; National Provident Institution; Nuffield College Library; Percy Bilton plc; Slough Estates plc; Slough Museum; and Welwyn Garden City Library were also of immense help and assistance.

John Armstrong, Jeremy Burchardt, Tony Corley, Eric Jones, Tim Leunig, Peter Miskell, Lucy Newton, Andrew Popp, and Tim Rooth provided comments on individual draft chapters, which were of great help when it came to revising them.

Thanks are also due to Nick Crafts for giving me access to his estimates of pre-1914 regional GDP per capita prior to their publication and to Stephen Ward for allowing me to reproduce two maps. Particular thanks are due to my commissioning editor, Derek Aldcroft for his help, advice, and encouragement, and to the staff at Ashgate. Finally, but very far from least, I would like to thank my partner Fong, to whom this book is dedicated, for her support, patience, and love.

Chapter One

Introduction

A rapidly modernising, regionally-divided, nation

On the eve of the First World War Britain remained, essentially, a nineteenth-century society. Capital was highly concentrated in the hands of the very few, less than one per cent of the population commanding almost two thirds of its total wealth.[1] Similarly, it had one of the highest levels of income inequality among the industrialised nations with the result that – despite being among the world's wealthiest countries – average life expectancy at birth stood at only 53 years (several years below less affluent nations such as the Netherlands, Denmark, and Sweden).[2] A large proportion of the population were so malnourished as to be stunted in height, while most people lived in houses that lacked indoor plumbing and were often subject to severe dampness, chronic overcrowding, vermin infestation, or other unsanitary conditions.

Britain's provincial regions remained dominated by a narrow range of export-orientated staple industries – particularly coal, cotton and woollen textiles, iron and steel, and shipbuilding – often using production technologies and skills that had changed little in generations. For example, coal mining remained the largest national employer of male labour, with around one in twelve of Britain's population being directly dependent on it. Much of the industry's working practices would have been recognisable to miners two centuries earlier – most coal being manually cut from the face with a pick and then transported to the shaft via a combination of human and animal power.

London had a more broadly based economy, but one that produced a starker polarisation between rich and poor than was evident in the provincial industrial areas. It had perhaps the world's largest concentration of wealthy individuals, together with a relatively high proportion of middle-class salaried workers (on account of its highly developed service sector). Yet it was notorious for its large numbers of casual and 'sweated' workers, facing low and irregular earnings and regarded almost as a species apart by its more affluent inhabitants.[3] Poverty in rural Britain was even more widespread than in the towns and cities. Agricultural workers faced both very low wages and semi-feudal working and living conditions – often being reliant on

1 Roger Middleton, *Government Versus the Market. The Growth of the Public Sector, Economic Management and British Economic Performance, c. 1890–1979* (Cheltenham, 1996), p. 238.

2 See Table 3.2.

3 However, recent historical work has questioned contemporary perceptions that poverty in London was more severe than in other parts of Britain. Michael Ball and David Sunderland, *An Economic History of London 1800–1914* (London, 2001), pp. 94–117, reviews this literature.

their employer for both work and housing (from which they could be evicted at will). Landed families expecting their farm workers to attend their church in the same way that their household servants were obliged to, while in northern England, Scotland, and Wales, older rural children were still 'sold' to farmers by their parents at local hiring fairs, for six months or a year at a time.

When Britain went to war again in 1939, vestiges of this nineteenth century world were still evident. Yet the outstanding feature was the extent and rapidity of economic and social change during the intervening quarter century. In 'outer-Britain' – Scotland, Wales, and Northern England – change largely manifested itself in the negative. The old staple industries had experienced heavy falls in exports, output, and employment. Meanwhile the growth of new and expanding sectors had largely by-passed these regions, with the result that their industrial areas were characterised by high and long-term unemployment, widespread poverty (relative to the South), and high rates of out-migration.

By contrast the south and West Midlands had witnessed rapid economic growth and modernisation, largely based around industries and services aimed at the growing domestic market and activities that were 'new' – either in the products they supplied or the production methods used. Centres such as Slough, Dagenham, Welwyn, Letchworth, Luton, Watford, Coventry, Acton, and Willesden witnessed spectacular growth, drawing in substantial numbers of workers from as far as South Wales, Northumberland, and Clydeside. Meanwhile rising working and lower-middle class living standards were evident in trends such as the rapid growth of modern suburban housing; increased ownership of early consumer-durables such as radios, gramophones, and bicycles; and an expansion in commercialised leisure and tourism.

It was the pace of change in the South, as much as the relative stagnation and poverty of the north, which uneased contemporary observers. For example, while George Orwell famously highlighted the grim reality of conditions for many ordinary people in industrial Yorkshire and Lancashire in *The Road to Wigan Pier*, his novels *Keep the Aspidistra Flying* and, particularly, *Coming up for Air*, focus on what he saw as the soul-destroying effects of modernisation in and around London. In *Coming up for Air* George Bowling, a middle-aged insurance salesman, returns to his native Lower Binfield (loosely based on Orwell's boyhood world of Shiplake and Henley-on-Thames) in an attempt to escape the dullness of modern suburban life in the world of his childhood. When he arrives there, he finds it transformed beyond recognition, from a market town of around 2,000 people to a manufacturing centre of some 25,000. Modern council houses mark its outskirts, the chimneys of busy factories puncture its skyline, the main pub is transformed into a smart hotel with the fake heritage trappings of hunting prints, copper warming pans, and medieval décor, while his parents' seed-merchants business has been re-developed as a sham-antique tea shop. No one recognises his local surname, while his requests for directions receive replies in Lancashire and Cockney accents: 'I had that feeling of a kind of enemy invasion having happened behind my back.'[4]

J. B. Priestley's 1933 *English Journey* revealed a broadly similar picture. Priestley concluded that there were three Englands – the rural, heritage, tourist England, the

4 George Orwell, *Coming up for Air* (London, 2000), p. 192.

nineteenth century industrial England 'of coal, iron, steel, cotton, wool, railways', that had become 'a nasty mess', and a new, modern, third England:

> of arterial and by-pass roads, of filling stations and factories that look like exhibition buildings, of giant cinemas and dance-halls and cafes, bungalows with tiny garages, cocktail bars, Woolworths, motor-coaches, wireless, hiking, factory girls looking like actresses, grey hound racing and dirt tracks, swimming pools, and everything given away for cigarette coupons.[5]

Priestley expressed revulsion at the superficial, Americanised, nature of this new England, 'a trumpery imitation of something not very good even in the original'. Four years later Sir John Betjeman famously called down the bombers to annihilate Slough for very similar reasons, rejecting its bright new world of assembly factories, 'bogus Tudor bars', modern, affordable, labour-saving homes, and commercialised leisure.[6]

As Priestley noted, the dividing line between the new and old worlds was not purely a regional one. Throughout Britain those areas of the countryside that did not benefit from substantial tourist trade remained in a state of stagnation, low wages, poor housing, and semi-feudal relations, with migration to the towns and cities representing the only real hope of substantial material advancement for most farm-workers. Meanwhile a torrent of modernisation was crashing through high streets throughout Britain, uprooting local traders and depositing near-identical Woolworths, Marks & Spencer, British Home Stores, Burtons, Boots, Fifty Shilling Tailors, and the other mushrooming chains. Radio, cinema, and the new, mass-circulation magazines similarly promulgated 'Americanised' tastes throughout the nation.

Yet the regional divide between inner- and outer-Britain nevertheless marked a clearer and deeper fissure between areas of stagnation and growth than at any time since the industrial revolution. This was strikingly evident in both the economic statistics and in even the most casual observation by a traveller taking a train journey from London or Coventry, to, say, Bradford, Bolton, Newcastle, Swansea, or Glasgow. The more limited growth of modern suburban housing and relative absence of new factories as one entered the suburbs would provide the first indication that things were different. On arrival this would be starkly confirmed by the site of shiftless, gaunt, shabbily-dressed unemployed men and the general air of poverty and stagnation. Some centres which had been regarded as hives of industry in 1914 had been reduced to industrial scrapyards in the space of a few years. Many were never to truly recover.

An outline of this book

Unlike some previous studies of interwar regional development and policy, this book aims not only to focus on the problems of 'outer-Britain', but to explore

5 J. B. Priestley, *English Journey* (London, 1934), pp. 400–401.

6 John Betjeman, 'Slough', 21–3 in Earl of Birkenhead (ed.), *John Betjeman's Collected Poems* (London, 1958).

the cumulative processes of development which allowed the South East and West Midlands to emerge as the main centres for dynamic, modern, industry – a status that the South East at least has retained and consolidated over subsequent decades.

As Chapter Two demonstrates, medieval and early modern Britain was characterised by a strong division between a relatively prosperous metropolitan hub and a less developed northern and western periphery. This pattern was interrupted during the eighteenth century by industrialisation, shifting the focus of industry to what had hitherto been sparsely-inhabited low-wage rural areas of poor quality land. This era witnessed the development of the great provincial industrial cities and conurbations, based around strong local and regional specialisation in particular industries. Wages in the provincial industrial areas gradually caught up with those of London until by the late nineteenth century the capital had become only one of a number of high-wage areas that also included parts of northern England, Scotland, and Wales.

Yet, as Chapter Three discusses, from around the middle of the nineteenth century the provincial model of economic development, based around a narrow range of export-orientated staple industries, faced growing competition from other industrialising nations. Meanwhile provincial industry became increasingly 'crowded out' by Britain's growing comparative advantage as an exporter of London-based financial and business services and a recipient of huge and rapidly-growing incomes from overseas investments. These progressively squeezed out Britain's visible exports via 'Dutch disease' effects similar to those evident in modern oil-rich nations. London's mercantile activities, which initially had a complementary relationship with provincial export industries, assumed an increasingly competitive role, threatening to eventually transform Britain into a commercial and rentier state. Meanwhile incomes from services and foreign investment accrued primarily to individuals based in London and the South, rather than the industrial provinces.

Chapter Four discusses the impacts of the next major shock to Britain's long-term development, the First World War and its aftermath. Changes in the international and domestic economy are shown to have increased the relative importance of services and manufactures aimed at UK markets, as overseas investment earnings fell and exports of services and, especially, commodities, faced a much harsher international climate. Meanwhile war-time developments in infrastructure, production methods, and labour endowments gave Greater London and its hinterland a new competitive advantage as a centre for the types of standardised branded consumer goods, produced using assembly methods, that were to experience particularly rapid growth during the following years.

Chapter Five examines the impacts of the new conditions on the staple industries which dominated the industrial areas of northern Britain. Problems of over-capacity, reckless post-war speculative acquisitions, and technological 'lock-in' to labour-intensive craft-based production methods are shown to have been magnified by government macroeconomic policy. Under pressure from City interests, which identified the restoration of the gold standard at Sterling's pre-war parity as key to re-establishing the City's international hegemony, government embarked on a process of deflation to bring British prices into line with international ones. Yet despite this Sterling returned to gold in 1925 at what proved to be a substantial over-valuation. This hit the exports of the price-sensitive staple industries with particular severity, while defending Sterling's unrealistic parity entailed further deflationary measures that accentuated the deep depression of the staple industries and outer-Britain.

Patterns of new industrial development in 'outer-Britain' are then reviewed in Chapter Six. Most of Britain's provincial industrial regions are shown to have attracted relatively few new plants. Meanwhile their new factories were concentrated in traditional specialisations rather than those sectors that were experiencing rapid national growth. The most successful centres within these regions, such as the inner-areas of Leeds and Manchester, were those that were fortunate enough to have existing specialisations in one of the few traditional sectors that tied into expanding home demand (such as clothing and hosiery).

Chapters Seven to Eleven provide a detailed examination of the factors underpinning industrial prosperity and economic expansion in the South East and West Midlands. Chapters Seven and Eight examine patterns of new industrial development in these regions (together with new developments in service industries). Greater London is shown to have benefited from growth in three key areas. The first two: the growing concentration of domestically-orientated services in and around central London, and the expansion of craft-orientated consumer goods sectors such as clothing, furniture, and printing – concentrated in inner-London industrial districts, were essentially continuations of long-established trends. Conversely, the third involved a major break with pre-war patterns: the development of new industrial areas around outer-London, producing a diverse range of branded consumer goods using standardised, assembly, methods. These emerged mainly in the areas that had hosted war-time munitions factories and used similar production methods and labour to those which had been employed in the munitions plants. The West Midlands also experienced relative prosperity on the basis of a range of (mainly metal-using) assembly industries, though these partly represented the continuation of developments already evident before 1914 and by the 1930s even this region was losing ground to the South East – at least with regard to new plants.

Chapter Nine then examines the growth of new industrial centres within these regions and the reasons behind their success in attracting firms in a diverse range of branded and assembly consumer goods industries. Tight clustering of plants in particular centres is shown to have stimulated strong locational externalities (factors promoting firm growth) through input-output linkages and knowledge-spillovers between firms in different sectors sharing common product or process characteristics. Common labour requirements are identified as being of particular importance. These are further explored in Chapters Ten and Eleven, which show that these areas drew workers not primarily from the established manufacturing workforce but from a 'reserve army' of cheap, 'flexible' workers. These were initially recruited from local sources – such as women, juveniles, and agricultural labourers – but as the most rapidly-expanding areas outgrew local labour supplies long-distance migrants from Britain's depressed areas became of crucial importance to their continued expansion. Meanwhile government encouraged, and effectively subsidised, migration to these areas via its industrial transference programme. So great was the inflow of workers to the most rapidly expanding areas that they managed to combine huge increases in their working populations with wages that were below the national average for the sectors concerned.

Chapter Twelve then examines the interwar development of rural and coastal Britain. British agriculture is shown to have experienced a depression that mirrored that of the staple industries. Yet rural areas surrounding prosperous urban centres gained major benefits from the boom in suburban and ribbon development, while areas that combined scenic beauty with good longer-distance transport links to prosperous population centres were able to tap into the new market for rural leisure and tourism. Similarly, those coastal resorts that were accessible from the South and Midlands often ranked among Britain's most prosperous towns, as rising living standards and the growth of holidays with pay led to a major expansion in domestic tourism.

Britain's first steps towards the development of an explicit regional policy are reviewed in Chapter Thirteen. These are shown to have been important mainly as successful experiments, which set precedents for post-war policy, while the scale of activity was insufficient to make any real impact on unemployment in the depressed areas. Rearmament expenditure (which had a much greater impact on employment in these areas) is also reviewed.

Finally, Chapter Fourteen both draws together the analysis and briefly discusses the ways in which developments during the interwar period laid the foundations for Britain's pattern of regional growth during the mid- and late-twentieth century. It also restates one of the major arguments to emerge from the chronological chapters – that the problems of Britain's peripheral regions stemmed not only from their inherent economic weakness, but from the relative strength of London as an international financial and commercial centre. From the mid-nineteenth century a growing conflict emerged between the development path of Britain's commercial metropolitan hub and that of its provincial manufacturing periphery. Economic policy generally prioritised the interests of the former – a trade-off which usually proved correct when judged from the perspective of national economic growth, though less so in terms of the living standards, opportunities, and economic security of ordinary wage-earners.

Chapter Two

British regional development before the twentieth century

Introduction

Britain has always been a regionally divided nation. Throughout the middle-ages the English counties south of the Humber, Trent, and Mersey contained at least 80 per cent of England's tax-paying population and five sixths of its taxable wealth. They were also much more urbanised; with the exceptions of York and Newcastle, the south contained all of England's largest towns and the vast majority of its urban population (probably around 90 per cent of people living in towns of at least 10,000 inhabitants during the fourteenth century).[1]

While the concentration of the best agricultural land in the fertile plains of England's southern and eastern counties constituted one reason for this imbalance, a factor of increasing, and eventually key, importance was the dominance of Britain's political, commercial, financial, and industrial, life by a single city – London. Accounting for only one in 90 of England's population at the time of the doomsday book, the metropolis rose to encompass one in 75 by 1180, one in 60 by 1300, one in 50 by 1500 and one in 25 by 1600.[2] By 1300 it was already the second largest Christian city north of the Alps, after Paris. Furthermore, to the extent that the English economy was integrated during the middle ages, it was integrated around London, which acted as the hub for trade, credit, migration, wealth, and political power. The contours of high value industrial activity during the sixteenth and seventeenth centuries radiated out from the metropolis – for example the pre-industrial textile trade was mainly based in Essex, Norfolk, and around the Cotswolds. Evidence regarding the geography of wealth distribution during the six centuries following the Norman Conquest all shows the same general pattern, with wealth generally rising with proximity to London and the northern counties all ranking among the poorest in England.[3]

By the early modern period London dominated Britain to an extent that had no counterpart among other major nations. On the eve of Britain's industrialisation, in

1 Bruce M. S. Campbell, 'North-South dichotomies, 1066–1550', 145–74 in Alan R. H. Baker and Mark Billinge (eds), *Geographies of England. The North-South Divide, Material and Imagined* (Cambridge, 2004), pp. 159–60.

2 Ibid, p. 171.

3 John Langton, 'South, North and nation: regional differences and conciousness in an integrating realm, 1550–1750', 112–44 in Baker and Billinge, *Geographies of England*, p. 119; Campbell, 'North-South dichotomies', p. 152.

1700, it was the largest city in Western Europe, with a population of around 575,000, and was wholly exceptional among British cities both in terms of its rate of growth and relative size. London's population had risen ten-fold since the 1520s and now encompassed around 11 per cent of the population (or around two thirds of the urban population).[4] Meanwhile Norwich, England's second city, had a population of only 30,000, and Bristol, its third city, had around 20,000. Newcastle, with around 16,000 inhabitants, and York, with some 12,000, were the only cities outside the South of England[5] that boasted over 10,000 inhabitants. Meanwhile eighteenth-century Scotland, despite being 'a veritable mosaic of regional societies',[6] over-laid by the well-known Highland/Lowland distinction, was characterised throughout by low urbanisation, an agriculturally-based economy, poor wages, and low life-expectancy compared to southern England.

London played a key unifying role in the economic life of early modern Britain, representing its only truly national city prior to the industrial revolution. It acted as Britain's main international trading centre, some 80 per cent of England's imports and 70 per cent of exports passing through the capital. Together with its strong coastal connections and national market hub status it constituted the only British city demonstrating nationwide economic functions over a significant range of activities. London constituted the focal point for movements of goods, capital, and people; for example freemen and apprentices migrated there from all British regions, while by the eighteenth century shopkeepers from as far as Lancashire travelled there for supplies.[7] Meanwhile, London's hegemonic political, commercial, and cultural position increasingly drew in wealthy families from throughout Britain, its ambit even extending to Scotland. The Act of Union merely accelerated an established trend for the Scottish aristocracy to winter in London, as a means of advancing their social and political position.[8]

London's joint status as Britain's national and international trading centre, political and administrative capital, and social hub for elite society, generated high demand for a range of financial, business, and personal services. The growth of money, securities trading, commodity, insurance, and banking markets produced one of the most highly developed financial centres in seventeenth- and eighteenth-century Europe and started Britain on a development path which would see financial and business services playing a pivotal role in shaping and constraining Britain's long-term economic development.

London was also a major manufacturing centre. Its high concentration of wealthy individuals led to the rapid growth of craft industries such as high quality furniture,

4 Penelope Corfield, 'Urban developments in England and Wales in the Sixteenth and Seventeenth Centuries', 214–47 in D. C. Coleman and A. H. John (eds), *Trade, Government and Economy in Pre-Industrial England: Essays Presented to F. J. Fisher* (London, 1976), p. 217. The urban population is here defined as those living in settlements of 5,000 or more.

5 Defined to include the South East, South West, and East Anglia.

6 T. M. Devine, 'Scotland', 388–416 in R. Floud and P. Johnson (eds), *The Cambridge Economic History of Modern Britain. Volume 1: Industrialisation, 1700–1870* (Cambridge, 2004), p. 389.

7 Langton, 'South, North and nation', p. 131.

8 Devine, 'Scotland', pp. 397–8.

while other high value activities such as sugar processing capitalised on both the large and affluent London market and its unparalleled transport connections.[9] London played a key role in British industrial development, in particular by acting as a nursery for new industries – which subsequently migrated to the provinces in search of cheaper land and labour. Out-migrants in the seventeenth and early eighteenth centuries included fustian weaving, framework knitting, and silk throwing.[10]

London's dominance was not lost on contemporaries and by the early modern period a strong popular tradition had emerged, criticising its growth as unhealthy and abnormal. In 1703 Andrew Fletcher put the argument in an unusually sophisticated form, noting that, 'if, instead of one, we had twelve cities in these kingdoms possessed of equal advantages, so many centers of men, riches and power would be more advantageous than one.'[11] Yet economic forces appeared to have anchored British prosperity to the metropolis, its hinterland, and neighbouring regions.

Industrialisation and the rise of the North

The industrial revolution marked the most significant break in the geography of British economic development since the Norman Conquest. As Maxine Berg has noted, 'the most striking change in the industrial structure of the country between the end of the seventeenth century and the middle of the nineteenth was its geography.'[12]

The focus of industrial development experienced a decisive shift from long-established manufacturing centres in southern and eastern England, often based on coastal locations, to more northerly, and sometimes more inland, areas such as the West Midlands, the West Riding of Yorkshire, Lancashire, and South Wales – the one exception being London, which continued its relentless growth.

The reasons behind this process are complex and controversial. Changes in transport, industrial power sources and technology, plus the comparative advantage of the fertile southern and eastern counties in agricultural production, all clearly played a role.[13] However, institutional factors were also important. Established textile communities in areas such as Essex and Norfolk displayed strong institutional rigidities in accepting, and adapting to, the new technological and organisational forms of the industrial revolution. Craft workers proved resistant to radical changes in working conditions that threatened to undermine the value of established skills, while entrepreneurs and merchants were also less flexible in embracing the new production systems than their northern counterparts (possibly partly due to the

9 P. J. Cain and A. G. Hopkins, *British Imperialism: Innovation and Expansion 1688–1914* (London, 1993), p. 62.

10 Langston, 'South, North and nation', p. 132.

11 Cited in Corfield, 'Urban developments in England and Wales', p. 215.

12 Maxine Berg, *The Age of Manufactures. Industry Innovation and Work in Britain 1700–1820* (Oxford, 1985), p. 110.

13 Eric L. Jones, 'The constraints on economic growth in southern England 1650–1850', *Third International Conference on Economic History* (Paris, 1965), 423–30, p. 429.

influence of guilds in blocking new entrants and techniques).[14] New production methods proved much easier to introduce in 'new' manufacturing regions with low wages and plentiful supplies of pliable labour, while the hilly topography of areas such as the West Riding of Yorkshire and Lancashire, that had disadvantaged their growth in an age governed by agriculture and poorly-developed inland transport, now gave them access to plentiful water power to run the new machinery.[15]

A radically new geography of British manufacturing industry and urbanisation emerged. The triangular zone of seventeenth-century industry and high urbanisation, with Bristol, London, and Norwich as its corners,[16] was replaced by a coffin-shaped 'factory belt' extending diagonally from the London area to Merseyside, south Lancashire, and the West Riding of Yorkshire. While some areas outside this zone were important foci of industrialisation, such as South Wales, Tyneside and (prior to the mid-nineteenth century) Cornwall, these were based around extractive industries and became dominated by the coal – iron and steel – shipbuilding nexus of heavy industry, rather than factory trades.

The rise of the factory belt is illustrated in Table 2.1, which shows the regional distribution of Britain's population over the eighteenth and nineteenth centuries. Figures prior to 1801 are based on estimates that are less reliable than the census-based nineteenth-century data, and may underestimate growth in the first half of the eighteenth century and over-estimate it during the latter half.[17] However this is unlikely to affect the broad regional trends shown. During the first half of the eighteenth century the northern-south dimension of population change dominated the factory belt/industrial periphery dimension. The proportion of people living in Britain's northern regions rose from 53.6 to 55.6 per cent, while that living in the 'factory belt' regions remained stable. While southern regions outside the belt experienced relative population declines, the main area of population growth was the northern 'industrial periphery' rather than the northern factory belt. Meanwhile London and Middlesex also experienced a rare episode of relative population decline.

Yet during the following 150 years the factory belt/industrial periphery dimension clearly dominated. Factory belt regions, which accounted for less than half of Britain's population in 1751, made up almost two thirds in 1901, while the proportion of people in Britain's northern regions experienced a more modest increase – from 55.6 to 61.7 per cent. The 'southern periphery' experienced the largest declines, falling from over a fifth of the national population in 1751 to a tenth in 1901, though the 'northern periphery' also experienced a progressive fall in its share of Britain's population. London resumed its long-term trend of rapid relative population growth

14 Ibid., pp. 428–9; Eric L. Jones, 'La deindustrializzazione come forma di aggiustamento economico: il case dell'inghilterra sud-occidentale', *Quaderni storici* N.S. 73 (1990), pp. 247–68; Berg, *The Age of Manufactures*, pp. 118–22.

15 Peter Garrod, 'The Bradford worsted industry and foreign competition, 1870–1939', unpublished M.Phil thesis, University of Leeds, 1981, p. v.

16 Jones, 'The constraints on economic growth in southern England', p. 423.

17 Clive H. Lee, *The British Economy Since 1700: A Marcroeconomic Perspective* (Cambridge, 1986), p. 127. The original source for the eighteenth century estimates is P. Deane and W. A. Cole, *British Economic Growth 1688–1959* (Cambridge, 1967), p. 103.

during the nineteenth century, while the rest of the South East (much of which lay outside the belt) experienced a relative population decline – though this was partially reversed during the second half of the century, as the growth of the metropolitan economy spilled over into the home counties.

Table 2.1: The distribution of the British population, 1701–1901 (per cent)

Year	1701	1751	1801	1851	1901
South East					
London & Middlesex	8.5	8.0	7.9	12.1	14.4
Other South East	14.9	14.8	15.9	12.4	14.0
Total	23.4	22.8	23.8	24.5	28.4
Other factory belt regions					
West Midlands	7.5	7.5	8.1	8.2	8.1
East Midlands	8.5	7.5	7.6	6.8	6.5
North West	4.9	5.8	8.3	12.0	14.1
Yorkshire & Humberside	4.5	5.1	6.7	7.7	8.7
Total	25.4	25.9	30.7	34.7	37.4
Southern 'periphery'					
East Anglia	7.5	6.6	5.9	4.9	2.9
South West	15.5	15.0	13.0	10.7	7.0
Total	23.0	21.6	18.9	15.6	9.9
Northern 'periphery'					
Northern region	7.0	6.7	6.1	5.6	6.8
Wales	6.0	6.1	5.6	5.7	5.4
Scotland	15.2	16.9	14.9	13.9	12.1
Total	28.2	29.7	26.6	25.2	24.3
Total factory belt	48.8	48.7	54.5	59.2	65.8
Total periphery	51.2	51.3	45.5	40.8	34.2
Great Britain	100.0	100.0	100.0	100.0	100.0

Source: Adapted from Clive H. Lee, The British Economy Since 1700: A Macroeconomic Perspective *(Cambridge, 1986), p. 127.*

The factory belt encompassed that area of England and Wales that offered transport 'nodality', both regarding international trade – dominated by London and (as the industrial revolution progressed) Liverpool – and links to Britain's major urban centres.[18] London represented a barrier to road (and, to some extent, rail) accessibility, while the estuarine barriers of the Humber, Severn, and to a lesser extent Morecambe Bay, also seriously impeded inland transport, thus framing the boundaries of the factory zone.[19] The development of canal, and, later, rail networks,

18 E. G. R. Taylor, 'Discussion of the Geographical Distribution of Industry', *Geographical Journal*, 92 (1938), 22–39.

19 Ibid.

reinforced the nodality of the factory belt which, as the following chapters will demonstrate, was to define the major locations for factory production in England and Wales until after the Second World War. It also constituted England's main area of urbanisation, as demonstrated in Table 2.2 and Figure 2.1, which show the growth of London, England's seven largest provincial cities in 1700, plus its seven most rapidly expanding major urban centres during 1700–1850. Of the seven largest provincial cities in 1700, only one – Coventry – lay within the belt. Yet all the seven most rapidly expanding urban centres during the following 150 years lay within it.

Scotland had its own transport nodality, which became increasingly focused around the central Glasgow-Edinburgh industrial belt. As in northern England, industrialisation had a revolutionary impact on industrial structure and economic development. The seventy years from 1760 witnessed the growth of a substantial Scottish cotton and woollen hosiery industry, together with a massive expansion of linen production. This was followed from the 1830s by the growth of mining and iron manufacture, capitalising on the wealth of coal and ironstone in the central lowlands, and an emerging development bloc of heavy industry – which soon included engineering, railway construction and shipbuilding.[20] Industrialisation and urbanisation were dominated by the massive expansion of Glasgow, which eventually came to account for an even larger proportion of Scotland's population than London did for England and Wales.

One consequence of industrialisation was a marked reduction of regional disparities in working class incomes. Analysis by E. H. Hunt suggests that during the mid-eighteenth century wages were highest in the South East, particularly in and around London, and declined as distance from the capital increased – especially to the north.[21] However industrialisation transformed regional wage differentials and by the end of the eighteenth century new industrial areas in the northern counties had higher wages than many areas in the South (particularly the South West). By the closing decades of the eighteenth century the old adage 'the further from London, the further from prosperity' was beginning to ring less true.[22] Yet, in contrast to the rural South, wages in London and adjacent counties remained relatively high. Industrialisation also gave rise to a substantial provincial middle class, whose upper strata eventually came to play a major role in local and regional political elites. These were distinguished from their southern counterparts by their more capitalist outlook, weaker connections to the aristocracy, and, in many cases, protestant nonconformism – though for the very successful, co-option into the southern elite and Church of England often occurred within a few generations.

The rapid growth of new industrial centres continued during the nineteenth century, transforming Britain from a nation uniquely dominated by its capital to one noted for great provincial industrial cities. In 1800, with the exception of London, there were no cities in England and Wales with populations in excess of 100,000;

20 Devine, 'Scotland', pp. 399–400.

21 E. H. Hunt, 'Industrialization and regional inequality: wages in Britain, 1760–1914', *Journal of Economic History* XLVI, 4 (1986), 935–66, p. 937.

22 Mark Billinge, 'Divided by a common language: North and South 1750–1830', 88–111 in Baker and Billinge, *Geographies of England*, p. 95.

by 1891 there were 23. On the eve of the First World War Britain had some 38 cities of more than 100,000 people, including Glasgow with a million inhabitants, Manchester/ Salford with 945,000, Birmingham with 840,000, and Liverpool with 753,000.[23] Many were essentially new cities; for example Manchester, which became a city in 1853, had not been incorporated as a borough until 1838; Birmingham, also incorporated in 1838, did not become a city until 1896, while Liverpool and Leeds did not achieve formal city status until 1880 and 1893. Large provincial cities often acted as hubs for agglomerations of smaller, yet substantial, new industrial centres, giving rise to the conurbations of the West Midlands, Greater Manchester, Merseyside, Clydeside, West Yorkshire, South Yorkshire, and Tyneside.

Table 2.2: Population growth of the leading established, and new, major English urban centres, 1700–1850 (thousands)

Date	1700	1800	1850
London	550	860	2,320
Seven major provincial centres in 1700			
Norwich	29	36	67
Bristol	25	61	150
Newcastle	25	33	110
Exeter	14	16	16
York	11	16	35
Colchester	8	10	12
Coventry	7	16	36
Total	119	188	426
Seven most rapidly-growing centres 1700–1850			
Birmingham	10	71	230
Liverpool	6	76	422
Manchester	9	81	404
Leeds	7	52	185
Sheffield	8	45	141
Bradford	4	13	100
Stoke	3	22	65
Total	47	360	1,547
Total urban population	880	2,100	8,000

Source: Paul Bairoch, Cities and Economic Development. From the Dawn of History to the Present *(London, 1988), p. 254.*

The dramatic change in English regional wage differentials during the early decades of the industrial revolution was followed by relative stability during the nineteenth century; yet differentials did show some further narrowing.[24] The main

23 Lee, *The British Economy Since 1700*, p. 128.

24 Hunt, 'Industrialization and regional inequality'.

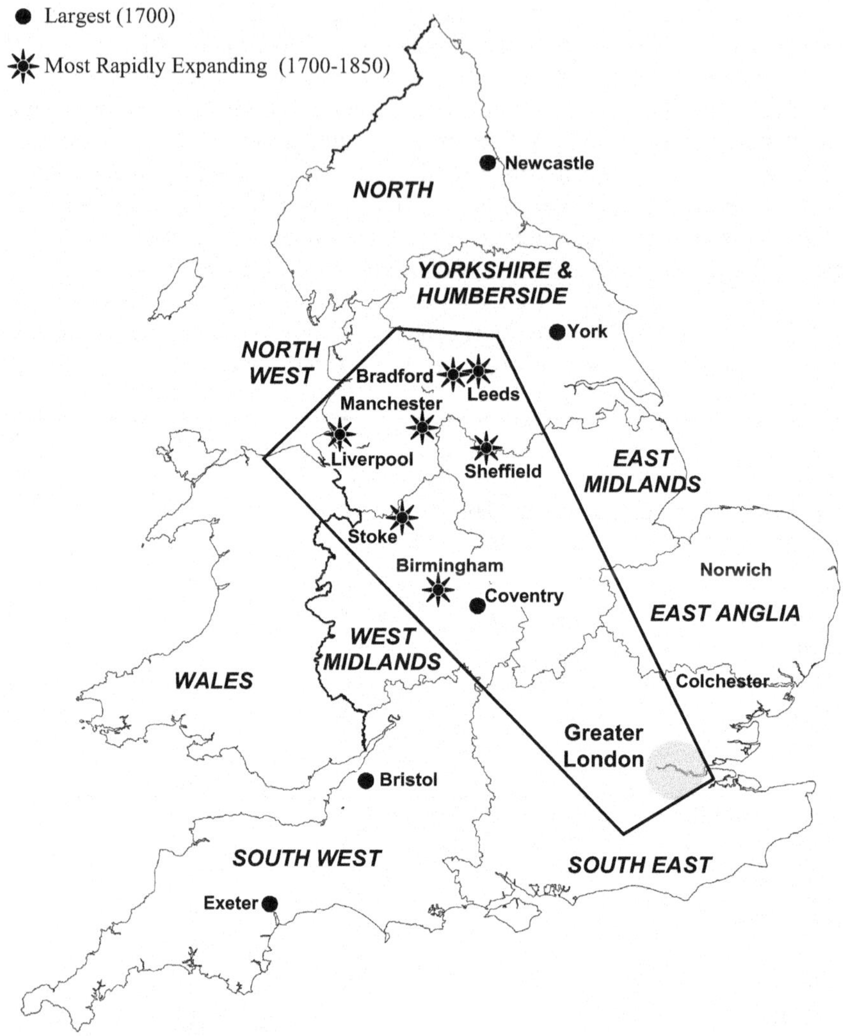

Figure 2.1: England's largest, and most rapidly expanding, provincial centres, 1700–1850

change occurred in British, rather than English, differentials, with a reduction in the previously considerable wage gaps between England and the 'celtic fringe'. Scotland experienced continued rises in relative wages, its central industrial belt constituting a high-wage area by the late nineteenth century. Scottish wage levels had generally been some 16–19 per cent lower than those in England and Wales for the same trades during the 1860s, but were only 9–13 per cent lower by the 1890s and by 1906 they had overtaken the UK average, for most sectors. Yet higher Scottish living costs meant that real wages were still significantly lower than in England.[25] Data for Wales are sparse prior to the mid-nineteenth century; yet it appears that it was during the second half of the century that the principality's very low wages began to show substantial increases.

For individual skilled trades, nominal, and especially real, wages showed relatively little variation between Britain's prosperous industrial areas. A Board of Trade inquiry indicated that in 1905 real wages for skilled male workers in London were not substantially out of line with those in Lancashire and Cheshire, the Midlands, Yorkshire, Wales, and the Northern counties. London's higher nominal wages, found to be around 14 per cent above wages in these centres, were offset by the higher cost of living in the capital.[26] The Edwardian era was to be the last time during which London represented merely one of a number of high-wage areas, encompassing both North and South.

The organisational structure of Victorian industry

One key feature distinguishing the nineteenth-century industrial geography of Britain from its modern pattern was its extreme local and, to a lesser extent, regional specialisation by sector. Provincial industrial towns and cities generally specialised in a narrow range of products and their associated services, such as the cotton in Manchester and Liverpool, coal in Cardiff, worsted in Bradford, metal-working trades in Birmingham and Sheffield, and the coal, iron and steel- shipbuilding nexus of Newcastle and Glasgow.

Sectoral specialisation appears to have been originally developed as a means of coping with Britain's poor inland transport links. Prior to the development of the railways, Britain was essentially a series of canal-based regional manufacturing economies. A reliance on the slow, costly, and incomplete canal network for much inland transport encouraged short-distance hauls, or hauls between inland production centres and coastal ports. Thus industries with strong input-output linkages tended to cluster together. Areas around nodal or terminal points on the canal network developed economies that were highly integrated, while being poorly integrated with other parts of the national economy. Such self-contained canal-based manufacturing clusters developed their own service sectors, tailored to the needs of their major industries and concentrated in their major provincial cities.[27] This pattern persisted during the railway era and, in many cases, well into the twentieth century. Sectoral clustering, initially developed through necessity, was found to have a number of important benefits that compensated for the small size of individual firms and allowed

25 Clive H. Lee, 'Scotland 1850–1939: Growth and Poverty', pp. 428–55 in R. Floud and P. Johnson (eds), *The Cambridge Economic History of Britain. Volume 2: Economic Maturity, 1860–1939* (Cambridge, 2004), p. 435.

26 For an analysis of this data see Michael Ball and David Sunderland, *An Economic History of London 1800–1914* (London, 2001), pp. 109–110.

27 John. Langton, 'The industrial revolution and the regional geography of England', *Transactions of the Institute of British Geographers*, 9 (1984), 145–67, pp. 162–3.

Britain to compete on world markets without developing the larger corporations and factories characteristic of German and American export industries.

The key unit of production in this system was the 'industrial district', based around a particular sector (and, often, a narrow range of products within that sector). Districts often encompassed both a myriad of small, highly-specialised, firms, together with a much smaller number of larger producers (each employing perhaps several hundred people) which were bound together with these small enterprises through sub-contracting relationships. In some trades, such as clothing and jewellery, goods might pass through the hands of several factories, workshops, and out-workers during the course of production. Such a system required very close geographical proximity, in order that the costs of monitoring and transport did not exceed the economic gains from clustering. Thus individual districts were generally limited in size to a few dozen, or at most a few hundred, acres, though tens of thousands of people might be employed within these small, dense, agglomerations.

Meanwhile, individual districts were often located within broader, less specialised, agglomerations of related and supporting industries, such as the south Lancashire cotton district (comprising a rectangle spanning around 30 miles east–west and 20 miles north–south); the Potteries; or the Birmingham conurbation's complex of metal-working trades. This second, broader, level of agglomeration provided a range of benefits that were not so tightly constrained by distance, such as specialist machinery suppliers, raw materials markets, and merchanting, financial, and other business services.

Typical firms in such districts were generally very small; in many light trades they might employ only a hand-full of workers, while even in some heavier sectors most firms employed no more than a few dozen. The spread of larger-scale enterprises was generally confined to sectors that produced massive or complex products (such as shipbuilding, the heavy glass trades, and some branches of heavy engineering), that required large scale for efficient operation (such as mines or iron works), or where mechanised technology was particularly advanced (such as machine-made nails, wire, and some sections and processes of the textile trades).[28] From around the 1860s a cluster of related technological developments in metallurgy, machine tools, production methods, and motive power (such as the diffusion of the gas engine) extended factory production to a much broader range of industries.[29] However, despite a marked growth in the number of factories, and medium-large enterprises, most industrial production remained organised on the basis of industrial districts, a high degree of process specialisation, and what were (by the standards of Britain's competitors) relatively small firms.

---

28 G. C. Allen, *The Industrial Development of Birmingham and the Black Country, 1860–1927* (London, 1929); pp. 112–41; Lucy Newton, *The Victorian Economy in Transition: A Regional Perspective* (Aldershot, forthcoming), Chapter 2.

29 Allen, *The Industrial Development of Birmingham*, pp. 229–30; Newton, *The Victorian Economy in Transition*, Chapter 2.

The advantages of local and regional clustering by sector were famously outlined by Alfred Marshall, from his observations of the Lancashire cotton trade.[30] In modern economic parlance, firms accrue static externalities (factors which enhance productivity at a particular point in time) by creating thick markets for inputs, outputs and ancillary services. Such thick markets allow firms to specialise in particular stages of the production process, providing economies of scale by increasing each firm's throughput for its particular process. Meanwhile districts develop pools of production factors with characteristics particularly suited to the industry, such as skilled labour, 'second-hand' or rented factories and plant, and trade credit. These both further lower production costs and facilitate firm entry (and exit).[31]

In addition to these static location externalities, Marshall also highlighted what became known as dynamic externalities (factors increasing the growth potential of clustered firms). Dynamic externalities occur principally through knowledge-spillovers between firms: 'The mysteries of the trade become no mysteries; but are as it were in the air, and children learn many of them unconsciously.'[32] Knowledge regarding incremental innovations in production methods, organisation, and product design is commonly vague, difficult to codify, and only serendipitously recognised, thus placing a premium on close and frequent observation of one's competitors.[33] Transmission mechanisms for the diffusion of knowledge between clustered firms can include spying, imitation, and taking on skilled workers previously employed in other firms.[34]

External economies of scale are of particular importance to industries producing non-standardised goods, where the alternative path of internal economies of scale through long production runs is inhibited by the differentiated and variable nature of demand. Most of Britain's major export industries faced such conditions. In addition to sectors where fashion played a major role, such as pottery, clothing & footwear, leather goods, cutlery, and parts of the textile trade, producer-goods sectors such as steel manufacture and shipbuilding were also characterised by 'batch' rather than standardised production. Yet even in sectors where output was more uniform, such as cotton thread or coal mining, production was still concentrated in clusters that bore most of the features associated with industrial districts – as firms derived important benefits from the pooling of skilled workers and from the presence of related and supporting industries.

30 Alfred Marshall, *Elements of Economics of Industry*, 4th edn. (London, 1907), pp. 151–5.

31 Ibid; Andrew Popp, Business *Structure, Business Culture and the Industrial District. The Potteries, c. 1850–1914* (Aldershot, 2001).

32 Marshall, *Elements of Economics of Industry*, p. 152.

33 David B. Audretsch, 'Agglomeration and the location of innovative activity', *Oxford Review of Economic Policy*, 14 (1988), 18–29, p. 21; Marshall, *Elements of Economics of Industry*, pp. 152–3.

34 See E. L. Glasser, H. D. Kallal, J. A. Scheinkman, and A. Shleifer, 'Growth in Cities', *Journal of Political Economy*, 100 (1992), 1126–52, p. 1130; V. Henderson, A. Kuncoro and M. Turner, 'Industrial development in cities', *Journal of Political Economy*, 103 (1995), 1067–90.

Strong commonalities in production methods were an important feature of such districts. Most firms within a district undertook production using compatible machinery, generally designed for 'flexibility' – the ability to produce different styles of goods. Production was typically labour-intensive, relying on a combination of simple, flexible machinery and highly skilled workers to produce a range of variegated goods. Workers generally acquired their skills on the shop floor, from childhood, as a by-product of working under the supervision of more senior workers. Common machinery thus maximised local pools of workers trained in the relevant skills, in turn minimising firms' training costs.

Common production methods also facilitated sub-contracting and process specialisation, as the technology of each stage of production was often interrelated with that of earlier and subsequent stages, as discussed in the following chapter. A common production technology also provided a large local market for machinery, encouraging the development of local capital goods manufacturers who designed machines to suit the technological requirements of the locality, particularly the skills of its workforce.[35] This, in turn, maximised local pools of second-hand machinery and factory premises (the design of which was often strongly linked to the machinery used), while encouraging the growth of firms that rented out factories and plant – in a number of areas manufacturers commonly rented space and power, occupying sections of larger factory buildings.[36]

Process specialisation, rented or low-cost second-hand machinery and plant, the ready availability of trained workers, local circuits of trade credit, and networks of subcontracting, outworkers, and ancillary industries, jointly acted to greatly ease firms' entry to, and exit from, production in the district, together with frequent and substantial changes in the scale of a firm's production. Many industrial districts experienced considerable turnover in firm numbers, artisans sometimes moving from being employees to masters and back again several times over the course of their working lives. Industrial districts could thus prosper in the aggregate despite numerous business failures, as there were always new contenders ready to take the place of unsuccessful incumbents.

The coordination of production within these districts was often undertaken either by the larger manufacturers or by merchants – the distinction between the two sometimes being rather vague. For example, factors and merchants played a key coordinating role in Birmingham's jewellery quarter, combining wholesale and retail marketing and sales functions with putting out work to 'small master' contractors (based on designs, and using materials, provided by the merchant), while merchants

---

35 See Popp *Business Structure*, 88–9; William Mass and William Lazonick, 'The British cotton industry and international competitive advantage: the state of the debates', *Business History*, 32, 4 (1990), 9–65, p. 13.

36 Walter Bennett, *The History of Burnley from 1850* (Burnley, 1951), p. 97; M. J. Lewis, 'The growth and development of Sheffield's business structure, 1880–1930', unpublished Ph.D. thesis, Sheffield City Polytechnic, 1989, pp. 41–2; J. M. Hunter, 'Factors affecting the location and growth of industry in Greater Nottinghamshire', *East Midland Geographer*, 3 (1964), pp 340–41.

sometimes even undertook manufacture on their own account.[37] Similarly, in the East End furniture districts strong vertical specialisation was coordinated by 'manufacturers', who received orders from wholesalers, purchased the necessary wood, had it cut and planed by sawyers, and then passed on to turners, fret cutters, carvers, and other craftsmen before merely undertaking final assembly.[38]

While industrial districts provided important benefits in terms of flexibility, low capital costs, and economies of scale, they also contained a number of negative features that impeded their ability to adjust to radical changes in production technologies, methods, and markets. As the following chapter will demonstrate, these features came to constitute important barriers to modernisation from the late nineteenth century, when many districts faced vigorous competition from newly-industrialising nations using more mechanised production methods and typically producing longer runs of standardised products.

Industrial specialisation was also evident at the regional level. Research by Clive Lee, using county level census data, has identified three basic types of 'growth regions' in Victorian Britain (in addition to a large number of stagnating rural areas).[39] The first type, typified by Durham and South Wales, were 'export-orientated mineral and raw material exploiting areas' – characterised by extensive development of coal mining. Other major activities were typically heavy manufacturing industries strongly linked to coal, such as metal manufacture, mechanical engineering, and shipbuilding. Such areas tended to have poorly-developed service sectors and very low female employment – as Britain's main female-employing sectors were strongly underrepresented.

The second type of region, best characterised by Lancashire, the West Riding of Yorkshire, and Tayside, were manufacturing export regions, heavily committed to textiles (but less dominated by textiles than the mineral-exploiting areas were by mining). Other important local industries often included clothing, mechanical engineering (partly textile machinery), mining, and metal manufacture. Female participation rates were much higher in this type of region (due to heavy female employment in textiles and clothing). Service sector employment was more important than in the mining regions, but still below the national average.

Both these types of regions were heavily dependent on export markets and had employment structures dominated by a narrow range of industries. Analysis by Ron Martin, at the broader geographical level of Standard Economic Regions, has divided them into the 'manufacturing heartland,' of the West Midlands, North West and Yorkshire & Humberside (which broadly corresponds to Lee's manufacturing exporting regions) and the 'industrial periphery' of Wales, Scotland, and the Northern region (which broadly corresponds to the export-orientated mineral and raw material

37 John Cattell, Sheila Ely and Barry Jones, *The Birmingham Jewellery Quarter. An Architectural Survey of the Manufactories* (Swindon, 2002), pp. 31–2.

38 Ball and Sunderland, *An Economic History of London*, pp. 302–12.

39 Clive H. Lee, 'Regional growth and structural change in Victorian Britain', *Economic History Review*, 34 (1981), 438–52.

exploiting areas).[40] During the late Victorian and Edwardian eras the manufacturing heartland progressively increased its share of national manufacturing employment. Conversely, the industrial periphery's share of manufacturing employment actually declined, as it became increasingly specialised in coal mining.[41]

One unifying feature of the manufacturing heartland and industrial periphery was an industrial structure that generally offered better paid and less casual work than was the case for many London trades, but at the cost of a much greater risk of unemployment during downturns in the business cycle. Analysis by Humphrey Southall, based on data from trade union unemployment insurance schemes, indicates that the main provincial industrial regions contained more than twice the proportion of employees in export-orientated industries strongly influenced by the trade cycle than was the case in London, making them especially vulnerable to cyclical downturns.[42] While in London poverty for able-bodied workers was associated with irregular and poorly paid employment, such as dock work, in the provincial cities the main danger stemmed from the vicissitudes of international competition and the world market. Unemployment (as opposed to underemployment or poverty) thus appears to have been higher in Britain's northern industrial areas than in the south even prior to the First World War.[43]

Lee's final class of growth region was a single continuous 'metropolitan' region, based on London and its hinterland. In terms of population growth, this metropolitan area was more important than the collective growth of either all the mining regions or all the textile regions. The export staples were strongly under-represented, while growth was based around service industries – encompassing some 66.1 per cent of new jobs created in the South East between 1841 and 1911 – together with a broad range of consumer and market-orientated manufacturing trades, including a substantial over-representation of 'new industries'.[44] While the textile and mining regions looked principally to markets outside their regions, much of the metropolitan economy's growth was internally generated by its buoyant consumer and producer markets.

During this period London consolidated its position as the world's main financial and commercial centre and as the administrative capital of Britain and a huge and growing Empire. Meanwhile integration of the national economy was accompanied by the concentration of many domestic financial services in London. For example, the 1860s witnessed the onset of a merger movement among clearing banks in England and Wales, which intensified from the 1880s. This centralised much banking business in large firms, headquartered from London, which serviced the provinces only through their branch networks; by 1911 London-based banking groups controlled

40 Ron Martin, 'The political economy of Britain's north-south divide', *Transactions of the Institute of British Geographers*, New Series, 13 (1988), 389–418, p. 391.

41 Ibid, pp. 391–2.

42 Humphrey Southall, 'The origins of the depressed areas: unemployment, growth and regional economic structure in Britain before 1914', *Economic History Review*, XLI (1988), 236–58, p. 255.

43 Ibid. For evidence regarding Scotland, see T. M. Devine, *The Scottish Nation 1700–2000* (London, 1999), p. 263.

44 Lee, 'Regional growth and structural change', pp. 450–51.

56 per cent of UK branches and 65 per cent of deposits.[45] Insurance companies also became increasingly clustered in and around the City, partly on account of their growing investment in overseas securities during the late nineteenth century.

London's domination of spending by Britain's elite continued to bolster its service sector – reflected in increased employment in areas such as retailing and domestic service. Britain's landed elite (who comprised over half the wealthiest people in Britain until the 1880s) divided their time between their country estates and London, spending substantially in the capital to meet the social demands of the season and enjoy easy access to English landed society's major institutions, such as the ancient universities, public schools, and elite sporting events. This London-centric aristocratic social sphere also proved attractive to those with non-landed wealth, who found fewer social barriers to entry than was the case for their counterparts in most continental countries. London's pull even stretched beyond Britain, drawing wealthy people from the Empire, Europe, and the United States into what was regarded as the leading international playground for the world's rich. These could enjoy its social and sporting facilities while using its unparalleled financial services to manage their portfolios.[46]

The concentration of wealthy individuals in the south is reflected in regional differences in income tax per head (then restricted to high and middle income individuals), which amounted to £22.50 for the South East in 1879–80, compared to the national average of £16.41 and significantly lower levels in most provincial industrial regions.[47] The southern-orientation of high income earners was reflected in the national distribution of service sector employment. After London and the South East, the South West and East Anglia were next in the league of services employment per capita, while the Midlands, northern England, Scotland, and Wales all had substantially lower proportions of service sector jobs.[48] Largely as a result of its high number of 'white collar' service sector employees, London and the Home Counties also had a disproportionate and rising share of Britain's middle classes.[49]

London's expanding manufacturing base was dominated by sectors that gained substantial benefit from location at Britain's services and distribution hub. Major London industries such as clothing (its largest manufacturing trade by 1900) and leather goods were strongly influenced by fashion, London firms being concentrated in particularly fashion-orientated lines such as women's dresses and handbags, for which close contact with markets was vital. Proximity to West End showrooms and department stores facilitated observation of domestic demand, while access to City merchants increased information flows regarding overseas markets. Partly as a consequence, these trades were highly concentrated in boroughs close to the West

45 Ball and Sunderland, *An Economic History of London*, pp. 338–46; Michael Collins, *Money and Banking in the UK. A History* (London, 1988), pp.78–9.

46 Ranald Michie, 'Options, concessions, syndicates, and the provision of venture capital, 1880–1913', *Business History*, 23 (1981), 147–64, p. 159.

47 Clive. H. Lee, 'The service sector, regional specialization, and economic growth in the Victorian economy', *Journal of Historical Geography*, 10 (1984), 139–55, p. 149.

48 Ibid.

49 W. D. Rubinstein, *Capitalism, Culture, and Decline in Britain 1750-1990* (London, 1993), pp. 26–8.

End and City. Another over-represented London industry, printing, derived much of its demand from the City's business and financial services firms, as well as the newspaper and journal trade (which demonstrated a growing metropolitan focus) and was again centrally clustered, in and around the City.

As a result of its booming services and consumer-goods trades, London continued to enjoy vigorous population growth over the nineteenth century, increasing its proportion of the total population of England and Wales from 12 to 20 per cent. By 1911 its population equalled the combined total for Britain's six other largest population centres.[50] London had become the world's first city; in 1890 the 4.2 million inhabitants of even its core area, the County of London, dwarfed those of the world's other largest cities – its nearest rival, New York/New Jersey, boasting only 2.7 million.[51]

Conclusion

British industrialisation had involved a complementary relationship between export-orientated staple industries, concentrated in the new industrial areas of northern Britain, together with the expansion of London's established role as a national and international commercial and financial services hub. The City's worldwide financial, commercial, and shipping links facilitated access to overseas markets for the export-orientated staples, while a high volume of industrial exports contributed to the international-orientation of the British economy and the rise of sterling as the major international currency, thus facilitating Britain's management of the international gold standard system. Yet, as the British economy expanded during the late nineteenth century, its comparative advantage in internationally-traded services progressively undermined that as an industrial nation, during a period when the staple industries faced growing problems from international competition and 'technological lock-in' to existing production systems. This conflict between Britain's industrial and commercial activities, and its impact on regional development and equality, form the topics of the next chapter.

50 Cain and Hopkins, *British Imperialism*, pp. 115–16.
51 Ball and Sunderland, *An Economic History of London*, p. 44.

Chapter Three

The new regional divide: 1870–1914

Introduction

As Cain and Hopkins noted, while 'between 1750 and 1850, the economic tide had run in favour of the industrial provinces it swung decisively back again, to the traditional centre of wealth and power, in the Victorian and Edwardian epoch.'[1] It was not so much changes in the geography of British manufacturing, where the staple industries continued to dominate production and, especially, exports, but the continued growth of the service sector and overseas investment that was decisive in producing this shift. Victorian Britain was, by nineteenth century standards, a peculiarly service-orientated economy. According to estimates by Lee, services accounted for 41.4 per cent of British employment in 1911 (with manufacturing comprising 50.5 per cent and agriculture only 8.1 per cent). Meanwhile their contribution to national income was substantially larger, being estimated at over 50 per cent by 1900.[2]

Services and income from overseas investments made a large and growing contribution to Britain's balance of payments, progressively 'crowding out' its visible exports. In every year from 1822 Britain experienced a deficit on its visible trade, which grew progressively larger over time. Yet Britain's balance of payments remained healthy on account of a huge and expanding surplus on invisibles, which in turn became increasingly dominated by receipts from overseas investments. During the third quarter of the nineteenth century overseas investment income had averaged 30.6 per cent of the overall invisibles surplus and services exports alone comfortably exceeded the visibles deficit. Yet by 1901–13 Britain's £136 million average annual surplus on services was insufficient to cover its £153 million trade deficit and it relied on a massive surplus on overseas investment income, averaging £151 million, to produce an overall surplus of £134 million. Much of this surplus went, in turn, on new overseas investment, which by 1913 was equal to around 8.5 per cent of Britain's GNP.[3]

While services surged ahead, manufacturing growth faltered. Table 3.1 shows Charles Feinstein's estimates of annual growth in real output per worker by sector over 1856–1913. The decline in agricultural productivity growth is easily explained

---

1 P. J. Cain and A. G. Hopkins, *British Imperialism: Innovation and Expansion 1688–1914* (London, 1993), p. 116.

2 Clive. H. Lee, 'The service sector, regional specialization, and economic growth in the Victorian economy', *Journal of Historical Geography*, 10 (1984), 139–55, pp. 139–40.

3 C. N. Harley, 'Trade 1870–1939: from globalisation to fragmentation', 161–89 in Roderick Floud and Paul Johnson (eds), *The Cambridge Economic History of Modern Britain. Volume II: Economic Maturity 1860–1939* (Cambridge, 2004), pp. 170–71; Cain and Hopkins, *British Imperialism*, p. 170.

by the rapid expansion of food imports and the consequent depression in profits, which lowered incentives for new investment. However industry also witnessed a dramatic and progressive fall in annual labour productivity growth, from 1.61 per cent during 1856–73 to 0.74 per cent over 1899–1913. While productivity in services cannot be measured directly, the indirect estimates demonstrate no clear trend, while productivity growth for internationally traded services is likely to have been substantially higher than that for all services (which include sectors such as domestic service, then a very large employer, with very limited potential for productivity gains).

Table 3.1: Annual growth in real output per worker by sector, 1856–1913

	Agriculture	Industry	Total (excluding services)*	Services**
Two long-swings				
1856–82	0.79	1.53	1.41	0.44
1882–1913	0.74	0.83	0.85	0.47
Four phases				
1856–73	1.13	1.61	1.52	0.20
1873–82	0.14	1.38	1.20	0.89
1882–99	1.02	0.90	0.96	0.44
1899–1913	0.41	0.74	0.71	0.51
Whole period (1856–1913)	0.76	1.15	1.10	0.46

Source: Charles Feinstein, 'What really happened to real wages?: trends in wages, prices, and productivity in the United Kingdom, 1880–1913', Economic History Review, *XLIII, 3 (1990), 329–55, p. 339.*

Notes:

* Excluding the following services: public administration and defense; professions; insurance, banking, and finance; miscellaneous services; ownership of dwellings.

** Output cannot be directly measured for most services and is estimated from the change in employment on the basis of an assumed annual productivity growth of 0.5 per cent for government, finance, miscellaneous services, and the professions. For defence, catering, and domestic services it is assumed that there was no change in productivity. Ownership of dwellings is excluded from the figures, as there is no measured labour input.

Meanwhile Britain's commodity exports were concentrated in a narrow range of products – those staple industries in which it had established an international lead during the eighteenth century. On the eve of the First World War three industries – textiles, iron and steel, and coal – accounted for some two thirds of commodity export earnings. Similarly, these industries were heavily dependent on exports. An extreme example is cotton, where exports represented 89 per cent of the linear yards of piece goods produced in 1912 and some 70 per cent of the weight of raw cotton inputs.[4]

In some respects Britain's invisible and staple industry exports displayed a symbiotic relationship. There was considerable overlap between the markets they served; overseas investments often fed back, directly or indirectly, into demand for British staple goods; and the bulk commodities that comprised much of the staple industries' output were extensive users of, mainly British, shipping space. However Cain and Hopkins argue that this positive relationship became less important over time, in the face of rising international competition in commodity trade.[5]

Britain's growing invisibles surplus progressively weakened its comparative advantage in the staple industries and, therefore, the price-competitiveness of their exports. If Britain was to avoid progressively draining the world of sterling (and gold), surpluses on invisibles had to be matched by deficits in commodity trade. The only alternative was to send the excess income back abroad in the form of additional overseas investment. Yet, despite the fact that no major nation has ever invested so large a proportion of its GNP abroad as Britain did during this period, overseas investment failed to keep pace with its invisibles surpluses. Furthermore, foreign investment could only postpone, and, in the long-term, accentuate, the need to redress the payments imbalance, as investments soon generated revenues, which further increased the invisibles surplus.

Britain thus faced a problem analogous to the 'Dutch disease' effect identified in modern oil-rich countries, where high export earnings from a major sector making little direct contribution to domestic employment crowd-out the development of other activities by appreciating the exchange rate.[6] As Britain was under a fixed exchange rate regime, other mechanisms operated to reduce the competitiveness of British industry in world markets (and thus correct the balance of payments surplus). Two main mechanisms have been identified in the literature, involving the impact of the invisibles surplus on British prices, and on national income.

A payments surplus might be corrected via its impact in raising British export prices, relative to those of other countries, thus raising the 'real exchange rate' for sterling during a period when the actual exchange rate was fixed by the pound's gold standard parity. The second, 'absorption' effect, on national income, occurred via the impact of receipts from the invisibles surplus on domestic consumption. Recipients would increase their consumption, producing an increase in imports and a reduction in exports (due to their consumption of domestically-produced goods otherwise destined for export) and thus generating a deterioration in Britain's visible trade balance. Research on Britain's Dutch disease problem has generally focused on receipts from overseas investments, rather than on invisible exports in general. Most early work focused on the price effect.[7] However, a more recent study by Rowthorn

4 William. Lazonick, 'The Cotton Industry', 18-50 in B. Elbaum and W. Lazonick (eds), *The Decline of the British Economy* (Oxford, 1986), p. 18.

5 Cain and Hopkins, *British Imperialism,* p. 180.

6 C. N. Harley, 'Trade 1870–1939', p. 174.

7 R.C.O. Matthews, C.H. Feinstein, and J.C. Odling-Smee, *British Economic Growth 1856–1973* (Oxford, 1982), pp. 455–56; Angus Maddison, *Phases in Capitalist Development*

and Solomou found that the absorption effect dominated the balance of payments correction over 1872–1913, more than accounting for the 2.4 per cent of GDP deterioration in the trade balance. This may have been reinforced by a price effect, though until the Edwardian period its impact was filtered out by other influences.[8]

This squeezing out of manufactured exports by invisibles can be viewed as merely reflecting Britain's comparative advantage in services and investment, as argued, for example, by W. D. Rubinstein.[9] Yet such a prognosis, while correct according to the impersonal calculus of neoclassical economics, disregards the distributional effects of Britain's drift towards becoming a rentier and services economy. Despite its smaller contribution to national income, manufacturing was the core sector for high-wage working-class employment in Britain, whereas internationally traded services generated fewer jobs relative to the value of their output and made a proportionately larger contribution to lower-middle class employment, in clerical and similar occupations.[10] Furthermore, such jobs were highly concentrated in and around London. Such a shift in employment opportunities is corroborated by data on real per capita incomes, which indicate a more rapid growth in average salaries than in wages.[11]

Distributional questions are of even greater importance with regard to overseas investment incomes, which expanded from 2.8 per cent of GDP during 1855–73 to 9.2 per cent on the eve of the First World War and constituted the lion's share of the invisibles surplus.[12] These generated little in the way of jobs other than via the 'trickle down' effect of spending by their recipients (again, highly concentrated in London).[13] From the perspective of most of Britain's population, a progressive drift towards an economy analogous to one of the modern Gulf States, with the major 'export' item, overseas investment incomes, directly benefiting only a relatively small minority of the population; services generating a limited number of predominantly white collar jobs, concentrated in and around the capital; and the vast majority deriving no direct benefit from its exports; did not constitute an attractive long-term prospect.

(Oxford, 1982), p. 38; Sidney Pollard, *Britain's Prime and Britain's Decline. The British Economy 1870–1914* (London, 1989), pp. 107–110.

8 R. E. Rowthorn and S. N. Solomou, 'The macroeconomic effects of overseas investment on the UK balance of trade, 1870–1913', *Economic History Review*, XLIV, 4 (1991), 654–64.

9 W. D. Rubinstein, *Capitalism, Culture, and Decline in Britain 1750–1990* (London, 1993).

10 Ibid, p. 32.

11 Charles H. Feinstein, 'What really happened to real wages?: trends in wages, prices, and productivity in the United Kingdom, 1880–1913', *Economic History Review*, XLIII, 3 (1990), 329–55, pp. 344–46.

12 Pollard, *Britain's Prime*, pp. 61–2.

13 While there was some feedback into British manufacturing employment via purchases of British goods by the recipients of overseas investment, this became of diminishing importance in the face of rising international competition in commodity trade, as noted above.

Britain's staple industries in retreat

Britain's staple industries were particularly vulnerable to the Dutch disease effect on relative UK prices, as overseas purchasers could easily substitute foreign for British goods. Many key exports, such as coal, cotton yarn, or bulk iron and steel goods, were simple, low value-added products, near-identical to those produced overseas and offering few 'first mover advantages' to protect British output, such as branding or restrictive patents. Meanwhile, Britain was facing an upsurge in foreign competition in these industries. Newly-industrialising nations found it relatively easy to undertake production of staple industry goods (compared to the capital-intensive, high-tech, sectors in which much U.S. and German export production was concentrated) as they did not require particularly advanced scientific or technical skills, or large, expensive, plant.

The new industrialisers lacked Britain's pool of workers trained in the sector-specific skills of the staple industries, but this could be circumvented by the use of more mechanised techniques and standardised, rather than flexible, production. Paradoxically, even manufacturers in low wage countries found labour-saving capital investment in mechanisation more attractive than their British counterparts. Labour costs are determined not only by wages but by the efficiency of labour. Thus, efficient craft methods may have offered British manufacturers low labour costs despite higher wages (relative to continental Europe), whereas newly-industrialising European nations lacking similarly skilled craftsmen had a greater incentive to undertake labour-saving investment, despite lower wage rates.[14] Yet in the long-term capital investment offered dynamic productivity grains that eventually outstripped the productivity growth potential of craft techniques. Furthermore, Britain's craft methods necessarily produced a higher ratio of labour to total costs than mechanised techniques and, given their limited long-run productivity growth potential, became increasingly incompatible with increases in living standards for the workers concerned.

Yet by the time such pressures became evident many British staple industries had become 'locked in' to existing production techniques (that, in some cases, would have been recognisable to their eighteenth-century predecessors) through mechanisms that have been highlighted in the economic literature on 'path dependence'. Thorstein Veblen famously pioneered this concept, using the example of Britain's small railway coal wagons. During the decades prior to the First World War, when the nations of Europe and North America introduced large rail wagons for moving coal, of 20 tons or greater capacity, Britain continued to use much smaller wagons, typically of 10 tons or less. Veblen argued that Britain's railway system was locked-in to the small coal wagon, as introducing larger wagons would entail the modification of a wide-range of interrelated infrastructure that could not presently accommodate them: 'terminal facilities, tracks, shunting facilities, and all the ways and means of handling freight on this oldest and most complete of railway systems.'[15]

---

14 Pollard, *Britain's Prime*, p. 50.

15 Thorstein Veblen, *Imperial Germany and the Industrial Revolution* (London, 1915), p. 130.

Charles Kindleberger further developed Veblen's concept of 'interrelatedness', noting that it could refer both to technical interrelatedness – the need to modify various stages of a production or distribution process to accommodate a new technology – and institutional interrelatedness – the additional obstacles that fragmented ownership of that system placed in the way of modification.[16] Recent research on Britain's small coal wagons has highlighted the importance of institutional interrelatedness. Early British railways had followed the precedent of the canals in allowing private firms to supply their own wagons and, once established, private wagon-owners proved unwilling to give up these rights. As late as the 1920s some 600,000 coal wagons, around three quarters of the national total, were owned by some 5,000 separate collieries, coal distributors and users, and specialist wagon supply firms. Most were incompatible with modern, high capacity, wagons – on account of their more primitive braking systems and gear boxes and general poor state of repair. Yet, despite an estimated saving of around 56 per cent from the replacement of the national wagon fleet with modern 20 ton wagons, in unified ownership, the additional costs of compensating private owners for the value of their wagons, on top of the costs of modernising associated infrastructure, made the expected return on the necessary investment unattractive. Fragmented ownership thus transformed obsolete wagons from a sunk to a real cost, thereby preventing a modernisation programme that would have substantially reduced haulage costs.[17]

Similar problems inhibited technical change in other staple industries. In coal mining, which ranked as Britain's largest employer of male labour, the main production tasks – the hewing of coal, loading it into tubs, and (in the main) moving these underground – were still largely done by hand.[18] As late as 1913 only 8.5 per cent of British coal was mechanically cut and a negligible proportion was mechanically conveyed. Meanwhile over 40 per cent of American coal was being cut by machine.[19] British mine engineers had been among the first to experiment with coal-cutting and conveying machinery. Yet they found that mechanical undercutting of coal-seams produced an output at the coalface that exceeded the maximum throughput capacity of existing underground haulage systems, while British underground roadways proved unsuitable for the mechanised haulage technology required to deal with this throughput.

Mechanised underground haulage was blocked by Britain's practice of developing roadways along the coal seam, which produced tunnels that were too curved and uneven in incline for underground locomotives or conveyors. Thus coalcutters (and conveyors at the coalface) often proved uneconomic, as their output could simply

16 C. P. Kindleberger, *Economic Growth in France and Britain, 1851–1950* (Cambridge, MA, 1964), pp. 142–43.

17 Peter Scott, 'Path dependence and Britain's "coal wagon problem"', *Explorations in Economic History*, 38 (2001), 366–85. The political economy of railway operation and regulation in Britain prevented the railways from simply prohibiting the further operation of private wagons on their tracks.

18 W. H. B. Court, 'Problems of the British coal industry between the wars', *Economic History Review*, XV (1945), 1–24, p. 5.

19 A. J. P. Taylor, 'Labour productivity and technological innovation in the British coal industry, 1850–1914', *Economic History Review*, XIV (1961), 48–67, p. 58.

not be moved through the mine fast enough. Meanwhile institutional interrelatedness with Britain's unique system of private and fragmented mineral royalty ownership inhibited the switch to the continental practice of 'horizon mining' – involving driving straight underground roadways through rock (for reasons that are explored in Chapter Five).[20] Thus, despite Britain's early development of coal-cutting and conveying machinery (with some British machines achieving substantial export sales), Britain proved unsuccessful in applying this technology to its own coal industry.

Britain's largest staple industry in terms of overall (male and female) employment, cotton, displayed similar inertia in adapting to technological change. The industry retained its traditional mule spindle and power loom technologies at a time when all its major competitors were adopting the newer ring spindle and automatic loom. The new technologies were labour-saving. Automatic looms required less supervision than power looms. Meanwhile the ring spindle offered higher output per hour than the mule as it spun continuously – spinning and winding in a single action – while the mule did these separately. Furthermore it required less skilled (and much cheaper) female workers than the skilled, male, mule spinners. Yet mule spinning entailed higher materials costs, as it subjected the cotton to greater friction, and thus required better grades of raw cotton for any given count of yarn.

The ring spindle and automatic loom were strongly interrelated, as were the mule spindle and power loom. Ring-spun yarn was substantially stronger than mule-spun yarn, and thus more suitable for automatic looms (which required break-resistant yarn). Meanwhile mule-spun yarn could be placed directly into a power-loom shuttle, whereas ring-spun weft yarn (which was attached to a wooden bobbin) had to be re-wound prior to weaving.[21] Britain also faced interrelatedness between its incumbent technology and its incumbent labour force and capital stock. Unlike its new competitors it already had a workforce that was trained in the difficult task of mule spinning, thus reducing the immediate cost advantages of ring spinning technology. Furthermore, it had large existing stocks of mule spindles and power looms, which appeared capable of an almost infinitely extendable lifespan and were recycled to new firms via an active second-hand market.

These skill and sunk cost endowments encouraged the industry to respond to competition from new, low-wage, competitors, via an adaptive strategy, which capitalised on existing technologies and organisational structures and sought to cut costs via the use of cheaper cotton that was more prone to breakages. This economised on the industry's major material cost (raw cotton), but did not substantially raise labour costs, as workers were paid on piece rates and would therefore bear the

20 Peter Scott, 'Path dependence, fragmented property rights, and the slow diffusion of high throughput technologies in interwar British coal mining', *Business History*, 48 (2006), 18–36.

21 Tim Leunig, 'New answers to old questions: explaining the slow adoption of ring spinning in Lancashire, 1880–1913', *Journal of Economic History*, 61 (2001), 439–66, p. 442.

burden of adjustment by intensifying effort in order to maintain output in the face of the more frequent breakages.[22]

The character of incumbent labour arrangements has also been put forward as a reason preventing the adoption of the automatic loom, which would have allowed firms to accrue the full productivity advantages of break-resistant ring-spun yarn. Automatic looms required fewer weavers (where they used such yarn) – as dealing with breaks was one of the weaver's main duties. In addition, automatic looms negated a major weaving labour cost of using ring-spun cotton on power looms – imposed by the small amount of yarn on a shuttle-ready bobbin and the consequent frequent need for the weaver to replenish the loom shuttle. Yet in the absence of these labour-saving effects automatic looms were not cost-effective, as their fixed cost per worker was about three times that of power-looms.[23] Mass and Lazonick have argued that restrictive union practices in Lancashire, which generally limited the number of power looms a weaver controlled to four, negated these potential labour cost savings and thus made the power loom unprofitable.[24]

Similar problems were evident in some traditional industries producing variegated consumer goods, such as pottery and cutlery. However, unlike producers of standardised industrial commodities, firms in these sectors had clear lines of retreat from the mass market, through concentrating on higher quality lines where their craft skills still commanded a premium. In the Potteries mechanisation threatened not just the skilled labourer, but the entire structure of the industry. Both owner-managers and skilled workers possessed knowledge and skills that were highly specific to existing working practices and technology. Furthermore, the incumbent labour-intensive technology underpinned the Potteries' system of personal capitalism, by greatly simplifying the managerial tasks of recruiting, training, supervising, and disciplining labour. These were largely organised by key workers and working families, through gang-working and sub-contracting.

Owner-managers also valued their independent status, viewing their firms as being held in trust for future generations of their families, and regarding trained managers and technologists as potential threats to this trust. Attempts to introduce radically new working methods associated with the new technology met opposition from determined unions that sought to protect established practices. Given that both workers and manufacturers felt threatened by the new methods, such conflicts usually resulted in compromises designed to ensure the continuation of existing practices and their underlying relationships of skill and status.[25] Thus the industry began a slow withdrawal into higher quality lines that could command a price commensurate with its higher-cost techniques.

---

22 William Lazonick, 'Public relations, labor productivity, and the choice of technique: British and U.S. cotton spinning', *Journal of Economic History*, XLI (1981), 491–516, p. 504.

23 William Mass and William Lazonick, 'The British cotton industry and international competitive advantage: the state of the debates', *Business History*, 32 (1990), 9–65, pp. 54–5.

24 Ibid, p. 54.

25 Andrew Popp, *Business Structure, Business Culture and the Industrial District. The Potteries, c. 1850–1914* (Aldershot, 2001), pp. 106–19.

Sheffield followed a similar trajectory. It had developed as Britain's premier centre for steel goods, and in particular cutlery, on the basis of the classic industrial district pattern of skilled labour, extensive out-work and sub-contracting, highly-developed local merchanting activities, and the production of differentiated items for order rather than stock. These features, together with trade credit and rented factory-space, produced low fixed costs and were suited to a strategy of specialisation in high-quality, differentiated, goods, in which Sheffield already had an outstanding reputation. Yet they necessarily impeded the introduction of mechanisation and the retention of the mass market.[26]

From the 1880s Sheffield's firms faced a growing economic crisis as a result of overseas competition, particularly from German and US manufacturers producing long runs of cheap, standardised goods. They felt unable to copy the methods of their competitors, fearing mechanisation would dilute quality and, therefore, erode the value of established brands and Sheffield's general reputation. Volume production would also impose high fixed costs, that would prove onerous if sales fell well below capacity during cyclical down-turns. Unlike their overseas competitors, Sheffield firms had not evolved strategies for stabilising production levels (which would, necessarily, involve a move to longer production runs of standardised goods), instead relying on laying off outworkers during such cyclical troughs to reduce output without incurring fixed cost penalties.[27] Skilled workers were understandably hostile to the adoption of technology that might displace skills they had invested many years in developing and which formed the basis of both their wage differentials compared to unskilled workers and their autonomy and artisan status.[28] A further obstacle to radical technological change was the current system of specialisation by process, which placed such a transition beyond the ambit of any individual firm (unless it was prepared to expand into processes it was currently unfamiliar with).[29]

Even heavy industries such as shipbuilding retained traditional, labour-intensive, techniques. Vessels were built to order, and to individual designs, using flexible production methods. Jobs were strictly demarcated along craft lines, partly as a means of facilitating the dismissal of workers when they were not needed. Demarcations became entrenched via the development of no fewer than 17 separate craft unions by the end of the nineteenth century. These played important functional roles in the industry, administering and regulating the acquisition of craft skills through the apprenticeship system, and helping to retain workers in this particularly volatile sector by providing unemployment, sickness, and superannuation benefits, together with labour exchange services through the union branch network.[30]

---

26 M. J. Lewis, 'The growth and development of Sheffield's business structure, 1880–1930', unpublished Ph.D. thesis, Sheffield City Polytechnic, 1989, p. 40.

27 Lucy Newton, *The Victorian Economy in Transition: A Regional Perspective* (Aldershot, forthcoming), Chapter 2.

28 Lewis, 'The growth and development of Sheffield's business structure', p. 110.

29 Ibid, p. 140.

30 E. H. Lorenz, 'An evolutionary explanation for competitive decline: the British shipbuilding industry, 1890–1970', *Journal of Economic History*, 51 (1991), 911–35, p. 920.

Yet, partly in response to the chronic job insecurity, unions jealously defended craft demarcations and resisted new methods that broke with existing practices and might undermine traditional skills. They thus inhibited the introduction of new, labour-saving, technologies, such as pneumatic riveting, imposing manning restrictions and piece-rate terms that removed any labour-saving benefits. Yet, as in the Potteries and the Sheffield cutlery industry, employers also remained wedded to existing methods. Labour-intensive production allowed shipbuilders to avoid the higher costs of new, capital-intensive plant, which would be under-utilised during cyclical downturns in an industry that still built to order. They also allowed firms to keep their capital requirements within the funding limits of owning-families and thus avoid the loss of control involved in creating public companies.[31] Meanwhile tight family control increased their ability to resist change and amalgamation into larger shipyards that would have been better suited to the new methods.

The slow growth of new manufacturing sectors

Interrelatedness, existing endowments of plant and skilled labour, plus workforce and – often – employer resistance to new standardised, capital-intensive, methods, jointly acted to inhibit the adoption of the new technologies employed by Britain's overseas competitors in the principal staple industries. Yet as the world's wealthiest nation and the hub of international trade, commerce, and finance, Britain might have been expected to have shifted resources from these labour-intensive, and often low-value added, sectors to more capital and science-intensive industries such as chemicals, electrical engineering, motor vehicles, and machine tools, which comprised a rising proportion of world trade in manufactured goods. However as late as 1911 only 2.13 per cent of British manufacturing workers were employed in the chemicals industries; 1.76 per cent in electrical engineering; 3.35 per cent in vehicles (excluding shipbuilding), and 0.67 per cent in instrument engineering.[32] The structure of Britain's political economy, and in particular the dominant role of London-based services and overseas investment activities, resulted in British developments in these sectors occurring more slowly, and generally on a smaller scale, than in Germany and the USA.

Britain's large service sector and major surplus on invisibles impeded the development of new industries via a number of mechanisms. One involved the 'Dutch disease' effect, discussed earlier. Others were indirect. These included restricting the effective size of the British mass market (compared to what would be expected given Britain's high per capita GDP). Table 3.2 compares British GDP and three measures of living standards with those of nine other major trading nations in 1870 and 1913. In 1870 Britain had both the world's highest per capita GDP and one of the highest levels of inequality among western nations. While the other countries in the Table

31 Clive H. Lee, 'Scotland 1860–1939: growth and poverty', 428–55 in Roderick Floud and Paul Johnson (eds), *The Cambridge Economic History of Modern Britain. Volume II: Economic Maturity 1860-1939* (Cambridge, 2004), p. 438.

32 Clive H. Lee, *British Regional Employment Statistics 1841–1971* (Cambridge, 1979), Part III, Series B.

Table 3.2: GDP per capita and three indicators of living standards for Britain and other industrial nations in 1870 and 1913

	1870				1913			
	GDP per Capita	Real wage index	Life expectancy At birth	Literacy rate	GDP per capita	Real wage Index	Life expectancy at birth	Literacy rate
	(Britain =100)		(Years)	(%)	(Britain =100)		(Years)	(%)
Britain	100.0	100.0	41.3	76.0	100.0	100.0	53.4	96.0
Belgium	80.9	90.0	40.0	66.0	82.1	92.0	49.6	86.0
Netherlands	80.9	85.0	38.9	78.0	78.5	81.0	56.1	97.0
USA	75.3	172.0	44.0	75.0	105.5	179.0	51.6	92.0
Denmark	59.1	54.0	45.5	81.0	74.8	104.0	57.7	99.0
Germany	58.6	87.0	36.2	80.0	76.2	92.0	49.0	97.0
France	56.9	75.0	42.0	69.0	68.6	75.0	50.4	92.0
Sweden	51.0	42.0	45.8	75.0	61.5	105.0	57.0	98.0
Canada	49.6	148.0	42.6	79.0	83.7	216.0	52.5	94.0
Italy	45.0	39.0	28.0	32.0	49.8	53.0	47.2	62.0
Average (excl. Britain)*	61.9	88.0	40.3	70.6	75.6	110.8	52.3	90.8

Source: Adapted from George R. Boyer, 'Living standards, 1860–1939', 280–313 in Roderick Floud and Paul Johnson (eds), The Cambridge Economic History of Modern Britain. Volume II: Economic Maturity 1860–1939 *(Cambridge, 2004), Tables 11.1 & 11.6.*

Note: * Simple average, not weighted by population.

had an average per capita GDP almost 40 per cent lower than Britain's, their average wages were only 12 per cent lower. Furthermore, Britain achieved only sixth place out of the ten countries in terms of life expectancy at birth and only fifth place in terms of literacy. By 1913 Britain's relative gap between GDP per capita and average wages had further widened. Average GDP per capita for the nine other countries in the Table had risen to around three quarters of the British level, yet they managed to pay wages that exceeded Britain's by an average of 10 per cent.

Britain's extremely skewed income distribution had a substantial impact in constraining the growth of working-class expenditure. Even in the Edwardian era a considerable proportion of its population could not afford to properly feed themselves – evidence concerning the body mass of military recruits suggests that perhaps a third of young working-class males were underweight to such an extent that their risk of death was significantly increased.[33] While life expectancy had risen over the previous decades, this owed more to improvements in sanitation and water supply, and consequent reductions in infectious diseases, than to better nutrition.

Britain's poor literacy rate, relative to its per-capita GDP, points to a further factor inhibiting the development of new, science-based sectors – the under-developed state of its education system. While education provision improved substantially over the decades to 1913, Britain still ranked only fifth out of the ten countries in the table in terms of literacy, while other evidence also points to the continuation of a real, if reduced, gap between education provision in Britain and some of its leading competitors. For example, in 1910 only 54.2 per cent of British people aged 5–19 were enrolled in primary or secondary schools, compared to a 'European norm' of 62.6 per cent.[34] Data on the proportion of people with advanced or intermediate scientific and technical qualifications paint a similar picture. In 1901–1902 there were only 3,370 technology graduates in Britain, compared to 10,740 in Germany and 13,465 in the USA.[35]

Under-provision of education reflected a lack of demand on the part of Britain's dominant sectors. Skill acquisition in the staple industries was essentially a process of 'learning by doing', with workers entering employment at a young age and acquiring skills though interaction with more senior workers rather than via formal training programmes. Employers were therefore uninterested in, or even hostile to, state education as it offered them little benefit and might even be detrimental – by delaying the age at which children entered employment. Meanwhile the business and financial services sectors required only a limited number of workers, with clerical rather than technical skills. Britain thus suffered from both a general under-provision

33 George R. Boyer, 'Living standards, 1860–1939', 280–313 in Floud and Johnson, *The Cambridge Economic History of Modern Britain. Volume II*, p. 294.

34 Roger Middleton, *Government Versus the Market. The Growth of the Public Sector, Economic Management and British Economic Performance, c. 1890–1979* (Cheltenham, 1996), p. 22.

35 Mary B. Rose, 'Investment in human capital and British manufacturing industry to 1990', 339–71 in M. W. Kirby and M. B. Rose (eds), *British Enterprise in Modern Britain from the Eighteenth to the Twentieth Century* (London, 1994), p. 353.

of education and a smaller proportion of people with either advanced scientific,[36] or lower-grade technical, qualifications. Many British engineers received only sector-specific training in the established techniques of their industries, via apprenticeships or industry-based professional associations. Slow technological change in the staple industries in turn limited the demand for engineers with wider skills. The pool of people with the necessary aptitudes to develop new, capital-intensive, industries such as motor vehicles, chemicals, and electrical goods was thus constrained by the lack of demand for such skills on the part of established sectors.

Measures to address Britain's high levels of inequality and relative under-investment in education were impeded by government policies of laissez-faire and 'cheap government', designed to maintain confidence in Sterling, maximise the volume of international economic activities conducted through London, and avoid any potential conflict in monetary policy between domestic considerations and Britain's management of the international gold standard. Britain had a particularly unified political elite, its (by European standards) open and forward-looking landed elite having successfully integrated the City-based financial elite and, later, the richest and most prominent industrialists, into their ranks. Following the abolition of the protectionist corn laws, this elite had successfully united around an economic doctrine based on the three key pillars of classical liberal political economy– the gold standard, minimal balanced budgets, and free trade. These were viewed as essential to maintaining confidence in Sterling and London's central role in an open world economy. A large and growing amount of world trade and finance was being conducted in sterling and through London – underpinned by international confidence in the permanent free convertibility of sterling into gold at fixed parity. Low direct taxation was viewed as a barometer of Britain's social and political stability and, therefore, as vital to maintaining this confidence. Meanwhile free trade, though less central to City interests than currency stability, also buttressed the City's international role. It supported Britain's overseas investments, by enabling debtors to earn sterling via commodity sales to Britain. Moreover, it reinforced sterling's status as the world's key currency – by maintaining Britain's high ratio of exports and imports to GDP and supporting London's substantial entrepot trade.

Britain's leading industrialists generally shared these policy goals, as most operated in export-orientated staple industries that relied on free access to markets and international currency stability. Costly developmental policies such as substantial extensions in education provision or social transfers to people experiencing income loss through unemployment and illness (which would have boosted working-class demand, by stabilising incomes) were thus opposed, as were tariffs. In contrast to Britain, most other major industrial nations had introduced tariffs to protect their growing manufacturing sectors. Tariff protection reduced the risks faced by manufacturers contemplating costly long-term and large-scale investment in mass production plant. Thus major U.S. and German producers of electrical goods, motor vehicles, chemicals, and machinery had been able to achieve the 'minimum efficient

---

36 With the exception of activities such as medicine, that had already achieved professional respectability.

scale' for mass production in the relative safety of protected home markets, before turning to international sales.

The hegemonic position of the City and Britain's internationally-traded services also undermined the development of new capital-intensive industries in more subtle ways. As Sidney Pollard noted, 'a rentier's mentality ... [acted] to keep down innovatory activity in Britain while making the export of capital more attractive to British capitalists.'[37] Substantial and continuing balance of payments surpluses tempered the perceived need for the development of new industries or the modernisation of existing ones. Most importantly, high returns on overseas investments (which are generally agreed to have been superior to those on UK stocks, after adjustment for risk) allowed investors to avoid British investments that offered a lower *private* rate of return, but might have produced a higher *social* rate of return.

New manufacturing enterprises are inherently high risk, and every Ford or General Motors emerged from a much larger number of (generally unsuccessful) competitors. Yet successful 'first movers' in these sectors developed into major multinational corporations that went on to play important roles in the long-term international success of the United States, Germany, and other major industrial nations. It is notable that a high proportion of the world's largest manufacturing enterprises in the late twentieth century were founded during the final quarter of the nineteenth century.[38] If Britain's mechanisms for deploying savings overseas had not been so highly developed, it is more likely to have witnessed the sort of finance-backed development of modern corporations, operating in capital-intensive sectors and undertaking mass production of standardised goods, that characterised the early history of the major American and German multinationals.

The impact on regional growth

To what extent are the trends outlined above reflected in regional growth differentials? Estimates of regional GDP per capita and its composition, by Nick Crafts, allow us to examine whether movements in regional incomes corroborate the hypothesis of a relative concentration of incomes in London-based services and overseas investment revenues, at the expense of domestic manufacturing. As Table 3.3 shows, London already had a strong lead over the rest of Britain in terms of GDP per capita in 1871, while this increased substantially over the next four decades. Conversely, the 'industrial heartland' regions of Britain's lighter staple industries – the Midlands, Yorkshire & Humberside, and the North West, all experienced significant falls in relative per capita GDP.

The heavy-industry 'industrial periphery' presents a more mixed picture, due to the rapid expansion of coal exports during this period (the tonnage exported increasing by 4.6 per cent per annum over 1873–1913).[39] Scotland experienced a substantial

37 Pollard, *Britain's Prime*, p. 110.

38 Alfred D. Chandler, *Scale and Scope. The Dynamics of Industrial Capitalism* (Cambridge, Mass., 1990), p. 18.

39 Matthews, Feinstein, and Odling-Smee, *British Economic Growth*, p. 667.

improvement in its relative per capita GDP, Wales had a modest improvement, and the northern region faced a substantial relative decline (possibly due to its older coalfields). Meanwhile the predominantly agricultural regions of East Anglia, the South West and 'rest of the South East' all experienced declining relative GDP per capita. Overall regional differentials, as measured by the coefficient of variation, are shown to have widened substantially between 1871 and 1911 (particularly if London is treated as a separate region).

Table 3.4 provides a breakdown of regional GDP per capita into wage and non-wage incomes. The results are striking. The increase in the coefficient of variation between regions is entirely accounted for by movements in non-wage incomes.[40] Meanwhile there are substantial differences between relative movements in wages and other incomes. The industrial heartland regions fare much better in terms of wage than non-wage incomes throughout the period, while the decline in their relative GDP is mainly accounted for by deteriorating non-wage incomes. For example, the North West retained its place as the second-highest wage region of Britain, while in terms of non-wage income it fell from second to fifth place. The industrial periphery regions of the North, Wales and Scotland again show a more mixed pattern, while the predominantly agricultural regions all record improvements in wages, together with substantial relative falls in non-wage incomes.

Table 3.3: Regional GDP per capita, 1871–1911 (Britain = 100)

Region	1871	1881	1891	1901	1911
South East	117.4	119.9	122	121.7	124.6
London	147.3	144.3	154.9	154.9	165.6
Rest of South East	88.5	93.1	86.1	87.4	86.3
East Anglia	92	87.2	79.1	76.9	76.8
South West	86.2	87.2	81.6	81.5	85.7
West Midlands	83.6	79.5	78.4	81.7	78.4
East Midlands	102.3	98	93.8	90.3	90.6
North West	108.1	104.5	101.9	97.9	97.2
Yorkshire & Humberside	94.4	93.4	94.7	91.9	89.5
North	91.4	85.9	82.3	82.9	79.2
Wales	87.7	89.5	94.6	90.7	90.1
Scotland	89.9	95.1	97.9	104.9	102.1
CV 1	0.107	0.114	0.137	0.138	0.148
CV 2	0.176	0.172	0.215	0.216	0.249

Source: Nicholas Crafts, 'Regional GDP in Britain, 1871–1911: some estimates', Scottish Journal of Political Economy, *52 (2005), 54–64, Table 4.*

Notes: CV = coefficient of variation. CV1 treats the South East as a single region while CV2 treats London and the rest of the South East as separate regions.

40 Nicholas Crafts, 'Regional GDP in Britain, 1871-1911: some estimates', *Scottish Journal of Political Economy*, 52 (2005), 54–64.

Table 3.4: Regional wage and non-wage incomes per capita, 1871–1911 (Britain = 100)

Year	1871	1881	1891	1901	1911
a) Wage income per person					
South East	113.5	115.8	111.5	116	116.7
London	139.7	139.5	133.3	136.3	137.7
Rest of South East	88.4	89.0	87.7	95.0	97.0
East Anglia	77.7	73.2	71.4	76.9	79.6
South West	76.2	82.8	76.3	79.7	82.8
West Midlands	84.9	86.8	87.0	89.6	90.2
East Midlands	93.0	89.4	93.8	89.1	90.3
North West	122.3	116.1	114.4	105.6	105.6
Yorks & Humberside	100.0	98.9	102.0	96.9	97.7
North	96.9	90.7	94.3	89.4	86.5
Wales	95.8	95.9	97.5	91.2	90.0
Scotland	88.1	89.8	94.1	98.2	94.3
b) Non-wage income per person					
South East	121.2	123.8	132.5	127.4	132.6
London	154.8	148.6	176.6	173.5	193.4
Rest of South East	88.5	96.5	84.5	79.8	75.8
East Anglia	106.6	101.3	86.8	77.1	74.0
South West	96.0	95.3	87.1	83.2	88.7
West Midlands	82.4	79.9	69.9	73.7	66.6
East Midlands	111.7	104.8	93.9	91.5	91.0
North West	93.6	92.0	89.5	90.2	88.8
Yorks & Humberside	88.4	86.5	87.5	86.9	81.3
North	85.7	79.2	70.5	76.5	71.9
Wales	79.6	83.8	91.8	90.1	90.1
Scotland	91.5	99.4	101.5	111.6	110.1

Source: Nicholas Crafts, 'Regional GDP in Britain, 1871–1911: some estimates', Scottish Journal of Political Economy, *52 (2005), 54–64, Table 5.*

Yet the outstanding feature of the Table is the rapid rise in non-wage incomes in London, which already had per a capita non-wage income 54.8 per cent in excess of the national average in 1871 and increased this lead to 93.4 per cent by 1911. Meanwhile per capita wages in London actually fell slightly relative to the national average. London-based non-wage incomes thus appear to have comprised a large, and growing, share of British GDP, consistent with the hypothesis that the services and investment sectors concentrated incomes both spatially and among higher-income, non-wage-earning, groups. As Davis and Huttenback's analysis of shareholdings on the London Stock Exchange has demonstrated, London's non-wage incomes were more strongly linked to overseas investment revenues than were provincial non-wage incomes. Londoners had less than a quarter of their shares in domestic securities; compared to about half the portfolios of provincial investors. Meanwhile the domestic securities in Londoners' portfolios appear to have been more strongly weighted towards services and away from industry than those of their provincial counterparts.[41] An analysis of all wealth holdings, including land, property, shares quoted on provincial stock exchanges, and local and regional credit networks, would almost certainly show a stronger overseas, and metropolitan, focus for investors in London and the Home Counties relative to their provincial counterparts.

One puzzling feature revealed by the tables is the resilience of wage incomes in Britain's provincial industrial regions, which experienced much more modest declines (relative to the national average) than non-wage incomes. This suggests that the burden of adjustment to the deteriorating position of the staple industries fell primarily on profits, rather than wages. Increasing relative wages in the agricultural regions probably reflect improvements in transport and communications which made farm workers (who had wages considerably below those of urban workers) more aware of opportunities for better-paid industrial employment. By 1900 labour shortages were reported even in the arable counties of the south and east.[42] Farmers may thus have found themselves obliged to increase wage rates in order to retain their workers, despite the depression in agricultural (and particularly arable farming) profits.[43]

With regard to the provincial industrial regions, the most likely explanation for the superior performance of wages, relative to other incomes, is the growing strength of trade unions in the staple industries. Feinstein's analysis of movements in money wages during the Edwardian period suggests that an increasingly assertive trades union movement enjoyed some success in defending its members' real wages during an era of rising prices. The staple industries generally had strong and well-developed unions; for example, the mining, cotton, and shipbuilding industries featured prominently in the 1908–14 upsurge in industrial disputes. Data for the mining industry indicate that wages out-stripped productivity and profits, supporting the hypothesis that employers in such strongly unionised industries found it difficult to pass on deteriorating profits to workers via wage cuts.[44]

The political consequences of uneven development

The upsurge in industrial disputes represented only one facet of growing social and political unrest in Edwardian Britain, demonstrated in such diverse phenomena as the campaign of public protest in support of women's suffrage; Joseph Chamberlain's tariff reform movement; the election of a radical liberal government committed to social welfare reforms funded by land taxes; campaigns for Irish Home Rule and

41 Lance E. Davis and Robert A. Huttenback, *Mammon and the Pursuit of Empire. The Economics of British Imperialism*, abridged edition (Cambridge, 1988), pp. 178–79.

42 Alun Howkins, *The Death of Rural England. A Social History of the Countryside since 1900* (London, 2003), p. 23.

43 Crafts, 'Regional GDP in Britain'.

44 Feinstein, 'What really happened to real wages'.

devolution for Wales and Scotland; and calls for radical new social and economic measures to counter the growing military threat from Germany.

A common thread running through these campaigns was explicit reference to issues of poverty, inequality, and social welfare. Both the tariff reformers and the Liberals promised increased social transfers, funded respectively through tariff revenues and land taxes. The suffragettes sought the vote, in part, to improve the economic and social status of women, while the prospect of a major war with Germany raised fears that the poor physical state of military recruits evident during the Boer War might again impede Britain's military effectiveness. Irish Home Rule advocates also stressed the economic advantages of political autonomy and Alan O'Day has speculated that the intensity of the Home Rule debate might have been muted, had not the post-1870 United Kingdom been seen to be such a poorly-performing economic union.[45]

Chamberlain's 1903–1906 Tariff Reform campaign is particularly interesting, as it was based on an explicit critique of Britain's progressive transformation from a manufacturing to a service and rentier-dominated economy and the likely long-term consequences with regard to working-class employment, Britain's world power status, and domestic social order.[46] However, the proposed solution – closer links with Britain's white colonies through a system of tariff preferences and an Empire external tariff wall – was of doubtful practicality. The colonies had only limited enthusiasm for an economic federation along these lines (which threatened their own industrial ambitions) and it was feared that tariffs might benefit weak firms in declining sectors, rather than strengthen new firms in expanding ones. Tariff Reform failed to achieve an alliance between industrialists and the working-classes. Despite considerable support from the 'newer' sections of British industry, who saw Germany as both a model of success and a powerful threat (some even advocating continental-style government intervention in industry), the most politically influential industrialists, generally in mature export-orientated sectors such as cotton, retained their free-trade stance.[47] Meanwhile working-class voters were deterred from the movement by claims that Tariff Reform would lead to higher food prices.

Yet Britain was moving, albeit slowly, away from the 'cheap government' Victorian liberal consensus. The introduction of limited old age pensions and health and unemployment insurance in the years immediately preceding the First World War reflected the growing political strength of the working-class and other hitherto marginalised groups. Political liberalism, which had extended the franchise to the 'losers' from Britain's gradual transition to a London, services, and rentier economy, was proving a long-term threat to the economic liberalism that had underpinned that transition. In the event, the potential crisis of these conflicting currents of domestic and international policy was prevented by the onset of the First World War. After 1918 a very different Britain was to face a very different world.

---

45 Alan O'Day, 'Irish home rule and liberalism', 113–32 in A. O'Day (ed), *The Edwardian Age: Conflict and Stability 1900-1914* (London, 1979), p. 131.

46 Cain and Hopkins, *British Imperialism*, pp. 210–12.

47 Ibid., p. 219.

New industrial areas

While the growth of capital-intensive, science-based 'new' industries in Britain lagged behind the United States and Germany, there were a number of major developments prior to the First World War. One of the first successful pioneers of mass production in Britain was the sewing machine manufacturer Singer. Tellingly, Singer was the subsidiary of an American corporation and was thus able to circumvent obstacles such as the under-developed state of the corporation in Britain, the shortage of managers with high-level technical qualifications, and the lack of familiarity with mass production techniques on the part of British managers and engineers.

Singer, which has been described as the first modern multinational enterprise,[48] established an assembly plant in Glasgow in 1867. While this initial investment was motivated by a desire to improve its position in the British market, Singer soon identified Glasgow's strategic value as a distribution centre for Europe and the advantages of the area's low wage engineering workforce. Its assembly plant was therefore replaced by a larger factory, undertaking full-scale manufacture and serving all the firm's British, European, and Empire markets.[49] This was, in turn, eventually replaced by a still larger factory in near-by Clydebank, from where Singer produced over a million machines per year by 1914, with around seven eighths for export. This became one of Britain's largest factories, with a workforce of 14,500. While labour productivity was lower than in Singer's U.S. factories, this was more than offset by lower British labour costs. Plans were even made to export sewing machines from Clydebank to the USA, following cancellation of the U.S. tariff.[50]

Singer constituted an early example of what was to become a long-term pattern of U.S. (and, to a lesser extent, German) multinationals succeeding in the mass production of modern, science-based, consumer and producer goods in Britain, in sectors where British-owned firms were generally less successful. This trend was to become much more important during the interwar and post-war years. Yet by 1914 overseas-based firms in parts of the chemicals, mechanical engineering, and electrical engineering sectors, such as Singer, Siemens, General Electric, Westinghouse, Hoechst, and Ciba, already dominated British output of certain products. The entry of overseas multinationals gathered pace during the Edwardian era, a time when evidence points to a dip in the rate of productivity growth for domestic industry. Some 75 overseas firms instigated British production during 1900–1909, compared to 30 in the 1890s and eight in the 1880s.[51]

A substantial proportion of the in-coming multinationals located in 'new' industrial areas rather than traditional centres for the industries in question. These included a new form of industrial area – the industrial estate. In 1896 the world's first industrial estate was established on a 1,200-acre site at Trafford Park, Manchester,

48 Andrew C. Godley, 'Pioneering foreign direct investment in British manufacturing', *Business History Review*, 73 (1999), 394–429, p. 394.

49 After 1907 other plants were opened, in Canada, Germany, Russia, and the USA – though the Clydeside plant still constituted Singer's largest factory.

50 Godley, 'Pioneering foreign direct investment'.

51 Frances Bostock and Geoffrey Jones, 'Foreign multinationals in British manufacturing, 1850–1962', *Business History*, 36, 1 (1994); 89–126; pp. 96–100.

alongside the newly-opened Manchester Ship Canal and Manchester docks. The promoting company, Trafford Park Estates Ltd, offered industrialists a planned campus environment, with a well developed power and transport infrastructure, together with proximity to other firms in new, capital-intensive sectors. One of the first major firms attracted to the estate was British Westinghouse (a subsidiary of the American Westinghouse Corporation), which established a major factory at Trafford Park in 1899, based on the American parent's famous Pittsburgh plant.[52] This rapidly became the largest engineering factory in Britain and attracted a number of other firms that supplied British Westinghouse (or aspired to do so) to the estate.[53] Promoted as an '"Americanised" island in cotton-based Manchester', Trafford Park soon attracted other multinationals, most notably Ford, which established its first plant outside North America there in 1911.[54]

In 1899 the Hayes Development Co. launched Britain's second industrial estate, at Hayes in West London. This again attracted a number of overseas multinationals, including the German company J.A. King and Co. (1900), the Chicago printing machine manufacturer Goss Printing Co. (1904) and the German-based Gramophone and Typewriter Co. (1906).[55] It also attracted firms moving out from more congested areas of central London – often following a transition to more mechanised processes. Firms of this type also began to decentralise to satellite towns around London. These included Letchworth, Britain's first 'garden city,' developed some 35 miles north of London alongside the Great North Road by the Garden City and Town Planning Association – in an attempt to implement the visionary urban planning ideas of the social reformer Ebenezer Howard. Letchworth proved attractive to industrialists on account of relatively low land costs, the zoning of industry on an industrial estate, good transport links and a 'healthy environment' – advertised to industrialists via a concerted promotional campaign.[56] A number of other towns around the fringes of the London conurbation similarly promoted themselves as attractive centres for firms who wished to decentralise from the metropolis, including Luton (which had launched a new industries promotional initiative as early as 1899) and Watford. [57] The overall magnitude of such decentralisation was still relatively small, but it foreshadowed the much more vigorous centrifugal movement of London's assembly industries to such centres after 1918.

The other main area of new industrial development for capital-intensive science-based industries was the West Midlands. Victorian Birmingham had encompassed both

52 Trafford Park Estates Ltd, *Trafford Park. Past and Present. And Ship Canal Guide* (Manchester, 1902), p. 32.

53 Ian McIntosh, *Ford at Trafford Park: 'An American Corner of Old Jog-trot England*', Manchester Sociology Society Occasional Paper No.30 (January 1991), p. 8.

54 Ibid., p. 12.

55 'The Development of Hayes', *Middlesex and Buckinghamshire Advertiser* (16 February 1907), p.5.

56 Mervyn Miller, *Letchworth: The First Garden City* (Chichester, 1989) pp. 113–16.

57 Stephen Bunker, '"A small town outside Vauxhall": Luton in the twentieth century', unpublished paper, presented at ESRC Colloquium on Industry and Urbanisation, University College London, 8 May 1993, p. 2; W. Francis Goodrich, *Watford: Its Advantages as an Industrial and Residential centre* (Watford, c. 1908), pp. 10 and 12.

a heavy industrial base of coal and iron, together with a substantial agglomeration of diverse metal goods and light engineering trades, characterised by small firms, skilled labour, and industrial districts. These firms and their skilled artisans successfully adapted themselves to the production of a range of new industries during the quarter century to 1914, such as bicycles, motor vehicles and components, and electrical engineering. From an insignificant base in 1890, the West Midlands' motor vehicle, cycle, and components industries employed some 40,000 people on the eve of the First World War.[58] There was also considerable additional employment in associated industries, such as machine tools (which only became a large Midlands industry during this period) and tyres, together with some development of other modern science-based sectors such as office equipment and rayon.

Plants began to specialise by product, rather than process, in contrast to the extensive vertical specialisation that had hitherto characterised Birmingham's metal-bashing industries. This was accompanied by a growth in firm size and the start of a process of decentralisation from inner-urban industrial districts to new suburban industrial areas. These offered both lower land costs and weaker unionisation, allowing firms to substitute un/semi-skilled female workers on some hitherto skilled tasks, via mechanisation.[59]

In nearby Coventry an inherited base of artisan workshop industry again provided the necessary skills for the foundations of what rapidly grew into a factory-based industrial structure of product-orientated firms in a range of engineering-related trades. Cycle manufacture initially led this process, later being joined, and eventually dwarfed, by motor vehicles and components.[60] Work initially continued on the basis of small groups or gangs, often coordinated by 'small master' artisan industrialists, following the precedent of Coventry's traditional ribbon and watch industries. However, as demand shifted from a luxury to a mass market, mass production and de-skilling quickly followed.[61]

The initial development of Coventry's cycle industry was assisted by its location within a wider industrial area following a similar technological trajectory, enabling firms to draw on components supplies from Birmingham and other nearby centres.[62] Yet inter-sectoral linkages within Coventry assumed growing importance, with the emergence of its own substantial components industry. Local engineering firms constituted a mutually-reinforcing development bloc, for example its motor vehicle industry had strong initial links with its cycle trade, sharing many components. The first Coventry car firm, Daimler, moved to Coventry to take advantage of skills developed in the local cycle trade and other car manufactures relied extensively

58 G. C. Allen, *The Industrial Development of Birmingham and the Black Country, 1860–1927* (London, 1929), p. 302.

59 Ibid., pp. 330–42.

60 G. L. Marson, 'Coventry: a study in urban geography', unpublished M.A. thesis, University of Liverpool, 1949, p. 135.

61 P. W. Carr, 'Engineering workers and the rise of labour in Coventry, 1914–1939', unpublished Ph.D. thesis, University of Warwick, 1978, Chapter One.

62 Ibid., p. 5.

on local components suppliers. Meanwhile a number of Coventry's bicycle firms developed into motor vehicle manufacturers.[63]

Prior to 1914 the concentration of 'new' industries in the South was not nearly as obvious as was the case after 1918. The north hosted a number of major developments, including Singer at Clydebank; the rapidly growing industrial complex at Trafford Park; Boots, Raleigh, and Players at Nottingham; and Lever Brothers at Port Sunlight on Merseyside. Yet London and its hinterland had already established a strong position in most of the new, rapid-growth, sectors, albeit generally involving firms using craft rather than standardised production methods. For example, 48.0 per cent of new jobs in instrument engineering between 1841 and 1911, and 41.4 per cent of new electrical engineering jobs, were in the South East.[64] During the interwar years both the southern-concentration of new industrial development, and the need for such development in the north, were to be thrown into much sharper relief.

63 Ibid., pp. 9–11.

64 C. H. Lee, 'Regional growth and structural change in Victorian Britain', *Economic History Review*, 34 (1981), 438–52, p. 450.

Chapter Four

The First World War

Introduction

On 4 August 1914 Britain was reluctantly dragged into the first general European war for a century, in order to honour its treaty obligations and meet the perceived threat to British interests from German military expansionism. The following four years proved to be one of the bloodiest episodes in world history. While Britain suffered fewer casualties than some of the other belligerents, the British army and navy nevertheless lost at least 616,382 men (excluding troops from Britain's dominions and colonies), while 1,656,735 were wounded – many facing a lifetime of disability or disfigurement.[1]

The economic costs of the War were also considerable. While historians have noted both major gains and losses for British industry, there is a consensus that, on balance, the First World War and its aftermath had a severe negative impact. Much analysis has focussed on the damage to the staple industries (and those regions that relied on them) as a result of war-time over-expansion, indebtedness from speculative amalgamations during the short post-war boom, and the loss of overseas markets that Britain could not supply during war-time. The economic impact of the War and its aftermath on the South have received less discussion. As this chapter will show, particularly in the London region, the War played an important role in creating modern factory and transport infrastructure, boosting the supply of female factory workers, extending mass production techniques, and fostering the growth of new, science-based, industries. Areas of major war-time development, such as Slough, West and North Middlesex, the Lea Valley, Hertfordshire, Birmingham, and Coventry, were to become the main foci of interwar industrial development, attracting the type of production-line industries that had witnessed massive expansion there during the war years. While a regional divide in British industrial development was already evident by 1914, events during the following four years were to considerably widen it.

The War's direct impacts on British industrial development

Pre-war planning had rejected the idea of raising a continental-size army in favour of a strategy based around a naval blockade, which would require only a small volunteer army and limited mobilisation of wider economic resources, thus allowing government to pursue a 'business as usual' economic policy. In addition

1 Alan S. Milward, *The Economic Effects of Two World Wars on Britain*, 2nd Edn. (Houndmills, 1984), p. 12.

to strategic arguments, the naval strategy avoided conscription (which was initially regarded as politically impossible) and placated the Treasury, whose contribution to pre-war defence planning had been to try and keep expenditure as low as possible, while avoiding any interventionist measures that might threaten the government's laissez-faire, free trade, orthodoxy. This had impacted most acutely in munitions production. Sir George Murray, Joint Permanent Secretary of the Treasury, had used his chairmanship of the Government Factories and Workshops Committee in 1906/7 to develop recommendations that both reduced the size of the Royal Ordnance Factories and starved private manufacturers of orders (so that remaining Royal Ordnance factory capacity could be kept as fully employed as possible). Thus, when war broke out, there was a serious shortage of munitions capacity.[2] Even following the outbreak of hostilities the Treasury continued to oppose state intervention and control over the key resources required for the war effort and to feed the civilian population.[3]

Meanwhile during the early months of the War General Kitchener successfully out-manoeuvred the advocates of the navy-centred strategy, rapidly raising an army of over a million men. Moves toward 'total war', rather than the short, limited, conflict that military planners had envisaged, soon forced Whitehall to abandon the 'business as usual' strategy in favour of unprecedented economic intervention. For example, by the end of the War government had taken responsibility for marketing some 80 per cent of domestic food consumption and had control over the vast majority of consumer prices.[4] One of the most important areas of intervention was in the planning, financing, and direction of industry. This was to have a number of major impacts, by far the most fundamental being the transformation of the engineering-related trades from production systems based around skilled labour, flexible machinery, and batch production, to systems of unskilled labour, specialised automatic and semi-automatic machinery (or simplified labour-intensive assembly processes), and the mass production of standardised goods.

The onset of War created immediate problems for munitions production, by cutting off supplies of many items for which Britain relied on continental (usually German) producers, such as magnetos, synthetic dyestuffs, and optical glass. Such was Britain's reliance on German imports that the government actually entered into negotiations with Germany, through the neutral office of Switzerland, to obtain chemical dyes and optical instruments in return for British commodity supplies. While the expansion of British optical glass production made this bizarre transaction unnecessary, khaki dyes for British uniforms were obtained via such barter trade.[5]

2 G. C. Peden, *The Treasury and Public Policy, 1906–1959* (Oxford, 2000), p. 56.

3 David French, 'The rise and fall of "Business as usual"', 7–31 in Kathleen Burk (ed.), *War and the State. The Transformation of British Government, 1914–1919* (London, 1982).

4 Barry Eichengreen, 'The British economy between the wars', 314–43 in Roderick Floud and Paul Johnson (eds), *The Cambridge Economic History of Modern Britain. Volume II: Economic Maturity 1860–1939* (Cambridge, 2004), p. 320.

5 Roy Macleod and Kay Macleod, 'War and economic development: government and the optical industry in Britain, 1914–18', 165–204 in J. M. Winter (ed.), *War and Economic Development. Essays in Memory of David Joslin* (Cambridge, 1975), p. 175.

The first year of the War revealed serious and widespread deficiencies in the ability of Britain's private enterprise system to meet the demand for 'munitions' (defined as arms and ammunition, fighting and supply vehicles, and optical instruments).[6] Munitions producers were faced with the challenge of supplying a fighting force that rapidly expanded from 100,000 men to many times that number – ultimately three million. Meanwhile the initial rush to join the forces drew in many skilled engineers; by June 1915 19.5 per cent of male workers in the engineering trades had enlisted, few of whom could be recalled to civilian duties.[7] Despite government steps to prevent the enlistment of further engineering workers, a massive and rapid expansion of munitions-related industries and personnel became imperative.

Dissatisfaction at the organisation of war production administration under the War Office culminated in a political storm over serious munitions shortages on the Western Front, when Field Marshal French released details of his wholly inadequate armaments supplies to the press. French's action precipitated both the collapse of the Asquith government and the major supply innovation of the War – the establishment of the Ministry of Munitions in June 1915. By this time the inadequacies of a private enterprise solution to war production, and demands for state intervention, were also evident in a range of other war-related sectors.[8] The Ministry of Munitions proved successful in increasing both the volume of war-supplies and the efficiency of the supply system. In the process it rapidly expanded the scale and scope of its activities until by November 1918 it had a staff of 65,000, controlled the employment of some two million workers directly (and 3.4 million all told), managed or supervised around 20,000 establishments, and had disbursed some £2,000 million by March 1919.[9]

Britain had experienced an earlier war-induced boost to the munitions sector at the end of the nineteenth century, the Boer War having led to a major extension in armaments capacity – much of which was redeployed following the cessation of hostilities via diversifications into motor vehicle production.[10] The impact of the First World War was to have much stronger and broader impacts on the cluster of war-related 'new industries' – motor vehicles, aircraft, electrical engineering, machine tools, synthetic chemicals, non-ferrous metals, and scientific instruments. These occurred largely through government-fostered initiatives to modernise the manufacturing processes in the major munitions industries; boost the role of scientific research in product and process development; and encourage the diffusion of best practice managerial techniques.

From the perspective of the shop-floor worker, government-fostered process innovations had the most visible impact. Prior to this period many of the key sectors involved in war-production, such as scientific instruments, optical glass, and many

6 Sidney Pollard, *The Development of the British Economy, 1914–1950* (London, 1962), p. 44.

7 Pollard, *The Development of the British Economy*, p. 45.

8 See, for example, Macleod and Macleod, 'War and economic development'.

9 Pollard, *The Development of the British Economy*, p. 46.

10 Ranald Michie, 'The finance of innovation in late Victorian and Edwardian Britain: possibilities and constraints', *Journal of European Economic History*, 17, 3 (1988), 491–530, p. 521.

branches of engineering, had been essentially craft industries, undertaking batch production using flexible-specialisation systems. For example, the official history of the Ministry of Munitions claimed that, compared to the pre-war British engineering industry:

> ...no country in the world could show such a high level of workmanship or so much out-of-date machinery. Repetition work on a large scale was comparatively rare in England, and a well-equipped engineering firm produced an endless variety of articles, not always on a commercial scale. Labour-saving devices were frequently neglected and the industry placed more reliance upon skilled workers than upon automatic machinery.[11]

While the early months of the War saw a great increase in the demand for skilled labour, government progressively found ways of mitigating labour scarcity via labour-saving capital investment, assisted by machinery imports from the USA. The introduction of American-style mass production techniques, based on capital-intensive specialised machinery, enabled tasks to be simplified so that production could be undertaken largely using un-skilled and semi-skilled workers. This, in turn, enabled women with little manufacturing experience to be brought into the workforce, freeing up male workers for the trenches. Over the course of the War female employment in industry, transport, commerce, and the professions increased by over 1.5 million, to around 4,950,000. Many found jobs in the munitions industries, where female employment rose from 212,000 to 945,000.[12]

Under 'dilution' agreements, introduced from 1915, trade unions accepted de-skilling and the employment of women on tasks traditionally undertaken by men, in return for guarantees that traditional working practices would be reinstated after the War. Under these agreements new production methods were introduced, based on automatic machines and the mechanised production line.[13] As George Hodgkinson, a skilled turner and shop steward at the Daimler factory in Coventry, noted, while the limited skills of dilutees initially: 'confined them to the roughing-out operations on metal to be machined, the kind of "hewers in wood" in the engineering trade... high specialisation [subsequently] broke down operations, and the skills required were simpler in form. Automation... eliminated the need for production skills...'[14]. Similar developments were evident in other war-related industries, for example shipbuilding witnessed increased standardisation, together with the introduction of pneumatic and electrical tools.

Unskilled workers' wages consequently rose and wage differentials between them and their skilled counterparts narrowed. For example, in the engineering and shipbuilding industries wage rates for unskilled labourers were estimated to have risen by some 113 per cent of their July 1914 values by July 1918, while rates for representative skilled trades had risen by only 69–73 per cent. Male/female wage differentials also narrowed markedly. As Sidney Pollard noted, while this trend

---

11 Ministry of Munitions, *History of the Ministry of Munitions*, Vol. VII, part 1 (London, 1918–1922), p. 94.

12 Pollard, *The Development of the British Economy*, p. 78.

13 Milward, *The Economic Effects of Two World Wars on Britain*, pp. 38–9.

14 George Hodgkinson, *Sent to Coventry* (Bletchley, 1970), p. 44.

was superficially largely the result of flat-rate wage increases, it also represented the underlying reality in most industries of the declining importance of traditional skills and the growing predominance of semi-skilled or virtually unskilled machine minders.[15] This pattern of high demand for un/semi-skilled labour and narrowing differentials between men and women was to be resurrected in the areas of former munitions production around London and the West Midlands during the interwar years, as discussed in Chapters 8–11.

The government-fostered introduction of machine tools sometimes produced spectacular productivity improvements. For example in optical glass (a small-scale craft-based industry in 1914, dwarfed by its German counterpart), mechanisation brought about a reduction in the manufacturing time for a binocular prism from eight or nine hours to half an hour. Automatic machinery and the employment of semi-skilled workers allowed the industry to expand some twenty-fold during the war years, while greatly increasing its product range.[16] The Ministry of Munitions also played a key role in diffusing best-practice managerial and accounting techniques throughout National Factories and controlled firms, including cost accounting, American-style 'scientific management' techniques of time and motion study, and productivity-based systems of worker remuneration such as 'premium bonus'.

New production techniques and systems of labour monitoring and remuneration often provoked a hostile response from workers and unions. Yet over the course of the war restrictive practices were significantly reduced. In the immediate post-war period these changes appeared transitory – government being forced by the unions to honour its pledge to return to pre-war norms.[17] Yet some de-skilling innovations remained, such as the introduction of automatic welding and the use of limit gauges by unskilled labour.[18] More importantly, despite the government's initial efforts to be seen to honour its commitment, many working practices introduced during the War years were soon re-introduced into engineering, metal-working, and other sectors involving analogous production processes, in the harsh business climate of the interwar years. As *The New Survey of London Life and Labour* noted, while production methods in London's engineering trades had been transformed by the War, 'only when their demobilisation was fairly complete did they reveal the full extent of the technical and economic revolution which had meanwhile been in progress...'[19]

One key innovation that permeated much of British industry was the accelerated diffusion of electricity. Prior to 1914 Britain had generally lagged behind other leading industrial nations in this area, the majority of factories remaining steam-powered.[20]

15 Pollard, *The Development of the British Economy*, p. 86.

16 Macleod and Macleod, 'War and economic development', p. 177.

17 B. W. E. Alford, 'Lost opportunities: British business and businessmen during the First World War', 205–227 in N. McKendrick and R. B. Outhwaite (eds), *Business Life and Public Policy: Essays in honour of D.C. Coleman* (Cambridge, 1986), pp. 223–4.

18 Pollard, *The Development of the British Economy*, p. 20.

19 London School of Economics *The New Survey of London Life and Labour. Volume II: London Industries I* (London, 1931), p. 41.

20 Ministry of Munitions, *History of the Ministry of Munitions*, Vol. VIII, part 3, p. 92.

Conversely some 95 per cent of new munitions factories were electrically powered.[21] The war required substantial restructuring of Britain's fragmented and non-standardised electricity supply industry along lines more similar to those of its German adversary. Shortages of fuel and generating plant necessitated rationalisation to prevent the duplication of equipment in small, inefficient, stations. Following the establishment of the Ministry of Munitions, the Ministry's Gun Ammunition Department was given the remit of overseeing power supply. Capacity was extended following the principle that electricity should be obtained from public supply stations where possible rather than generated independently in private stations – thus concentrating generation in large units and facilitating their future incorporation into any post-war power supply programme.[22] However, other government departments did not always follow this policy for their own power needs and this lack of coordination between the main power-using ministries limited the effectiveness of the policy.

Despite these problems, concentrating generation in larger power stations produced substantial scale economies – assisted by an emphasis on modern, high-capacity, plant. Pressure to economise on the use of coal led to government encouragement of the linking up of electricity networks and greater use of bulk supply arrangements, which further increased productivity. Yet modernisation was largely limited to areas of high munitions demand.[23] Meanwhile Treasury pressure for financial restraint blocked some of the most ambitious rationalisation schemes in favour of cheaper short-term expedients. For example, in 1918 a Ministry of Munitions project, to provide four generating plants at a cost of £3 million, led to Treasury objections that the underlying rationale was:

> *not* to provide for War necessities but to equip the country for after-the-war trade. It is a form of 'State Capitalism'. The commercial gentlemen who have got a footing in the ministry – possibly with quite disinterested and patriotic motives – think they will never get such another opportunity – with unlimited credits, Defence of the Realm Act powers and all the rest of it, to re-equip the country on the most modern lines at the expense of the general taxpayer.[24]

During the War years the average size of generating unit increased from 522 to 7,000 KW. While output growth was no higher than had been the case during the pre-war period, the rate of growth of industrial sales was undoubtedly accelerated by the war; between 1913 and 1920 these expanded from 1,000 to 2,545 GWh. Industrial demand, which had constituted about half the pre-war electricity supply market, accounted for nearer two-thirds by 1920.[25] This was accompanied by major new process applications. For example, electric air compressors for riveting proved key to productivity advances in shipbuilding. Meanwhile electric steel furnaces facilitated the use of domestic and

---

21 Leslie Hannah, *Electricity before Nationalisation: A Study of the Development of the Electricity Supply Industry in Britain to 1948* (London, 1979), pp. 57–9.

22 Ministry of Munitons, *History of the Ministry of Munitions*, Vol. VIII, part 3, p. 93.

23 Hannah, Electricity before Nationalisation, pp. 54–5.

24 NA, T1/12207/39120, George Barstow to John Bradbury, 21 Feb. 1918, cited in Peden, *The Treasury*, p. 118.

25 Ibid, pp. 59–60 and Table A1.

Spanish ore and scrap metal, after Britain lost its supply of Swedish ore, and offered important advantages for the production of high-grade steel.[26] In 1918 there were 117 electric furnaces in existence (74 in Yorkshire – many in Sheffield), very few of which had been installed before the War.[27]

Government played a key role in promoting scientific research in the main war-related industries. In June 1915, alarmed at Germany's technical lead in a range of key sectors, it established a department to promote scientific research in industry (in 1916 this acquired its familiar name of the Department of Scientific and Industrial Research – DSIR). DSIR helped industries to form research associations, while itself establishing research stations to undertake research considered of national importance but unsuitable for industry-wide private enterprise.[28] Government initiatives fostered the accelerated technological development of several research-intensive or engineering-related industries, including aircraft, radio, scientific instruments, chemicals, explosives, petroleum, ball bearings, and motor vehicles. For example, Macleod and Macleod found that government initiatives to mobilise capital and technical assistance in the optical instruments sector liberated a hitherto unexploited capacity for technical innovation and diffusion – the forced collaboration between skilled technicians, scientists, and manufacturers sending, 'a quickening impulse along the entire route of innovation from "pure" research to product and process development, to manufacture and to diffusion.'[29] Similarly in a number of other sectors government-fostered collaborations between universities, scientists, and industry, often fostered by the new research associations, were to prove an enduring legacy of the War.

The influence of the War on industries previously served from Germany is illustrated by the case of tungsten production. Before the war the British tungsten industry was negligible, manufacturers of high-speed steel relying on German supplies – despite the fact that the raw material, wolfram ore, was largely produced in the British Empire. War demand resulted in the establishment of a significant tungsten industry in Britain. This received further financial support after the War, to reduce the impact of the sudden reduction in military demand, while the industry was further supported with a one third ad valorum duty under the 1921 Safeguarding of Industries Act.[30] Similar impacts were evident in some much larger industries. For example, the War transformed both the scale and methods of the motor vehicle industry, encouraging the adoption of interchangeable parts and modern production techniques (assisted by the demonstration effect of Ford's new Trafford Park plant).[31] In common with some other government-supported science-intensive sectors, the industry received tariff protection from 1915, under the McKenna duties. Although ostensibly temporary war-time measures, these duties were continued throughout the

26 Ibid, pp. 55–6.

27 Ministry of Munitions, *History of the Ministry of Munitions*, pp. 104–5.

28 R. S. Sayers, 'The springs of technical progress in Britain, 1919–39', *Economic Journal*, LX (1950), 275–91, pp. 280.

29 Macleod and Macleod, 'War and economic development', p. 191.

30 Ministry of Munitions, *History of the Ministry of Munitions*, Vol. VII, part 1, p. 83.

31 Alford, 'Lost opportunities', p. 214.

interwar years and encouraged both domestic producers in these sectors and inward foreign direct investment by American and other tariff-jumping overseas firms.[32]

Meanwhile higher working class incomes and the elimination of unemployment and under-employment boosted the general level of domestic consumption and the potential demand for the types of consumer goods that the munitions factories might convert to in peacetime. Bernard Alford's survey of the impact of the War on leading British firms found that such effects benefited both munitions producers and consumer-goods firms serving the war effort, such as Courtaulds, Lever Brothers, Imperial Tobacco, Boots, and the oil companies.[33] Domestically-focused consumer-goods production, underpinned by rising mass incomes, was to provide the main engine of industrial growth in Britain during the 1920s and 1930s.

Of the staple industries, the War had the largest impact on technology and capacity in the iron and steel sector. The Ministry of Munitions fostered the introduction of a number of new techniques, including the spread of the basic and open hearth processes, the extension of special alloy steel production, and heat treatment technology.[34] However, new steel capacity was generally built alongside existing plant and thus had the effect of perpetuating existing location patterns, which were often poorly suited to the needs of the modern industry (see Chapter Six). Furthermore, the industry did not experience the radical changes in the organisation of production witnessed in the metal goods and engineering-related sectors. This is illustrated by the example of the West Midlands, where the War years greatly accelerated an existing divergence between the development paths of the region's heavy iron and steel bloc and its lighter metal goods and engineering base.[35] Prior to the War there had been a broad division of functions between Birmingham and the Black Country. The Black Country had specialised in the making of iron and steel, forging, founding, and heavy engineering, with a labour force heavily dominated by men.[36] Meanwhile Birmingham had concentrated on the production of machinery, engines, and, especially, small metal goods, employing a substantial proportion of women and using 'flexible specialisation' production methods, characterised by:

> 'divisible' as opposed to 'lumpy' investment. Thus a plant might have – perhaps running from a single power source – a whole series of stamping, or capstan lathes, or spinning, or sheet metal working etc., machines... With this kind of technical equipment, the internal economies of scale were slight enough to permit small firms to be efficient and a wide variety of combinations of different processes within, and between, firms was possible.

32 Peter Scott and Tim Rooth, 'Protectionism and the growth of overseas multinational enterprise in interwar Britain,' *Journal of Industrial History*, 3, 2 (2000), 31–50.

33 Alford, 'Lost opportunities', pp. 211–15.

34 Ministry of Munitions, History of the Ministry of Munitions, Vol. VII, part 1, pp. 87–8.

35 G. C. Allen, *The Industrial Development of Birmingham and the Black Country, 1860–1927* (London, 1929), p. 374.

36 NA, BT177/2330, report to the Clay Committee on the industrial development of the West Midlands Conurbation in the interwar years, by M. Beesley, May 1955.

> Thus, many kinds of assembled products could be made, each process-specialist firm contributing to the activities of many assemblers.[37]

The First World War led to an expansion in the Black Country's traditional iron and steel manufacture and goods industries, using conventional skills, together with some expansion in the use of unskilled (partly female) labour. When the post-war boom ended these heavy industries resumed a decline which had been already evident by 1914.[38] In Birmingham, by contrast, there was a large expansion of assembly processes, hitherto undertaken only on a small scale in the Birmingham area and involving a considerable extension of the female workforce. Many traditional trades, such as silversmiths and jewellery, button, and pen producers, turned to munitions manufacture. War-time restructuring gave rise to some major companies. For example, at the start of the War the engineering firm Lucas decided to move into magneto production, where it anticipated heavy demand, as 98 per cent of peacetime UK demand had been supplied by the German firm Robert Bosch. It thus acquired the manufacturing side of the only current British magneto manufacturer, the small Birmingham firm Thomas-Bennett Ltd. Raising output levels from about 1,500 magnetos in 1914 to 100,000 in 1919 entailed the introduction of standardised and assembly production methods, which laid the foundations for Lucas's subsequent success as the main sub-assembler of electrical equipment for the motor vehicle industry.

Lucas's new mass production workforce included a high proportion of women, many of whom had transferred from Birmingham's declining jewelry quarter.[39] Similarly, workers in other Birmingham factories were introduced to new processes and a range of skills (including some related to electrical engineering) were added to the workforce.[40] A new class of 'general workman', emerged, with knowledge of many kinds of machinery and sufficient engineering skill to set their own machines, together with a new class of women workers, experienced in a range of repetition metal-working and assembly tasks. These changes appear to have weakened unionisation in Birmingham. Meanwhile the Black Country's labour structures were relatively undisturbed, perhaps contributing to its stronger unionisation and higher level of industrial conflict during the early 1920s.[41]

Another important contrast between Birmingham and the Black Country concerned their legacies of war-time product and process innovation. The War stimulated development of a wide variety of engineering machinery in Birmingham, some embodying new processes, such as improved methods for cutting metals. The introduction of magneto production in the motor vehicle industry laid the foundations for a local ancillary industry in electrical parts production for motor vehicles. War-time gear cutting developments also found peacetime applications in the motor

37 Ibid.

38 Allen, *The Industrial Development of Birmingham*, p. 389.

39 Michael Beesley, 'Changing industrial advantages in the British motor car industry', *Journal of Industrial Economics*, 6 (1957), 47–57; Harold Nockolds, *Lucas: The First Hundred Years. Vol.I: The King of the Road* (Newton Abbot, 1976), pp. 143–55.

40 NA: BT177/2330.

41 Ibid.

vehicle industry, while in rubber goods (mainly tyres) employment expanded almost four-fold between 1911 and 1921. This period also witnessed the development of a local aluminium casting industry to supply aircraft producers, which again survived after the war by supplying motor vehicle firms.[42] Conversely, the Black Country experienced relatively little industrial diversification.

Birmingham's industrial complex derived further benefit from munitions production via the introduction of very large-scale factories, producing standardised items, and moves towards vertical integration in some sectors. Michael Beesley argued that the War was the key factor behind Birmingham's move from small-scale production to a significant base of very large engineering plants (together with the survival of a large mass of specialist suppliers and sub-contractors).[43] The contrasting war-time experiences of the Black Country and Birmingham, which became strongly reflected in their interwar performance, was repeated on a national scale. As the following chapters will show, Britain's expanding manufacturing industries generally shared the key features of assembly operations, the displacement of craft skills by general production skills, a significant expansion in the employment of women and non-apprentice juveniles, and new production methods aimed at the rapid throughput of standardised goods. While these trends were evident in some companies and sectors prior to 1914, the decisive shift in production techniques often occurred during the War years. Meanwhile the impact of war on the staple industries had largely concerned the volume, rather than nature, of their production.

War-time infrastructure development

The impact of the War on physical and human capital development again demonstrated a strong regional divide. While Britain's outer regions capitalised on their proximity to the coalfields and their existing industrial base by undertaking heavy war production, such as iron and steel manufacture, shipbuilding, and heavy engineering, the South East and West Midlands received a particularly large share of production involving light assembly work. This both boosted their supply of female and other semi-skilled workers and gave them a considerable physical legacy of modern factories and plant.

One major source of new infrastructure development was the government's 'National Factory' programme. By November 1918 there were over 200 National Munitions Factories, while the addition of stores, depots, etc. brought the total to 305. Some were developed from privately-owned establishments, commandeered by government, though the majority were purpose-built, involving an aggregate government expenditure of some £60 million.[44] In designing the National Factories, considerations of efficient production flow took priority over safety measures – such as building in separate units so as to contain explosions. Factories were also designed to facilitate the employment of women – for example by avoiding operations that

42 Ibid; Allen, *The Industrial Development of Birmingham*, pp. 403–404.

43 NA: BT177/2330.

44 NA: BT106/21, 'Disposal of factories at the end of the last war', memorandum, 7 October 1943.

would entail heavy lifting. The first National Factories were often poorly designed, partly due to the speed of their construction. However, over the following years the Ministry of Munitions gained considerable experience in factory building and increasingly applied scientific management criteria to plant layout.[45] Most proved efficient production units, generally supplying munitions more cheaply than private contractors (even after allowing a good margin for depreciation of plant).[46]

The National Factory programme boosted the diffusion of a new model of factory design and location, which was beginning to emerge in a few areas even prior to 1914, but was undoubtedly greatly accelerated during the war years. Previously even many factories in 'new' sectors, such as branded packaged foods and cigarettes, had been developed as traditional multi-storey factories in inner-urban areas, as shown by the examples of Player's Castle tobacco factory at Nottingham, and Huntley & Palmer's biscuit factory at Reading, in Figure 4.1.

National factories generally adopted the modern 'shed' factory model, which had been pioneered in the American motor vehicle industry by architects such as Albert Kahn. Efficient production-line technology required production to flow horizontally across a factory floor unencumbered by excessive internal pillars and walls. The solution was to develop single-storey factories, steel or reinforced concrete skeletons being used to create sheds of large roof-spans and minimal internal supports, which were lit naturally throughout via windows in the north-light or single span roofing. Such factories were economical and simple to build, adaptable and easily capable of extension, facilitated rapid construction and incurred low maintenance costs.[47] An example of the new production conditions facilitated by this type of well-lit, open, factory floor is shown in Figure 4.2. Given their high volume of production and single-storey premises, the National Factories required very large sites. They were thus generally developed in 'green field' areas, accelerating the trend towards the suburbanisation of industry.

Southern firms were much more extensively involved in munitions production than the textile and clothing firms that dominated light industry in many northern areas. As such they benefited from widespread remodelling of buildings and up-to-date machinery, while their northern counterparts were often barely touched by wartime modernisation initiatives.[48] London proved one of the most important centres for munitions production. Government factories and depots within the metropolis were principally concentrated in 'green field' areas on the fringes of the conurbation, where industrialisation was only just beginning in 1914, such as Acton, Willesden, Hayes, Greenford, the Lea and Wandle Valleys, Croydon, and the Lower Thames. Availability of labour was an important consideration in selecting these sites, which

45 Ministry of Munitions, *History of the Ministry of Munitions*, Vol. VIII, part 1, pp. 66–8.

46 NA: BT106/21.

47 James Marshall, *The History of the Great West Road* (Hounslow, 1995), p. 56.

48 E. D. Smithies, 'The contrast between north and south in England 1918–1939: a study of economic, social and political problems with particular reference to the experience of Burnley, Halifax, Ipswich, and Luton', unpublished Ph.D. thesis, University of Leeds, 1974, p. 64.

were in expanding residential areas with good public transport links both to central London and to agricultural areas beyond London's fringes.

Following the end of the War some 130 government factories were ear-marked for disposal to industry. These were generally well-suited for civilian assembly production and were rapidly converted to the manufacture of goods such as dynamos, electrical fittings, drop stampings, oil engines, lace, engineering, railway wagons, bottle machinery, and propellers.[49] National factories formed the nuclei of a number of major industrial agglomerations in and around the London area. For example, war-time munitions plants at Park Royal (spanning the West Middlesex boroughs of Acton and Willesden) were acquired by a number of developers and formed the basis of the giant Park Royal industrial estate that employed some 30,000 people by 1938.[50] Aircraft and munitions plants also formed the core of successful interwar industrial estates at the Hyde in Colindale, West Middlesex, and at Croydon. War-time depots also proved well suited for civilian factory production. A 72 acre R.A.F. depot at Feltham (originally developed by the Whitehead Aircraft Co.) became occupied by a variety of firms including Citroen's first English car assembly plant (and, later, by Aston Martin).[51] At Slough, where some £2 million had been invested by government during 1918 and 1919 in constructing a national repair depot for war transport vehicles, the sale of the depot to a private consortium led to the establishment of the Slough trading estate – accommodating some 210 firms and around 28,500 workers by 1938.

War developments also boosted these areas' human capital endowments. Local female workers received training and experience in assembly production, while many workers, who initially commuted in from inner-London, later moved into these areas.[52] War-time human capital and physical infrastructure development initiated a cumulative, self-sustaining, process of development, encouraging further factory-building and in-migration into what became Britain's most important centres for standardised, assembly, production, as discussed in Chapters 8–9.[53]

The long-term impact of the War

Until the final months of the War it had been assumed that the outcome would probably be a stalemate, with a strong Germany having the potential to continue its conflict with Britain on an economic, rather than military, plane.[54] The Ministry of Reconstruction had made extensive investigations regarding ways in which war-time

49 NA: BT106/21.

50 NA: HLG52/746, report by London Passenger Transport Board and main line rail companies to the Technical Committee of the Standing Conference on London Regional Planning, 18 November 1938.

51 J. E. Martin, *Greater London: An Industrial Geography* (Chicago, 1966), p. 32.

52 D. E. Keeble, 'Industrial growth in North West London: A geographical analysis', unpublished Ph.D. thesis, University of Cambridge, 1967, pp. 21–2.

53 Ibid, pp. 41–2.

54 Peter Cline, 'Winding down the war economy: British plans for peacetime recovery, 1916–19', 157–81 in Burk, *War and the State*.

Figure 4.1: The pre-1914 model of large-scale factory development – Player's Castle tobacco factory, Nottingham, and the Huntley & Palmer biscuit factory, Reading.

state intervention in industry could be developed into an effective post-war state-led industrial modernisation strategy to counter this threat. Increased social welfare expenditure was also envisaged, partly do avoid heavy post-war unemployment and political unrest by creating 'homes fit for heroes'. Meanwhile the Treasury had developed a very different policy, based around a return to the pre-war gold standard and requiring both an end to government borrowing and the imposition of deflation

Figure 4.2: The new model of large-scale factory development – the machine shop of the Chester Engineering Co. in 1917

and higher interest rates. As the Minister of Reconstruction, Sir Auckland Geddes, pointed out at a February 1919 ministerial conference, the Treasury's financial policy was incompatible with the 'social (better Britain) policy' of active post-war reconstruction.[55] Meanwhile Germany's sudden collapse in the months leading to the Armistice had undermined the strategic arguments in favour of continued economic intervention and massively strengthened the hand of the advocates of a return to pre-war 'normalcy'.[56] During the following months high inflation, rising government debt, deteriorating industrial relations, and the City's desire for a return to free trade and Glastonian finance, all lent weight to the Treasury view. Thus, with the exception of a few initiatives to promote key industries, the war-time framework of intervention and planning was rapidly demolished, while social welfare measures were largely shelved.

In macroeconomic and financial terms, Britain came out of the War a considerably weakened nation. War-time inflation and production dislocations had massively raised British export prices; the ratio of British to US prices having increased by an estimated 49 per cent between 1913 and 1917–18.[57] British industry thus faced a major readjustment problem if it was to regain competitiveness in world markets. This was to prove a long and painful process. Econometric analysis by Greasley and Oxley indicates that the First World War represented a major negative shock to Britain's long-term growth, the effects of which persisted during the interwar years: while British industrial growth was faster after 1920, the gap between potential output (based on extrapolating pre-1914 growth trends) and actual industrial production was not eradicated until 1937.[58] They also found that the main decline in Britain's industrial competitiveness occurred during the First World War, rather than the 1919–20 readjustment, which had been identified as the crucial period in earlier work by J.R. Dowie.[59] Yet the long-term detrimental impact of the War did not become evident until around 1920, when the transition to peacetime trading relationships required sharp cost reductions on the part of British industry if it was to regain its competitiveness in overseas and domestic markets. Post-war inflation exacerbated the adjustment problem, while the obvious solution of a major devaluation of sterling was regarded as politically unacceptable (in the face of vigorous opposition from City interests). Given that sterling's real exchange rate is estimated to have been over-valued by more than 30 per cent in the immediate post-war years, the prognosis for British industry was bleak.[60]

---

55 Peden, *The Treasury*, p. 125.

56 William R. Garside, 'The economic legacy of conflict: Britain in the aftermath of the First World War', 25–36 in Harmut Berghoff and Robert von Friedeburg (eds), *Change and Inertia. Britain under the Impact of the Great War* (Bodenheim, 1998), pp. 27–9.

57 David Greasley and Les Oxley, 'Discontinuities in competitiveness: the impact of the First World War on British industry', *Economic History Review*, XLIX, 1 (1996), 82–100, p. 95.

58 Ibid.

59 J. R. Dowie, '1919–20 is in need of attention', *Economic History Review*, XXVIII (1975), 429–50.

60 Greasley and Oxley, 'Discontinuities in competitiveness', p. 98.

Yet the impact of this over-valuation did not hit all industries equally. Firms producing branded goods could differentiate their products from those of competitors in the eyes of their consumers and thus enjoyed some measure of protection against an uncompetitive exchange rate. Another group of industries for which overvaluation had a lesser impact were manufacturers of goods facing limited overseas competition, such as clothing (where proximity to markets was vital to keeping pace with changing consumer tastes) and printing (where the need for face-to-face contact and rapid turn-around times again required a market-based location). Conversely, the industries most sensitive to overvaluation were those producing standardised commodities and semi-manufactureds. Unfortunately many of the industries that formed the back-bone of the industrial economies of northern and western Britain fell into this category, such as coal mining, much iron and steel production, and most branches of the textile industry.

Much of the new munitions complex, concentrated around London and the West Midlands, switched to manufacturing branded goods (or to supplying branded goods producers). The relatively low prices at which much factory and plant passed from government to civilian hands eased these companies' competitive positions. Meanwhile the war-time introduction of new machinery, production methods, and forms of cheaper labour offered them major competitive advantages. Mass production methods pioneered in Britain during the War years proved particularly useful for firms producing standardised, branded, goods, enabling them to maintain large-scale production. Meanwhile, smaller components plants in these areas generally moved towards specialisation in a narrower range of goods for a smaller number of (individually larger) customers than had been the case pre-war, leading to the displacement of flexible machinery and methods by more specialised equipment for standardised production.

The War had lowered the risks associated with conversion to mass production, highly profitable war contracts having provided a substantial and (temporarily) safe market for standardised products. These developments eased the transition of long-established sectors in the south and midlands to new products and production methods. For example, many of Birmingham's metal-working industries, despite being in sectors that faced depression nationally, prospered by transforming themselves into components manufacturers for its expanding electrical apparatus and vehicle industries. These changes were accompanied by sharp declines in traditional sub-contracting relationships, continuing the war-time trend from craft to mass production.[61]

The staple industries, by contrast, had not undergone any similar radical transformation in production methods during the War years and an over-valued currency was only one of the problems they faced. For four years naval hostilities had shut off foreign markets, while foreign neutrals and indigenous producers had seized their opportunity to capture markets previously served from Britain. For example, in South America and South Asia, where British exports had hitherto reigned supreme, American and Japanese producers gained important footholds. Having established these 'beachheads', Britain's new competitors proved extraordinarily difficult to

61 Allen, *The Industrial Development of Birmingham*, pp. 400–24.

dislodge, especially by a country that was deliberately raising its export prices in an attempt to restore its pre-War gold standard parity.

War-time technological changes also reduced demand for some staple industry products; for example the demand for coal was weakened by the promotion of technical change based on oil and electricity. Meanwhile several of the major staple industries, particularly iron and steel and shipbuilding, had substantially extended their capacity during the war years. High war-time profits had offered opportunities for post-war structural adjustment, while inflation reduced accumulated over-capitalisation in the form of fixed-interest debt. Yet, rather than taking advantage of these opportunities, the staple industries – following a commonly held, but (with hindsight) outrageously optimistic view of their post-Armistice international market position – instead embarked on a spree of speculative investment, much of which served only to bid up the value of existing plant. This further extended over-capacity, though its main effect was to increase overcapitalisation, saddling these industries with debt burdens that were to considerably weaken them for the rest of the inter-war years. Following the return to normal trading conditions this mis-match between capacity and demand was to become painfully obvious.

War and the transport revolution

A further major impact of the First World War on the geography of industrial development involved accelerating the switch of inland freight transport from rail to road. The War witnessed a revolution in mechanical road transport. At its outbreak the War Office had only 47 motor lorries in use, while it could call on a further 700 civilian-owned vehicles.[62] Meanwhile the technical development of motorised road haulage was very limited, services over distances that would rival the railways still being at the experimental stage.[63] War transformed the sector, military demand for vehicles stimulating both production and technical development on an unprecedented scale. Following the close of hostilities the War Disposals Committee sold around 60,000 lorries and vans at low prices, whilst war-time duties had trained at least as many men to drive them.[64]

At the close of the War it was still generally believed that road and rail transport were complementary, road vehicles fulfilling their traditional role of short distance transport and feeder traffic for the railways.[65] However, the purchase of war-surplus vehicles (often suitable for medium-distance transport) by demobilised servicemen who set themselves up as haulage contractors, together with the expansion of established firms, led to a mushrooming of the sector. So great was the demand

62 Michael Cassell, Long Lease! The Story of Slough Estates 1920 – 1991 (London, 1991), p. 3.

63 G. L. Turnbull, *Traffic and Transport: an Economic History of Pickfords* (London, 1979), pp. 150–53.

64 Alfred Plummer, *New British Industries in the Twentieth Century* (London, 1937), p. 75; Philip Bagwell, *The Transport Revolution from 1770* (London, 1974), p. 224.

65 C. T. Brunner, *The Problem of Motor Transport: an Economic Analysis* (London, 1928), p. 18.

for vehicles that despite war-surplus disposals the order book of at least one major manufacturer, Fodens, remained full throughout 1919 and 1920.[66] From March 1919 to August 1921 the number of goods vehicles rose from 62,000 to 128,200.[67] Their area of operations had also greatly expanded – in 1921 it was estimated that motorised vehicles had extended the effective radius of road goods haulage from 10–12 to 50–60 miles.[68] As a memorandum prepared for the Minister of Transport in June 1920 noted, war-time demands had brought motorised road freight 'to a state of development which in the normal course it would probably not have reached for many years to come, and the railways are now faced with a situation which in any event would have arisen sooner or later but which the war has greatly accelerated.'[69] The inflationary post-war boom led to rapidly rising demand for commodities and a consequent growth of demand for goods transport. The railways were still under government control and subject to restrictions on the acceptance of traffic that, together with the 1919 railway strike, provided the road hauliers with initial market opportunities.[70] Big increases in railway rates from 1920, during a period when boom turned to depression and manufacturers were therefore particularly keen on minimising costs, led traders to re-evaluate this experience and, in many cases, make a longer-term switch to road transport.[71]

Meanwhile the effects of the War on Britain's railways were largely structural rather than technological. In August 1914 government commandeered the railway network, bringing it under unified control for the first time. Government control, with railway ownership and day to day management, persisted until 1921. It was widely perceived that the railway network gained substantial benefits from unified control, which should be preserved. Nationalisation was seriously considered, but eventually rejected in favour of restructuring as a regulated legal and collusive oligopoly with regional monopolies. Under the Railways Act, 1921, Britain's 120 railway companies were amalgamated into four regional companies, the 'Big Four'.

The significance of road competition was not taken into account, the 1921 legislation being based on the assumption of a regulated monopoly.[72] It included a system of freight charges based on the 'what the traffic will bear' system that had underpinned previous railway freight pricing, both in Britain and overseas.[73] Goods were classified into 21 categories, each charged a standard rate. Classification was primarily based on selling value per ton, with further modifications to take account

66 Harold Nancollis, *Foden. My Life with the Company* (Glossop, 1995), p. 25.

67 British Road Federation, *Basic Road Statistics, Great Britain, 1950* (London, 1950), pp. 10–11.

68 NA: MT33/1, Committee on Road Conveyance of Goods by Railway Companies, report A to Geddes, Minister of Transport, 8 March 1921.

69 Ibid.

70 R. J. Howley, 'Road transport in relation to the general transport problem of the country', *Journal of the Institute of Transport* (March 1924), pp. 192–208, comment by J. L. Clewes, p. 204.

71 Railways v. road transport', *The Commercial Motor*, 31 (10 August 1920), pp. 714–15; NA, RAIL 421/146, LMS memorandum, 31 December 1926.

72 K. G. Fenelon, *Railway Economics* (London, 1932), p. 114.

73 K. G. Fenelon, *British Railways Today* (London, 1939), p. 39.

of factors such as bulk in relation to weight, cost of handling, risk of damage, and large consignments. What the traffic will bear pricing was untenable in the long-run if a serious competitor charging prices based on marginal cost should emerge. The railway companies had been extensively consulted regarding the 1921 Act. In framing the new pricing structure they neglected the looming threat from road competition; an important failure, for which they were to pay dearly during the following years.

Pressure of competition within the road haulage sector ensured that road charges approximated marginal cost.[74] They were thus lower than rail rates for more valuable goods, and higher for less valuable commodities. In this respect the advent of motorised road haulage had transformed the 'privatisation' of control over the railways from a situation analogous to privatising the gas, electricity, or water industries, where monopoly power was conferred by ownership of an expensive network without access to which it was impossible to compete, to a situation more akin to that which would be faced by the Post Office – charges did not reflect marginal cost but it was now possible (in the absence of regulation) for competitors to enter the field using marginal cost pricing. The inevitable result was a rapid loss of the most remunerative traffic to the roads, a situation which, the railways correctly perceived, could only be effectively redressed via a revision of the legislative framework governing freight transport.

Following pressure from the railways, government eventually introduced a restrictive system of road haulage vehicle licensing under the Road and Rail Traffic Act 1933. Yet this only eased the pace of growth of road, relative to rail, freight. The volume of road merchandise and mineral traffic potentially conveyable by rail (i.e. excluding short hauls) is estimated to have expanded from 6.3 per cent of total road and rail tonnage in 1921 to 25.1 per cent in 1932 and 30.8 per cent in 1938.[75] Yet the percentage was much higher for goods with a high value in relation to their bulk, such as electrical consumer goods, cosmetics and toiletries, furniture, and branded, packaged, foods – as these were most disadvantaged by the railways' pricing policies. Road haulage also offered major qualitative advantages for the conveyance of such products, including faster delivery times and a seamless, door-to-door, service – avoiding the need for expensive and time-consuming transhipment (a particular problem with freight passing through London). Partly in consequence, speed of delivery was considerably faster,[76] pilferage rates were lower (largely because the same people were responsible for a cargo throughout its journey), and breakages were less of a problem.[77] Such factors were particularly important for high value

74 Ministry of Transport, *Transport Advisory Council: Report on Services and Rates* (London, 1937), Appendix 1.

75 Peter Scott, 'The growth of road haulage, 1921–58', *Journal of Transport History*, 19, 2 (1998), 138–55. The data exclude coal haulage (which was virtually all conveyed by rail).

76 British Library of Political and Economic Science Archive, Ward Papers, Transport Sub-committee minutes, Management Research Group No. 1, 20 March 1929.

77 Royal Commission on Transport, *Minutes of Evidence*, Vol. 3 (London, 1930) p. 824. With regard to breakages, the stresses involved in shunting were probably the prime cause.

goods, such as radios (that were particularly vulnerable to pilferage) and for items such as furniture, that were easily scratched or damaged during trans-shipment.

The rise of road transport had a major impact on industrial location, not so much on account of its lower cost (transport costs typically comprised only around 1–2 per cent of total costs),[78] but due to its important service, marketing, and logistical advantages. As a 1936 report by consulting engineers Alexander, Gibb & Partners for North Eastern Trading Estates Ltd, noted, road transport offered: 'ease of handling in and out of the factory, daily – almost hourly – delivery to customers' own premises; the ability to send out, or collect, the smallest consignment at short notice; the much smaller quantities of materials and manufactured articles that have to be kept…'[79] These were generally of greatest importance for outputs, as these tended to be dispatched more frequently and in smaller quantities. There was also generally a greater premium on rapid delivery, while inventories of inputs could compensate for slower and less punctual rail deliveries. The balance of location factors thus moved further in favour of markets, as road transport proved most efficient over relatively short distances and the generally poor state of Britain's road network encouraged proximity to major market hubs (which generally had better road links). Sites offering proximity to major national and international marketing and distribution centres, and nodality with respect to both road and rail networks, such as the western and northern fringes of London (and, to some extent, the southern West Midlands) proved particularly attractive.

Conclusions

The First World War had a major long-term impact on regional disparities. Defence production concentrated light munitions work in the south and West Midlands, while increasing the relative specialisation of 'outer-Britain' in its narrow range of dominant staple export industries. Crafts and Mulatu found that the average Krugman index of regional specialisation for Britain, which had experienced a slow decline over 1871–1911, rose sharply from 0.61 in 1911 to 0.79 in 1921 (subsequently falling back to 0.72 by 1931).[80] More importantly, over the course of the War government made what amounted to huge investments in the physical and human capital of manufacturing industry the South East and southern West Midlands. Boosting munitions output in these areas involved developing skills, production methods, factories, and plant that were to anchor inter-war assembly production to these areas (while war-time transport developments further boosted their locational advantages). Much new industrial development during the 1920s and 1930s was literally built on the foundations of war-time munitions production.

78 S. R. Dennison, *The Location of Industry and the Depressed Areas* (London, 1939), pp. 64–7.

79 NA: BT104/31, report on sites for trading estates, prepared by Sir Alexander Gibb & Partners for North Eastern Trading Estates Ltd, March 1936.

80 Nicholas Crafts and Abay Mulatu, 'What explains the location of industry in Britain, 1871–1931?', *Jourrnal of Economic Geography* (forthcoming), Table 5. Based on regional employment data; average of 10 standard regions.

Conversely the staple industries entered the 1920s having experienced generally incremental, rather than radical, technological change, together with major capacity increases and debt burdens that left them extremely vulnerable in a world economy characterised by rising competition and growing protectionism. Yet, as the next chapter will show, the interwar plight of the staple industries arose not only from the shadow that the War had cast on them, but from the longer shadow of the pre-war 'golden age'. Attempts by government, on the advice of the City, to re-establish pre-war 'normalcy', by returning to the gold standard at sterling's traditional parity, were to plunge them into deep and protracted depression, which accentuated their inherent problems of overcapacity, obsolete production methods, and deteriorating markets.

Chapter Five

Depression and decline in 'outer-Britain'

Introduction

The 1920s witnessed the onset of high and persistent unemployment concentrated in the industrial areas of 'outer Britain'; their staple industries being plunged into deep depression which, while varying in severity, was not to lift until the Second World War. Depression in these dominant industries sapped local purchasing power, thus further depressing economic conditions. In 1929 unemployment in the northern English,[1] Welsh, and Scottish Ministry of Labour divisions averaged 15.0 per cent, compared to an average of only 7.7 per cent in the London and South East, South West, and Midlands divisions. By the next cyclical peak, in 1937, differentials had widened still further – unemployment averaging 17.3 per cent in outer, and 7.1 per cent in inner, Britain.[2] Meanwhile new industrial development had largely by-passed the north; during 1932–38 Scotland, Wales, and England's northern region[3] accounted for only 8.32 per cent of new British manufacturing plants with an initial employment of 25 or more.[4]

This chapter outlines the factors that led to the severe decline of Britain's principal staple industries, the impact of this decline in widening regional differentials, and the limited success of industry, bank, and government-sponsored initiatives in addressing the crisis in the staple industries. The following chapter then examines patterns of new industrial development in the regions of outer-Britain and the extent to which their resources of human and physical capital were suitable for re-deployment to other sectors.

The impact of the post-war boom and slump

As noted in the last chapter, war-time production had boosted capacity in the staple industries. Even prior to 1914 they had been heavily reliant on overseas markets and a combination of chronic world over-capacity and rising international protectionism during the 1920s made a substantial decline in their output and employment inevitable. Yet in the immediate aftermath of the War a potent cocktail of pent-up demand and what proved to be a wholly-unfounded optimism regarding the buoyancy and

1 Comprising the North, North West, and North East regional divisions.

2 D. E. Pitfield, 'Labour migration and the regional problem in Britain, 1920–1939', unpublished Ph.D thesis, University of Sterling, 1973, p. 23.

3 Using the modern Standard Economic Region definition.

4 Peter Scott and Peter Walsh, 'New manufacturing plant formation, clustering, and locational externalities in 1930s' Britain', *Business History*, 47, 2 (2005), 190–218, Table 1.

openness of post-war markets fuelled a major boom. In an atmosphere of inflation, speculative activity, and liberal bank credit, many firms were tempted into costly acquisitions that were to handicap them for the rest of the interwar period.

Britain's demobilisation and conversion to a peacetime economy initially appeared relatively successful – particularly in terms of employment. Despite concerns regarding the dangers of severe economic dislocations and social unrest from the rapid entry of millions of demobilised servicemen into the civilian labour market, in the event their re-absorption occurred relatively smoothly. Trade union figures indicate an unemployment peak of only 2.9 per cent during the demobilisation period.[5] This was facilitated by the exit of three quarters of a million women workers from the labour market during the year following the Armistice, while others left manufacturing and commerce to resume careers in domestic service.

Yet the post-war boom proved short-lived. Inflation raised British export prices and producers began to develop a more realistic appreciation of the true state of international markets. A number of commentators, following J.A. Dowie, have also highlighted the introduction of an eight hour working day in 1919 (reducing the average working week by around 13 per cent) as a major additional factor eroding Britain's international competitiveness.[6] Yet evidence suggests that its importance has been exaggerated. For example, in coal mining Britain's principal European competitors also instigated hours reductions after the First World War, that generally exceeded Britain's both in absolute terms and as a proportion of 1914 shift lengths.[7]

By April 1920 bank credit was beginning to dry up, high prices tempered consumer expenditure, and firms began to reassess their position in the light of rising indebtedness. Government accentuated the slump, by raising bank rate to 7 per cent in April 1920 and cutting back on public expenditure. Conditions deteriorated markedly during the second half of the year and by the middle of 1921 Britain was in deep recession. Yet its severity did not demonstrate any pronounced regional divide. Some regions suffering from above average unemployment during the post-war depression were to become relatively prosperous by the 1930s, such as the West Midlands. Conversely, until 1925 Wales – the area of most severe unemployment during the 1930s – had an unemployment level below the national average.[8] However, as the decade progressed the markets for Britain's export staple industries steadily deteriorated and they began a long and painful process of readjustment. Meanwhile their difficulties

---

5 Sidney Pollard, *The Development of the British Economy, 1914–1950* (London, 1962), p. 88.

6 J. A. Dowie, '1919–20 is in need of attention', *Economic History Review*, XXVIII (1975), 429–50; S. N. Broadberry, 'The emergence of mass unemployment: explaining macroeconomic trends in Britain during the trans-World War 1 period', *Economic History Review*, XLIII (1990), 271–82.

7 International Labour Office, *The World Coal-mining Industry, Volume 1: Economic Conditions* (Geneva, 1938), p. 109; David Greasley, 'The Diffusion of a Technology: The Case of Machine Cutting in the British Coal Industry, 1900–38', unpublished Ph.D. thesis, University of Liverpool, 1979, p. 73.

8 M. E. Daly, 'Government policy and the depressed areas in the inter-war years', unpublished D.Phil thesis, University of Oxford, 1978, p. 34.

were accentuated by the City's successful advocacy of a recovery policy based around returning Sterling to the gold standard at its pre-war $4.86 parity.

The gold standard, deflation, and depression

During the 1920s Treasury financial orthodoxy remained firmly wedded to the pre-war classical liberal pillars of the gold standard, minimal balanced budgets, and free trade. Indeed restoring the free convertibility of sterling into gold at its pre-War parity was held to be key to re-establishing the economic 'normalcy' that the War had interrupted. Yet changes to both the British and international economy during the War years proved less reversible than many advocates of the return to gold appreciated. War debts and finance had necessitated the liquidation of a substantial part of Britain's overseas investment portfolio, seriously weakening its invisible balance and role as international creditor. Meanwhile Britain's established patterns of international financial services exports and shipping had also been disrupted. These developments reversed the long-term trend towards the growing domination of the British economy by services exports and overseas investment revenues. As Figure 5.1 shows, after 1914 the steadily growth in the UK invisibles surplus (as a percentage of GNP) was replaced by a downward trend, the ratio eventually falling to less than half that of the late Edwardian period.

Meanwhile the United States had moved from the position of a net international borrower to the world's most important international creditor, with the nations of Europe tied to it via a network of war debts and reparations. France also became a major international creditor and both New York and Paris developed money markets in competition with London. Whereas in 1914 London had reigned as the undisputed financial capital of the world, the international financial system now had three centres.

The gold standard system had effectively been a managed system, managed by Britain (with the cooperation of other major trading nations). This had involved allowing monetary and fiscal policy to prioritise external stability – a stable international gold standard and the maintenance of international liquidity and confidence in sterling (as the main international currency) – over internal economic requirements. Britain was peculiarly well-placed to undertake this role, on account of its domination by financial and commercial, rather than industrial, interests and a political consensus that what was good for the City was good for Britain. As W.R. Garside noted, 'The strength of the gold standard... dependended upon the inherent strength of London as an international financial centre, not the reverse.'[9]

Neither America nor France were well-placed, or even willing, to take on this management role. The United States lacked the strong central bank necessary to manage the gold standard; its equivalent, the Federal Reserve, was a decentralised system designed to meet the Unites States' internal needs rather than to manage international credit and payments. Furthermore, American financial policy was dominated by domestic, rather than international, considerations. The structure of

9 William R. Garside, *British Unemployment 1919–1939. A Study in Public Policy* (Cambridge, 1990), p. 116.

the French financial system also militated against effective management of the gold standard. French overseas investment was concentrated in short-term assets that could be easily converted to gold, while the Bank of France was narrowly limited in the type of assets it could hold – to gold, bills of exchange of a very high quality, or loans secured by gilts. Gold stocks thus constituted the main medium by which adjustments in assets could take place – thus threatening international liquidity.

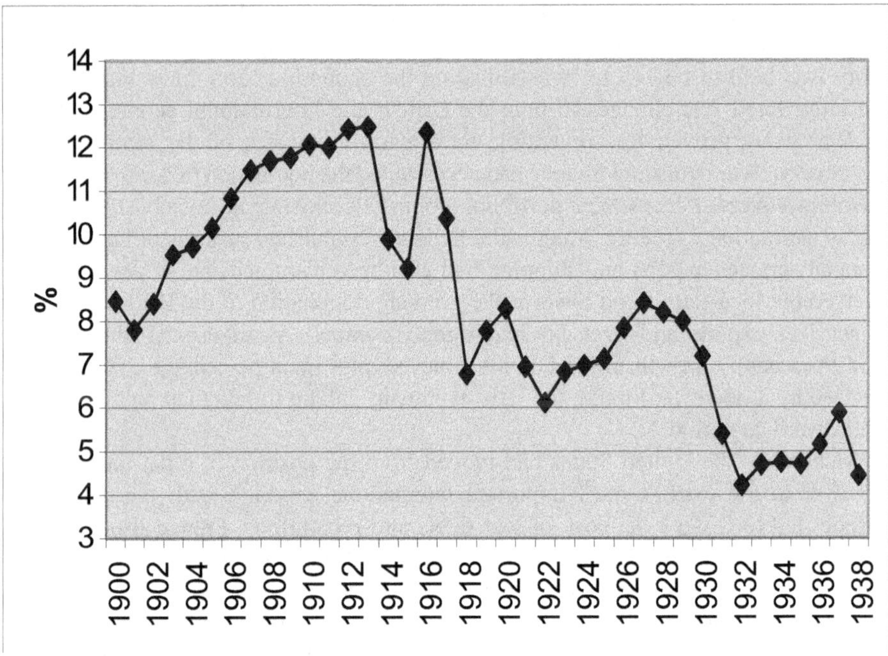

Figure 5.1: The UK invisibles surplus as a proportion of GNP, 1900–1938

Source: C. H. Feinstein, National Income, Expenditure and Output of the United Kingdom, 1855–1965 *(Cambridge, 1982), pp. T8 and T82.*

Note: Data from 1920 exclude southern Ireland.

Meanwhile, the War had represented a huge shock to the international financial system, the reverberations of which continued to threaten its stability. These included divergent movements in the imports, exports, and interest rates of major industrialised countries, of a magnitude that had not been evident during the Victorian and Edwardian periods. Even Britain had lost much of the economic stability and price-flexibility (already coming under pressure from increased unionisation and other influences prior to the First World War) that had underpinned its management of the gold standard.

During the War the gold standard's function as an adjustment mechanism between exchange rates, international prices, and international payments had effectively been suspended. From 1915 sterling's exchange rate was pegged by official borrowing and intervention with the proceeds to preserve the pound's gold value. Domestic prices rose and the cost of intervention became considerable, despite Britain being partially shielded from gold outflow by government controls and the submarine threat to shipping. The major allies had also pegged their currencies; thus an artificial market in currency had been created, backed by government intervention. This, together with war-time inflation and economic dislocations, led to large discrepancies between exchange rates, international prices, and payments flows.

January 1918 saw the appointment of the Cunliffe Committee on Currency and Foreign Exchanges after the War. The Committee's first interim report recommended that government should create conditions conducive to the re-establishment of the gold standard by reducing government borrowing and raising interest rates. In other words, it advocated a temporary sacrifice in internal stability, through fiscal and monetary policies that would depress output and employment, in order to bring about long-term external stability via a resurrected gold standard. Yet the magnitude of current economic dislocations made this politically impracticable in the short-term. War-time inflation, followed by the vigorous post-war boom, had raised prices to such a level that deflationary policies would have to be so severe as to risk massive unemployment and serious social unrest. Consequently, in March 1919 the gold standard was formally abandoned. Sterling's value was allowed to be determined by the market and fell to a low of $3.20 in February 1920.

To return the currency to its pre-war $4.86 parity seemed a formidable task – yet government soon resolved to do so. Domestic inflation was addressed via a deflationary 'dear money' policy; Bank Rate was raised from 5 per cent to 6 per cent in November 1919 and to 7 per cent in April 1920. By autumn 1920 boom had turned to slump and prices were falling. Yet Bank Rate was not lowered for almost a year, intensifying the slump. Government then wavered in its determination to further pursue the drastically deflationary policies which its policy required, especially in the light of severe criticism from J. M. Keynes and others regarding the unemployment that this first wave of deflation had already caused. However from July 1923 it moved decisively in favour of restoring sterling's pre-war parity. Deflation, reinforced by speculative activity in anticipation of restoration, drove up sterling's value, and on 28 April 1925, despite his own misgivings, the Chancellor of the Exchequer, Winston Churchill accepted the weight of Treasury and Bank of England opinion and announced Britain's return to gold.

Historians have condemned those involved in this policy for paying insufficient attention to the massive domestic costs in terms of lost jobs and output; ignoring international conditions that made the likelihood of maintaining sterling at its $4.86 parity remote (in the absence of policies that would further cripple the domestic economy), and failing to consider alternative measures such as a return to gold following a sterling devaluation.[10] Some have also argued that the return to gold reflected the economic interests of that section of the City concerned with international finance.[11] Certainly the main 'players' in providing the key reports

10 Ibid, p. 121.

11 For example, Sidney Pollard (ed.), *The Gold Standard and Employment Policies between the Wars* (London, 1970), editor's introduction.

and advice in favour of this policy represented City interests. The Bank of England (whose governing body was dominated by international banking interests) played a pivotal role, while the main official committees which examined the issue, the Cunliffe and Bradbury Committees, were dominated by bankers. Re-establishing the gold standard was a central priority for these groups, as it was seen as key to restoring the City to its prime international role, which was being progressively undermined by Paris and New York. As Garside noted:

> To the Bank of England restoration of gold was synonymous with the restoration of its own pre-eminence. Whether the exchange rate was appropriate in terms of its likely effects on employment and the balance of payments was not an issue which troubled the Bank unduly. Stability of the exchanges was able to be presented as a meaningful alternative to full employment because it was associated with the restoration of London as an international financial centre.[12]

Any hopes that the return to gold would herald the revival of a stable, open, world economy, in which Britain's staple industries could regain their former prosperity, were rapidly dispelled. Instead, what proved to be a substantially over-valued exchange rate hit the price-sensitive staple industries with particular severity. Keynes, who estimated that the restored pound was over-valued relative to the dollar by some 10 per cent, famously outlined the obvious consequences for British industry:

> [W]henever we sell anything abroad, either the foreign buyer has to pay 10 per cent more in his money or we have to accept 10 per cent less in our money. That is to say, we have to reduce our sterling prices, for coal or iron or shipping freights … by 10 per cent in order to be on a competitive level, unless prices rise elsewhere. [13]

Historical research has generally confirmed this 10 per cent overvaluation (in terms of purchasing power parities), while suggesting that in terms of measures of domestic costs such as GNP and consumer expenditure the over-valuation may have been as much as 11–14 per cent. The pound was even more over-valued relative to a basket of non-dollar foreign currencies, by as much as 20–25 per cent in 1925 and 15–20 per cent in 1929.[14] Mark Thomas has estimated (assuming a 22 per cent overvaluation and a multiplier of 1.2) that job losses from the return to gold could be conservatively put at over one million, with a corresponding output shortfall of 5 per cent.[15] Research by M. E. F. Jones has demonstrated that these losses were concentrated in the staple industries and the export-orientated industrial areas of 'outer-Britain'.[16]

---

12 Garside, *British Unemployment*, p. 123.

13 J. M. Keynes, 'The economic consequences of Mr Churchill', abbreviated reprinted version, 27–43 in Pollard *The Gold Standard and Employment Policies*, p. 23.

14 For a review of this literature, see Garside, *British Unemployment*, p. 124.

15 Mark Thomas, 'The macro-economics of the interwar years', 320–58 in R. Floud and D. McCloskey (eds), *The Economic History of Britain since 1700. Volume 2: 1860–1939*, 2nd edn. (Cambridge, 1994), p. 341.

16 M. E. F. Jones, 'The regional impact of an overvalued pound in the 1920s', *Economic History Review*, XXXVIII (1985), 393–401.

Britain's combination of severe deflation in preparation for the gold standard restoration, and continued deflationary policy to support the over-valued currency in its aftermath, contributed to a particularly poor growth record during the 1920s (a period of relative prosperity for most industrial nations). Analysis by Barry Eichengreen has shown that national growth rates during 1920–27 generally display an inverse relationship with growth rates during the First World War, as countries heavily involved in the War caught up with lost war-time growth. Yet Britain performed poorly during 1920–27 relative both to other European countries and to what would be expected given this relationship – with a growth rate some 22 percentage points below that predicted for a country in its position.[17]

British wages and prices proved less downwardly-flexible than the neoclassical theory which underpinned the logic of the government's policy predicted and the impact of overvaluation was expressed largely via unemployment. The protracted state of depression which ensued was one of the main inspirations for Keynes's brilliant corrective to orthodox economic theory, *The General Theory of Employment, Interest and Money* (1936). Meanwhile events in other countries accentuated sterling's overvaluation. U.S. prices did not rise to meet Britain's after 1925, while during the following years a number of countries, including France and Belgium, returned to gold at parities which undervalued their currencies with respect to sterling – thereby improving their international competitiveness at Britain's expense. Meanwhile the U.S. and France added considerably to their gold reserves, increasing the scarcity of gold and therefore putting further pressure on sterling's gold exchange rate. All of these events could, however, have reasonably been predicted at the time of Britain's return to gold.

Sterling and the UK balance of payments consequently came under repeated pressure. Meanwhile policies aimed at boosting the domestic economy were ruled out by the need to protect the pound. The onset of international depression from 1929, which further damaged Britain's balance of payments and gold reserves, made the defence of sterling even more difficult and costly. In 1931 there was a loss of international confidence in sterling and Britain's minority Labour government, politically divided in the face of calls for harsh deflation to restore confidence, collapsed in August, being replaced by a new, Conservative-dominated, 'National' coalition government. The new government instigated limited cuts in unemployment benefits and public sector salaries, but ran into significant resistance from the groups affected – most famously the 'mutiny' of sailors at the Invergordon naval base. International confidence in sterling thus took a further knock and, with Bank of England reserves approaching exhaustion, the new government abandoned the gold standard on 19 September, less than a month after taking office.[18] Two months later it introduced general tariff protection under the Abnormal Importations Act (later consolidated by the 1932 Import Duties Act) – thus undermining a second major pillar of pre-war liberal economic orthodoxy.

By December 1931 the pound had fallen by about 30 per cent against the dollar, though the effective devaluation against all currencies amounted to only around 13 per cent, as some 25 countries with strong economic or imperial ties to Britain

17 Eichengreen, 'The British economy between the wars', pp. 322–3.

18 Ibid, p. 335.

pegged their currencies to sterling.[19] From April 1932 the Bank of England managed sterling's value (with Treasury advice and consent), using the Exchange Equalisation Account. A managed, floating, currency also facilitated the government's new cheap money policy, by allowing balance of payments deficits to be addressed via changes in the exchange rate rather than interest rates.[20] Ironically, while the high pound/dear money strategy of the 1920s had hit the staple industries and outer-Britain with particular severity, the low pound/cheap money strategy of the 1930s – while benefiting the whole of Britain – offered the greatest boost to the south. By this time Britain's staple industries had already lost many of their overseas markets to nations that were determined to retain them, particularly in a climate of excess international capacity. An intensification of international protectionism also limited the scope for regaining lost overseas markets. Conversely the south's manufacturing base of light, domestically-orientated, 'new' industries gained substantial benefit from British tariffs, while cheap money both boosted domestic consumer demand and made expansion finance both cheaper and more freely available.

Depression and decline in 'outer-Britain'

Unemployment data provide the best available indices of changing disparities in regional prosperity. Yet even these are problematic. Official data, available by region from 1923, are based on the number of people who were both covered by the government's unemployment insurance scheme and registered as unemployed. This excludes workers aged under 16, non-manual workers earning more than £250 a year, together with workers in agriculture, forestry, horticulture, private domestic service, teachers, nurses, the police, established civil servants, some local authority employees, railway workers, and members of the armed forces.[21] Further problems arise from the boundaries of the Ministry of Labour's administrative regions. For example the South Eastern division includes the post-1945 East Anglian counties (which were then not particularly prosperous); the South West includes Hampshire and Oxfordshire; and the North East includes Yorkshire.[22]

While the data only start in 1923, evidence suggests that during the depression of the early 1920s there were patterns of high unemployment throughout Britain and no marked 'north-south divide'. This situation persisted during the recovery years of 1923 and 1924, as shown in Table 5.1 and Figure 5.2. However, from the mid-1920s stronger regional disparities emerged, while during the 1929–32 depression unemployment increased substantially across Britain, peaking at over 35 per cent in Wales, around 28 per cent in Scotland and Northern Britain, 20 per cent in the Midlands, and 14 per cent in London and the South East. Yet regional differentials (as measured by the coefficient of variation) actually narrowed during the 1929–32

19 Mark Thomas, 'The macro-economics of the interwar years', p. 351.

20 Garside, *British Unemployment*, p. 135.

21 For further information on the limitations of the official data see Garside, *British Unemployment*, pp. 3–7.

22 See Department of Employment, *British Labour Statistics. Historical Abstract 1868–1968* (London, 1971), p. 424.

depression, then widened during the recovery – when rates dropped sharply in the South East but remained high in outer Britain. This, and the evidence of low regional disparities during the slump of the early 1920s, suggests that regional unemployment differentials moved inversely with the economic cycle. This contrasts with the post-1945 period, when regional disparities rose during each recession (until the early 1990s).

Widening regional disparities are also reflected in Census of Production data on regional shares of national net output and regional net output per employee, shown in Table 5.2. By 1935 Greater London's contribution to UK net output had risen by 38.5 per cent (relative to its 1924 level). The other gainers were Warwickshire – the centre of the motor vehicle industry – and the 'rest of England'. Of the staple industry areas, the West Riding fared the best, with a decline of around 6.7 per cent. This was the centre of the woollen textile industry, which was less export-orientated than its cotton counterpart and included a relatively prosperous coalfield (by the standards of the industry) together with a significant engineering base. Northern Ireland and west central Scotland experienced declines of just over 10 per cent, and Lancashire, which had previously topped the output league table, had declined by 13.4 per cent. The agriculturally-dominated 'rest of Scotland' and 'rest of Wales' both experienced still heavier declines, as did the coal-iron/steel dominated Northumberland & Durham and South Wales. Overall, the figures show a clear relationship between geographical peripherality and economic decline.

In terms of growth of net output per employee, the 'rest of England' fared best in percentage terms, followed by Warwickshire and West central Scotland. London, which had the highest 1924 labour productivity in Britain, had growth below the national average. This reflects the expansion of assembly manufacturers employing un/semi-skilled labour, and heavy in-migration of such labour from other regions, as discussed in the Chapters 8–11. South Wales, the rest of Scotland, and Northumberland & Durham also had productivity growth rates below the national average. Lancashire and the West Riding recorded slight absolute declines in labour productivity (probably reflecting changes in the sectoral composition of employment in favour of lower productivity industries), while the rest of Wales and Northern Ireland experienced larger productivity falls – of 6.0 and 6.5 per cent respectively.

As Sean Glynn has noted, the problems of outer-Britain's depressed staple industries can be decomposed into two basic elements – a market access problem and a cost problem.[23] Market access posed growing difficulties during the interwar period, the initial war-time shock of new competition and import-substitution being reinforced by the raising of ever-higher tariff walls. Shipbuilding provides an extreme example. Between 1914 and 1920, when British launchings reach an all-time peak tonnage, capacity had expanded by almost 40 per cent.[24] Replacing war-time shipping losses (which amounted to some 30 per cent of the world's pre-war merchant fleet) produced a post-war boom which temporarily masked the impact of a considerably expanded overseas shipbuilding capacity, particularly in the US, Japan,

23 Sean Glynn, 'The nature of the problem', 3–16 in Sean Glynn and Alan Booth, *The Road to Full Employment* (London, 1987), p. 15.

24 T. M. Devine, *The Scottish Nation 1700–2000* (London, 1999), p. 266.

Table 5.1: Insured unemployment rates by administrative division, 1923–38

Year	London	South East	South West	Midlands	North East	North West	Northern	Scotland	Wales	Coefficient of variation[c]
1923	10.1	9.2	10.6	10.7	12.2	14.5		14.3	6.4	0.24
1924	9.0	7.5	9.1	9.0	10.9	12.9		12.4	8.6	0.19
1925	7.8	5.9	8.5	9.1	15.0	11.4		15.2	16.5	0.35
1926	6.9	5.4	8.4	11.0	17.2	14.7		16.4	18.0	0.41
1927	5.8	5.0	7.2	8.4	13.7	10.7		10.6	19.5	0.47
1928	5.6	5.4	8.1	9.9	15.1	12.4		11.7	23.0	0.51
1929	5.6	5.6	8.1	9.3	13.7	13.3		12.1	19.3	0.43
1930	8.1	8.0	10.4	14.7	20.2	23.8		18.5	25.9	0.43
1931	12.2	12.0	14.5	20.3	27.4	28.2		26.6	32.4	0.37
1932	13.5	14.3	17.1	20.1	28.5	25.8		27.7	36.5	0.35
1933	11.8	11.5	15.7	17.4	26.0	23.5		26.1	34.6	0.39
1934[a]	9.2	8.7	13.1	12.9	22.1	20.8		23.1	32.3	0.46
1935[a]	8.5	8.1	11.6	11.2	20.7	19.7		21.3	31.2	0.49
1936[a]	7.2	7.3	9.4	9.2	16.8	17.1		18.7	29.4	0.53
1937[a]	6.4	6.7	7.8	7.3	11.1[a]	14.0[b]	17.9[a]	16.0	23.3	0.51
1938[a]	8.0	8.0	8.2	10.3	13.6[a]	17.9[a]	18.4[a]	16.4	24.8	0.45

Sources: W. R. Garside, British Unemployment 1919–1939. A Study in Public Policy *(Cambridge, 1990), p. 10.*

Notes: [a] Figures exclude juveniles under 16 and persons insured under the Agricultural scheme. These first became subject to National Insurance in September 1934 and May 1936 respectively.

[b] Northern division created from parts of North-Eastern division (Northumberland, excluding Berwick district; Durham; and the Cleveland district of Yorkshire) and parts of the North Western division (Cumberland and Westmorland).

[c] Excludes Northern division.

the Netherlands, and Sweden. The resulting chronic capacity surplus – accentuated by poor growth in demand as tariffs reduced the volume of international goods shipments – led to a decline in world shipbuilding output from a peak of six million tons in 1920 to an annual average of two million tons during 1924–38 (British yards alone having a capacity of three million tons).[25] Sluggish demand for merchant vessels was matched by the slashing of military orders following the Washington Treaty for the Limitation of Naval Armaments in 1921; large naval orders did not re-emerge until the late 1930s.

Table 5.2: Regional contributions to UK net output, and regional labour productivity, in 1924 and 1935

Region	Share of national net output (%)			Net output per employee (£)		
	1924	1935	% change	1924	1935	% change
Greater London	14.50	20.08	38.5	262	271	3.4
Lancashire	19.50	16.88	-13.4	204	202	-1.0
West Riding	11.73	10.94	-6.7	203	200	-1.5
Northumberland & Durham	6.25	4.91	-21.4	186	190	2.2
Warwickshire	10.51	12.20	16.1	211	221	4.7
Rest of England	18.49	19.77	6.9	212	227	7.1
South Wales	5.21	3.38	-35.1	200	207	3.5
Rest of Wales	0.98	0.75	-23.5	201	189	-6.0
West central Scotland	5.32	4.73	-11.1	205	214	4.4
Rest of Scotland	5.35	4.45	-16.8	208	213	2.4
Northern Ireland	2.15	1.92	-10.7	153	143	-6.5
Total	100.00	100.00	0.0	212	222	4.7

Source: James Foreman-Peck, 'Industry and industrial organisation in the inter-war years', 386–414 in R. Floud and D. McCloskey (eds), The Economic History of Britain Since 1700. Volume 2 1860–1939, *2nd Edn. (Cambridge, 1994), p. 411.*

The shipbuilding industry's fortunes largely followed the unstable course of world demand. During 1920 Britain had launched 2.1 million gross registered tons of shipping; in the worst inter-war year, 1933, this had fallen to a mere 0.1 million. Yet as a percentage of world output, British tonnage had only fallen from 35 to 27 per cent. Indeed following the recovery in demand during the mid and late 1930s annual British launchings, while less than half their 1920 tonnage, constituted a

25 Clive. H. Lee, *Scotland and the United Kingdom. The Economy and the Union in the Twentieth Century* (Manchester, 1995), p. 78.

higher proportion of world demand.[26] Access to overseas markets was impeded by the protectionist policies of overseas governments, including both tariffs and subsidies. British shipbuilding thus became increasingly dependent on the state of the British shipping trade, where it gained preferential access on account of a strong tradition of British shipping lines commissioning vessels in Britain.

The importance of domestic demand is further illustrated by the textile industry. Employment in the cotton textiles (spinning, doubling, and weaving), which had stood at 612,500 in 1912, declined to only 359,700 by 1937, a fall of 42.1 per cent. Meanwhile the smaller and more domestically-orientated woollen and worsted industry, which had employed 279,600 people in 1912, experienced an employment fall of only 10.6 per cent by 1937. Furthermore, in contrast to the continued decline of the cotton industry, employment in the woollen industries actually increased during the 1930s, partly due to the influence of tariff protection in reducing the access of overseas producers to the British market.[27]

Table 5.3: British exports of cotton piece goods by type and destination (million yards)

	Average 1900-13	1937	% change
By Type:			
Grey	2,150	317	-85.3
Bleached	1,828	572	-68.7
Printed	1,203	413	-65.7
Piece dyed	1,026	506	-50.7
Yarn died	268	112	-58.2
By Destination:			
India & Burma	2,507	356	-85.8
Other British Empire	724	768	6.1
China & Far East	973	74	-92.4
Near and Middle East	744	88	-88.2
Europe	454	269	-40.7
Non-empire Africa	187	51	-72.7
Latin America	766	295	-61.5
Other	122	22	-82.0
Total	6,476	1,921	-70.3

Source: adapted from S. N. Broadberry and Andrew Marrison, 'External economies of scale in the Lancashire cotton industry, 1900–1950,' Economic History Review, *LV (2002), 51–77, p. 70.*

26 J. R. Parkinson, 'Shipbuilding', 79–102 in N. K. Buxton and D. H. Aldcroft (eds), *British Industry between the Wars: Instability and Industrial Development 1919–1939* (London, 1979), p. 82.

27 J. H. Porter, 'Cotton and wool textiles', pp. 25–47 in Buxton and Aldcroft, *British Industry between the Wars*, p. 27.

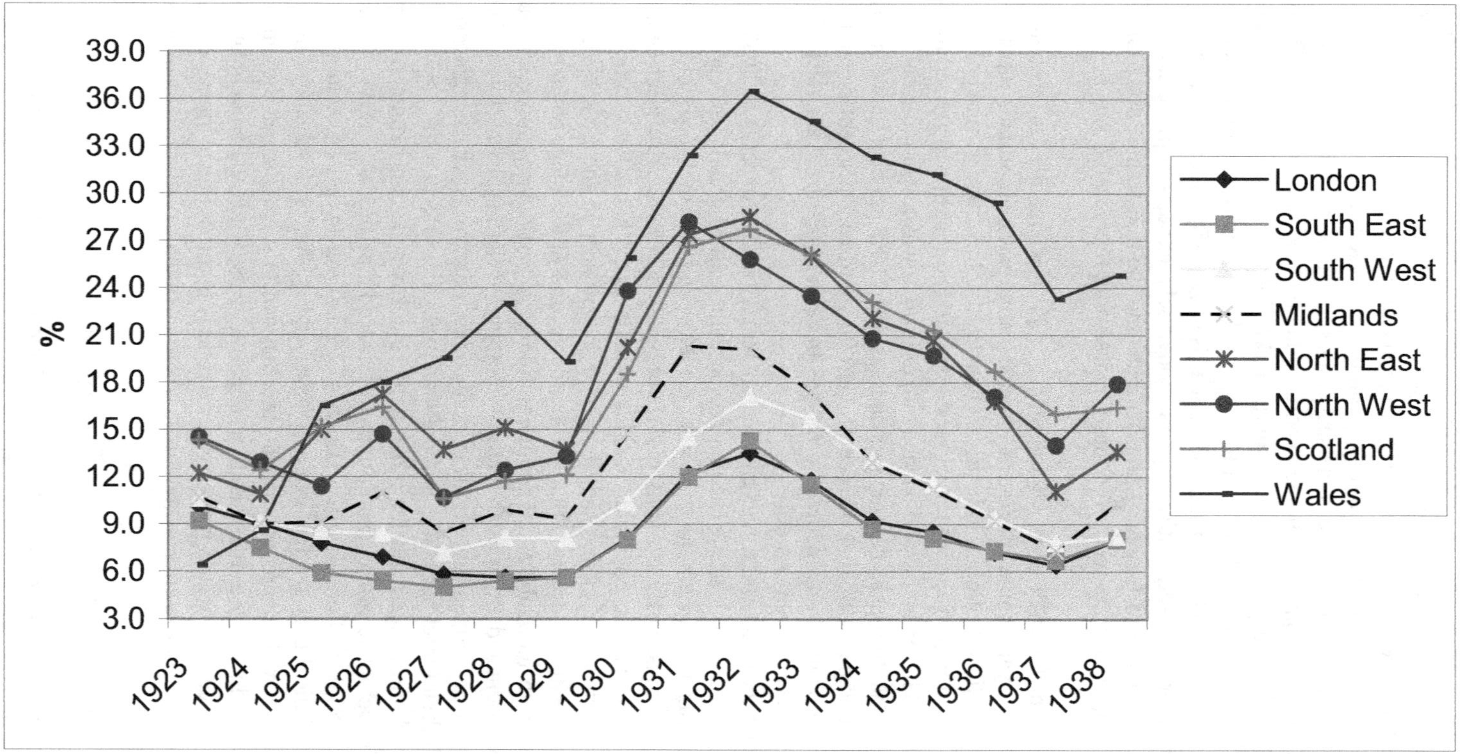

Figure 5.2: Unemployment rates by administrative division, 1923–38

Source: Table 5.1.

Cotton faced particularly severe demand-side problems, as it was extremely export-orientated and, as a basic semi-manufactured good, was particularly vulnerable to the price impacts of rising international protectionism, overseas import-substitution strategies, and new, low-wage, competitors, such as Japan. Simpler, less differentiated, products experienced the sharpest export falls, as shown in Table 5.3. 'Grey' goods, Britain's largest volume export market by type of product, and Burma and India, Britain's largest volume export market by destination, both suffered particularly severe declines. It was in these areas that competition from low-wage producers, such as Japan, bit hardest, while the rise of tariff-protected Indian home production further squeezed British exports. Conversely, exports of piece and yard-died fabrics, and those to Europe, Latin America and the non-India/Burma British Empire, held up relatively well. Yet these had always represented much smaller markets for Britain.

Steel fared better than most of the staple industries, mainly on account of the relatively buoyant home market, as steel constituted an important input into expanding, as well as declining, industries. Over 1920–24 average annual per capita domestic consumption of finished steel products was 180 lbs; this increased to 242 lbs in 1928 and 338 lbs in 1936.[28] Hence output growth was respectable compared with Britain's main European competitors, increasing by 61.5 per cent between 1913 and 1936–37, compared to 36.4 per cent in Germany and 36.5 per cent throughout Europe. Yet there were home demand problems in certain important sections of the industry, such as ship plate and rails.

The importance of domestic market-orientation to regional prosperity is illustrated by the two most prosperous staple industry regions – the East Midlands and Yorkshire. Coal mining was a major employer in both these regions, yet their coalfields were relatively prosperous, partly as a consequence of being more domestically-orientated than Britain's other major coalfields. Similarly, their textile industries – principally woollen & worsted in Yorkshire and hosiery and knitwear in the East Midlands, were more domestically-focused than the textile sectors of the other outer-regions. Furthermore, both had substantial representation of a particularly successful and domestically-orientated traditional sector – clothing. Relative prosperity in these dominant industries helped support the region's other industries such as engineering, both through their direct purchases and regional multiplier effects.

Yet even domestic demand for most staple industries lagged behind Britain's GDP growth. Domestic coal consumption experienced a particularly heavy decline, falling from 183.4 million tons in 1913 to 172.3 million in 1927–29, largely on account of technical changes favouring other fuels, together with advances in fuel economy. For example, increases in fuel efficiency led to a doubling in the amount of electricity produced by a ton of coal between the wars, while the amount of coal required to produce a ton of steel was halved.[29] Similarly in shipbuilding, improvements in design and a trend towards larger ships reduced demand, relative to the volume

28 K. Warren, 'Iron and steel', 103–28 in Buxton and Aldcroft, *British Industry between the Wars*, p. 107.

29 G. W. Williams, 'From grand slam to great slump: economy, society and rugby football in Wales during the depression', *Welsh History Review 11* (1983), 338–57, p. 341.

of world trade, as ships became more efficient carriers ton-for-ton. Meanwhile depression in some staple industries reverberated to others that supplied their inputs. For example, the collapse of shipbuilding hit its major steel suppliers and, in turn, the collieries who supplied them.

Yet even if market access had been unobstructed and demand had been more buoyant, much British production would have been priced out of foreign markets, on account of Britain's high production costs. The over-valuation of sterling constituted one major element of this problem. However, structural and organisational impediments to modernisation also imposed a major competitive disadvantage on Britain's staple industries. One obstacle involved their high levels of corporate indebtedness – a legacy of the post-war speculative mania. For example, in cotton a huge inflow of capital during 1919–20 had been largely directed to the refloatation or recapitalisation of concerns embodying second-hand plant – which was thus effectively re-valued at inflated prices. In the latter half of 1919 alone some 150 cotton mills had changed hands; more often than not these were later refloated at vastly inflated capitalisations. During the boom 46 per cent of Lancashire's spindles were traded, in an orgy of speculation that saw share prices peak at seven or eight times their original value.[30] The brevity of the boom meant that there was insufficient time to develop a substantial volume of new plant; the effect of this interval of easy credit was, therefore, an increase in capital liabilities without any significant modernisation of the capital stock. A similar pattern was evident in the other staple industries, saddling them with debts that were to prove an enduring burden. By 1929 heavy industry accounted for 14 per cent of non-government overdrafts.[31]

Britain's combination of labour-intensive techniques and relatively high wages (compared to some of its overseas competitors) produced an unusually high ratio of labour to total costs. For example, an International Labour Office enquiry found that labour costs per ton of coal mined, relative to those in Britain, amounted to only 48 per cent in Poland, 61 per cent in the USA (for bituminous coal), 68 per cent in German West Upper Silesia, 81 per cent in Belgium, and 96 per cent in the Ruhr.[32] Wage rates in these countries spanned a very broad range; yet their unifying feature was a successful reduction of the ratio of labour to total mining costs, through mechanisation. Conversely, British industrialists emphasised driving down wage rates as the main means of lowering labour costs – as evidenced by the mining industry submissions to the 1925 Royal Commission on the Coal Industry. Given that Britain had particularly high living costs, and that some major components of living costs, such as rents, could not be expected to display the same downwards flexibility that was being sought of wages, this was a very bitter pill for the workers concerned to swallow. Indeed, in some industries, such as textiles, a policy of driving

30 Mary B. Rose, *Firms, Networks, and Business Values. The British and American Cotton Industries since 1750* (Cambridge, 2000), pp. 208–209.

31 Stephen Tolliday, 'Steel and rationalization policies, 1918–1950', 82–108 in B. Elbaum and W. Lazonick (eds), *The Decline of the British Economy* (Oxford, 1986), p. 94.

32 Cited in N. K. Buxton, 'Coalmining', 48–78 in Buxton and Aldcroft, *British Industry Between the Wars*, p. 57.

wages down to meet the levels of low-wage competitors such as Japan would have required British workers to accept wages below subsistence levels. Yet pursuing the alternative strategy of lowering labour costs through productivity-enhancing capital investment faced formidable barriers from 'technological lock-in' to existing production methods, through path dependence effects.

Path dependence and slow technological change in the staple industries

Technical change was inhibited, in part, through the sheer volume of over-capacity, heavily weighted towards early vintages of factories and plant. Existing capacity represented a formidable obstacle to modernisation, as it represented a sunk cost (often with low, if any, re-sale value outside the industry) and would thus remain in operation even if run at a loss, so long as operating costs were covered. Mining constituted an extreme example. The re-sale value of the industry's plant was negligible, neither pits nor machinery having alternative uses. Thus coalowners ceasing production were faced with having to completely write-off their sunk capital stock.[33] Marginal interwar collieries demonstrated an amazing capacity to continue in business in the hope of better times ahead, even if this meant selling at a loss of 1s or 2s per ton, or closing down temporarily, rather than abandon their fixed assets.[34] Even if profits fell so low that operating costs could not be covered, mines were often kept open so as to save on 'start-up' costs in the event of an improvement in market conditions.[35]

Similar problems were encountered in the steel industry, where capacity utilisation fell as low as 30 per cent during 1921 and 1927 and rarely rose above 60 per cent over during 1921–33.[36] Much of this capacity was technologically backward, the industry having been in a state of relative technological stagnation for around half a century by 1920. For example, a survey of 1904 found that plants currently considered important had all already been important in 1880 and had generally experienced little subsequent growth.[37] Moreover, a substantial proportion of this older capacity was located in areas that had become unsuitable with respect to either markets and/or raw materials, as discussed in the next chapter.

Meanwhile older plant often inhibited the introduction of interrelated new machinery. A survey by the Factory and Storage Control during the Second World

33 N. K. Buxton, 'Entrepreneurial efficiency in the British coal industry between the wars', *Economic History Review*, XXIII (1970), 476–97; N. K. Buxton, 'Avoiding the pitfalls: entrepreneurial efficiency in the coal industry again', *Economic History Review*, XXV (1972), 669–73.

34 Barry Supple, *The History of the British Coal Industry. Volume 4. 1913–1946: The Political Economy of Decline* (Oxford, 1987), pp. 264–5.

35 Barry Supple, 'The political economy of demoralization: the state and the coalmining industry in America and Britain between the wars', *Economic History Review*, XLI (1988), 566–91, p. 568.

36 Tolliday, 'Steel and rationalization policies', p. 83.

37 D. L. Burn, *The Economic History of Steelmaking 1867–1939. A Study in Competition* (Cambridge, 1940), p. 219.

War indicated that 67 per cent of buildings in the cotton spinning sector and 69 per cent in weaving (representing 61 and 69 per cent of floorspace, respectively) had been constructed before 1900, while a 1947 survey indicated that 77 per cent of wool factory space was built prior to the twentieth century.[38] The more modern factories of their American competitors allowed better spacing of machines to give greater freedom of movement, together with electric lighting and air conditioning. Meanwhile the substitution of noisy and dangerous overhead shafting with electric driving in modern factories reduced the weight that the roof had to support, thus facilitating natural lighting and removing the need for cumbersome internal columns which constrained machinery layouts.[39] Modernisation of the UK cotton and woollen industries was inhibited by the unsuitability of many plants for highly-mechanised equipment, due to factors such as pillar-spacing, layout, restricted floorspace, lighting, and other interior conditions.[40] This raised the operating costs for new plant and/or increased its installation costs by requiring plant modifications. The interrelatedness between mule spindles, power looms, and incumbent labour skill endowments, discussed in Chapter Three, also continued to inhibit technological change.

Coal mining provides a classic example of the problems caused by interrelatedness between new types of machinery and other elements in the production system, which is worth examining in depth. The industry experienced a particularly severe interwar decline; by 1937 its employment and tonnage exported had fallen to only 63.1 per cent and 66.3 per cent of their 1924 values.[41] While market factors played an important role, the industry's extremely poor productivity growth relative to its major competitors, closely associated with its strong lag in mechanisation, undermined its competitive position. Between 1913 and 1936 the Netherlands increased output per man-shift by 117.20 per cent, while increases of 81.34 per cent were recorded in the Ruhr; 72.46 per cent in Polish Upper Silesia; 50.57 per cent in Belgium; 50.31 per cent in Czechoslovakia, 22.40 per cent in France (Pas de Calais); but only 9.63 per cent in the UK.[42] A similar pattern is evident for individual British coalfields. Over 1913–37 no British coalfield other than the Lancashire, North Staffordshire and Cheshire field managed to beat the output per man-shift growth of any continental coalfield for which data are available, while even this region failed to match the European average.[43]

Britain was particularly slow to mechanise processes downstream from the extraction of the coal at the face, involving the conveyance of the coal from the

38 Porter, 'Cotton and wool textiles', pp. 33–7.

39 Ibid, p. 37.

40 Ministry of Production, *Report of the Cotton Textile Mission to the USA* (London, 1944), p. 33; Board of Trade, *Jute Working Party Report* (London, 1948), p. 40; Marvin Frankel, 'Obsolescence and technological change in a maturing economy', *American Economic Review*, 45 (1955), 296–319, pp. 313–14.

41 Supple, *History of the British Coal Industry*, pp. 8–9.

42 International Labour Office, *World Coal-mining Industry*, p. 109.

43 Peter Scott, 'Path dependence, fragmented property rights, and the slow diffusion of high throughput technologies in interwar British coal mining', *Business History*, 48 (2006), 18–36.

face and then along subsidiary and main haulage systems to the shaft. Its principal competitors introduced underground locomotives for coal haulage, which economised on labour, reduced haulage costs, and, crucially, substantially increased throughput – enabling new, more powerful machines for extracting coal at the face to operate at capacity. Yet in British mines the proportion of coal conveyed beyond the face did not exceed a third of total output until 1938. Meanwhile locomotive or conveyor haulage further downstream, on secondary and primary roadways, represented a negligible proportion of output throughout the interwar period. On the eve of the Second World War there were only 16 locomotive in use throughout Britain's 1,870 pits.[44]

British mine engineers identified major potential savings from the adoption of underground locomotives or main roadway conveyors, but found that Britain's underground roadways were unsuitable for these technologies and could only be modified at prohibitive cost. Traditional British mining practice involved developing underground roadways in the course of mining operations, along the line of the coal seam. This had been an efficient system prior to the advent of mechanisation, as British seams were relatively flat and it was cheaper to mine through coal than rock. However, it produced uneven and curved roadways, which were unsuitable for mechanised haulage. Continental mines, by contrast, generally used the 'horizon mining' system – involving concentrating coal extraction at one, or few, faces, reached by straight underground roadways cut through the rock at a slight upward incline from the shaft bottom (which was usually the lowest point in the mine). Horizon mining was originally developed to cope with steeply inclined seams; yet as mine size grew its haulage, ventilation, and roadway maintenance advantages progressively outweighed its greater initial costs and it became widely-adopted even in European coalfields with relatively flat seams.[45]

Part of Britain's problem stemmed from the great age and extensive legacies of previous workings of many British mines. Yet this still left a substantial proportion of more recent mines, developed over the period when European coalfields had adopted horizon-mining. Britain's retention of its traditional mining practice during this period can be traced to its unique system of fragmented mineral royalties. European royalty systems generally developed from a tradition of crown mineral ownership, the state owning mineral royalties and granting concessions to mining concerns.[46] Britain, by contrast, maintained its system of vesting mineral ownership with the owners of the surface land. Britain's current and former colonies mainly followed British practice, but as land was generally held in very large estates this imposed few problems regarding fragmentation.

Privately-owned mineral royalties had not impeded efficient operation in an era of small, unmechanised mines, as the British pattern of land-holding was substantially less fragmented than that of most European countries and each colliery thus typically had to deal with one, or few, royalty owners. Yet as mine size grew, the fragmentation

44 H.M. Chief Inspector of Mines, *Annual Report* (London, 1922), p. 48; NA: COAL 22/174, T.A.C./9, 3 October 1944.

45 C. H. Fritzche and E. L. Potts, *Horizon Mining* (London, 1954), pp. 7–8.

46 Royal Commission on Mineral Royalties, *Final Report With Appendices* (B.P.P., 1893, XLI), pp. 50–59.

problem increased. By the mid-1920s collieries wishing to introduce mechanised mining, through switching to a system of horizon mining and concentrated workings, required the agreement of an average of five (and, for larger mines, possibly as many as 20) separate royalty owners.[47] Each owner wanted to maximise the amount of coal taken from their royalty (as royalty payments were generally based mainly on the tonnage extracted). Thus, if a royalty was required purely for wayleave (underground haulage), they would insist on being compensated for the lost value of their un-mined coal. Owners of royalties through which main haulage tunnels had to pass also had considerable potential for 'strategic hold-up' to extract as much of the potential profit from the scheme via increased royalties as they felt they could get away with. Evidence from interwar colliery rationalisation proposals suggests that problems of securing the agreement of fragmented royalty holders constituted a major barrier to such programmes.[48] Systems of minimum rents, payable regardless of whether any coal was mined from the royalty, also encouraged the continuation of extensive, rather than concentrated, workings. British royalties thus impeded both to the concentration of extraction in particular faces that was essential for employing high throughput machinery at capacity and the development of haulage facilities capable of dealing with this high throughput.

Industrial intervention and support initiatives

One potential solution to the problems of very slow retirement of excess and obsolete capacity through market mechanisms was the development of industry-wide rationalisation initiatives. Potential sponsors included leading firms within the industry; the banking sector; or government. All three agencies played some role in efforts to restructure the interwar staple industries, but none achieved any great measure of success.

Corporate-led initiatives faced considerable difficulties due to the atomistic structure of the staple industries and the extent of their over-capacity. They were typically characterised by very large numbers of, generally small, firms, with few – if any – that were sufficiently large to have managerial structures capable of efficiently running the large corporations that might arise from multi-firm mergers involving a significant proportion of the industry's capacity. Steel and shipbuilding constitute at least partial exceptions, with sufficient large enterprises for firm-led restructuring to be contemplated, at least at the regional level. Such regional mergers proved most successful in Scotland, where they were initiated during the post-war boom. Euphoric expectations that war-time shipping losses would provide the industry with huge markets led to a scramble among the large Scottish yards to absorb steel-manufacturers in order to secure supplies of ship plate. By 1920 only one Scottish steel manufacturer, Stewart & Lloyds, remained independent of the shipbuilders.[49] One major firm, Colvilles, pursued a longer-term strategy of aggressive mergers, that

47 Royal Commission on the Coal Industry (1925), *Report* (B.P.P., 1926, XIV), p. 77; Political and Economic Planning, *Report on the British Coal Industry* (London, 1936), p. 92.

48 Scott, 'Path dependence, fragmented property rights'.

49 T. M. Devine, *The Scottish Nation 1700–2000* (London, 1999), p. 267.

gave it control over 80 per cent of Scottish steel production by 1936, thus enabling it to pursue a modernisation strategy.[50]

Yet initiatives in other major steel-producing regions proved less successful. On the North East coast the fragmented structure of the region's heavy steel industry and the survival of old plant persisted during the interwar years, despite the obvious benefits from merger and rationalisation and the development of a series of merger proposals. Stephen Tolliday has attributed this to historical rivalries between firms headed by 'irritable genrontocracies' who had long memories of old animosities; together with rival interests within these firms, with powers that could be more easily exercised to block change than to compel it.[51]

In less concentrated sectors industry-wide associations attempted to fill the role that might otherwise have been taken by leading firms, but generally achieved little more than short-term holding operations. For example in cotton, the Federation of Master Cotton Spinners' Associations attempted to address over-capacity via the temporary expedient of organising short-time work during 1921–26, in the hope of better times ahead. Yet the improvement in demand did not occur and the initiative merely acted to preserve both excess capacity and less efficient producers.[52] The Federation also tried to set minimum prices, though its attempts to regulate prices and output were not particularly successful, as firms had an incentive to stay outside the agreements and undercut them.

In general, industry-led initiatives met with only limited success. As Barry Supple noted, with regard to initiatives in the coal industry, the basic obstacle confronting firm-led rationalisation was that it was rarely in any particular firm's private interest to spend money in buying up surplus productive capacity merely in order to close it.[53] Meanwhile collective agreements, sponsored through industry-wide bodies, relied on the voluntary cooperation of individual firms, while each firm had an incentive to avoid cooperation, and thus gain from whatever reduction in rival capacity, or output, was agreed by those who participated, without having to bear a share of the cost.

Bank-sponsored rationalisation initiatives appeared to offer better prospects, on account of the highly concentrated structure of the banking sector and the high degree of collusion between the major clearing banks. Having provided considerable overdraft finance to the staple industries during the 1919–20 boom, once the speculative mania subsided the banks found that they had saddled themselves with debtors who could not repay them and who would require long-term support if they were ever to recoup their capital. They thus had a strong incentive to promote integration. Yet pressurising firms into bank-led integration programmes went against the grain of British banking practice. The clearing banks saw themselves as having an arms-length, professional-client, relationship with their corporate debtors, rather than the more interventionist approach taken by German, other European,

50 Ibid, p. 270.

51 Tolliday, 'Steel and rationalization policies', pp. 86–8.

52 W. Lazonick, 'The Cotton Industry', 18–50 in B. Elbaum and W. Lazonick (eds), *The Decline of the British Economy* (Oxford, 1986), p. 31.

53 Supple, *The History of the British Coal Industry*, p. 203.

and American banks. Furthermore they lacked the relevant expertise to design and sponsor effective rationalisation initiatives.

Bank of England support for rationalisation looked likely to tip the scales in favour of action. The Bank of England was particularly well-placed to persuade the banks to engage in restructuring, on account of its supervisory role over the British financial system and its intermediary role between the clearing banks and government. The Bank's influential Governor, Montague Norman, became interested in the possibility of bank intervention and the establishment of institutional frameworks to promote this. In November 1929 the Bank of England launched the Securities Management Trust, to supervise the financing of rationalisation schemes that received the Bank's support. During the following year it launched the Bankers Industrial Development Company (BIDC), in cooperation with the major issuing houses and merchant banks, to increase the supply of credit for mergers and rationalisation in the staple industries. City cooperation was encouraged by a belief that these programmes might forestall more far-reaching government-inspired intervention in private industry, that might set unwelcome precedents for further government interference.

In Lancashire, where the stability of the local banks was threatened by the decline of the cotton industry, the Bank of England intervened during 1929 by sponsoring the formation of the Lancashire Cotton Corporation (LCC) for the 'American' section of the industry. The plan was to organise a systematic reduction of the industry's capacity in order to increase profitability.[54] Between 1929 and 1932 the LCC absorbed almost 100 firms, representing the largest inter-war industrial amalgamation initiative. Similarly the banks established Combined Egyptian Mills Ltd in 1929 for the smaller 'Egyptian' section of the industry, which acquired capacity equal to three million spindles. Yet these initiatives had very limited success in terms of fundamental rationalisation of the sector. The Lancashire Cotton Corporation failed to develop a managerial structure capable of effectively coordinating such a large organisation; indeed in 1932 its chief executives resigned following a decision by its board that local mill managers should be given more autonomy.[55]

Other Bank of England-led initiatives also produced results which, while positive, had only limited impact. For example, efforts during the 1920s to sponsor rationalisation in the shipbuilding industry led to the development of National Shipbuilders' Security Ltd, with the support of the Bank of England, in 1930. Member shipbuilding firms contributed a levy of 1 per cent on the price of vessels commenced from 1 November 1930 in order to fund the purchase and scrapping of redundant and bankrupt yards.[56] This led to the removal of 1.4 million tons of shipbuilding capacity, more than a third of the industry's total, encompassing some 38 yards. Yet capacity still substantially exceeded demand.

Government-sponsored intervention was impeded by Britain's strong tradition of laissez-faire, that even the two brief inter-war minority Labour administrations proved unwilling to challenge. Furthermore, intervention raised the prospect of government financial support, which threatened the Treasury orthodoxy of minimal

54 Garside, *British Unemployment*, p. 213.

55 Lazonick, 'The Cotton Industry', p. 33.

56 Garside, *British Unemployment*, p. 234.

balanced budgets. Yet by the early 1930s, and particularly after the collapse of the gold standard (which reduced pressure to keep expenditure down in order to maintain international confidence in sterling), the government slightly modified its non-interventionist stance – though without any substantial financial commitment. Derek Aldcroft estimated that total public expenditure on aid to industry and agriculture amounted to less than £29 million in 1935, over two thirds of which was directed towards agriculture.[57]

Government intervention faced a fundamental problem – action aimed at eliminating excess capacity would add to unemployment in the short term, while employment-generating measures would preserve excess capacity. In practice government responded to the demands of the staple industries with measures that tried to achieve both aims, generally with the result that neither was properly addressed. The new policy framework followed the precedents set by the Bank of England and the banks, in trying to encourage amalgamation of the major firms in each of the staple industries or raise prices and profits via some form of cartel. Tariff protection facilitated this, by partially shielding domestic markets from world competition.

Some initiatives were successful in reducing capacity. For example, in 1936 government intervened in the cotton industry via the Cotton Industry (Reorganisation) Act. This established the Spindles Board, with powers to raise a compulsory levy on the industry for the acquisition and scrapping of redundant capacity. By the eve of the Second World War, of 13.5 million spindles considered redundant, the Board had scrapped some 6.2 million. Other measures proved less successful, such as the 1930 Coal Mines Act. This introduced statutory cartel provisions and production quotas, together with mechanisms for promoting compulsory restructuring initiatives, with the establishment of the Coal Mines Reorganisation Commission under Part II of the Act. Yet, as Kirby has noted, the cartel provisions inhibited market pressures towards amalgamation, while those for compulsory restructuring were a total failure – largely due to opposition from some mining interests.[58]

Efficiency losses from government-sponsored cartelisation schemes were not limited to coal mining. For example, in the steel industry the British Iron and Steel Federation (BISF) was launched in April 1934, with government backing, to facilitate schemes of industrial reorganisation and help raise prices – a process aided by tariff protection. In practice the BISF proved most active and successful in suppressing new sources of competition, by allocating production quotas to existing firms and pursuing policies which effectively subsidised high cost producers.

State subsidies offered another potential avenue of government support, but one that raised the spectre of indefinite financial commitment to what later generations would come to know as 'lame ducks'. In one industry internationally characterised by extensive state subsidies, shipbuilding, the government did move towards very limited subsidisation. The first significant measure was the granting of a £8 million

57 D. H. Aldcroft, *The British Economy. Volume 1: The Years of Turmoil 1920–1951* (Brighton, 1986), p.125. This figure does not include expenditure on interest and loan guarantees, or on housing subsidies.

58 M. W. Kirby, 'The control of competition in the British coal-mining industry in the thirties', *Economic History Review*, XXVI (1973), 273–84.

low-interest loan to Cunard towards the construction of the liners Queen Mary and Queen Elizabeth in 1934. In 1935, following lobbying from the Chamber of Shipping to provide a temporary subsidy for the most depressed sector of the industry, tramp shipping, government launched the British Shipping (Assistance) Act, 1935. Under the Act cargo tramp shippers received favourable Treasury loans for ship purchases, on condition that they scrapped two tons of existing tonnage for every one ton of new construction.

Direct subsidies were also paid to the tramp shipping industry under another section of the Act, on condition that ship-owners cooperated to collectively reduce competition and raise rates. The direct subsidy had the perverse effect of discouraging the scrapping of excess capacity and capacity modernisation that the legislation was designed to foster. Indeed only 50 vessels were built under the scheme, of 186,000 gross tons, less than a third of the modern tonnage that the programme was designed to produce. Perversely, British owners were allowed to buy and scrap overseas shipping under the scheme, thus diverting some of the subsidy to foreign shipowners who welcomed the opportunity to sell redundant vessels to UK shippers. Yet the direct subsidies did help to foster international cooperation to raise freight rates over certain routes and by 1937 rates had improved sufficiently to allow the subsidy provisions (which were tied to shipping rates) to lapse.[59]

Government intervention in the rationalisation of the staple industries has been widely criticised on account of its very limited effectiveness and contradictory impacts. However, more thoroughgoing rationalisation would have raised major political problems. Any radical restructuring, short of nationalisation, would have involved favouring certain 'champions' among the main producers, which would have raised loud complaints from the remaining firms and involved a degree of coercion of private companies for which there was no precedent in Britain during peacetime. Furthermore, it would have left government open to aggressive lobbying from particular business interests for rationalisation projects that it lacked the technical competence to objectively assess. Radical restructuring would also almost certainly have involved higher unemployment, at least in the short-term, together with greater concentrations of unemployment in certain areas which had lost their initial production advantages. While the failure to foster effective rationalisation in the staple industries damaged their long-term future, it had the positive effect of keeping larger numbers of people in some form of employment.

Workers' responses to industrial decline

Faced with a mis-match between production costs and world market prices, and constrained from lowering costs through modernising capital investment, employers in the staple industries turned to the only cost that seemed under their direct control – labour. As wages formed a high proportion of total costs, wage cuts appeared an attractive means of restoring price competitiveness. Reducing wages also fitted in with the government's strategy of deflation; during the 1920s it sought

59 Aldcroft, *The British Economy*, p. 126.

a reduction in British prices and wages to bring them into line with international prices at the gold standard's pre-war parity. Workers and their unions understandably resented employers' attempts to throw the burden of cost reductions onto them by imposing a substantial fall in their living standards. However, their power to resist wage reductions was limited by the high unemployment and low profitability of their industries. Internal divisions among the unions, and inept industrial tactics, compounded their economic weakness, with the result that the two major concerted attempts to resist wage cuts rapidly became subject to internal splits, with severe and long-term adverse impacts on union numbership and negotiating strength.

Britain's trades unions had emerged from the War in a particularly strong position. Union membership had risen from 4,145,000 in 1914 to 7,926,000 in 1919 (though this partly reflected the continuation of a trend of rapid membership growth already evident during the late Edwardian period). War conditions had necessitated an unprecedented level of government consultation and negotiation with the union movement, to enable the employment of un/semi-skilled non-apprenticed labour on jobs hitherto undertaken by skilled workers, under 'dilution' agreements. Full employment further strengthened their negotiating position, while the adverse impact of inflation on real wages led workers to look to the unions to win them compensating increases in money wages.

Union power maintained its strength during the post-war boom. Government honoured its pledge to abolish war-time dilution agreements, while workers were granted an eight hour working day and other concessions. Meanwhile continuing inflation led to further wage conflict, with national strikes in the railways and coal mines; even the police engaged in strike action. Then, following the downturn in economic conditions from the summer of 1920, the unions' position rapidly deteriorated. Even the much-vaunted 'Triple Alliance' of the Miners, Railwaymen, and Transport Workers unions broke ranks when faced with a major challenge. On 31 March 1921, the date of government decontrol of the coal mines, the miners were 'locked out' by the employers over their refusal to accept severe wage cuts. Joint strike action by the Miners, Railwaymen and Transport Workers was agreed, from Saturday 16 April. Yet before the strike commenced the Miners broke off a fresh attempt to establish negotiations. The moderate J. H. Thomas of the Railwaymen demanded that the Miners return to the negotiating table; when they refused, the other two unions cancelled their sympathetic strikes. The Miners continued what was now a unilateral strike action, but were forced to concede defeat at the end of June.[60] Following this episode the number of days lost through strikes fell considerably and union membership, which had peaked at 8,348,000 in 1920, declined to 5,506,000 by 1925.

The events of April 1921 were replayed on a larger scale, and with even more disastrous consequences for union negotiating strength and solidarity, during the 'General Strike' of May 1926. The strike was called in response to attempts on the part of the mine-owners to enforce further cuts of 13 per cent in the standard wages of miners, together with an increase in the working day from seven to eight

60 Henry Pelling, *A History of British Trade Unionism* 4th edn. (Harmondsworth, 1987), pp. 154–5.

hours (both exclusive of winding time).[61] This produced a major national strike, encompassing around three million workers at its peak, while the suspension of most public transport disrupted the work of several million others. The number of people willing to strike was much larger than those who actually did, as the TUC's strategy was to concentrate on a number of key industries such as transport, rather than calling out all its members.

In the event the government proved itself far more unified, organised and prepared for a General Strike than were the unions. While government officials had been planning for such a strike since July 1925, the TUC General Council had only begun its detailed planning a week before the strike commenced. Moreover, while the government was clear in its objectives – the defeat of the strike – the TUC General Council was far from clear. As Henry Pelling noted:

> having no revolutionary purpose in mind, they were as much afraid of a state of political chaos as the Government was; and as the days went by ... they could see no solution except through the resumption of negotiations. Several of them ... seemed afraid that they might lose control of their followers ... they were all the more anxious to grasp at any chance to resume talks with the Cabinet.[62]

Differences in political temperament between militant miners' leaders and influential moderates in the TUC leadership provided a further source of division. This led to the remarkable outcome that, after only nine days of strike action, the General Council agreed to a return to work on the basis of an agreement with the Chairman of the 1925 Royal Commission on the Coal Industry, Sir Herbert Samuel. This followed the recommendations of the Commission's report – which included wage reductions and had already proved unacceptable to the miners. The strike was cancelled without securing any commitment whatsoever from the government, even regarding protection of strikers against victimisation, and has generally been viewed by contemporary and historical commentators as a complete surrender on the part of the union movement.

Not surprisingly, the miners rejected the settlement and remained on strike for almost seven months in what proved one of the longest and most bitter major disputes in British trade union history. By September some miners in the Derbyshire and Nottinghamshire coalfields were beginning to drift back to work, having been offered slightly better terms by the mine-owners in an attempt to break the strike. By November a general drift back to the pits became evident, by miners who had been starved into submission. Finally, on 30 November the South Wales and Yorkshire miners returned to work, followed by the Durham miners on 1 December. The cost of this long process of attrition was one of severe, in some cases permanent, damage to the physical health of miners and their families; for example, half those who applied to join the army during the next few years were declared unfit.[63]

---

61 Winding time was the time taken to lower or raise an entire shift of men. This was estimated to vary between about 30 and 43 minutes for the main British coalfields in 1925 – Supple, *History of the British Coal Industry*, p. 429.

62 Pelling, *A History of British Trade Unionism*, pp. 165–6.

63 R. J. Cootes, *The General Strike 1926*, 2nd edn. (Harlow, 1983), p. 69.

The following years witnessed a low level of industrial militancy and a decline in union membership from 5,506,000 in 1925 to a trough of only 4,392,000 in 1933. The Great Depression, the 1931 Labour government split, and Labour's catastrophic defeat in the following election, further eroded the movement's industrial and political strength. While union membership recovered during the late 1930s, to 6,053,000 by 1938, there was no return to industrial militancy. Yet the stigma of militancy still hung around the staple industry areas, deterring new industrial development.[64] For example, a proposal by Lord Weir, with Ministry of Transport backing, that new power stations should be erected on the South Wales coalfield, exporting electricity to central and southern England, was rejected by the Central Electricity Board, partly due to fears that militant South Wales miners might pose a threat to the security of power supplies.[65]

Employers' opposition to unions did not generally centre on their influence on wage rates per se, but on their efforts to impose restrictions on the organisation of production and the displacement of skilled adult males by cheaper un/semi-skilled workers.[66] Skilled workers had much to lose from new, de-skilling, production methods and employment practices, as they had made lifetime investments in skill and seniority, which had both monetary and status value to them. For example, cotton weavers opposed the 'more looms' initiative, in which each worker was asked to double the number of looms they monitored, with their work at each loom being restricted to certain functions and unskilled workers doing their remaining tasks. In coal mining, studies have found relatively little specific worker opposition to the introduction of mechanisation, conflict instead focussing on the working arrangements and remuneration that accompanied it.[67] Alan Campbell's review of industrial unrest associated with mechanisation in Scottish collieries found that much industrial action stemmed from grievances rooted within the labour process, concerning effort, pay, discipline and job control.[68] Similarly, studies by Trevor Boyns and A. Renfrew revealed considerable resistance to new working methods accompanying mechanisation, that were seen to violate traditional practices and threaten established skills.[69] In addition to de-skilling, conflict also arose as a result of the introduction of new working methods that increased the intensity of work, or

64 S. R. Dennison, *The Location of Industry and the Depressed Areas* (London, 1939), p. 80.

65 Leslie Hannah, *Electricity Before Nationalisation* (London, 1979), pp. 138–9.

66 See, for example, Peter Scott, 'The wolf at the door: the trade union movement and overseas multinationals in Britain during the 1930s', *Social History,* 23, 2 (1998), 195–210.

67 Roy Church, *The History of the British Coal Industry, Volume 3, 1830–1913: Victorian Pre-eminence* (Oxford, 1986), p. 351; Supple, *History of the British coal industry*, p. 439; A. Renfrew, 'Mechanisation and the miner: work, safety and labour relations in the Scottish coal industry, c. 1890–1939', unpublished Ph.D thesis, University of Strathclyde, 1997, p. 203.

68 Alan Campbell, *The Scottish Miners 1874–1939. Volume One: Industry, Work and Community* (Aldershot, 2000), pp. 109–51.

69 Trevor Boyns, 'Jigging and shaking: technical choice in the South Wales coal industry between the wars', *Welsh History Review*, 17: 2 (1994), 230–51; Trevor Boyns, 'Of machines and men in the 1920s', *Llafur*, 5 (1989), 30–9; Renfrew, 'Mechanisation and the miner', p. 233.

led to deterioration in working conditions (such as shift work). Yet it was precisely by altering working methods and substituting skilled workers with 'cheap' un/semi-skilled workers that employers in the expanding manufacturing sectors obtained their competitive advantage, as discussed in Chapters 9–11.

Chapter Six

New industrial development in outer-Britain

Introduction

Depression for many established firms in Britain's outer regions was mirrored by a relatively low volume of new plant formation. During 1932–38 the South East – which had accounted for only 21.3 per cent of British manufacturing employment in 1911 – received 47.9 per cent of new manufacturing plants, while Scotland, Wales, and England's northern region received only 3.9, 1.6 and 2.8 per cent respectively.[1]

Partly in response to perceptions of a widening regional divide in plant formation, the Board of Trade published a series of annual surveys of new industrial development. This and the following chapter draw on a database assembled from these surveys to examine the changing geography of plant formation in Britain.

The Surveys of Industrial Development (hereafter SID's), conducted annually during 1932–38, covered all new manufacturing plants established, or extended, throughout Britain, where this involved the employment of 25 or more people (with the exception of government factories set up under the late 1930s' rearmament programme).[2] Information was provided on each plant's production, location, initial employment (within bands of 100), and whether it arose as the result of a transfer from another locality or through the establishment of a branch plant. Data from the SID's have been entered into a database, each plant being coded by UK Standard Economic Region (SER) and 3-digit 1980 Standard Industrial Classification (SIC). SIC coding was based on product/process descriptions; these were usually sufficiently specific, though ambiguities were encountered in some cases. The SID's also included a few non-manufacturing plants, such as servicing and repair facilities; these were excluded from the analysis. Plants were grouped into a number of 'districts', each of which was usually further divided into fairly small 'localities'.[3] Locality-level data generally separated the central areas of major cities and each of their suburban industrial zones; for example, the 'Leeds' locality did not include suburban areas such as Armley and Stanningley; 'Sheffield' excluded similar areas

1 Source: Table 6.1 and Appendix 2. Estimate for new plants refers to plants with an initial employment of at least 25 people.

2 Board of Trade, 'Survey of industrial development in 1932', *Board of Trade Journal* (29 June 1933), pp. iii–xv; Board of Trade, *Survey of Industrial Development* (London, 1934–39); NA: HLG71/1330, memorandum, n.d., c. 1943.

3 Appendix One discusses those exceptional cases where locality-level data were not provided, at least for some years.

such as Intake, Attercliffe, and Ecclesfield; and 'Glasgow' excluded areas such as Pollokshaws and Govan. Further details of the SID's and the database developed from them are provided in Appendix One.

Industrial inheritance and new plant formation

Previous studies of new industrial development in interwar Britain have highlighted the strong links between inherited industrial structures and new industrial development.[4] Yet the reasons underlying these relationships have not been fully explored. Links between a region's current, and inherited, patterns of plant formation may not necessarily be causal. For example, an inherited base of resource intensive, export-orientated, industries might reflect factor cost and market access conditions which, if they remain unchanged, might be similarly reflected in new plant formation.

Yet evidence suggests that causal links are also likely to be strong. One important relationship concerns locational externalities. As discussed in Chapter Two, industrial districts offered clustered firms in the same sector a number of major advantages, including thick markets for inputs, outputs and ancillary services – that facilitate process specialisation and, therefore, economies of scale; pools of industry-specific production factors such as skilled labour, 'second-hand' or rented factories and plant, and trade credit; and knowledge spillovers between firms regarding new product and process innovations and changes in the character of market demand.

A further link between a region's industrial inheritance and current pattern of plant formation, of particular importance during periods of substantial unemployment and excess capacity, concerns the 'asset specificity' of its physical and human capital. Asset specificity, a central concept of transactions cost economics, is defined as 'the degree to which an asset can be redeployed to alternative uses and by alternative users without sacrifice of productive value'.[5] Districts with declining industries whose plant displays low asset specificity are more likely to attract firms from other sectors. For example, a vacant weaving shed is more likely to be redeployed to a different industry than a coal mine, shipyard, or steel mill. Human capital displays analogous features; for example, during this period firms in expanding manufacturing sectors preferred labour with experience of simple, repetitive, tasks to redundant craft workers from the heavy staple industries.[6]

Information on the inherited industrial structures of Britain's regions, together with London and Middlesex (the closest approximation to Greater London using county-level data) is provided in Appendix Two – based on 1911 and 1931 Census employment data compiled by Clive Lee. The 1911 Census provides the best

---

4 S. R. Dennison, The *Location of Industry and the Depressed Areas* (London, 1939), p. 148; J. H. Jones, 'Memorandum on the location of industry', 249-79 in *Royal Commission on the Distribution of the Industrial Population*, Report (London, 1940); Carol E. Heim, 'Uneven regional development in interwar Britain', unpublished Ph.D. thesis, Yale University, 1982, p. 110.

5 O. E. Williamson, 'Transactions cost Economics', in R. Schmalensee and R. D. Willig (eds), *Handbook of Industrial Organisation*, Vol. 1 (Amsterdam, 1989), p. 142.

6 See Chapter 10.

available benchmark just prior to the dislocations caused by the First World War and post-war readjustment, while the 1931 data show regional employment structures immediately prior to the SID's. Both the broad distribution of employment between all activities, and the distribution within manufacturing, are examined. 'Coefficients of regional specialisation' are also included, for manufacturing sectors only – based on the coefficient of localisation (calculated by summing the positive deviations of the regional percentage of workers in a sector from the corresponding regional percentage of workers in all industries and dividing the total by 100). An industry with a regional distribution reflecting that of the workforce in general would have a coefficient of zero, while a sector entirely based in a single region would have a figure approaching 1.[7] The coefficient of regional specialisation uses the same approach, but sums the plus deviations of sectoral variations in manufacturing workforce composition for a particular region, relative to that for Britain, to provide an index of regional specialisation within manufacturing.

New plants established in each region over 1932–38 are examined in Tables 6.1–6.3. Table 6.1 shows the number of plants (including transfers between localities) and regional 'new plant quotients', calculated by dividing the ratio of new plants in each region to new plants nationally by the same ratio for 1931 manufacturing employment. Data are also provided on the proportion of plants representing branch premises, or transfers between localities, together with the ratio of plant extensions (involving at least 25 additional jobs) to new plants. Table 6.1 also shows the proportion of new plants with an initial employment of over 100, 200, and 500. Mean regional employment levels cannot be accurately estimated from the SID's, as these only published plant-level employment data within bands of 100. However, Table 6.2 shows estimates based on a contemporary official analysis of the original returns (grouped according to the regions used in the SID's, rather than the SER's used elsewhere in the analysis). The Table also includes regional estimates of net output per employee in 'factory trades' – from the 1935 Census of Production.[8]

In order to examine local plant clustering within regions, Table 6.4 provides details of 'substantial' clusters in Britain's provincial regions – each involving the establishment of more than 25 plants in the locality during the period of the surveys (the locations of all British clusters outside the London conurbation are also shown in Figure 6.1). Variables include the sectoral concentration of each cluster in its largest two and three digit SIC classes and its degree of industrial diversification (measured using two proxies – the proportion of plants in two digit SIC classes other than the three largest; and the number of SIC classes over-represented relative to new plants nationally). The Table also shows the proportion of plants in each cluster with an initial employment of over 100 and the proportions of branch premises and transfers.

---

7 P. S. Florence, Investment, Location, and Size of Plant (Cambridge, 1948), pp. 34–5.

8 Assuming that regional differentials for new plants were broadly similar to those for all plants – given that regional plant formation patterns generally mirrored existing sectoral specialisations.

Table 6.3 examines the industrial composition of new plants in each region, by 2-digit SIC. The Table again includes coefficients of regional manufacturing specialisation, though these are calculated in terms of the number of plants (given the absence of precise employment data).

New plant formation in regions outside the axial belt

The broadest geographic divide in new plant formation was that between the concentration of new factory (as opposed to manufacturing plant) development in a coffin-shaped axial belt extending diagonally from London to Merseyside and the West Riding of Yorkshire, illustrated in Figure 6.1. As noted in Chapter Two, this area had encompassed the main locations for manufacturing centres dominated by factory trades since the Industrial Revolution. During the interwar period the belt continued to define that area of Britain offering good nodality for Britain's main centres of population and factory production, the rise of road transport and decline of coastal shipping after 1918 having increased the importance of land-based goods transport.

As noted in Chapter 2, areas outside the belt had constituted an 'industrial periphery', dominated by heavy 'export-orientated mineral and raw material exploiting' industry.[9] Scotland represented a partial exception, with its own transport nodality, centred around the Glasgow-Edinburgh axis. Scotland had a substantially more diverse inherited manufacturing base, with a coefficient of specialisation in 1911 of only 0.13, compared to rates of between 0.26 and 0.34 for the other industrial periphery regions (see Appendix Two). Yet by 1931, while it was still more diversified than its periphery counterparts, the coefficient had increased to 0.19, with a significant shift from textiles and clothing to food and raw materials processing industries.

New plant formation during the 1930s further reflected this shift; while plant formation in the other periphery regions also reinforced their bias towards resource-exploiting, non-factory production. As Table 6.5 shows, even if Greater London is removed from the analysis, the axial belt still accounts for 80.00 per cent of new plants in the rest of England and Wales during 1932–38, while its inclusion brings this figure to 88.25 per cent. While this partly reflected their traditional non-manufacturing bias, all five periphery regions attracted substantially fewer new plants during 1932–38 than would be expected given their share of 1931 manufacturing employment. Those plants which were established were even more dominated by industries making intensive use of local primary inputs, such as metal manufacture, non-metallic mineral products, bulk chemicals, wooden goods, and food & drink processing, than had been the case before 1914. A further unifying characteristic of these regions, largely stemming from the 'heavy' nature of their principal industries, was low female participation rates compared to regions within the axial belt.[10]

9 C. H. Lee, 'Regional growth and structural change in Victorian Britain', *Economic History Review*, 34 (1981), pp. 438–52.

10 C. E. V. Leser, 'Men and women in industry', *Economic Journal*, 62 (1952), 326–44, p. 339.

Table 6.1: A profile of new manufacturing plant formation in Britain (with an initial employment of 25 or more), 1932–38

Region	No. of new plants	New plant quotient*	Percentage with initial employment of over:			% Branches	% Transfers	Ratio of plant extensions to new plants (%)
			100	200	500			
Greater London	1,408	N/A	18.39	5.61	1.07	9.02	25.28	17.90
Other South East	295	N/A	24.41	10.85	2.37	12.88	11.86	45.42
All South East	1,703	1.84	19.44	6.52	1.29	9.69	22.96	22.67
South West	95	0.62	26.32	9.47	3.16	22.11	6.32	34.74
East Anglia	45	0.79	28.89	13.33	2.22	17.78	6.67	60.00
West Midlands	294	0.69	25.85	11.56	4.42	18.37	6.46	50.68
East Midlands	193	0.70	17.10	4.15	1.04	24.87	2.59	51.30
Yorkshire & Humerside	230	0.58	18.26	6.96	1.30	31.74	7.39	51.30
North West	700	1.03	24.86	9.29	1.71	18.29	10.00	31.71
Northern	99	0.76	26.26	8.08	4.04	16.16	2.02	37.37
Scotland	140	0.33	17.86	7.86	0.00	20.71	4.29	30.71
Wales	57	0.68	33.33	19.30	3.51	19.30	3.51	29.82
Britain	3,556	1.00	21.48	7.85	1.74	15.55	14.65	31.81

Source: UK Data Archive, AHDS History, SN5192, Peter Scott and Peter Walsh, 'National data on new interwar manufacturing plants and extensions, 1919–1938', deposited 2005.

Notes: N/A – not available (employment data for 1931 are not available for the Greater London region). * Regional new plants/national new plants divided by regional 1931 manufacturing employment/national 1931 manufacturing employment.

Table 6.2: The initial employment generated by new plants, and their estimated annual net output, 1932–37

Region*	Number of plants	Initial employment	Average employment per plant	Net output per employee (£)**	Total net output (£)**
Greater London	1,400	111,700	80	276	30,829,200
Other South East & South West	152	12,250	81	256	3,136,000
Midlands	456	48,050	105	227	10,907,350
Eastern counties	111	10,500	95	254	2,667,000
North West	530	70,000	132	200	14,000,000
North East	272	26,000	96	206	5,356,000
Wales & Monmouthshire	39	5,000	128	259	1,295,000
Scotland	125	10,000	80	217	2,170,000
Total	3,085	293,500	95	231	67,798,500

Source: NA: HLG 71/1330, memorandum, September 1943; Board of Trade, Fifth Census of Production 1935, Final Summary Tables *(London, 1944).*

Notes:
* Regions correspond to the original SID classifications. North East includes Yorkshire.
** Estimates, based on 1935 Census of Production data for factory trades only (assuming that new plants in each region had a net output per employee roughly similar to that for all plants). Census of Production regions were matched with SID regions using guidance notes in NA, HLG71/1330, memorandum, September 1943.

Table 6.3: The sectoral distribution of new manufacturing plants with 25 or more employees, by region, 1932–38

SIC	GL	Other SE	Total SE	SW	EA	WM	EM	YH	NW	N	S	W	Total
22 Metal Manufacture	0.78	1.36	0.88	1.05	0.00	4.42	1.55	4.35	1.00	6.06	3.57	17.54	1.97
24 Non-metallic mineral products	2.77	11.86	4.35	6.32	2.22	8.84	7.25	5.22	5.00	16.16	16.43	8.77	5.96
25 Chemicals	3.76	6.78	4.29	5.26	2.22	1.36	0.52	4.35	2.86	7.07	2.86	7.02	3.63
26 Man-made fibres	0.07	0.34	0.12	0.00	4.44	0.34	0.52	0.87	0.43	0.00	0.00	5.26	0.39
31 Other metal goods	4.55	5.76	4.76	4.21	4.44	22.45	2.59	9.13	3.43	7.07	2.86	10.53	6.19
32 Mech. engineering	4.33	3.73	4.23	5.26	4.44	11.22	3.11	5.22	3.29	6.06	5.71	7.02	4.81
33 Office machinery	0.28	0.00	0.23	0.00	0.00	0.34	0.00	0.00	0.00	0.00	0.00	0.00	0.14
34 Electrical engineering	10.51	6.10	9.75	2.11	11.11	5.10	2.59	1.74	3.00	4.04	5.71	7.02	6.58
35 Motor vehicles	2.13	2.03	2.11	0.00	0.00	4.08	1.04	0.87	0.86	2.02	1.43	0.00	1.74
36 Other transport	1.56	7.80	2.64	8.42	2.22	6.46	0.52	2.17	2.00	2.02	0.71	5.26	2.78
37 Instrument engineering	2.70	1.69	2.52	2.11	0.00	0.34	0.00	1.30	0.29	0.00	1.43	0.00	1.49
41/2 Food, drink, tobacco	5.47	8.81	6.05	15.79	40.00	4.76	5.18	5.22	5.29	5.05	17.86	8.77	6.86
43 Textiles	2.63	2.71	2.64	4.21	0.00	4.08	37.31	26.09	27.57	7.07	19.29	3.51	11.87
44 Leather goods	2.20	1.69	2.11	3.16	2.22	3.06	3.63	0.87	2.14	2.02	0.71	1.75	2.17
45 Clothing/footwear	30.04	16.95	27.77	17.89	15.56	9.18	28.50	22.61	28.86	12.12	10.00	1.75	24.18
46 Timber & furniture	13.35	9.15	12.62	10.53	11.11	4.76	1.04	6.52	6.14	16.16	3.57	3.51	9.20
47 Paper/paper products	7.17	8.81	7.46	9.47	0.00	4.08	4.15	1.30	4.57	4.04	5.00	3.51	5.74
48 Rubber & plastics	1.85	2.37	1.94	3.16	0.00	1.36	0.00	0.87	2.29	2.02	0.71	1.75	1.74
49 Other manufacturing	3.84	2.03	3.52	1.05	0.00	3.74	0.52	1.30	1.00	1.01	2.14	7.02	2.56
Total	100.00	100.00	100.00	100.00	100.00	100.00	100.00	100.00	100.00	100.00	100.00	100.00	100.00
Coefficient of Specialisation*	0.19	0.20	0.15	0.25	0.44	0.36	0.33	0.21	0.21	0.27	0.31	0.42	0.00

Source: UK Data Archive, AHDS History, SN5192, Peter Scott and Peter Walsh, 'National data on new interwar manufacturing plants and extensions, 1919–1938', deposited 2005.

Note: * For definition see text.

Table 6.4: Provincial clusters with over 25 new plants, 1932–38

	Number of plants	Largest 2-digit SIC		Largest 3-digit SIC		% in 2 digit SIC classes excluding 3 largest	No. of 2 digit SIC's with LQ>1	% plants with 100+ employees	% Branch plants	% Transfers
		Class	% in class	Class	% in class					
North-West England										
Manchester*	53	45	67.9	453	62.3	18.9	3	13.2	15.1	1.9
Blackburn	34	43	41.2	432	29.4	32.4	5	23.5	14.7	2.9
Burnley	26	43	53.8	432	53.8	23.1	5	30.8	19.2	3.8
Salford	29	45	51.7	453	51.7	27.6	6	17.2	27.6	13.8
Yorkshire & Humberside										
Bradford	28	43	78.6	431	60.7	0.0	1	14.3	35.7	0.0
Leeds	38	45	84.2	453	81.6	2.6	2	28.9	28.9	5.3
Sheffield	40	31	47.5	316	37.5	30.0	6	17.5	35.0	7.5
East Midlands										
Leicester	46	43	71.7	436	63.0	4.3	3	10.9	23.9	0.0
Scotland										
Glasgow	37	45	21.6	453	18.9	51.4	7	10.8	16.2	2.7

Source: UK Data Archive, AHDS History, SN5192, Peter Scott and Peter Walsh, 'National data on new interwar manufacturing plants and extensions, 1919–1938', deposited 2005.

Note: Disaggregated data were not available for the Birmingham area. * Excluding 1933 and 1934, for which no disaggregated data are available.

Meanwhile the limited base of factory industry within the peripheral regions contracted markedly, as illustrated by clothing & footwear – the largest factory-based sector in three of the periphery regions in 1911 and a substantial employer in all five. By 1931 national clothing employment had declined by 27.7 per cent despite buoyant demand, largely as a result of productivity improvements. Yet this decline was much more severe in the periphery regions (63.2 per cent in Wales, 55.4 per cent in the Northern region, 54.3 per cent in Scotland, 51.2 per cent in the South West, and 30.0 per cent in East Anglia) compared to 10.3 per cent in Yorkshire & Humberside, 13.4 per cent in the North West, 15.5 per cent in the East Midlands, and 21.2 per cent in the South East. While depressed consumer demand in the periphery clearly played a role, the trend towards nationwide production from large, sectorally-specialised, clusters within the factory belt, such as the central areas of Leeds, Manchester, and London, appears to have been the chief influence.

Regions outside the axial belt can be divided into two broad types: those with an inherited industrial structure based around the coal-iron/steel-shipbuilding nexus – the Northern region, Wales, and Scotland – and regions that were largely agricultural in 1911 – East Anglia and the South West. The coal-iron/steel-shipbuilding nexus was particularly dominant in the Northern region and Wales. In 1911 mining & quarrying, metal manufacture, and shipbuilding accounted for 53.12 per cent of primary and secondary sector employment in the Northern region and 55.80 per cent in Wales, compared to only 19.57 per cent for Britain. Partly as a result, these regions had an unusually low proportion of females in their workforce (just over two thirds the national average). Scotland had a substantially more diverse base, with only 24.54 per cent of non-tertiary sector employment in these industries and a significant representation of textile and clothing firms, together accounting for 24.93 per cent of 1911 non-tertiary sector employment. It thus had some similarities to the textile-based regions discussed below (though they were much more strongly weighted towards these sectors). However, by 1931 its employment had shifted significantly away from textiles and clothing, which accounted for only 18.14 per cent of non-tertiary sector employment, compared to 26.59 per cent for mining & quarrying, metal manufacture, and shipbuilding.

Substantial expansion of Scotland's coal-iron/steel-shipbuilding base during the First World War had increased its reliance on this strongly-interrelated heavy industry nexus, while the 1919–20 boom accentuated this trend. The growth of nationally-based companies, headquarted south of the border, also played some role in the decline of its light manufacturing sector. For example, by 1929 the Calico Printers Association had closed all the Scottish factories inherited from the companies that had merged to form it. Corporate amalgamations also had a negative impact on its heavy industry base; for example the reorganisation of Britain's railways into the 'Big Four' companies was followed by the closure, or scaling down, of the workshops of the former Scottish railway firms.[11]

All three coal-iron-steel regions fared badly during 1932–38. The Northern region, Wales, and Scotland, attracted only 2.78, 1.60, and 3.94 per cent of new plants recorded in the SID's, well below what would be expected given their share

11 C. L. Mowat, Britain *Between the Wars 1918–1940* (London, 1955), p. 468.

Figure 6.1: 'Substantial' clusters of new manufacturing plants in Britain, 1932–38

Source: UK Data Archive, AHDS History, SN5192, Peter Scott and Peter Walsh, 'National data on new interwar manufacturing plants and extensions, 1919–1938', deposited 2005.

Notes: 'Substantial' clusters each contain more than 25 new plants with an initial employment of 25 or more people. The Greater London area contains 13 such clusters. Data for the Birmingham area are not disaggregated by locality; the area as a whole encompasses 132 new plants.

of 1931 manufacturing employment. The Northern region and Wales attracted a higher proportion of large plants than the national average, though Scotland had both a small number of new plants and a low proportion of large plants. These regions received a higher proportion of branch plants than the national average, but a very low proportion of wholesale transfers of production. With the exception of the Northern region, they also had ratios of plant extensions to new plants slightly below the national average, indicating that they fared poorly in terms of employment growth via both new and existing plants.

Table 6.5: The number and sectoral distribution of plants in the 'factory belt' and the rest of Britain, 1932–38

	Factory Belt	Factory Belt (excl. Greater London)	Non-Factory Belt (England & Wales)	Scotland
Number	3013	1605	401	140
SIC Distribution (%)				
22 Metal Manufacture	1.43	1.99	5.24	3.57
24 Non-metallic mineral products	4.91	6.79	9.98	16.43
25 Chemicals	3.45	3.18	5.24	2.86
26 Man-made fibres	0.40	0.69	0.50	0.00
31 Other metal goods	6.51	8.22	4.99	2.86
32 Mechanical engineering	4.75	5.11	4.99	5.71
33 Office machinery	0.17	0.06	0.00	0.00
34 Electrical engineering	6.87	3.68	4.74	5.71
35 Motor vehicles	1.86	1.62	1.00	1.43
36 Other transport	2.49	3.30	5.74	0.71
37 Instrument engineering	1.53	0.50	1.25	1.43
41/2 Food, drink, tobacco	5.01	4.61	16.96	17.86
43 Textiles	12.45	21.06	4.99	19.29
44 Leather goods	2.29	2.37	1.75	0.71
45 Clothing/footwear	26.35	23.12	12.97	10.00
46 Timber/wooden furniture	9.39	5.92	9.73	3.57
47 Paper/paper products	5.77	4.55	5.74	5.00
48 Rubber & plastics	1.76	1.68	2.00	0.71
49 Other manufacturing	2.62	1.56	2.24	2.14
Total	100.00	100.00	100.00	100.00

Source: UK Data Archive, AHDS History, SN5192, Peter Scott and Peter Walsh, 'National data on new interwar manufacturing plants and extensions, 1919–1938', deposited 2005.

Meanwhile their new manufacturing plants reinforced their export-orientated mineral and raw material exploiting industrial inheritance, based around the coal-iron-steel nexus. Many of their manufacturing plants were not 'factories' in the conventional sense, but enterprises such as iron foundries, steel mills, shipyards, brick kilns, and bulk chemical facilities, undertaking production which was often both raw-material and energy intensive. Despite the development of a 'national' electricity supply grid from 1926, the grid initially operated more as a series of regional grids (with interregional emergency tie lines) than as a truly national system and industrial power costs remained lower in the coalfield regions than in the South.

All three regions were over-represented in SIC's 22 (metal manufacture) and 24 (non-metallic mineral products). The Northern region and Wales were also over-represented in SIC 25 (chemicals). Metal manufacturers were concentrated in iron and steel goods (particularly in the Northern region and Wales), while the non-metallic mineral plants were dominated by energy-intensive activities such as brick production and concrete products. Meanwhile their chemical plants mainly represented bulk chemicals; these generally required cheap fuel inputs, easy access to raw materials, plentiful supplies of water, and good facilities for effluent disposal, thus making sparsely-populated coastal areas near coalfields particularly attractive.[12] Other over-represented sectors were mainly 'heavy', mature, producer-goods industries, most consumer-goods sectors being strongly under-represented.

Apart from bulk chemicals, 'new' industries were weakly represented in all three regions. The main exception, artificial fibres in Wales, concerned three plants in the extreme north east (at Holywell and Flint), within the axial belt and in an area with greater proximity and stronger economic links to Merseyside and Cheshire than to most areas of Wales. The importance of appropriate water supplies and effluent disposal for artificial fibre production may also have influenced the choice of these relatively sparsely-populated coastal locations.

Another characteristic of these regions was a low level of plant clustering. Wales demonstrated no significant clustering other than the Treforest industrial estate, with 13 plants, all established during 1937 and 1938. The estate formed part of the government's experimental Special Areas policy of regional assistance, discussed in Chapter 13. The Northern region had a similar absence of substantial clusters, the largest being Gateshead with 12 plants – the majority based on another government-sponsored estate at Team Valley. Scotland exhibited some limited clustering, including Dundee will 11 plants (five connected with its traditional specialisation in jute). Meanwhile the central area of Glasgow, with 37 plants, was the only 'substantial' cluster (with 25 or more new plants) outside the axial belt. Glasgow attracted a diverse range of (mainly consumer goods) plants, in sectors such as clothing; paper & printing; food, drink & tobacco; electrical engineering; and instrument engineering. This reflected the city's industrial inheritance: despite Clydeside's dominance by the coal-iron/steel-shipbuilding nexus, Glasgow's central area had a diversified structure, with these industries already strongly represented.[13]

12 See W. F. Luttrell, *Factory Location and Industrial Movement. A Study of Recent Experience in Great Britain*, Volume II (London, 1962), Chapter 9; R. S. Edwards and H. Townsend, *Business Enterprise. Its Growth and Organisation* (London, 1958), p. 154.

13 Alec Cairncross, 'The economy of Glasgow', in R. Miller and J. Tivy (eds), *The Glasgow Region* (Edinburgh, 1958), pp. 219–41.

Although the core Clydeside heavy industries were severely depressed, central Glasgow nevertheless continued to benefit from classic urbanisation externalities stemming from its size, diversity, and metropolitan role as the centre of Scotland's consumer goods market and the base of many of its largest companies.

Another common feature of these regions was a low rate of closures for new manufacturing plants. Contemporary analysis of the SID's noted that plants which closed during the year after they opened amounted to only 3.0 per cent of the total in north-eastern England, Wales, and Scotland, compared to 7.0 per cent in the North West, 5.1 per cent in Greater London, and 3.1 per cent for the Midlands, South West, and eastern counties. When standardised for industrial structure, the differential between closures in the coal-iron/steel-shipbuilding regions and the national average widens further.[14] This may have been connected with the absence of large light-manufacturing industrial districts in these regions. In such districts sub-contracting networks and pools of rented premises, second-hand machinery, and skilled labour not only facilitated firm entry, but also eased firm exit by lowering sunk costs, thus encouraging more marginal entrants.

The two other non-axial belt regions, East Anglia and the South West, had inherited structures strongly biased towards agriculture. East Anglia had 28.69 per cent of its 1911 workforce in agriculture, forestry and fishing – the highest of any region – and only 20.17 per cent in manufacturing. The South West had a more diverse structure, but still had more than twice the national proportion of workers in agriculture, and a proportion in manufacturing more than ten percentage points below the national average. These regions also had similar manufacturing structures, with food-and-drink and clothing-and-footwear both heavily over-represented – together accounting for 47.17 of 1911 manufacturing employment in East Anglia and 45.85 per cent in the South West, compared to only 25.65 per cent throughout Britain. By 1931 the pattern of a small manufacturing sector, specialised in these two industries, was still evident, the main change being the growth of vehicle production in the South West.

Like the coal-iron-steel regions, they attracted few manufacturing plants, both relative to other regions and to their 1931 manufacturing populations, though these included a substantially higher proportion of large units than the national average. Again, branches were over-represented and transfers substantially under-represented. The composition of new plants largely conforms to the 'export-orientated mineral and raw material exploiting' model, while also reflecting these regions' inherited clothing specialisations. Of the 45 plants attracted to East Anglia, no fewer than 18 were in the food & drink sector; including 11 fruit canning and bottling plants – drawing on its specialisation in fruit growing. Meanwhile the only other sector with more than five plants was clothing & footwear. Similarly, the two largest sectors in the South West were clothing & footwear and food & drink.

Yet the South West's new plants had a somewhat broader composition than East Anglia's, with 10 sectors over-represented. This was probably a function of the greater distance of much of its population from manufacturing centres outside the region and the role of Bristol as a major port and regional capital. While East Anglia

14 NA: HLG71/1330, memorandum, 22 September 1943. Regional classifications are based on definitions current at the time of the SID's.

showed no significant evidence of clustering (even Norwich attracting only seven plants) Bristol represented Britain's second largest cluster outside the axial belt, with 20 plants – including seven of the region's nine paper and printing plants – thus playing a similar 'metropolitan' role to that of Glasgow.

Yet there were signs that both regions were beginning to develop a base of engineering-related industry of a type neither evident in 1911 nor typical of export-orientated mineral and raw material exploiting regions. The South West attracted seven plants in SIC 364 (aircraft and components), including one with an initial employment of over 2,700, one employing over 700, and three other large plants employing over 300, 200, and 100 respectively. All were clustered in a relatively small geographical area – four in or near Bristol, two in Cheltenham, and one in Gloucester.[15] Meanwhile East Anglia had attracted one aircraft manufacturer (with an initial employment of over 300), together with smaller plants making aeronautical instruments, motor vehicle lamp bulbs, spark plugs, and motor vehicle accessories. While these developments were on a very limited scale (and strategic concerns regarding vulnerability to bombing influenced the choice of western locations for aircraft plants) they do at least indicate that these regions were beginning to be considered as acceptable locations for such industries – foreshadowing the post-war emergence of the 'sunbelt' of high-tech, research-intensive, engineering-related plants in the area of southern Britain spanning Bristol to East Anglia.[16]

The 'industrial heartland'

Within the factory belt, three types of region can be identified, the 'industrial heartland' of the North West, Yorkshire & Humberside, and East Midlands; the diversified metal-fabricating base of the West Midlands; and Greater London. While the industrial heartland covers a much greater physical area than the latter two, its new plant clusters nevertheless possess broadly similar characteristics in terms of the narrowness of their sectoral specialisations and the nature of their locational externalities. Each region lies partly outside the axial belt, but all had most of their new interwar plants within the belt. Only five of the 193 new plants in the East Midlands and 10 of the 700 in the North West were located outside the belt, while even in Yorkshire & Humberside (which had the bulk of its territory outside the belt) they accounted for only 34 of 230 new plants.

These regions shared the inherited features of a high proportion of workers in manufacturing, service sector employment substantially below the national average, and a strong over-representation of textiles. As Appendix Two shows, textiles dominated manufacturing employment in the North West and accounted for over 40 per cent of Yorkshire & Humberside's 1911 manufacturing population. It was less important in the East Midlands, but still ranked second to clothing & footwear in 1911, and had become the region's largest manufacturing sector by 1931. Clothing

15 Five of the eight plants were established during 1937–38, probably indicating a military element to their production and, possibly, their choice of location.

16 See Doreen Massey, *Spatial Divisions of Labour: Social Structures and the Geography of Production* (London, 1984), pp. 137, 272, 277.

was also over-represented in Yorkshire & Humberside and the North West, as a proportion of total employment (but not in terms of manufacturing employment, on account of these regions' manufacturing bias).

Their coefficients of regional specialisation reveal more diversified inherited patterns of manufacturing employment than was the case for most industrial periphery regions; with the exception of the East Midlands this was also reflected in new plant formation during 1932–38. Yet only the North West attracted more plants than would be expected given its 1931 manufacturing employment, while the East Midlands and Yorkshire & Humberside both had low 'new plant quotients', as shown in Table 6.1.

Furthermore, unlike the North West, these regions attracted a smaller proportion of large plants than the national average. All three regions attracted a lower proportion of plant transfers than was the case nationally, but a higher proportion of branches. These were particularly important in Yorkshire & Humberside and the East Midlands, accounting for 31.74 and 24.87 per cent of plants respectively.

Carol Heim has argued that branch plant formation in Britain's provincial regions was not substantial during the 1930s and that most British firms lacked the organisational sophistication to divide production by process over long distances. Even if macroeconomic policy had been more expansionary, she argues, peripheral areas would not, therefore, have received a substantial number of plants.[17] Yet, as Table 1 shows, branch plants made up a substantial proportion of the (relatively few) new plants in Britain's peripheral regions. The SID's provide no indication of the location of branches' parent plants. However, there is evidence that, while Heim's arguments are correct at the national level, the dispersal of labour-intensive processes, not dependent on strong locational externalities, was beginning to emerge over smaller distances. For example, in the prosperous and expanding Leeds clothing district, industrial growth eventually produced labour shortages (especially regarding female workers) and rising wages, leading a number of the largest menswear manufacturers to establish satellite plants during the late 1930s in areas of high female unemployment and flexible 'green' labour such as South Yorkshire, the north-east, and Lancashire.[18]

These areas offered both cheap labour and increased flexibility regarding the organisation of production, such as evading union restrictions on the employment of females and juveniles. Montague Burton employed girls at his new Walkden factory in Lancashire on tasks performed by adult males at his Leeds factories, while John Barran opened a branch plant at the government's Team Valley trading estate, using the conveyor-belt system (which was not popular with Leeds workers) and only employing females.[19] Location at Team Valley provided the firm with government assistance, including both a rented factory and help with training – the Ministry of Labour having established a small factory of the estate to train women for the

17 C. E. Heim, 'Industrial organization and regional development in interwar Britain', *Journal of Economic History*, XLIII (1983), pp. 931–52.

18 Katrina Honeyman, Well *Suited. A History of the Leeds Clothing Industry 1850–1990* (Oxford, 2000), pp. 87–90.

19 Ibid, pp. 185–96.

clothing industry.[20] While it is not clear to what extent this formed part of a more general pattern, the example of Leeds nevertheless shows that, in at least one centre, when economic expansion became sufficiently vigorous to create labour scarcity, firms were prepared to move some production to neighbouring regions.

New plant formation in the industrial heartland reflected its inherited specialisation in textiles and clothing – these two sectors collectively accounted for 65.8 per cent of new plants in the East Midlands, 56.4 per cent in the North West, and 48.7 per cent in Yorkshire & Humberside, compared to 36.1 per cent nationally. The synthetic fibre sector was also over-represented, while engineering and transport were under-represented, with the exception of mechanical engineering in Yorkshire & Humberside. Plant clustering largely reflected inherited local specialisations and the presence of mature industrial districts; the sectoral composition, production methods, skill base and physical plant of new establishments either mirroring their predecessors or representing evolutionary developments of established techniques.

As Table 6.4 shows, eight of Britain's 23 'substantial' clusters (with 25 or more new manufacturing plants during 1932–38) were located within the industrial heartland – four in the North West, three in Yorkshire, and one in the East Midlands. These shared a number of key characteristics. All demonstrated a high degree of sectoral specialisation, both at the two and three digit SIC levels – reflecting specialisms not only in particular trades, but in particular lines of goods. All produced goods which were largely aimed at consumer markets and involved a significant element of fashion and product differentiation through design. Furthermore, all were characterised by strong Marshallian externalities, based around the tight clustering of factories; skilled labour operating simple, flexible, machinery; networks of vertical specialisation and sub-contracting; and strong information flows regarding the characteristics of styles that were currently selling well.[21] Many new plants had their activities described either in terms of vertically-specialised processes or the production of semi-manufactured goods that could have formed inputs for other local firms. Meanwhile qualitative surveys of these clusters indicate that they continued to thrive on the basis of labour with sector-specific skills and production systems characterised by 'flexible specialisation'[22] and networks of cooperative sub-contracting relationships.

The North West attracted some 700 new plants during the period of the SID's, making it the only region outside the South East to gain more plants (if only marginally more) than would be expected given its share of national 1931 manufacturing employment. This was assisted by the region's large local market; the Manchester-Liverpool area constituted the second-largest centre of population and purchasing power in interwar Britain.[23] The ready availability of disused textile factories and

20 Ibid, p. 196.

21 W. H. Chaloner, 'The birth of modern Manchester', 131–46 in C. F. Carter (ed.), *Manchester and its Region* (Manchester, 1962); J. Jewkes, 'The industries of the Manchester province', 81–122 in H. Clay and K. Russell Brady (eds), *Manchester at Work: A Survey* (Manchester, 1929).

22 See Michael J. Piore and Charles F. Sabel, *The Second Industrial Divide: Possibilities for Prosperity* (New York, 1984).

23 Heim, 'Uneven regional development', p. 175.

unemployed female textile workers also played a key role in attracting firms to the region.

Vigorous plant growth was matched by significant clustering, four of Britain's 'substantial' clusters – central Manchester, Salford, Blackburn, and Burnley – collectively accounting for 143 of the region's 700 new plants. These were long-established industrial districts, strongly specialised not only in particular sectors, but in particular lines of goods. New plant formation reflected this, as demonstrated in the region's two major clothing clusters. Two thirds of Salford's new clothing plants produced waterproof clothing, a local specialisation since the 1820s. Meanwhile Manchester's clothing plants were concentrated in its specialist area of women's ready-made blouses and light dresses. Factories were generally fairly small, having evolved from an industry originally dominated by out-workers and workshops, while studies of these districts highlighted strong Marshallian externalities, underpinned by common production methods and networks of vertical specialisation and sub-contracting.[24]

While clothing faced buoyant demand, the region's two other substantial clusters, Burnley and Blackburn, were dominated by particularly depressed trades. Not only were they highly specialised in cotton weaving (which was harder hit by the depression in cotton than was spinning), they were further specialised in coarse, low-quality, products largely serving Eastern markets – an area where foreign competition made particularly strong inroads into British exports.[25] Yet their physical and human capital proved readily transferable to both other areas of textiles and to non-textile trades, drawing in substantial numbers of new manufacturers. Burnley and Blackburn were the most important cotton weaving towns in Lancashire, accounting for 13 and 12 per cent of its loom (and, therefore, weaving shed) capacity respectively. Weaving sheds were suitable for a range of assembly industries, as they were single storey buildings, with north-light windows and a large working area, unencumbered by the internal pillars of multi-storey weaving mills. A tradition of factory ownership by independent companies who rented 'room and power' to manufacturers facilitated the transfer of vacant sheds to new occupiers.[26] Weaving also involved an unusually high proportion of females; in 1921 their representation in the occupied populations of Blackburn and Burnley stood at 44.5 and 42.6 per cent.

Contemporaries noted their success at switching production to the less depressed home market by diversifying into new product lines, such as more expensive and complex weaves.[27] Furthermore, they attracted a substantial proportion of, largely female-employing, plants outside their traditional cotton niche, including both mature sectors such as clothing, footwear, and leather goods, plus a diverse range of mainly light industries such as kitchen utensils, plastic mouldings, and confectionery. Yet this did not compensate for the decline of weaving; a study found that 22 of a sample

24 Chaloner, 'The birth of modern Manchester'; Jewkes, 'The industries of the Manchester province'.

25 Jewkes, 'The industries of the Manchester province', pp. 96–101; John K. Walton, *Lancashire. A Social History 1558–1939* (Manchester, 2002), pp. 338–41.

26 W. Bennett, *The History of Burnley from 1850* (Burnley, 1951), pp. 97–9.

27 Bennett, *The History of Burnley*, p. 108; Mary B. Rose, *Firms, Networks, and Business Values. The British and American Cotton Industries since 1750* (Cambridge, 2000), p. 220.

of 47 wholly or partly vacated Blackburn cotton mills were re-occupied before 1939, by 30 manufacturing, and seven service-sector, concerns. Yet their employment amounted to only a fraction of that which had been lost.[28]

Such redeployment contributed to the North West's general success in attracting new plants; S.R. Dennison, writing in the late 1930s, estimated that at least 200 disused spinning mills and weaving sheds in Lancashire had become occupied by new industries since 1931. Most of these, according to Dennison, would probably not have been established in Lancashire had the buildings concerned not been available at very low prices.[29] Yet, as the Chief Inspector of Factories noted, these conversions usually produced less employment than the plants' original activities.[30]

Reoccupied factories also accounted for almost all the region's new cotton plants; during the whole of the interwar period only five new British cotton spinning mills were built.[31] New concerns recycled machinery as well as factories. While much textile machinery was of considerable age, and therefore fully depreciated, it seemed capable of an almost infinitely extendable lifespan. Furthermore, the industry had a mature and stable technology, with older vintages of mules and power looms not being substantially less efficient in design than their more recent counterparts.[32] 'New' industrial developments in this sector therefore very largely constituted the recycling of established factories and plant among new owners. Plant formation in the North West may, therefore, have contributed to keeping its unemployment rate below that of the heavy-industry areas, but did little to augment its productive capacity.

The East Midlands had the highest concentration of new plants in clothing/footwear related industries of any region. Clothing and footwear, textiles, synthetic fibres, and leather goods made up 69.95 per cent of new plants, compared to 38.61 per cent nationally. Plants were strongly clustered, 47 of the region's 193 new plants being located in Leicester, 22 in Nottingham, and ten each in Kettering and Northampton. These were highly-specialised industrial districts. Eight of the ten new plants in Kettering produced footwear, while the other two undertook leather dressing. Similarly, seven of Northampton's ten plants produced boots, leather goods, or treated animal skins. Nottingham had witnessed the emergence of a number of major firms in new industries during the late nineteenth century,

---

28 J. R. Cotton, 'The changing industrial structure of an east-Lancashire town – Blackburn from 1919–1970', unpublished part II thesis, Geographical Tripos, University of Cambridge, 1970. There were another 13 wholly or partly empty cotton mills for which full information could not be found.

29 S. R. Dennison, *The Location of Industry*, p. 93.

30 H. M. Factory Inspectorate, Annual Report of the Chief Inspector of Factories and Workshops for 1934 (Cmnd 4931 of 1935), p. 17; ibid, 1935, (Cmd 5230 of 1936), p. 11; ibid, 1936 (Cmd. 5514 of 1937), p. 12.

31 J. H. Porter, 'Cotton and wool textiles', 25–47 in N. K. Buxton and D. H. Aldcroft (eds), *British Industry between the Wars: Instability and Industrial Development 1919–1939* (London:, 1979), p. 35.

32 M. W. Kirby, 'The Lancashire cotton industry in the inter-war years: a study in organizational change', Business History, XVI (1974), 145–59, p. 152.

including Boots, Raleigh, and Players.[33] Yet its new plants mainly reflected longer-established specialisations in lace, hosiery and knitwear: 16 of its 22 new plants produced underwear, lace, hosiery & knitwear, or other textile and clothing products, while there were no chemicals, bicycle, or cigarette plants.

Leicester, the region's only 'substantial' cluster, was also highly specialised. Some 70.2 per cent of new plants were in textiles, all of which appear to have involved hosiery and related trades.[34] This reflected an inherited specialisation, which tied in to an expanding market. Knitted goods and stockings both enjoyed the general buoyancy of domestic demand for finished 'clothing' goods and benefited from favourable changes in fashion, while during the 1930s tariff protection further reinforced domestic demand.[35] Indeed the local labour market was so buoyant that a 1936 League of Nations household earnings survey ranked Leicester the second most prosperous city in Europe.[36]

Yorkshire and Humberside had a concentration of new plants in textiles, but also attracted a significant number of metal-working firms. These were weighted towards 'up-stream' activities; the location quotient for new plants, relative to the national average, was 2.21 for metal manufacture, but declined to 1.48 for other metal goods and 1.08 for mechanical engineering. Meanwhile electrical engineering, vehicles, and instrument engineering were all significantly under-represented. The region's 230 new plants displayed strong clustering, with 106 in three 'substantial' clusters – the central areas of Leeds, Sheffield, and Bradford. Again, all were highly specialised industrial districts.

Leeds was Britain's main centre for men's clothing, particularly out-wear, with almost 85 per cent of its new plants in SIC 45. Between the First World War and the late 1930s the size of the Leeds clothing industry doubled to around 49,000 workers (including juveniles), dominating manufacturing employment in the city. Production mainly served the domestic market, which faced very little foreign competition during this period.[37] Expansion was based around the integration of production and distribution and strategies which extended the availability of suits to a nationwide working-class market, during an era which witnessed an increased blurring between working and middle-class standards of dress. These trends were spearheaded by the Leeds tailoring multiples, such as Montague Burton, Price's 'Fifty Shilling Tailors', and Joseph Hepworth, that developed nationwide retail outlets for suits produced in their Leeds factories. Meanwhile Leeds also had a number of large manufacturing-only clothing firms.

Despite the prevalence of large factories, the industry continued to rely significantly on sub-contracting and out-work during the inter-war years, on account

33 S. D. Chapman, 'Economy, industry, and employment', 480–512 in J. Beckett (ed), *A Centenary History of Nottingham* (Manchester, 1997).

34 For two plants, undertaking silk throwing and elastic web manufacture, this cannot be confirmed.

35 David Nash and David Reeder (eds), Leicester *in the Twentieth Century* (Stroud, 1993), pp. 49–52; S. D. Chapman, *Hosiery and Knitwear. Four Centuries of Small-Scale Industry in Britain, c. 1589–2000* (Oxford, 2002), Chapter 5.

36 Cited in Nash and Reeder, *Leicester in the Twentieth Century*, p. 54.

37 Honeyman, *Well Suited*, pp. 81–4.

of the irregularity of demand that was an inherent feature of the trade. This period saw the emergence of small factory units to perform this work, in competition with its longer-established 'sweatshop' and home production sectors. These small factories were particularly vulnerable to fluctuating demand, leading to a high rate of firm turnover. Firms employed common production methods, which facilitated sub-contracting, labour pooling, and knowledge spillovers.[38] As with the London and Manchester clothing trades, labour costs were kept low by the employment of a high proportion of women and girls.[39]

While Leeds continued to show strong signs of industrial district-type production and Marshallian externalities, it had progressed much further down the road towards large, hierarchical, firms and large factories using mechanised technology than either its London or Manchester/Salford counterparts. This was facilitated both by the internalising of distribution by several of the largest concerns, and the concentration on menswear – where changes in fashion were slower and the demand for goods much less variegated than was the case for women's clothing. The large manufacturer-retailers were consequently able to use highly mechanised production techniques, with considerable sub-division of tasks – which facilitated the satellite branch plant strategy adopted by some of the largest firms.

In contrast to Leeds, the central areas of Bradford and Sheffield were dominated by industries in secular decline. Yet they still managed to develop substantial numbers of new plants, largely based around their specialist sectors.

Bradford's development had some similarities to that of Blackburn and Burnley. The city dominated national worsted manufacture, with 88 per cent of Britain's 1918 worsted combing workforce; 39 per cent of spinners; and 48 per cent of weavers. [40] Depression during the 1920s, due to rising imports and adverse fashion changes, was followed by a substantial, if limited, recovery in the 1930s – based around favourable fashion trends and tariff protection.[41] This was mirrored by the widespread closure of mills during the late 1920s and early 1930s, many of which were later reopened – usually by new occupants who concentrated on finer-quality cloths.[42] There was also some redeployment to synthetic fibres, with the establishment of four textile plants using artificial silk. As with Blackburn and Burnley, physical and human capital had thus been transferred both to new manufacturers and product lines, though, in Bradford's case, without any significant transfer outside the textiles sector (possibly influenced by its more sector-specific factory stock, with a higher proportion of multi-storey buildings than the specialised weaving towns). Similar patterns of expansion during the 1930s, based on factories, machinery, and workers made redundant during the sector's earlier contraction, were evident in other West Yorkshire woollen and worsted centres.

38 Ibid, pp. 86–7, 131.

39 Ibid, p. 56.

40 Peter Garrod, 'The Bradford worsted industry and foreign competition, 1870–1939', unpublished M.Phil thesis, University of Leeds, 1981, p. vi.

41 Garrod, 'The Bradford worsted industry', pp. 121–201.

42 M. T. Wild, 'The Yorkshire wool textile industry', in J. G. Jenkins (ed.), *The Wool Textile Industry in Great Britain* (London, 1972), p. 227.

Sheffield was the only substantial cluster in the industrial heartland not based around textiles or clothing. Yet the factors attracting plants had close parallels to those in Bradford, Blackburn, and Burnley. Plant formation was dominated by 'other metal goods', especially SIC 316, hand tools and finished metal goods, together with other industries related to its inherited base of iron/steel – engineering – light metal trades. Despite depression in these sectors, an industrial structure characterised by complex networks of out-work and subcontracting, rented and second-hand buildings and plant, and pools of skilled labour, greatly facilitated firm entry during upturns in demand. Conversely, by minimising sunk costs, this structure also lowered exit costs, thus encouraging more marginal entrants and a high rate of plant turnover.[43]

The limits of new industrial development – iron and steel

Clusters of new manufacturing plants in Britain's provincial regions (excluding the West Midlands, discussed in the next chapter) were generally based around long established specialisations, involving mature industries, and constituted traditional, sectorally-specialised, industrial districts that had been well-known centres for their principal industries for many generations. For most staple industries there were no overriding changes in inputs, technology, or markets that might offer powerful incentives for moves to entirely new locations. The main exception among the classic manufacturing staples was steel.

British iron and steel production was subject to strong local clustering, as shown in Figure 6.2. Optimal locations, largely determined by the cost differential between the transport of coal and that of iron-ore to blast furnaces, had decisively shifted since the nineteenth century. Advances in fuel economy had reduced the volume of coal used to less than that of the ore smelted, shifting cost-minimising locations to areas offering proximity to ore rather than coal. Furthermore, some established production centres faced depleted local coal or ore reserves, while new domestic sources of both inputs were being developed elsewhere.

Scotland's steel industry suffered from inland locations, mainly in mid-Lanarkshire – using local coal supplies. Yet the increased importance of low transport costs for ore deliveries made coastal locations more efficient. According to estimates by Neil Buxton, the excess transport costs of mid-Lanarkshire locations imposed a cost penalty of several shillings per ton of steel produced.[44] Proposals to move to integrated coastal plants were considered, but foundered on the rocks of fears among steel-owning shipbuilders these might benefit competitor yards at their expense; concerns that any such plants would not operate sufficiently close to capacity to achieve greater efficiency than existing producers; and market uncertainties following the onset of the 1929 depression. Scottish producers thus persisted with fragmented, in-land, 'cold-metal' production, involving producing pig-iron at iron-works, allowing it to run cold, transporting it to steel plants, and re-heating it for conversion to steel, at a time when molten iron had already become

43 Sidney Pollard, *A History of Labour in Sheffield* (Liverpool, 1959), pp. 290–91.

44 N. K. Buxton, 'Efficiency and organization in Scotland's iron and steel industry during the interwar period', *Economic History Review*, XXIX (1976), 107–24, pp. 112–13.

the dominant technology for most other British steel-producing areas. Despite some savings from the use of scrap metal in the industry's open-hearth furnaces, this lack of integration between iron and steel production imposed a further significant cost penalty on the Scottish industry.[45]

Only in the late 1930s was this problem resolved by one major Scottish steel producer, Colvilles, who embarked on an ambitious project to develop an integrated 'hot-metal' works by amalgamating the Clyde Iron Works and Clydebridge Steelworks. Despite the fact that these were on different banks of the Clyde, an innovative solution was found, involving conveying iron from the iron-works across the river in molten form via a bridge, thus reducing steel production costs by around 10 per cent.[46]

At the inter-regional level, there was a trend towards the extension of capacity around the East Midlands ore-fields, at the expense of Britain's peripheral regions. Between 1920 and 1937 Northamptonshire, Lincolnshire, and the East Midlands coalfield increased their share of national pig iron production from 18.6 per cent to 35.0 per cent.[47] This included some inter-regional plant transfers, most famously that of Stewart & Lloyds. Having shifted their headquarters from Glasgow to London in 1927, Stewart & Lloyds moved their main steel production base from west central Scotland to Corby in Northamptonshire (building on their existing major Corby iron ore and blast furnace interests).[48] Another inter-regional project involved the transfer of a bar mill from Tredegar in South Wales to Redbourn in Lincolnshire in 1933.

Table 6.6: Geographical distribution of British steel production (%), 1913–37

Year	1913	1929	1937
North East Coast	28	23	22
South Wales & Monmouthshire	23	24	20
Scotland	19	16	15
North West Coast	5	2	3
Lancashire, Cheshire, etc.	7	8	8
Sheffield	11	13	13
Lincolnshire	3	8	10
Black Country	5	6	5
Northamptonshire	0	0	3
Total	100	100	100

Source: D. L. Burn, The Economic History of Steelmaking 1867–1939. A Study in Competition *(Cambridge, 1940), p. 484.*

45 Ibid, p. 115.

46 Ibid.

47 K. Warren, 'Iron and steel', 103–28 in Buxton and Aldcroft, *British Industry between the Wars*, p. 110.

48 Stephen V. Ward, *The Geography of Interwar Britain: The State and Uneven Development* (London, 1988), p. 114.

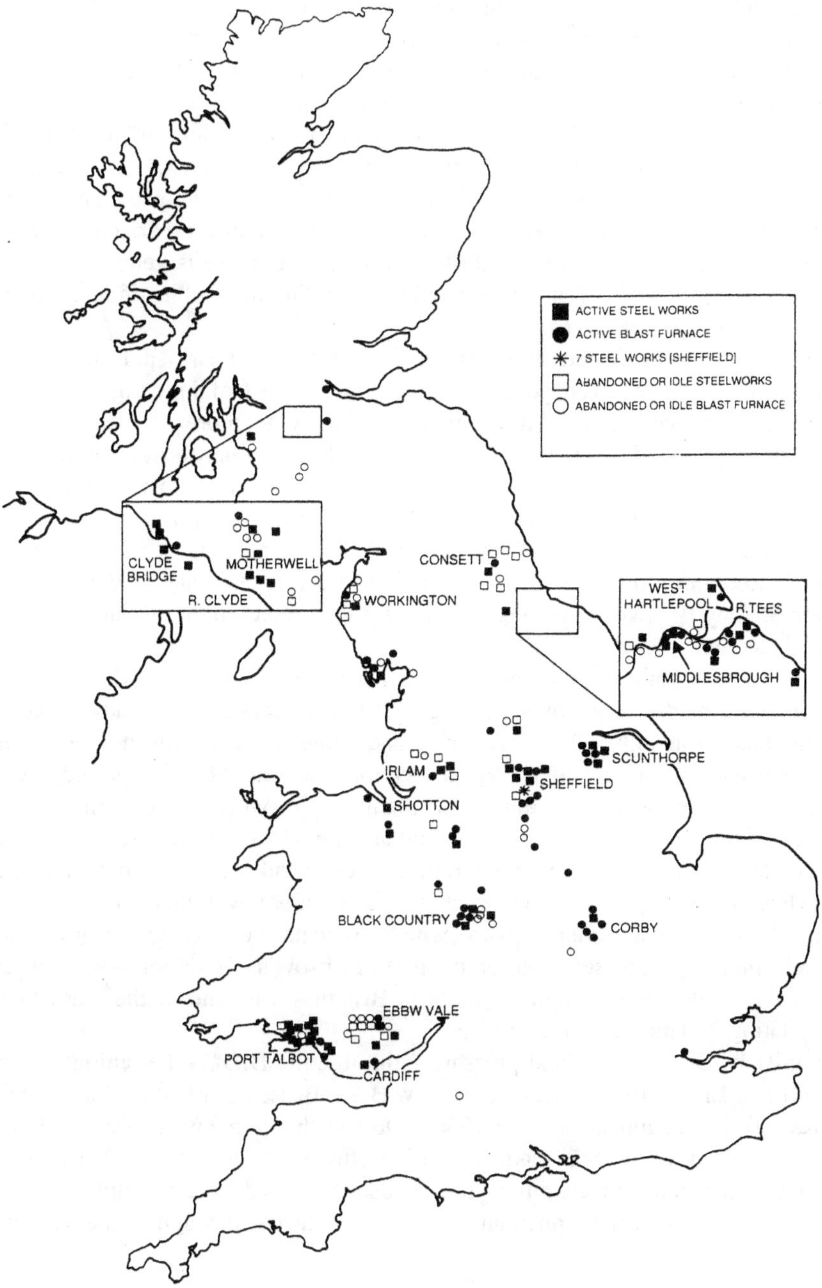

Figure 6.2: Active and abandoned/idle British iron and steel making sites in 1937

Source: Stephen V. Ward, The Geography of Interwar Britain: The State and Uneven Development *(London, 1988), p. 106.*

Table 6.6 shows the regional distribution of steel production in 1913, 1929, and 1937. The areas of the 'coal-based periphery' – Scotland, South Wales, and the east and west coasts of what became England's northern Standard Economic Region after 1945, all experienced significant declines in their contribution to total output, while gains were recorded in the 'industrial heartland' regions of the Midlands, Yorkshire, and Lancashire and Cheshire. Yet the North East Coast, South Wales, and Scotland retained their positions as Britain's three largest steel-producing regions and the overall magnitude of regional change was modest in comparison to the scale of the crisis that confronted the industry. Furthermore, there is general agreement that Midlands production failed to expand to the optimum level justified by the cost advantages of its ore reserves.

Opposition from vested interests, in the form of the British Iron and Steel Federation (which received government backing as part of its cartel policy) and the banks impeded plans to develop new capacity in more efficient locations. For example Richard Thomas & Co. had an ambitious plan to develop a modern strip-mill at Redbourn in Lincolnshire – producing steel at a cost well below the Federation's price. Yet this was so mauled by Federation opposition that Thomas was both eventually forced to join the cartel (thus producing at its price) and to abandon Redbourn in favour of a less efficient site at Ebbw Vale in Wales, in order to gain Stanley Baldwin's personal backing for the project in the run-up to the 1935 general election.

The inter-regional shift of production that the original plan (which involved closing some of the company's existing Welsh steel capacity) had advocated was thus avoided. Ironically, while this period had witnessed a shift of the South Wales steel industry to more efficient coastal locations, such as Port Talbot and Cardiff, together with the closures of almost all plants in the Welsh valleys, this political fix saddled the Ebbw Vale plant with an inland site which was realised to be a poor location at the time and imposed a permanent cost disadvantage.[49] Another casualty of the Federation's opposition was a scheme for a major new integrated steel plant at Jarrow, on the site of a former shipyard, which would have offered coastal advantages. The resulting popular resentment on the part of Jarrow's population – who suffered one of the highest unemployment rates in Britain – was one of the main factors precipitating its famous hunger march.[50]

Similarly, Bank of England pressure – through the BIDC – had initially forced Stewart and Lloyds to scale-back their new Basic Bessemer plant at Corby, though the revival of demand during the 1930s allowed the company to free itself from the BIDC and develop their plant on a more efficient scale.[51] As K. Warren noted, steel reconstruction projects during the 1930s established, 'the principle that really radical solutions could be postulated, and even carried through if they involved

---

49 Ibid, p. 105.

50 Noreen Branson and Margot Heinemann, *Britain in the Nineteen Thirties* (St. Albans, 1973), p. 57.

51 Stephen Tolliday, 'Steel and rationalization policies, 1918–1950', 82–108 in B. Elbaum and W. Lazonick (eds), The Decline of the British Economy (Oxford, 1986), p. 97.

re-equipment, but not if they implied wholesale abandonment of old metallurgical districts, or required new patterns of regional or firm product-specialisation.'[52]

Yet opposition from vested interests was not the only factor militating against new, larger, better-located, plants. During the interwar period the average capacity of UK blast furnaces more than doubled to 69,000 tons per annum. However this was dwarfed by the 128,000 tons average capacity in Germany, let alone the 280,000 in the USA. A plant capacity of 100,000 tons was regarded as the minimum for efficient operation, in a world of capacity output.[53] However, as Tolliday noted, the overheads of best-practice new plants could be crippling if they were forced to operate substantially below capacity, while fully-amortised old steel plants could attain remarkable longevity while remaining cost-effective in terms of variable costs.[54] Small furnaces had the advantage of 'flexibility' to serve a domestic market characterised by variable and non-standardised demand. Irregular demand was a particular problem in Scotland, where a major customer, the shipbuilding industry, was subject to considerable variations in output and little standardisation. Thus, even in steel, the continued advantages of running old plant, and thus not having to worry about fixed costs or high-volume output, often made investment in new plant an uneconomic proposition.

52 Warren, 'Iron and steel', p. 103.

53 Buxton, 'Efficiency and organization in Scotland's iron and steel industry', p. 117.

54 Tolliday, 'Steel and rationalization policies', p. 85.

Chapter Seven

The beautiful South

Introduction

> The termination of the Great War produced a reaction against the old order of things … 'pleasure and spending' came increasingly to the front … some of the older towns … were described as 'grim', 'dead and alive', etc. The popularity of the South of England, and London in particular, increased enormously: cheap travelling facilities had made the City's attractions known to millions and after the war people found it difficult to settle down to the old humdrum way of life. Manufacturers … preferred to be near London because they felt life there was more enjoyable … Life had much more glitter, sparkle, and show: it was more superficial and sensational than before the War … a beautiful factory decorated with brightly coloured lights in the evening was a necessity if success was to be won. The way was then open for the Land Development Companies to sell the idea of arterial road and Private Estate development.[1]

Thus S.A. Sadler Forster, who had been involved in industrial development promotion both in the North East and around London,[2] summed up the psychological appeal of the South in private evidence to the Federation of British Industries. The attractions of the new communities and lifestyles that emerged around the suburban fringes of London and other prosperous southern centres, to the 'lost generation' who returned from the trenches and to the generation that followed them, was a recurring theme in interwar literature. For example, in *The Lion and the Unicorn* George Orwell identified the emergence of a new England:

> in the light-industry areas and along the arterial roads. In Slough, Dagenham, Barnet, Letchworth, Hayes … In those vast new wildernesses of glass and brick the sharp distinctions of the older kind of town, with its slums and mansions, or the country, with its manor-houses and squalid cottages, no longer exist. There are wide gradations of income, but it is the same kind of life that is being lived at different levels, in labour-saving flats or Council houses, along the concrete roads and in the naked democracy of the swimming-pools… a rather restless, cultureless life, centring around tinned food, *Picture Post*, the radio and the combustion engine.[3]

---

1 Modern Records Centre, University of Warwick [hereafter MRC], MSS 200/F/3/S2/19/1, 'Location of Industry', paper presented by S.A. Sadler Forster to the Federation of British Industries' [FBI] Committee on the Geographical Distribution of the Industrial Population, 3 December 1937.

2 Having worked with the Tees District Development Board and North East Coast Development Board and, later, as manager of the Industrial Development Department of Welwyn Garden City Ltd.

3 George Orwell, *The Lion and the Unicorn: Socialism and the English Genius* (London, 1941), p. 54.

This was J. B. Priestley's 'third England', modern, democratic, and vaguely Americanised.[4] Some of its characteristics were evident in all but the most depressed of Britain's towns and cities, but it achieved its fullest expression in the South, and especially in the outer suburbs and satellite towns of London. Together with the South's traditional cultural, educational, and elite sporting attractions, it exerted a powerful pull on the location preferences of executives, technicians, and other key staff. For example, ICI encountered problems in retaining administrative staff at its giant new Billingham-on-Tees plant in County Durham, as they sought transfers 'to more attractive surroundings'.[5]

Meanwhile, there were strong factors of a purely economic nature pulling industry to the South and, in particular, within the orbit of London. Developments in transport, distribution networks, industrial infrastructure, business services, and production methods cumulatively reinforced the advantages of the metropolis as an industrial and business centre. As a result London experienced accelerated growth; while the conurbation had accounted for 17.5 per cent of Britain's population expansion during the decade to 1911, it comprised almost 35 per cent of national interwar population growth.[6] Beyond London's hinterland, only the West Midland's showed any similar developments and by the 1930s it was already beginning to lose ground, at least with respect to new plant formation. This chapter examines the general attractions of the South and West Midlands for both new manufacturing and service firms, while Chapter Eight discusses the extraordinary industrial growth of the Greater London region during this period. The specific attractions of the main centres of new industrial development within the South and West Midlands are then discussed in Chapter Nine, while Chapters Ten and Eleven examine the new industrial workforce who manned the shop floors of the South's growing assembly industries.

An important factor attracting new plants to the South, and especially around London, was the growing importance of the capital as a services hub, including both its traditional specialisms and the concentration of control over activities that had previously been at least partly decentralised. The development of the service sector therefore constitutes the first topic of analysis.

The interwar services boom

The proportion of Britain's employed workforce working in the services, construction, and utilities sectors increased from 51.2 per cent in 1911 to 55.4 per cent in 1931.[7] Middle-class services employment experienced a larger increase, the proportion of 'white collar' employees in Britain's workforce rising from 18 per cent in 1911 to 23 per cent by 1931.[8] The proportion of tertiary sector employees in London and Middlesex (the closest available proxy for Greater London using

4 J.B. Priestley, *English Journey* (London, 1934), pp. 400–403.

5 MRC, MSS 200/F/3/S2/19/1, minutes of meeting of FBI committee on the geographical distribution of the industrial population, 20 January 1938.

6 Royal Commission on the Industrial Population, *Report* (London, 1940), p. 162.

7 See Appendix Two.

8 A. Howkins and J. Lowerson, *Trends in Leisure, 1919–1939* (London, 1979), p. 6.

county-level Census data) declined marginally, from 68.8 to 68.0 per cent. However, as Table 7.1 shows, if miscellaneous services (which largely comprised domestic servants) are excluded, the tertiary sector's contribution to total employment in London & Middlesex actually rose substantially between these dates. Service sector employment elsewhere in Britain rose even more sharply, mainly on account of the growth of consumer-orientated services such as distributive trades (whose share of national employment increased by almost 50 per cent between 1911 and 1931) and professional and scientific services. Rising working-class incomes increased demand for these services throughout Britain, whereas previously London's higher percentage of middle and upper class households had given it a disproportionate share of their employment.

Yet while aggregate services employment was slightly less concentrated in London and the South East, high-level decision-making activities involving headquarters, purchasing, and marketing functions were becoming substantially more London-centred. One particularly important example concerns the clearing banks. While a trend towards the concentration of the banking sector into national firms, headquartered from London, had been evident for several decades by 1914, it accelerated markedly over the period during and immediately after the First World War. Some 27 banks disappeared due to mergers between 1917 and 1920, as high war-time banking profits were spent on speculative acquisitions. In some ways this mirrored the acquisition mania in the staple industries – but with one crucial difference – the banks succeeded in creating a tight, collusive, oligopoly over high street banking services. As a recent history of Barclays notes, if this oligopoly 'could reduce competition and raise sustainable long-run profits, the acquiring banks' shareholders might yet benefit. Fortunately for them (though arguably less happily for the banks' customers)... this condition was fulfilled.'[9]

Following the merger wave, control over banking policy towards industrial lending became further centralised in London, finally breaking the symbiotic relationship between local British banks and local industry that had been increasingly undermined since the late-nineteenth century. All of the 'Big Five' banks which emerged from this merger frenzy were based in London. Three of them – Midland, National Provincial, and Westminster – centralised control over all loans above a certain (very low) limit at Head Office; while Lloyds employed a less strictly centralised system and only Barclays pursued a policy of decentralisation. The extent of centralisation provoked widespread concern, even *The Economist* arguing that 'far too much goes to London'.[10]

Retailing also experienced a concentration of control into national concerns, mainly headquartered in London (with some notable exceptions – such as Burtons and Boots). By 1939 large-scale retailers probably accounted for over a third of national retail sales. Multiple chains experienced particularly rapid growth; their share of total

9 Margaret Ackrill and Leslie Hannah, *Barclays. The Business of Banking 1690–1996* (Cambridge, 2001), p. 69.

10 *Economist*, 21 May 1921, p. 1037, cited in W. A. Thomas, *The Finance of British Industry 1918–1976* (London, 1978), p. 57.

Table 7.1: Tertiary sector employment in London and Middlesex, and in Great Britain, as a proportion of all employment, 1911 and 1931

	London and Middlesex				Great Britain	
	1911	1931	1911 (%)	1931 (%)	1911 (%)	1931 (%)
Construction	173,625	161,694	7.18	5.73	6.62	5.01
Gas, electricity, water	15,522	44,320	0.64	1.57	0.50	1.21
Transport & communications	316,638	278,004	13.09	9.85	9.40	8.13
Distributive trades	299,074	495,929	12.37	17.58	9.73	14.56
Insurance, banking, financial services	55,606	107,879	2.30	3.82	1.41	2.07
Professional & scientific services	138,942	154,689	5.74	5.48	4.25	4.75
Miscellaneous services	582,210	511,079	24.07	18.11	16.78	14.24
Public administration & defence	81,655	164,352	3.38	5.82	2.54	5.47
Total services	1,663,272	1,917,946	68.77	67.97	51.23	55.43
Total (excluding miscellaneous services)	1,081,062	1,406,867	44.70	49.86	34.45	41.19

Source: C. H. Lee, British Regional Employment Statistics 1841–1971 *(Cambridge, 1979), Part III, Series B.*

Note: Excluding workers who could not be classified by sector.

retail sales roughly doubling over the interwar-period, to around 18–19.5 per cent.[11] Yet their influence on town centre high street trading was much greater, nationally-based chains such as Marks & Spencer, Woolworths, British Home Stores, Burtons, and Boots, squeezing local stores out of the best shopping pitches in high streets throughout Britain.

Many major retail chains had been founded by provincial firms, though the advantages of London as a centre for purchasing activities and expansion finance led to their concentration in the capital. Some, such as Marks & Spencer, moved their head offices from the provinces to London, though concentration of headquarters functions in the capital more commonly occurred as a result of mergers and acquisitions.[12] Many regional chains were absorbed by London-based national concerns, such as the various Scottish and North Eastern food multiples acquired by what became the Allied Suppliers group.[13] National retail chains also absorbed large numbers of single store local traders, by buying up their premises.

The growing concentration of headquarters functions in London stimulated the growth of ancillary service industries. For example, the multiple chains' demand for high street premises throughout Britain was met via the development of specialist commercial estate agents, based around Maddox Street in London's West End. These provided nationwide services regarding property acquisition, development, and finance (typically via mortgage or sale and leaseback arrangements with insurance companies) for the retail chains, who only had to visit a small area of London to gain information on available premises and new shopping parade developments throughout Britain.[14]

One particularly influential group of London-orientated services were the communications industries, the metropolis consolidating its position as the dominant centre for publishing, journalism, and new media such as film, radio and (from 1936) television. Charles Loch Mowat's classic history of inter-war Britain described mass communication as a 'monster with four heads … advertising, broadcasting, newspapers, and moving pictures'.[15] All four were drawn further into London's ambit. One of the most influential agents in promoting a London-centric view of Britain was the BBC. The British Broadcasting Company was founded at the end of 1922, being re-constituted four years later as a public corporation. From the outset it took an unashamedly metropolitan-orientated stance, which played an important role in accentuating the dominance of London and South East in the national consciousness. As the Corporation's official historian, Asa Briggs, noted, during the BBC's early years: 'London was thought of, almost without discussion, as the cultural metropolis, the place from which "the best" was most likely to come … [Provincial culture] was considered

11 J. B. Jefferys, *Retail Trading in Britain, 1900–1950* (Cambridge, 1954), pp. 72–4.

12 Goronwy Rees, *St. Michael. A History of Marks and Spencer* (London, 1969), p. 83.

13 Peter Matthias, *Retailing Revolution. A History of Multiple Retailing in the Food Trades based upon the Allied Suppliers Group of Companies* (London, 1967).

14 Peter Scott, *The Property Masters. A History of the British Commercial Property Sector* (London, 1996), pp. 38–48.

15 C. L. Mowat, *Britain Between the Wars, 1918–1940* (London, 1955), pp. 240–41.

to be inferior, except in very special cases, to the "universal culture" of the metropolis.'[16] Senior BBC staff, particularly its formidable Director-General, Sir John Reith, publicly advocated a policy of using the BBC as a means of promulgating 'the amenities of Metropolitan culture' to what were seen as provincial backwaters.[17] Even the London-focused national newspapers took exception to the BBC's London/Oxbridge bias. As Collie Knox, the *Daily Mail*'s wireless editor, noted, limiting the spoken radio voice to 'The Oxford Accent', effectively proposed this as the representative intonation of Britain's whole vigorous populace.[18]

Advertising also became increasingly concentrated among large agencies, located in the capital. The interwar years have been characterised as the 'golden age' of British advertising, national advertising expenditure having risen steeply from an estimated £31 million in 1920 to £57 million in 1928 (then, falling back during the depression before recovering to £59 million by 1938).[19] During the 1930s advertising expenditure varied from 1.1–1.3 per cent of GNP and was dominated by press advertising. Agencies thus located close to the newspaper companies, whose commissions accounted for most of their income. By 1918 national newspapers (with the exception of those serving Scotland) were already firmly based around Fleet Street, the *Manchester Guardian* constituting the sole example of a nationally-important newspaper edited from one of the English provinces. Yet the interwar years saw growing concentration, of both national and provincial newspaper ownership, into the hands of a small number of, mainly Home Counties-based, press barons. Film also became more London-centred, as sound and other technical developments raised costs and thus concentrated the production industry into a small number of studios. Britain's two main film producers, Gaumont British and Associated British Picture Corporation, made films reflecting their London studio locations (at Shepherds Bush and Elstree), while Britain's other significant film producers were also based in suburban London. Meanwhile the coming of sound, together with the 1927 Film Quota Act (which required cinemas to show a compulsory quota of British films, mainly produced by the two major British studios who had their own cinema chains) led to the concentration of film exhibition into three major groups by the late 1930s. All were headquartered in London (Odeon having transferred its head office from Birmingham in 1935).[20]

London also began to attract the business services functions of industrial companies, both regarding externally-purchased services and in-house managerial and administrative functions. The proportion of Britain's largest companies headquartered in the South East rose sharply, from about one third in 1919 to over half by 1930.[21] Meanwhile the

16 Asa Briggs, *The History of Broadcasting in the United Kingdom. Volume II: The Golden Age of Wireless* (London, 1965), pp. 306–307.

17 J. C. W. Reith, 'Broadcasting and a Better World', *The Spectator*, 22 November 1930, cited in Briggs, *The History of Broadcasting in the United Kingdom*, p. 308.

18 Cited in Robert Graves and Alan Hodge, *The Long Week-end. A Social History of Great Britain 1918–1939* (London, 1941).

19 T. R. Nevett, *Advertising in Britain. A History* (London, 1982), p. 145.

20 Robert Murphy, 'Oscar Deutsch', 89–93 in David Jeremy (ed.), *Dictionary of Business Biography*, Vol. 2 (London, 1984).

21 C. M. Law, *British Regional Development Since World War 1* (Newton Abbot, 1980), p. 159.

proportion of national output accounted for by these largest companies also increased substantially.[22] A few leading manufacturing companies, such as ICI and Unilever, established their head offices in the City, together with a larger number of trading and oil companies. However, most manufacturers still located their administrative headquarters alongside their main factories. This involved making joint location decisions for administrative and manufacturing activities: the optimality of London as a head office location typically reinforcing its attractions as a production centre.

Many co-located head offices and factories were built along the arterial road network of outer-London or in one of London's industrial satellite communities. The most visible examples concerned the British plants of major overseas multinationals, who developed prestigious offices on conspicuous roadside sites such as Brentford's 'Golden Mile' of art deco office palaces fronting the Great West Road, or along Western Avenue.[23] Offices such as the Hoover and Firestone buildings were as much advertising hoardings as functional exteriors to the less glamorous assembly operations that lay behind them, and acted as beacons for other companies. As the Czech immigrant manufacturer Eric Pasold recalled, passing along the Great West Road in search of premises he was singularly impressed by 'those breathtaking modern factories with their brilliant neon signs. Coty, Pyrene, Firestone, Macleans, and Jantzen ... This was the industry of the future'.[24]

The concentration of corporate control in and around the capital, together with the headquarters functions of new public-sector organisations such as the BBC and Central Electricity Board, further reinforced London's attractions as a market centre. As the Ministry of Labour stated, in evidence to the Barlow Commission on the geographical distribution of the industrial population, it was difficult to steer foreign manufacturers wishing to undertake production in Britain to the provinces, as they usually argued that a location around London was essential for marketing purposes: 'not only are prospective customers centred there, but in many types of business most buyers from the provinces and abroad do their buying in the capital'.[25] John Armstrong's study of multinationals on the Park Royal estate in West Middlesex indicated that the American electronics company British Rola located on the estate partly to facilitate access to the Air Ministry and semi-government organisations such as the BBC. Similarly the Swiss company Landis and Gyr was influenced in its choice of a London location by the fact that following the establishment of the national grid many electrical products required approval by the Central Electricity Board.[26] As the industrialist R. H. Roberts noted, in a 1938 discussion on regional development at the Federation of British Industries, a number of businesses in the Birmingham area with which he was associated:

---

22 Leslie Hannah, *The Rise of the Corporate Economy*, 2nd edn (London, 1983), pp. 91–2, 180.

23 James Marshall, *The History of the Great West Road* (Hounslow, 1995).

24 E. W. Pasold, *Ladybird Ladybird: A story of Private Enterprise* (Manchester, 1977), p. 286.

25 Royal Commission on The Distribution of The Industrial Population, *Minutes of Evidence* (London, 1940).

26 John Armstrong, 'International confluences on the development of London business: the case of the Park Royal industrial estate between the wars', unpublished paper.

> if he were starting them anew, would not be located there, since a majority of their orders were secured from London. London was increasingly important, not merely from the social but from the commercial point of view. It was a convenient centre in which to meet customers both from abroad and from other parts of the country, while many contracts even in the provinces were carried out by London firms.[27]

The concentration of head office and other key business and financial services functions in London was thus a cumulative and mutually reinforcing process. It both increased the solid business reasons for a metropolitan location and generated a perception that for ambitious, enterprising, people and firms, London was the place to be. As Sadler Forster noted:

> The Banks and many larger industrial firms had done much to encourage the view that London was the Mecca. Control had been removed from the provinces to London... Managements and staffs got accustomed to working in London. The provinces developed – in some senses – an inferiority complex. Constant reference to 'Head Office in London' was bad for the development of initiative… Behind all of this was the constant feeling that the 'plums' in business were in London.[28]

The southern consumer industries boom

As noted in Chapter 2, Britain's nineteenth-century consumer-goods trades had been traditionally concentrated around London (and, for some metal-working sectors, the West Midlands), while the regions of the 'industrial heartland' and 'industrial periphery' had been more focused on producer goods and export markets. The main exception had been manufacturers of standardised branded goods, who often located in the provinces to take advantage of lower factor costs. Interwar macroeconomic trends disadvantaged producer-goods and exporting industries (the contribution of exports to national income having declined from 33 per cent in 1907 to only 15 per cent in 1938) while boosting consumer goods sectors, which became increasingly focused on the prosperous domestic market. Rising real wages (for those in work) and declining fertility increased the proportion of household income available for 'discretionary spending';[29] by the late 1930s the average non-agricultural working-class family with a head of household in employment devoted around 41.3 per cent of income to items other than food, fuel, lighting, and accommodation.[30] Meanwhile the selective extension of tariffs during the First World War and 1920s, to goods such as motor vehicles and components, clocks and watches, gramophones, and silk, gave British manufacturers some degree

27 MRC, MSS 200/F/3/S2/19/1, minutes of meeting of FBI committee on the geographical distribution of the industrial population, 20 January 1938.

28 MRC, MSS 200/F/3/S2/19/1, 'Location of Industry', paper presented by S.A. Sadler Forster to the FBI's Committee on the Geographical Distribution of the Industrial Population, 3 December 1937.

29 Spending that does not involve essentials such as food, heating, and shelter.

30 NA: LAB17/7, 'Weekly expenditure of working-class households in the United Kingdom in 1937–38', report, July 1949.

of protection from foreign competition, while also boosting inward foreign direct investment (fdi) in these industries.

The changed macroeconomic conditions following Britain's departure from the gold standard in the autumn of 1931 further boosted the domestic consumer-goods sector. The low pound and the introduction of substantial general British manufacturing tariffs encouraged the growth of import-substituting industries and inward fdi in the newly-protected sectors. Between November 1931 and November 1932 the volume of manufactured imports fell by over 50 per cent;[31] while during the 18 months from November 1931 some 254 foreign-based enterprises established UK plants, generally producing consumer goods which the firms in question had hitherto exported to Britain.[32]

The government's new policy of 'cheap money' acted to further boost consumer goods' sales, both directly and indirectly. The direct impact occurred principally via encouraging the expansion of hire purchase (HP) and other credit sale trading. The Board of Trade estimated that by the late 1930s consumer HP transactions had an annual value of around £100–£120 million, about 3.5 per cent of retail sales and 2.5 per cent of total personal expenditure, while trade estimates put the annual number of new agreements at around 7 million. By this time the majority of purchases of cars, bicycles, working-class furniture, electrical household equipment, pianos, and sewing machines were undertaken using this method.[33]

Meanwhile cheap money had an indirect impact on consumer goods sales of probably greater magnitude, through stimulating house-building. As discussed in Chapter 12, the 1930s witnessed Britain's largest ever private-sector house-building boom, as low interest rates and liberalised mortgage terms extended the availability of house purchase to a substantially larger proportion of the population. New houses were more suited to expensive durable goods than the inner-urban accommodation their occupants typically moved from, as they generally had mains electricity, were of substantially larger average size, and were much less likely to be subject to problems such as dampness. Furthermore, meeting the social expectations of the new suburban estates often involved higher standards of 'conspicuous consumption', families feeling obliged to invest in smarter clothes and better furniture (at least for those areas of the house visible from outside) in order to 'keep up with the Jones's'. As Ruth Durant's survey of the London County Council's Watling Estate noted, 'The new house needs new linoleum, new curtains and even new furniture, and all is bought on hire purchase. In the old "mean street," people were not tempted by the example of their neighbours to acquire fresh impedimentia. At Watling … the wireless next door becomes an obligation to bring home a wireless.'[34]

---

31 Mark Thomas, 'The macro-economics of the interwar years', 320–58 in R. Floud and D. McCloskey (eds), *The Economic History of Britain since 1700. Volume 2: 1860–1939*, 2nd edn. (Cambridge, 1994), p. 352.

32 Peter Scott and Tim Rooth, 'Protectionism and the growth of overseas multinational enterprise in interwar Britain', *Journal of Industrial History*, 3, (2000), 31–50.

33 See Peter Scott, 'The twilight world of interwar hire purchase', *Past & Present*, 177 (2002), 195–225.

34 Ruth Durant, *Watling: A Survey of Social Life on a New Housing Estate* (London, 1939), pp. 7–8.

Meanwhile, just as cheap money (together with Treasury controls on overseas capital issues in Britain) increased the flow of capital to HP traders and building societies, it also facilitated enterprise formation and expansion in the consumer goods industries by increasing their access to, and reducing the cost of, capital. Firms also effectively gained capital benefits from the impact of low interest rates on building and mortgage costs, as many new consumer-goods producers rented or purchased new ready-made factories on the industrial estates that mushroomed alongside London's arterial roads.

The consumer goods boom benefited both long-established consumer goods sectors, such as clothing, footwear, furniture, and hosiery, plus a range of branded goods typically produced via assembly methods and often linked to relatively new product and/or process technologies, such as motor vehicles, bicycles, electrical goods, cosmetics, and toiletries. London derived considerable benefit from buoyant home demand for its long-established, craft-based, consumer goods sectors such as fashion clothing. However, in sharp contrast to nineteenth-century trends, it also managed to retain modern consumer goods producers, despite their moves to large-scale assembly production (which had previously been associated with migration out of the London region).

Thus London's domination of interwar industrial development cannot be explained simply in terms of its inherited industrial structure. Tim Hatton has shown that even when industry-specific factors are controlled for, the prosperous regions still performed better than average and the depressed regions worse than would be expected given their industrial composition, while 'regional' (as distinct from sector-specific) influences were particularly significant in the South.[35] Before considering the new factors which enabled London to dominate the growth of both craft and assembly consumer-goods industries, we will first examine patterns of new industrial development in the only other British region to attract a substantial base of 'new' assembly goods industries – the West Midlands.

New industrial developments in the West Midlands

The West Midlands had a unique industrial inheritance – with the highest coefficient of regional specialisation within manufacturing of any British region for both 1911 and 1931 – based around heavy concentration in the 'other metal goods' sector, together with related industries such as metal manufacture and vehicles. By 1931 a specialisation in electrical engineering had also emerged.

New plant formation during 1932–38 broadly reflected the region's industrial inheritance, with a similarly high coefficient of specialisation, due to the strong presence of metal-fabricating trades. Though its proportion of plants in metal manufacture was well below that of Wales, and just ahead of Yorkshire & Humberside, 'downstream' metal-using activities were much more heavily represented. The proportion of plants in SIC 31, other metal goods, was more than twice that of Wales

35 T. J. Hatton, 'Structural aspects of unemployment in Britain between the World Wars,' *Research in Economic History*, 10 (1986), 55–92.

and 3.6 times the national average. It also had location quotients for mechanical engineering, motor vehicles, other transport, and office machinery in excess of 2.3. Yet electrical engineering was under-represented, despite its over-representation in 1931 manufacturing employment.

The number of new plants in the West Midlands over 1932–38 was well below what would be expected given the region's existing manufacturing workforce. As Tables 6.1 and 6.2 show, even after taking account of its relatively high average employment per plant (and Britain's highest percentage of very large plants – with an initial employment of over 500), the region still received a ratio of new industrial development to 1931 manufacturing employment well below the national average. Rapid employment growth during the 1930s appears to have arisen primarily from existing, rather than new, plants. For example, despite Coventry's famous prosperity (with the most rapid population growth of any British city, from 128,152 in 1921 to an estimated 224,267 in 1939) it attracted only 14 new plants of 25 or more employees over 1932–38. In addition to an under-representation of new plants, the West Midlands shared two other features in common with the industrial heartland and industrial periphery regions – an over-representation of branch plants and a relatively low proportion of plant transfers between localities.

Analysis of clustering within this region is problematic, as new plants in the 'Birmingham district' recorded in the SID's were not disaggregated by locality. It was not therefore possible to separate plants located in central Birmingham, and in newer industrial areas on the fringes of the city, such as Aston, Balsall Heath, or Selly Oak. As such disaggregation was possible for other cities, Birmingham could not be included in the analysis of 'substantial clusters' as this would not involve comparing like with like. Yet as the district attracted 132 new plants (accounting for 44.9 per cent of all new plants in the West Midlands) dissagregated data would almost certainly have revealed several such clusters. Limited clustering was also evident in other centres, such as Wolverhampton (with 20 plants) and Coventry (14 plants). While part of the region fell outside the factory belt, this territory encompassed only six new plants.

Unlike the industrial heartland, where clusters were concentrated within particular sectors (and, generally, in a narrow range of products within those sectors), clustering in the West Midlands sometimes involved plants in a range of complementary metal-working industries. For example, in Wolverhampton 15 of the 20 plants were in SIC's 31–6, but the largest, mechanical engineering, only involved six of these. Similarly, 13 of Coventry's 14 new plants were in SIC's 32–6, but the largest, again mechanical engineering, only accounted for four. Conversely the Birmingham district, despite covering a much larger area, displayed stronger sectoral concentration (with regard to plants in metal-working sectors); 32.58 per cent of its new plants were in its traditional specialism of other metal goods, while SIC's 32–6 accounted for only 21.21 per cent. Meanwhile other West Midlands' centres, with inherited specialisations more narrowly focused on particular sectors, generally experienced low levels of plant formation and much higher interwar unemployment.[36]

Clustered firms in the main industrial centres of the southern West Midlands benefited from locational externalities that operated between, as well as within, related sectors. This formed part of a wider trend, evident from the late-nineteenth century, for firms in 'new' industries, or sectors experiencing rapid technological change, to cluster in localities accommodating plants in a range of different industries. Such firms derive static externalities via economies of urbanisation –advantages associated with urban scale and diversity (until outweighed by the negative externality of congestion).[37] Yet dynamic externalities, (typically referred to as Jacobs externalities) are generally viewed as being of greater importance. These capture knowledge-spillovers and other productivity enhancing benefits accruing from the clustering of firms in different, though complementary, sectors. [38] Complementarities can encompass both commonalities in physical technology, new methods of organising production, or other managerial innovations that can be applied to a range of industries facing similar problems.[39]

Nathan Rosenberg's seminal study of the American machine-tool industry identified a process of inter-sectoral 'technological convergence', whereby innovation was often characterised by the introduction of a small number of broadly similar processes to a range of complementary industries, generating strong inter-sectoral dynamic externalities. For example, technological requirements in the bicycle industry included the need for lightness, hardened precision parts, efficient power transmission and friction reduction. Solving these problems led to a range of broadly applicable innovations, such as the development of an effective technique for making ball bearings.[40]

This process was paralleled in the West Midlands; its metal-fabricating clusters having developed through a cumulative process of mutually reinforcing technological and input-output linkages between complementary sectors. For example, the cycle industry stimulated the local machine-tool industry, which developed innovations and capabilities later put to the service of motor vehicle manufacturers. Meanwhile cycle firms also engaged directly in innovation; for example the development of

36 G. C. Allen, 'Labour transference and the unemployment problem,' *Economic Journal*, 40 (1930), 242–8.

37 V. Henderson, A. Kuncoro and M. Turner, 'Industrial development in cities', *Journal of Political Economy*, 103 (1995), 1067–90, p. 1068; Jane Jacobs, *The Economy of Cities* (New York, 1969).

38 Jacobs, *The Economy of cities*; E. L. Glaeser, H. D. Kallal, J. A. Scheinkman, and A. Shleifer, 'Growth in cities', *Journal of Political Economy*, 100 (1992), 1126–52; Paul Bairoch, *Cities and Economic Development* (London, 1988); M. P. Feldman and D. B. Audreutsch, 'Innovation in cities: science-based diversity, specialization and localised competition', *European Economic Review*, 43 (1999), 409–29.

39 Glaeser et al., 'Growth in Cities'; Jacobs, *The Economy of Cities*; Nathan Rosenberg, 'Technological change in the machine tool industry, 1840–1940', *Journal of Economic History*, 23, 4 (1963), 414–43; Bairoch, *Cities and Economic Development*; Feldman and Audreutsch, 'Innovation in cities'.

40 Rosenberg, 'Technological change', pp. 414–43.

interchangeable parts by early cycle manufacturers stimulated similar innovations among machine-tool firms that were carried over to the local motor vehicle trade, while also finding wider application among engineering sectors.[41] Technical complementarities also produced strong input-output links; for example, Coventry's early motor vehicle industry shared many components with the cycle producers.

Interwar expansion was based around a complementary relationship between large-scale mass producers of standardised goods and traditional, flexibly-specialised metal-working firms – the latter generating new products and innovations, which were later incorporated into the mass production sector. For example, many of Birmingham's new 'other metal goods' plants were vertically specialised, process-based, firms in traditional product-specialised industrial districts within the city's central industrial zone; the SID's recording their activities in terms such as casting, founding, stamping, presswork, plating or finishing. Their range of flexible craft skills created an environment favourable to experimentation with product innovations via new combinations of parts.[42] Meanwhile the subsequent mass production of successful innovations arising from this process generally occurred outside central Birmingham (in areas on the fringes of the conurbation, or in other centres such as Coventry and Wolverhampton), by product-based firms using assembly processes and un/semi-skilled labour. Yet flexibly-specialised firms survived by applying their craft skills to a range of customers; for example, while motor vehicle gears were transferred to the mass production sector, small producers retained other markets – gears having a wide range of engineering applications.[43]

Yet technological and input-output linkages do not fully capture the functional complementarities between firms in these clusters. Larger, product-based, firms also shared strong functional complementarities through innovations in the organisation of production and systems of worker recruitment, monitoring, and payment. Production generally involved assembly operations, while innovations aimed at simplifying tasks, replacing skilled with unskilled workers, increasing the pace of work, and linking wages to output, proved key to productivity improvements. As noted earlier, trends towards mass production, standardisation, and the displacement of skilled men by semi-skilled female workers, were already evident among larger firms in the Birmingham area prior to the First World War and were greatly accelerated during the War years. Following the War firms successfully modified restrictions on the recruitment and deployment of labour to facilitate the retention of techniques originally introduced under tightly-regulated temporary war time 'dilution' agreements. For example, following defeat of the unions in the 1922 'employers' lock-out', Coventry's engineering firms rapidly moved towards the substitution

41 Roger Lloyd-Jones and M. J. Lewis, 'Business networks, social habits and the evolution of a regional industrial cluster: Coventry 1880s–1930s', 229–50 in John F. Wilson and Andrew Popp (eds), *Industrial Clusters and Regional Business Networks in England 1750–1970* (Aldershot, 2003), p. 240.

42 See Michael. Beesley, 'The birth and death of industrial establishments: experience in the West Midlands conurbation', *Journal of Industrial Economics*, 4 (1955), 45–61, p. 47.

43 Michael Beesley, 'Changing industrial advantages in the British motor car industry', *Journal of Industrial Economics*, 6 (1957), 47–57.

of skilled by semi-skilled labour and a substantial increase in the proportion of juvenile workers – mainly outside apprenticeships. This process was facilitated by encouraging large-scale in-migration of workers from outside the area's traditional workforce.

Industrial developments in the West Midlands thus demonstrated an evolutionary pattern in which predominantly metal-based new industries developed complementary relationships with traditional skilled metal-working trades – while gradually subsuming their output when demand grew to justify quantity production. Yet mass production metal-working activities were beginning to move beyond the pre-1914 West Midlands centres, to areas in London and the South East without any strong engineering tradition – such as Ford at Dagenham, General Motors at Luton, and the rapid expansion of Morris Motors at Oxford. While insured employment in motor car assembly in the Birmingham area expanded by 65 per cent over 1924–37, it was outpaced by the 77 per cent increase in national employment in this sector. New assembly methods and product standardisation appear to have been easier to introduce in areas without any strong engineering craft tradition.[44]

In addition to its poor record in attracting new plants during the 1930s, evidence indicates that the aggregate manufacturing growth of the West Midlands was already being outpaced by Greater London by the 1920s. The West Midlands' manufacturing workforce, of 611,850 in 1911, had increased by 20.49 per cent by 1931, while London and Middlesex (the closest approximation to Greater London using census data) had expanded its 1911 manufacturing workforce of 731,419 by 21.27 per cent.[45] Given that a significant proportion of Greater London's interwar manufacturing growth occurred in metropolitan Essex and Surrey, these figures underestimate Greater London's lead. The factors behind the spectacular interwar industrial growth of the metropolis form the topic of the next chapter.

44 Carol E. Heim, 'Uneven regional development in interwar Britain', unpublished Ph.D. thesis, Yale University, 1982, p. 133.

45 C. H. Lee, *British Regional Employment Statistics 1841–1971* (Cambridge, 1979), Part III, Series B.

Chapter Eight

New manufacturing industry in Greater London

Introduction

The drift of new manufacturing plants to the South was, essentially, a drift to Greater London. With the exception of a few centres with locations intermediate between London and the Midlands, such as Luton and Oxford, Greater London and its hinterland encompassed all the major areas of new industrial development in the South East. Despite the fact that much of the region was located outside the axial belt, including substantial population centres such as Southampton, Portsmouth, and Brighton, only 61 of the South East's 1,703 plants fell outside it (many involving raw material-intensive activities such as food & drink, non-metallic mineral products and ship/boat building).[1]

A major expansion in the conurbation's overall working population was accompanied by a relative shift in favour of manufacturing, which increased its share of total employment in London and Middlesex from 30.2 to 31.4 per cent between 1911 and 1931, during a period when the national ratio had declined slightly, from 33.5 to 32.5 per cent.[2] London's manufacturing growth accelerated during the 1930s; Greater London's employment in 'factory trades' rose by 18.4 per cent between 1930 and 1935, compared to only 6.0 per cent for Britain.[3] During 1932–38 the metropolis attracted no fewer than 1,408 plants with 25 or more employees, 39.6 per cent of the British total, while the rest of the South East received a further 8.3 per cent (concentrated in London satellites such as Slough, Welwyn, and Watford). Greater London's plants were relatively small, with an average initial employment of 80, compared to 95 for Britain (see Table 6.2); yet this was more than compensated by their greater net output per employee (£276, compared to £231 for Britain, in 1935).[4]

---

1 For a further plant the exact location was not clear.

2 Source: Clive H. Lee, *British Regional Employment Statistics 1841–1971* (Cambridge, 1979), Part III, Series B.

3 Board of Trade, *Fifth Census of Production 1935, Final Summary Tables* (London, 1944), p. 21, advises that an adjustment to remove 15,000 factory workers added to the 1935 figure by the incorporation of districts around Watford and Slough into the Census' definition of 'Greater London' should be made when comparing employment in 1935 and 1930.

4 Employment data are derived from NA: HLG 17/1330, memorandum, September 1943. These were based on the original SID returns, which gave more accurate employment estimates than the published versions. Data refer to plants with an initial employment of 25 or more, established from 1932–37. Net output data are derived from Board of Trade,

London's pattern of new plant formation was in stark contrast to Britain's provincial regions (see Table 6.1). It had an unusually low proportion of branch plants (9.02 per cent, compared with 20.94 per cent for plants outside the South East) and a much higher proportion of wholesale transfers of production from other localities (25.28 per cent, compared with 7.02 per cent for plants outside the South East). Meanwhile extensions of existing plants created employment equivalent to only 17.9 per cent of that created by 'new' plants (including transfers) in the metropolis, compared to 40.21 per cent for extensions in Britain's provincial regions (or 45.4 per cent for the rest of the South East). This appears to be largely due to the fact that London plants, in industries such as the metal-fabricating sectors or furniture, were more likely to combine plant extension with movement to new, outer-London, districts. During 1932–38 some 200 plants moved from the County of London to outer London (with only 17 moves in the opposite direction).[5] Meanwhile there were only 26 moves into the London region and 36 transfers out of the region (including 11 to areas on the fringes of London and eight to other parts of the South East), compared to 352 between localities within Greater London.

Of the 23 'substantial' clusters identified nationally, no fewer than 14 were in the South East; 13 within Greater London and one on its western border, at Slough. Given that London was classified into around 200 'localities', this represents very strong clustering. London's localities were generally smaller than individual boroughs – while many were named after boroughs, these often encompassed only part of the borough in question, distinct industrial zones within them being classified separately, such as the Park Royal estate, or the Perivale estate in Ealing (which, if included under Ealing, would have created a further substantial cluster).

Unlike the other British regions, new manufacturing plant formation within Greater London can be examined for the whole of the interwar period, using the SID data (for 1932–38) in conjunction with a register compiled by the Greater London Regional Development Committee [hereafter GLRDC] for the years 1919–31.[6] Their compatibility, and the organisations from which they drew their data, are discussed in Appendix One. The following analysis of plant clustering is based on this combined dataset (except when making comparisons with other regions, where the 1932–38 SID data are used). Given that the GLRDC data were classified by borough, the SID data were also re-classified by borough for the combined dataset. Using data sorted according to the borough boundaries of the 1930s also requires the use of the contemporary 'London region' (see Figure 8.1) rather than the modern 'Greater London' region – though the areas covered by the two are roughly similar (especially with regard to areas of significant industrialisation).

The analysis also draws on three contemporary surveys. The 1928–31 *New Survey of London Life and Labour* [hereafter *New Survey*], provides information on industrial development within the County of London, plus adjacent northern boroughs, from

Fifth Census of Production, using data for factory trades only. This assumes that regional differentials in net output per employee for new, and for total, plants are roughly similar.

5 Unlike the outer furniture boroughs, the electrical engineering boroughs did not draw most of their transfers from one part of inner-London.

6 London Metropolitan Archives, MCC/MIN/65/3.

Acton in the west to Barking in the east (with the exception of Hendon and Finchley). D. H. Smith's survey of industrial development in the north-west quadrant of outer-London, conducted during 1928–32, provides detailed information on the industrial development of this area.[7] Meanwhile more comprehensive geographical coverage, including reports on most individual London boroughs, is provided in the unpublished reports of the 1941–43 Nuffield College Social Reconstruction Survey.

Table 8.1: The sectoral distribution of new manufacturing plants with 25 or more employees in the London region, compared to that for Britain

	Percentage distribution			
SIC	Britain 1932-38	London 1919-38	London 1932-38	LQ for London plants 1932-38
22 Metal manufacture	1.97	0.68	0.78	0.39
24 Non-metallic mineral products	5.96	2.70	2.75	0.46
25 Chemicals	3.63	3.71	3.81	1.05
26 Man-made fibres	0.39	0.04	0.07	0.18
31 Other metal goods	6.19	4.21	4.59	0.74
32 Mechanical engineering	4.81	4.03	4.31	0.90
33 Office machinery	0.14	0.22	0.28	2.01
34 Electrical engineering	6.58	9.22	10.59	1.61
35 Motor vehicles	1.74	2.95	2.12	1.22
36 Other transport	2.78	1.66	1.69	0.61
37 Instrument engineering	1.49	2.20	2.68	1.80
41/2 Food, drink, tobacco	6.86	6.45	5.51	0.80
43 Textiles	11.87	2.45	2.61	0.22
44 Leather goods	2.11	2.45	2.19	1.04
45 Clothing/footwear	24.24	28.82	29.87	1.23
46 Timber/wooden furniture	9.20	12.50	13.35	1.45
47 Paper/printing	5.74	10.09	7.13	1.24
48 Rubber & plastics	1.74	1.30	1.84	1.05
49 Other manufacturing	2.56	4.32	3.81	1.49
Total	100.00	100.00	100.00	1.00
Total (number)	3,556	2,776	1,416	

Source: UK Data Archive, AHDS History, SN5192, Peter Scott and Peter Walsh, 'National data on new interwar manufacturing plants and extensions, 1919–1938', deposited 2005.

Table 8.1 shows the sectoral distribution of new manufacturing plants in the London region, together with their location quotients [hereafter LQ's] relative to

7 D. H. Smith, *The Industries of Greater London* (London, 1933).

new plants nationally.[8] LQ's could only be calculated for 1932–38, as national data are not available before 1932. Given that London plants made up almost 40 per cent of new plants nationally during this period, such a comparison understates the differences between London and the rest of Britain. Table 8.2 provides estimates of the initial employment generated by London's new manufacturing plants. As the SID's only provide employment estimates within bands of 100, the GLRDC (including data for 1932–35, not used elsewhere in the analysis) was used to estimate mean employment per plant, total employment being estimated by multiplying mean employment by the number of new plants during 1919–38.[9]

Table 8.2: Estimated initial employment for new London plants with 25 or more workers, 1919–38

SIC	Number of plants	Mean Employment*	Estimated total Employment* No	%
22 Metal manufacture	19	62.2	1,181	0.51
24 Non-metallic mineral products	75	96.2	7,217	3.12
25 Chemicals	103	83.5	8,596	3.72
31 Other metal goods	117	84.1	9,842	4.26
32 Mechanical engineering	112	71.4	7,994	3.46
34 Electrical engineering	256	120.0	30,712	13.30
35 Motor vehicles	82	113.0	9,262	4.01
36 Other transport	46	122.4	5,632	2.44
37 Instrument engineering	61	88.4	5,392	2.33
41/2 Food, drink, tobacco	179	125.2	22,408	9.70
43 Textiles	68	81.0	5,507	2.38
44 Leather goods	68	70.1	4,766	2.06
45 Clothing/footwear	800	65.7	52,533	22.74
46 Timber/wooden furniture	347	68.9	23,921	10.36
47 Paper/printing	280	86.5	24,210	10.48
48 Rubber & plastics	36	138.9	5,000	2.16
49 Other manufacturing	120	82.7	9,928	4.30
Total	2,769	83.4	230,966	100.00

Source: UK Data Archive, AHDS History, SN5192, Peter Scott and Peter Walsh, 'National data on new interwar manufacturing plants and extensions, 1919–1938', deposited 2005.

Notes: *Employment estimates are based on GLRDC data only, for 1919–35 (data for 1935 are incomplete). SIC's 26 and 33 are excluded, as the GLRDC listed no plants in SIC 26 and only three for SIC 33.

8 Location quotients are calculated by dividing the ratio of new plants in the sector, as a percentage of all new plants in London, by the same ratio for Britain. A figure in excess of one indicates that the sector is over-represented in London, relative to Britain as a whole.

9 Even the GLRDC employment estimates were imprecise, generally being rounded to the nearest five or ten employees (or the nearest 100 for very large plants).

London's largest sectors for new plants were clothing & footwear (by far the most important, with 28.8 per cent of plants and 22.7 per cent of estimated employment); timber & wooden furniture; electrical engineering; and paper & printing. These collectively comprised 60.6 per cent of new plants in the London region (or 60.9 per cent from 1932–38, compared to 45.8 per cent nationally). Clothing & footwear, furniture, and printing represented London's core nineteenth century manufacturing trades. Towards the end of the century the lighter sections of the nascent electrical engineering industry also developed a strong London focus and by 1911 these four sectors, together with leather & fur and instrument engineering, had the highest LQ's (for employment, relative to Britain) of all London's industries.[10]

Other over-represented sectors mainly included consumer or other branded goods, such as instrument engineering, office machinery, other manufacturing, and motor vehicles & components. Conversely, strongly under-represented sectors mainly concerned industries dominated by non-branded producer-goods, such as metal manufacture; non-metallic mineral products; artificial fibres; and textiles. This is confirmed when the analysis is undertaken at the 3-digit SIC level. For example, London's chemicals sector has a LQ (for 1932–38) of 1.05, but this rises to 1.81 for SIC 258 (soap, detergents, cosmetics, and toilet preparations). Similarly, the LQ for electrical engineering, 1.61, rises to 2.06 for SIC 345 (gramophones, radios, etc.). This division is evident even for under-represented sectors, the LQ for textiles rising from 0.22 to 0.52 for SIC 436, hosiery and knitwear, which was particularly orientated towards branded consumer products.

Greater London demonstrated strong local clustering of new plants, as shown in Figure 8.1. London's densest clusters – with more than 80 plants per borough – were Acton and Willesden in West Middlesex,[11] plus a contiguous group of seven boroughs in the central and north-eastern County of London, north of the Thames. These nine boroughs encompass 1,025 classified plants, while if unclassified plants (see Appendix 1) listed as 'central London' (a district that covered only boroughs in this group) and 'West End' (that mainly represented Westminster and St. Marylebone) are added, they contain an estimated 1,236 plants, some 44.5 per cent of all plants established in London's 93 boroughs.

Other areas of substantial industrialisation include boroughs immediately south of the Thames in the western half of the County of London; the western side of the Lea Valley; boroughs bordering Acton and Willesden to the north and West; the area immediately east of the County of London, north of the Thames; Dagenham; and Croydon. Boroughs with a significant number of new plants (8 or more over the 20 year period) form a contiguous group; there are no 'islands' of industrialisation surrounded by residential boroughs. Some 84.9 per cent of plants are located in 33 boroughs, each with 25 or more plants.[12] These boroughs, examined in Table 8.3, can be categorised into four groups – in which either clothing & footwear; timber

---

10 See Michael Ball and David Sunderland, *An Economic History of London 1800–1914* (London, 2001), pp. 75–6.

11 Analysis of that data which can be disaggregated into the Acton or Willesden boroughs reveals that they each contained over 80 plants.

12 Including some that could only be classified by broader geographical area.

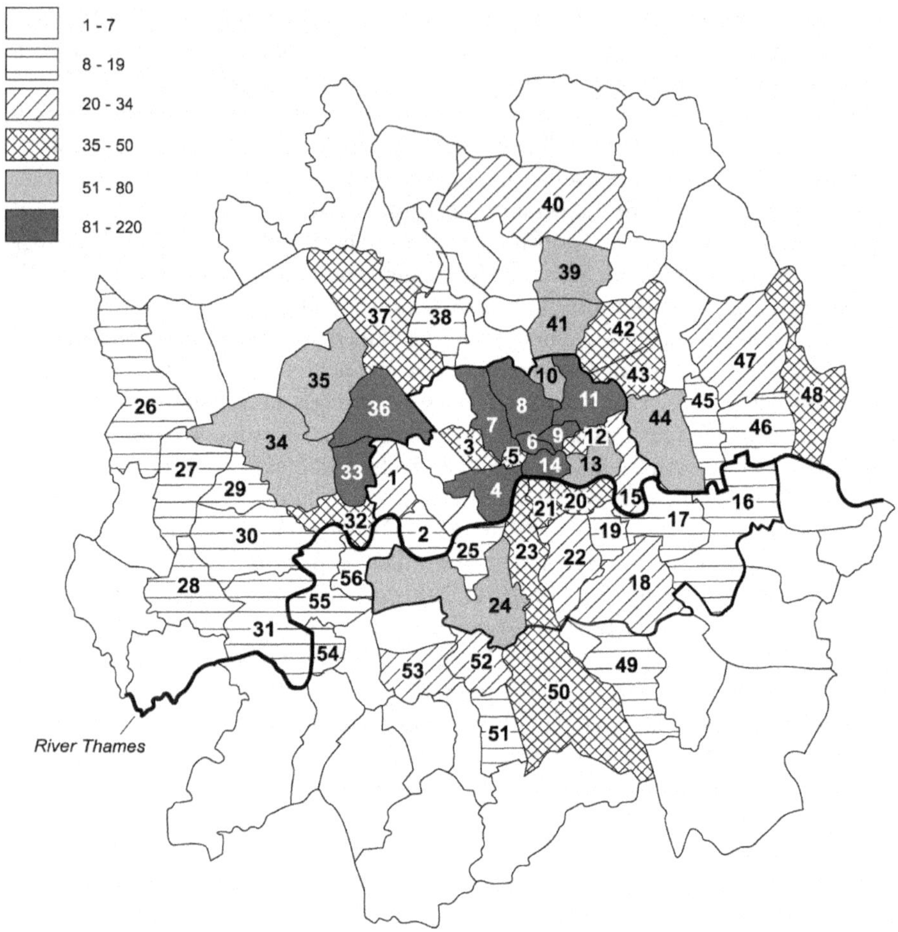

Figure 8.1: The distribution of new London plants by borough, 1919–38

Source: UK Data Archive, AHDS History, SN5192, Peter Scott and Peter Walsh, 'National data on new interwar manufacturing plants and extensions, 1919–1938', deposited 2005.

Key to boroughs: 1 Hammersmith, 2 Fulham, 3 St. Marylebone, 4 Westminster, 5 Holborn, 6 Finsbury, 7 St. Pancras, 8 Islington, 9 Shoreditch, 10 Stoke Newington, 11 Hackney, 12 Bethnal Green, 13 Stepney, 14 City, 15 Poplar, 16 Woolwich, 17 Greenwich, 18 Lewisham, 19 Deptford, 20 Bermondsey, 21Southwark, 22 Camberwell, 23 Lambeth, 24 Wandsworth, 25 Battersea, 26 Uxbridge, 27 Hayes & Harlington, 28 Feltham, 29 Southall-Norwood, 30 Heston-Isleworth, 31 Twickenham, 32 Brentford & Chiswick, 33 Acton, 34 Ealing, 35 Wembley, 36 Willesden, 37 Hendon, 38 Finchley, 39 Edmonton, 40 Enfield, 41 Tottenham, 42 Walthamstow, 43 Leyton, 44 West Ham, 45 East Ham, 46 Barking, 47 Ilford, 48 Dagenham, 49 Beckenham, 50 Croydon, 51 Beddington & Wallington, 52 Mitcham, 53 Merton & Morden, 54 Kingston, 55 Richmond, 56 Barnes.

and wooden furniture; electrical engineering; or paper, printing & publishing, were over-represented and formed the largest single sector.[13] Each group displays strong distinctive features.

Patterns of location and clustering for traditional London industries

Analysis of industrial clustering within London demonstrates the various spatial levels over which different kinds of locational externalities can operate. For example, distribution networks can be viewed as urbanisation economies, as they originate in urban diversity (while subsequently developing sector-specific characteristics).[14] Yet, particularly in large urban agglomerations, maximising 'communication economies' from such networks (and from the manufacturing networks that coalesce close to the marketing hubs of trades producing highly differentiated products) may involve location within small, specialised 'quarters'.[15] In such areas tight clustering enables inter-firm observation and communication to occur incidentally and on an almost continuous basis, producing the unconscious flow of ideas highlighted by Marshall. Meanwhile, aspects of localisation economies involving less frequent interactions between firms, such as access to local machinery producers or dealings with suppliers of standardised parts, may operate over larger spatial levels.

London's clothing trade provides a classic example of a compact group of sectorally-specialised industrial districts. Its 'clothing boroughs' (in which new clothing plants were over-represented and formed the largest single sector for new plants) formed a contiguous, centrally-located, group, as shown in Figure 8.2. Boroughs in this group had by far the highest average density of plants and were more dominated by their main sector than the other groups. Clothing & footwear accounted for an average of almost half the plants across these 11 boroughs. Other strongly-represented sectors were also traditional London industries; SIC's 44–47 & 49 (leather goods, clothing, furniture, printing, and other manufacturing) averaged 77.7 per cent of new plants, compared to only 26.9 per cent for the 12 boroughs in the electrical engineering group. Meanwhile engineering and metal-fabricating sectors (SIC's 22 and 31–37) averaged less than 10 per cent of new plants. Sectorally-based clustering is also evident at the sub-borough level. As a 1955 survey by J.E. Martin demonstrated, this area of London can be de-composed into specialised 'quarters', ranging in size from small, dense, clusters – such as the City's clothing quarters on its south-eastern fringe and in Aldergate – to much larger districts such as the

13 Walthamstow was included under furniture rather than clothing, despite having slightly more plants in clothing, as its location quotient for clothing was below 1. Bermondsey, classified as a paper and printing borough, had equal numbers of plants in this sector, in clothing, and in food, drink & tobacco.

14 S. N. Broadberry and Andrew Marrison, 'External economies of scale in the Lancashire cotton industry, 1900–1950', *Economic History Review*, LV, 1 (2002), 51–77, p. 54.

15 J. E. Martin, 'Industry in inner London', *Town and Country Planning*, 24 (1957), 125–8; A. R. Pred, 'The intrametropolitan location of American manufacturing', *Annals of the Association of American Geographers*, 54, 2 (1964), 165–80.

Stoke Newington/Hackney clothing area. Other industries localised in the clothing boroughs also had distinct quarters, such as printing around Fleet Street and in southern Shoreditch.[16]

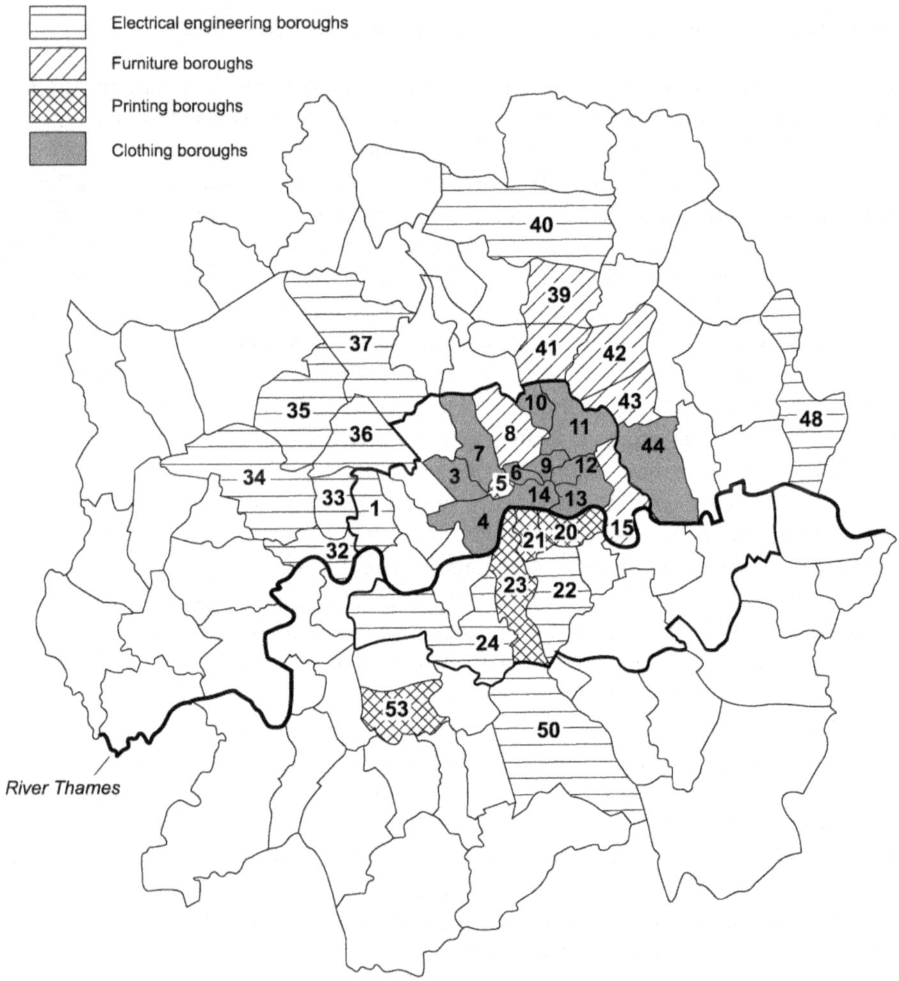

Figure 8.2: London boroughs with 25 of more new plants during 1919–38, classified by main sector

Source and key to boroughs – as for Figure 8.1.

16 Martin, 'Industry in inner London'; this includes a map of quarters in the north-east quadrant of inner-London.

While London's footwear industry had been in almost continuous decline since at least the 1860s (the displacement of traditional methods by quantity production techniques having been accompanied by firm out-migration to the provinces), clothing had experienced rapid growth. This was achieved via an industrial structure based on sub-contracting, extensive employment of female labour, and major process innovations – the sewing machine and band-saw.[17] Production was highly specialised in women's clothing, where demand remained buoyant during the interwar years – increasing roughly in line with incomes – while the importance of fashion and, therefore, proximity to markets, severely limited foreign competition. Yet the emphasis on fashion and variety meant that markets were subject to highly volatile and batch demand. These conditions placed a premium on flexible, limited-scale, production. Flexibility even straddled the major classes of tailoring: 'wholesale', bespoke, and made-to-measure; the *New Survey* reported that factories specialised in one of these divisions often accepted orders in the others when short of work.[18]

In common with other centres of the women's clothing trade in Europe and North America, manufacturers were clustered in areas close to the urban core. London's clothing industry had long been concentrated in the central and eastern County of London, North of the Thames, providing both proximity to City and West End markets and (particularly for the cheaper end of the trade, based around the East End) cheap labour and premises.[19] By the interwar period some boroughs in which new clothing plants were concentrated (particularly the City, Westminster, St. Marylebone, and St. Pancras) had high land values, while even the East End County of London clothing boroughs had higher land costs than areas such as Tottenham, Edmonton, and Walthamstow.[20] The clothing boroughs' labour cost advantages had also declined, due to minimum wage controls (under the 1909 Trades Boards Act) and the virtual cessation of Jewish immigration. Indeed some boroughs to their north east, such as Tottenham, Walthamstow, and Leyton, appear to have had a local supply of cheap workers at least as abundant as that of several clothing boroughs, together with substantially lower land costs.[21]

Yet London's clothing trade displayed remarkable locational stability, as demonstrated by data on 'new' plants formed as the result of the transfer of production from another locality (available for 1932–38).[22] Only 10.64 per cent of London's clothing & footwear plants owed their origins to such transfers, compared to 25.28 per cent for all new London plants (or 31.52 per cent for sectors other than SIC 45). Furthermore, in contrast to furniture (discussed below) there was no trend towards decentralisation to areas of lower land and labour costs; the majority of transfers represented either moves within established clothing districts, or sub-sectors that

17 Ibid.; P. G. Hall, *The industries of London since 1861* (London, 1962), p. 54.

18 London School of Economics [hereafter LSE], *The New Survey of London Life & Labour. Volume II: London's Industries* (London, 1931), p. 280.

19 Paul Johnson, 'Economic development and industrial dynamism in Victorian London', *London Journal*, 21 (1996), 27–37, p. 33.

20 Smith, *Industries of Greater London*, pp. 42–3.

21 Ibid., pp. 39–42.

22 As many localities were smaller than boroughs, a few transfers represent plant movement within the same borough, though these were not significant in number.

were not core specialities of these districts (such as boots & shoes). This stability was the product of particularly strong Marshallian externalities, constituting a 'glue' that held the industry's localisation in place when the conditions that had originally produced it became modified.[23] As Paul Johnson noted, clothing, together with other central London industries such as craft-based furniture and leather goods, were classic examples of flexible specialisation.[24] Indeed localisation economies were sufficiently strong to allow London's small, flexibly specialised, clothing plants to achieve higher productivity (in terms of net output per worker) than the larger and more mechanised provincial clothing centres.[25]

Central locations and tight clustering arose partly due to strong 'communication economies' – external economies derived from immediate access to centrally-based purchasers prior to the actual process of manufacture.[26] The tacit nature of knowledge regarding the key features of those products that happened to be selling well at any particular time; small batch orders and the ensuing frequency and volume of interactions with customers; and the informal nature of many contacts between manufacturers and their customers, collectively produced a high premium on locations that facilitated virtually continuous face to face communication with purchasers.

Extensive sub-division of production was facilitated by the industry's common production technology, based on the sewing machine – which was well-suited to small-scale units and small production runs.[27] Manufacturing technology thus allowed the industry to respond to differentiated and uncertain demand by developing an industrial structure characterised by extensive networks of vertical specialisation, sub-contracting, and home workers; indeed P.G. Hall noted their persistence even during the early 1960s.[28] The small distances over which most inter-firm linkages operated, together with the high number and frequency of linkages, also acted to temper the opportunism that is an inherent danger in cooperative production systems.[29] London's clothing districts lacked strong mediating institutions to control opportunism, of the kind highlighted in the industrial district literature, such as political parties, local government, employers associations, and trade unions,

23 V. Henderson, A. Kuncoro and M. Turner, 'Industrial development in cities', *Journal of Political Economy*, 103 (1995), 1067–90, p. 1069.

24 Johnson, 'Economic development', p. 33.

25 A. C. Godley, 'Immigrant entrepreneurs and the emergence of London's East End as an industrial district', *London Journal*, 21, 1 (1996), pp. 38–45; Ball and Sunderland, *An Economic History of London*, p. 304.

26 Pred, 'The intrametropolitan location', p. 175.

27 Godley, 'Immigrant entrepreneurs', p. 42.

28 Nuffield College, Oxford, Nuffield College Social Reconstruction Survey Archive, (hereafter NCSRS), C1/113, report by G. R. Mitchison, April 1943; Hall, *The Industries of London*, p. 65.

29 J. You. and F. Williamson, 'Competition and co-operation: toward understanding industrial districts', *Review of Political Economy*, 6 (1994), 259–78, p. 260.

relying instead on the market-based mechanism of self-enforcement in the context of repeated games among the same firms.[30]

Effective self-enforcement depends on a high probability of the game being repeated sufficiently frequently, or information flows between firms being sufficiently strong, for 'local reputation' to act as an effective deterrent to opportunism.[31] Reputation can be viewed as a form of personal capital, which incurs high development costs for the firm in question (through failing to accrue potential short-term gains from opportunism) and high identification costs for potential collaborators.[32] Tight geographical clustering reduces identification costs and thus maximises the firm's return on reputational investment.

Tight clustering also facilitates knowledge spillovers. The theory of knowledge spillovers, derived from the knowledge production function, suggests that clustering arising from spillovers will be strongest in industries where tacit knowledge plays an important role, as such knowledge can only be transmitted informally, typically via direct and repeated contact.[33] Such dynamic externalities were particularly important in a fashion-based sector such as the type of women's clothing in which London specialised, where rapid access to information regarding which styles were currently selling was vital to success. Knowledge regarding fashion can be viewed as an urbanisation externality, as it is fostered by urban scale.[34] Yet at the intra-metropolitan level it was strongly linked to communication economies, as many observations would be made incidentally, for example while making journeys on foot in the course of other business or via chance social contacts, such as in pubs frequented by the clothing trade. Furthermore, in addition to direct communication flows from distributors, much information on new and successful lines was transmitted between producers – through subcontracted work, 'gossip', observation, and inter-firm staff movement.

By encouraging the clustering of manufacturers, communication economies can foster other external economies.[35] Meanwhile firms facing markets characterised by volatile batch-demand and uncertainty also accrue other major advantages from clustering, not directly linked to communication economies. In a market highly subject to both fashion and product differentiation, where the demand for any particular item is extremely difficult to predict, sub-contracting constitutes an important means of reducing risk by facilitating the ease and speed by which the scale of output can be varied. In effect sub-contracting collectivises production tasks, both reducing the amount of uncertainty faced by any one unit and stabilising the flow of

---

30 G. Dei Ottati, 'Trust, interlinking transactions and credit in the industrial district', *Cambridge Journal of Economics*, 18 (1994), 529–46; You and Williamson, 'Competition'; David Feldman, *Englishmen and Jews. Social relations and political culture 1840–1914* (New Haven, 1994), pp. 201–3.

31 You and Williamson, 'Competition', pp. 272–3.

32 Dei Ottati, 'Trust', pp. 532–6.

33 Audretsch, 'Agglomeration', p. 23.

34 Henderson, Kuncoro, and Turner, 'Industrial development', p. 1068.

35 Ibid., pp. 175–6.

Table 8.3: London boroughs with 25 or more new plants during 1919–38

	No. of plants	% plants in main SIC class	LQ within London	SIC's with LQ>1	% SIC's 22 & 31-37	% SIC's 44-47 & 49	% plants with 100+ workers
Clothing boroughs							
Bethnal Green	39	35.90	1.25	6	7.69	82.05	28.21
City	89	65.17	2.26	4	2.25	91.01	10.11
Finsbury	220	53.18	1.85	4	9.55	81.82	18.64
Hackney	121	41.32	1.43	6	7.44	85.12	23.14
Shoreditch	100	33.00	1.15	6	5.00	81.00	23.00
St. Marylebone	48	77.08	2.67	2	8.33	85.42	10.42
St. Pancras	102	35.29	1.22	6	25.49	63.73	11.76
Stepney	56	64.29	2.23	4	1.79	80.36	35.71
Stoke Newington	57	43.86	1.52	5	19.30	70.18	22.81
West Ham	55	30.91	1.07	7	12.73	47.27	21.82
Westminster	98	68.37	2.37	3	7.14	86.73	18.37
Printing/paper boroughs							
Bermondsey	41	21.95	2.18	5	12.20	60.98	41.46
Holborn	36	30.56	3.03	5	22.22	75.00	13.89
Lambeth	41	21.95	2.18	10	26.83	41.46	24.39
Merton & Morden	30	20.00	1.98	8	46.67	43.33	26.67
Southwark	48	31.25	3.10	6	16.67	62.50	37.50
Furniture boroughs							
Edmonton	63	44.44	3.56	5	26.98	66.67	30.16
Islington	100	21.00	1.68	7	20.00	66.00	21.00
Leyton	38	28.95	2.32	6	13.16	71.05	52.63

Poplar	28	42.86	3.43	6	21.43	71.43	21.43
Tottenham	77	32.47	2.60	5	25.97	66.23	22.08
Walthamstow*	49	16.33	1.31	9	26.53	59.18	32.65
Electrical engineering boroughs							
Acton\Willesden	196	16.33	1.77	11	46.94	28.57	30.10
Brentford & Chiswick	42	16.67	1.81	11	57.14	21.43	26.19
Camberwell	25	24.00	2.60	6	32.00	56.00	28.00
Croydon	48	14.58	1.58	11	58.33	27.08	25.00
Dagenham	45	17.78	1.93	9	46.67	24.44	31.11
Ealing	51	19.61	2.13	8	45.10	17.65	23.53
Enfield	27	29.63	3.21	9	55.56	33.33	22.22
Hammersmith	26	30.77	3.34	8	53.85	30.77	38.46
Hendon	43	25.58	2.77	9	62.79	27.91	34.88
Wandsworth	53	20.75	2.25	9	47.17	11.32	37.74
Wembley	51	27.45	2.98	8	68.63	17.65	27.45
(Slough)	(77)	(18.18)	(1.97)	(10)	(44.16)	(15.58)	(19.48)
Average (clothing boroughs)	89.55	49.85	1.73	4.82	9.70	77.70	20.36
(printing/paper boroughs)	39.20	25.14	2.49	6.80	24.92	56.65	28.78
(furniture boroughs)	59.17	31.01	2.48	6.33	22.35	66.76	29.99
(elec. eng. boroughs)**	50.58	22.10	2.40	9.00	52.20	26.92	29.52

Source: UK Data Archive, AHDS History, SN5192, Peter Scott and Peter Walsh, 'National data on new interwar manufacturing plants and extensions, 1919–1938', deposited 2005.

Notes: Averages are simple averages (rather than being weighted by the number of plants). * Walthamstow is included under furniture boroughs, despite its largest single sector being clothing, since it has a LQ for clothing (relative to London) of below 1.

** Excluding Slough – which falls outside the London region. The average number of plants is adjusted to account for the fact that Acton and Willesden are separate boroughs. Other data treat Acton & Willesden as one borough.

work throughout the industrial district.[36] Yet sub-contracting in differentiated and rapidly changing product markets requires tight clustering, as spatial convergence minimises the potentially onerous transactions costs generated by the high volume and frequency of inter-firm linkages (minimising such costs is also a key feature of communication economies).

A spatial structure aimed at minimising transactions costs was particularly evident in the clothing districts. Vertical production chains generally involved passing on work-in-progress – in which a good deal of working capital was invested – to several different firms; thus minimising turn-around times had a major impact on costs and production chains generally operated over very short distances.[37] Meanwhile, by lowering linkage costs, spatial concentration in turn facilitated economies of specialisation and thus encouraged further disintegration of the production process.[38] Such specialisation increases efficiency and lowers costs, particularly for small firms, for example by ensuring that scarce and expensive skilled workers are employed only on skilled tasks.

Local linkages with other sectors were very limited, as materials and machinery could be easily purchased far from their points of production. The only significant local inter-sectoral linkage appears to have been with leather goods. Footwear plants (which traditionally had a similar geographical distribution within London to clothing) had strong input-output linkages with leather producers.[39] Furthermore, the manufacture of fancy leather goods, such as hand-bags, had some functional complementarities to clothing and footwear. Both sectors were based around the sewing machine and were subject to similar broad fashion trends and, to some extent, distribution outlets.[40]

Paper and printing constituted the largest sector for new plants in several London boroughs, though the 'printing boroughs' were smaller in number, and had a smaller average number of plants per borough, than was the case for the other groups in Table 8.3. Printing boroughs had a level of industrial diversification substantially higher than the clothing boroughs, but lower than the electrical engineering boroughs. Their proportion of new plants in metal fabricating sectors, or in SIC's 44–47 & 49 (clothing, leather goods, woodworking, paper & printing, and other manufacturing), similarly occupied an intermediate position between the clothing and electrical engineering groups.

London's printing trade had traditionally been clustered in, and on the fringes of, the City of London, in areas such as Fleet Street, Holborn and southern Shoreditch. By the interwar period the location of new plants was showing signs of movement, over distances that varied considerably according to the type of activity undertaken. For printers engaged in non-standardised batch production and/or work involving

36 A. J. Scott, 'Industrial organization and the logic of intra-metropolitan location: I theoretical considerations', *Economic Geography*, 59, 3 (1983), 233–50, pp. 244–5.

37 Ball and Sunderland, *An Economic History of London*, p. 301.

38 Scott, 'Industrial organization', pp. 241–2.

39 Ball and Sunderland, *An Economic History of London*, p. 309.

40 LSE, *The New Survey of London Life And Labour. Volume V: London Industries II* (London, 1933), p. 319.

rapid turn-around times, such as newspapers, magazines and most commercial work, communication economies were of considerable importance. Proximity to City (and, to a lesser extent, West End) based customers proved a key factor influencing location, in common with the core metropolitan clustering of similar printing activities in major U.S. cities.[41] As with clothing, communication economies dissipated rapidly with distance, especially in an era of primitive telecommunications.[42]

Meanwhile the non-standardised nature of this type of printing required a high proportion of skilled workers, while volatile market demand for job printing made it impractical to train all skilled workers in-house and then permanently retain them. Labour pooling provided the solution to this problem, assisted by the use of a small number of standard printing technologies, involving skills that were policed by tight apprenticeship systems and strong unions.[43] Features of the apprenticeship system – including the common practice of requiring workers to spend a period at another firm after completing their apprenticeships – cemented the common skill base and the interchangeability of workers between firms. Such labour pooling required geographical clustering, particularly in an industry such as printing where a substantial proportion of work was undertaken at night and thus required residential proximity to the workplace. [44]

New plants were concentrated in one traditional printing centre, Holborn, and three boroughs in a contiguous area of central London immediately south of the Thames – Lambeth, Southwark, and Bermondsey. These combined proximity, and, therefore, good communication economies, with London's business centre, together with the much lower land prices south of the river (an important factor given that some printers had very large plants). For example, Lambeth's printers were mainly based immediately south of Waterloo Bridge, around Stamford Street, separated from the southern border of the City by little more than the width of the Thames. These areas also had some of London's highest residential concentrations of printing workers, who, like the manufacturers, had identified their combination of good access to the city and low property costs. They were therefore centrally placed for the trade's key localisation externality of skilled labour pooling.

Meanwhile SIC 47 also encompassed activities for which proximity to markets and rapid turn-around times was of less importance, such as books, monthly periodicals, and standardised commercial printing;[45] together with non-printing activities – cardboard and paper products. Access to central London's pool of skilled printers was also less important for these activities – standardised printing involved a lower proportion of labour in type-setting and other skilled operations, while paper and cardboard manufacture were less skilled trades than printing. These activities, particularly cardboard and paper, were thus able to migrate further in search of

41 Pred, 'Intrametropolitan location', p. 175.

42 V. Henderson, 'Marshall's scale economies', *Journal of Urban Economics*, 53 (2003), 1–28, p. 2.

43 See, for example, S. A. Rosenthal and W. C. Strange, 'The determinants of agglomeration', *Journal of Urban Economics*, 50 (2001), 191–229.

44 LSE, *New Survey... Volume V*, pp. 267–8.

45 Hall, *Industries of London*, pp. 96–112.

cheaper land and labour. Plant transfers in paper & printing were concentrated among SIC's 471 and 472 (cardboard and paper products), which represented 56.25 per cent of the sector's transfers within Greater London, but only 38.21 per cent of all new London paper & printing plants. The 'printing/paper boroughs' in Table 8.3 include one reception borough for such transfers, Merton and Morden.[46] This had characteristics intermediate between the printing and electrical engineering boroughs: half its SIC 47 plants produced cardboard or papier mache goods, while its printing works were outnumbered by electrical engineering plants. Furthermore, it had a large base of metal-fabricating firms and its plants were mainly located on industrial estates.[47]

Like clothing and printing, furniture represented a traditional, craft-based, industry. Yet it experienced much more radical changes in production technology during the early twentieth century, with the rapid development of mechanised, standardised production, especially for the cheaper end of the market. However, despite decentralising to areas of cheaper premises and labour, the industry nevertheless maintained strong clustering. Four of the six boroughs in the furniture group were located in a contiguous area to the north east of the County of London, while the remaining two, Islington and Poplar, were close to the southern borders of this area. LQ's (relative to London) for furniture averaged 2.48 for the six boroughs, indicating strong localisation. Furniture boroughs had a density of plants second only to the clothing boroughs, while their furniture plants – though less dominant than clothing in clothing boroughs – nevertheless accounted for a significantly higher proportion of plants than electrical engineering, or printing and paper, where these formed the chief industries. The furniture boroughs had a more diversified structure of new plants than the clothing group, but were nevertheless dominated by traditional, non-metal-fabricating sectors; plants in SIC's 44–47 & 49 averaged around two thirds of the total. Yet mechanical engineering, other metal goods, and electrical engineering were also over-represented in several boroughs.

Furniture had been the most strongly clustered of London's major nineteenth century industries, largely due to the fact that its raw material and semi-manufactured inputs were both expensive and difficult to transport. Meanwhile, like clothing, its original location pattern had been strongly influenced by proximity to West End and City markets and the availability of cheap labour and premises. Prior to the twentieth century it had strong similarities with clothing in terms of small production units, specialisation, and relatively cheap, flexible, machinery. The production process was highly vertically specialised, the manufacture of a single item often involving passing it between sawyers, turners, fret cutters, carvers, and other craftsmen, the process being coordinated by 'manufacturers' whose direct production role was often limited to final assembly.[48] Marshallian externalities also included a range of

46 Some firms undertaking standardised printing also decentralised outside London, to take advantage of lower land costs and provincial printing wage scales.

47 NCSRS, C1/111, report on Surrey by P. J. Self, April 1943.

48 Ball and Sunderland, *An Economic History of London*, pp. 302–12.

ancillary and service trades, such as ironmongery parts, upholsterers, and specialist training facilities.[49]

The trade's traditional centre had been Shoreditch, but during the late nineteenth century it began to migrate in search of cheaper premises and labour, firstly eastwards to Bethnal Green, then northwards to Hackney.[50] During the interwar period migration continued northwards, to the Lea Valley, and eastwards, to Walthamstow and Leyton, again influenced by cheaper premises and labour, together with the use of the Lea Navigation for supplying timber. Transfers between localities comprised 36.51 per cent of all 'new' furniture plants in the London region, mainly representing moves from central London to the four outer-London furniture boroughs. For example, Enfield and Tottenham received 24 transfers in SIC 46, 23 of which moved from one of seven contiguous boroughs: Bethnal Green, the City, Finsbury, Hackney, Islington, Shoreditch, and Stoke Newington.

Craft-based, 'flexible specialisation' became increasingly associated with small-scale inner-London plants, producing higher quality goods.[51] Meanwhile in the outer boroughs there was a strong trend towards quantity production, stimulated both by demand factors (the growth of a mass-market for cheap furniture, sold by nationwide chains) and by technological change – the deployment of expensive machinery best suited to high, standardised, throughput. Mechanisation was accompanied by moves towards integrated production and a new general class of semi-skilled employee, the wood-cutting machinist, who undertook many tasks traditionally performed by the carpenter, joiner, or cabinet-maker, in some cases leaving little more than assembling and finishing to the skilled worker.[52]

Moves towards quantity production in the outer-London furniture boroughs were facilitated by their legacy of human and physical capital arising from the First World War. Local munitions factory development both boosted their supply of semi-skilled, often female, workers and created a pool of modern factory premises, later sold for civilian use.[53] Following the War a programme of arterial road development, introduced in part to combat heavy local post-war unemployment, greatly improved their transport links. The North Circular road brought Edmonton, Tottenham, and Walthamstow into London's new arterial road network, while the Cambridge Road increased accessibility northwards. Arterial roads, together with high demand for converted munitions factories, encouraged the further development of factories by industrial estate developers in all four outer boroughs.[54] Another legacy of war-time munitions development was the creation of a base of metal-goods and engineering plants. These and the furniture firms shared a common demand for relatively unskilled labour – using production methods with broad functional similarities

49 LSE, *New Survey... Volume II*, p. 12.

50 Ball and Sunderland, *An Economic History of London*, p. 311.

51 NCSRS, C1/122, report on Bethnal Green by E. Thomas, May 1941; LSE, *New survey... Volume II*, p. 25.

52 LSE, *New Survey... Volume II*, p. 8.

53 Smith, *Industries of Greater London*, pp. 42–50; NCSRS, C1/167, report on Walthamstow by C. J. Holloway, October 1941.

54 See Figure 9.3.

to those found in the munitions factories. As a study of Edmonton noted, one unifying characteristic of its manufacturing base was the prevalence of mechanised or simplified processes and the employment of un/semi-skilled, often adolescent, labour outside apprenticeships.[55]

Clustering in London's assembly goods industries

London's 'new' assembly and branded goods industries were clustered in boroughs beyond, or on the fringes of, London's traditional manufacturing area, in which electrical engineering constituted the largest single sector. These boroughs were less dominated by their largest sector than was the case for London's central industrial clusters. While electrical engineering provided an estimated 13.3 per cent of total employment created by London's new manufacturing plants, it accounted for only 9.2 per cent of their number. Yet, despite this there are no fewer than 12 boroughs in the electrical engineering group, even more than for clothing, which accounted for over three times as many plants. The electrical engineering boroughs had a much broader industrial composition than the inner-London clusters, with an average of nine sectors over-represented. Other heavily-represented sectors included motor vehicles; mechanical engineering; other metal goods, chemicals, and, to a lesser extent, non-metallic mineral products, food & drink, and textiles. Conversely, traditional inner-London industries were strongly under-represented, comprising only 26.92 per cent of plants, compared with 58.18 per cent for the London region.

Seven of the twelve electrical engineering boroughs formed a contiguous area stretching north and west from Hammersmith into Middlesex and including the large Acton/Willesden cluster. Three more – Wandsworth, Camberwell, and Croydon – were located in a contiguous area south of the Thames. The remaining boroughs – Enfield, in north London, and Dagenham, on London's eastern periphery – appear isolated, but were linked to the others by the arterial road network.

Analysis of the SID data indicates that, in addition to the London electrical engineering clusters, there was a further similar substantial cluster, Slough – located just beyond Greater London's western border, but linked to the West Middlesex electrical engineering clusters by the Great West Road – Bath Road and by rail links. This constituted the only substantial new plant cluster in the South East outside Greater London. As Slough was included within the area of the GLRDC register, it is possible to examine its new manufacturing plant formation for the whole of the interwar period. In the following analysis the Slough cluster is considered alongside the London electrical engineering clusters, but treated separately in the statistical analysis, as it fell outside London's borders (Table 8.3 includes comparative statistics for Slough and London's electrical engineering boroughs).

Plant formation in the new industrial areas of outer London and its hinterland outstripped that in the West Midlands. In order to compare the two it is necessary to revert to the SID data (covering 1932–38 only), and to clusters based on SID 'localities' rather than London boroughs. Four 'substantial' electrical engineering

55 G. W. Sturges, *Edmonton: Past and Present* (London, 1941), p. 37 of Chapter 7.

clusters are identified in outer-London and its environs using this data – Acton, Park Royal, Wembley, and Slough. The number of plants recorded in these localities by the SID's, 165, was almost as large as the collective total for the Birmingham district, Coventry, and Wolverhampton. Meanwhile, if outer-London and London satellite clusters of this type, with at least as many plants as Coventry, are added – Barking (15 plants); Brentford (17); Croydon (16); Dagenham (22); Enfield (14); Hendon (15); Luton (22); Perivale (24) and Willesden (23) – their total new plants substantially exceed the number established throughout the West Midlands.

During the First World War the electrical engineering boroughs underwent processes of war-related infrastructure development and the creation of a female assembly workforce similar to the outer-furniture boroughs, though on a more extensive scale. Several hosted large munitions projects: including the extension of the Enfield Small Arms factory and major new plants at Croydon, Hendon, Acton, and Willesden, while Wembley subsequently underwent site development for the 1924 Exhibition.[56] Meanwhile Slough hosted a major depot for reconditioning war-surplus vehicles. In common with the furniture boroughs they also received arterial road development following the cessation of hostilities, partly to combat heavy local post-war unemployment. Road projects – including Western Avenue (Ealing and Acton); the Great West Road (Brentford and Slough); North Circular Road (Willesden and Hendon); Edgeware Road (Hendon); Cambridge Road (Enfield), Purley Way (Croydon) and A13 (Dagenham) – eventually formed a network linking these boroughs and providing good access both to central London and to Britain's long-distance road network.

Arterial road construction was often closely synchronised with the onset of substantial factory development.[57] Land along the new roads was initially cheap, yet in those areas where large concentrations of factories emerged, prices rose several-fold. Smith found that in 1932 industrial land prices in outer-London averaged around £1,000 per acre, though for West Middlesex's largest concentration of factories, Acton, Willesden, and Cricklewood, prices had already reached £2,500.[58] At the beginning of 1935 estate agents Hillier Parker noted the appreciation of land values in one favoured location from £1,000 to £6,000 per acre and by 1937 prices of £8,000 per acre were being quoted for sought-after sites.[59]

Despite rapid appreciation of land values, and the availability of cheaper industrial land in other areas along the arterial road system, factories in the electrical engineering boroughs demonstrated very strong clustering. Buoyant demand for abandoned munitions factories stimulated industrial estate development, often on former munitions sites, on a more extensive scale, and sometimes involving much larger estates, than was the case in the outer furniture boroughs. The author has identified 20 industrial estates,

56 Martin, *Greater London*, p. 31; Smith, *Industries of Greater London*, p. 78; Croydon Reference Library, *The Waddon Factory Estate* (undated promotional brochure).

57 Smith, *Industries of Greater London*, p. 84.

58 Ibid., p. 163.

59 Hillier Parker, *Report on the Property Market during 1934* (London: Hillier Parker, 1935); Martin, *Greater London*, p. 34; 'Industrial site survey', *Business* (March 1937), 32–8, p. 33.

encompassing all the outer electrical-engineering boroughs. Twelve, for which 1938 employment data are available, are estimated to have accommodated some 92,000 people. Meanwhile Slough hosted a major industrial estate, that is estimated to have employed a further 28,500 on a 600 acre site.[60]

Industrial estates in the London electrical engineering boroughs constituted particularly dense concentrations of plants and employees, such as the 335 acre Park Royal estate in Acton/Willesden (about 302 firms and 30,000 workers); the 100 acre North Cricklewood estate in Willesden (around 45 firms and 9,700 employees); Ealing's 60 acre Perivale estate (around 63 firms and 6,100 employees); and the 25 acre Waddon Estate in Croydon (with firms employing around 4,300 workers).[61] The larger estates were of roughly similar size to the larger central London 'quarters' identified by Martin, and had higher employment densities (though this comparison is biased by the fact that inner-London quarters also contained large amounts of non-industrial buildings).[62] They also shared a further similarity with the inner-London quarters in that buildings were generally available to rent, increasing the speed at which firms could establish production and turning the capital cost of premises into a rental stream.

Table 8.4: Percentage distribution of new London plants between the County of London, the outer-London electrical engineering boroughs, and other outer-London boroughs, at employment ranges over 100, 1919–38

Initial Employment	County of London	Outer-electrical engineering boroughs	Other outer-London boroughs	Total (Number)
100-199*	55.4	18.1	26.6	448
200-299	50.0	27.8	22.2	108
300-399	46.7	43.3	10.0	30
400-499	26.9	30.8	42.3	26
500-599	33.3	20.0	46.7	15
600-899	52.9	0.0	47.1	17
900+	18.2	72.7	9.1	11

Source: UK Data Archive, AHDS History, SN5192, Peter Scott and Peter Walsh, 'National data on new interwar manufacturing plants and extensions, 1919–1938', deposited 2005.

Note: * Excludes two plants that could not be classified by area.

This heavy concentration of plants in compact estates casts doubt on the assumption that the availability of large sites was an overriding determinant of location for most plants that moved to these areas. In addition to the rapid escalation of land values, noted above, the high density of plants on these estates, together with the presence of some

60 See Chapter Nine.

61 Ibid.

62 Martin, 'Industry in inner London'.

very large plants that accounted for a significant proportion of their aggregate acreage, suggests that typical firms cannot have been particularly large. This is corroborated by Table 8.3, which shows that the proportion of plants with 100 or more employees was roughly equal to that in the furniture and printing boroughs (though well above that in the clothing boroughs). In order to discover whether plants become concentrated in the electrical engineering boroughs at some higher employment level, Table 8.4 examines the distribution of new London plants between the County of London, outer-London electrical engineering boroughs, and other outer-London boroughs, at employment ranges over 100. No simple relationship between size and location is evident; while the proportion of plants in the County of London drops considerably at the 400–599 employment range, the highest concentration of plants at this range is found in the other outer-London boroughs. Meanwhile the County of London's proportion of plants rises again at the 600–899 employment range. Plants with 900 or more workers are highly concentrated in the outer electrical engineering boroughs, though there are only eleven plants in this group.[63]

Table 8.5: Initial employment per plant in the County of London and in outer London, 1919–35

SIC	County of London			Outer London		
	Mean	Median	Coefficient of variation	Mean	Median	Coefficient of variation
22	74.8	57	0.57	51.3	50	0.49
24	108.3	50	2.18	88.6	56.5	1.25
25	87.3	51	1.05	79.9	52.5	0.96
31	86.1	50	1.08	82.7	60	0.88
32	80.8	55	0.74	63.7	46.5	0.85
34	97.7	50	1.24	137.1	60	1.74
35	78.4	66	0.50	130.6	60	1.57
36	83.5	70	0.50	135.4	72.5	1.05
37	89.5	78	0.58	87.1	62.5	0.82
41/2	113.9	60	1.20	140.9	57	2.67
43	68.8	55	0.60	96.3	50	1.09
44	58.9	50	0.63	139.8	100	0.83
45	62.9	50	0.94	85.4	50	1.00
46	62.0	50	0.86	78.3	60	0.86
47	88.2	57	1.24	81.9	60	0.73
48	56.3	50	0.40	194.0	90	1.35
49	69.7	50	0.73	111.1	62	1.32
Total	74.0	50	1.12	101.5	58	1.65

Sources and notes: As for Table 8.2.

63 With the exception of one aircraft plant, which was established in 1938 and could not therefore have significantly influenced local interwar industrial development, the highest initial employment of any London plant was 3,000.

Data on median initial employment per plant (derived from the GLRDC register, which provides more precise estimates than the SID's) also fail to show a strong relationship with location, as shown in Table 8.5. Median initial employment in outer London was only eight workers in excess of that in the County of London; the difference in mean employment is larger, but still only 27.5 workers. Differences in median employment are also small for individual sectors heavily concentrated in outer-London, though again differences in mean employment are sometimes substantial. Evidence regarding Slough casts further doubt on the argument that the development of these clusters was primarily driven by the need for large premises. From around 1927 Slough Estates pursued a policy of avoiding large firms, to limit potential losses arising from the departure of individual tenants.[64] As Table 8.5 shows, Slough had a smaller proportion of firms with an initial employment of over 100 than even the clothing boroughs. Yet its industrial structure was broadly similar to those of the outer-London electrical engineering boroughs.

Space requirements are determined not only by employment, but by single or multiple floor occupancy and floorspace per worker. While multiple-floor occupancy was common for smaller plants in clothing and other traditional inner-London sectors, it was of much less importance for substantial modern paper and printing or woodworking factories. Comparison of floorspace per worker ratios is more problematic, as the earliest British data concern firms on government industrial estates in the north-east of England and Wales, at September 1948 (covering 349 firms and 38,264 workers). These indicate that while clothing firms had a particularly low floorspace per worker (134 sq. ft.), most sectors strongly represented in the electrical engineering boroughs had ratios of between 212 and 262 sq. ft., while paper and printing and woodworking firms had ratios of 290 and 252 sq. ft. respectively.[65] Sectoral data on horsepower per worker in 1930, found by P. Sargant Florence to be the best available contemporary proxy for capital-intensity, provide another indicator of space-intensity, as capital-intensive sectors tend to be space-intensive. Again many sectors over-represented in the electrical engineering boroughs were not more capital-intensive, by this measure, than furniture or printing.[66] Significantly, electrical engineering does not appear particularly space-intensive by either measure and, as shown in Table 8.5, it did not have a high median employment per plant.

While factor endowments were key to the initial industrial development of these boroughs, locational externalities played an important role in fostering their continued expansion during the 1930s, despite rising land values and shortages of *local* supplies of *suitable* labour. These areas offered substantial intra-metropolitan urbanisation economies regarding market access; for example, Smith stressed the importance of access to the West End, which the new arterial roads brought within 25 minutes of most West Middlesex factories, as a factor attracting manufacturers of 'luxuries'. Good transport links to the London docks and City-based international

---

64 Michael Cassell, *Long Lease! The Story of Slough Estates 1920–1991* (London, 1991), p. 56.

65 See Peter Scott, 'British regional policy 1945–51: a lost opportunity', *Twentieth Century British History*, 8 (1997), 358–82, p. 374.

66 Florence, *Investment, Location, and Size of Plant*, pp. 90–100 and Appendix IV.

marketing facilities were also found to be important to many firms.[67] Yet, as these typically produced standardised, and often branded, goods, with long production runs, they did not face the same requirement for near-constant interaction with customers that characterised the clothing and job printing trades.

Proximity to other manufacturers appears to have been of greater importance; evidence points to the presence of dynamic externalities, operating at both the inter-sectoral and intra-sectoral levels. Such externalities were particularly important, as firms in these areas were still relatively small – the median London electrical engineering plant with 25 or more workers having an initial employment of only around 55. As such, they often relied extensively on other firms for components and services and, as their products were often subject to rapid technological change, proximity facilitated close cooperation regarding innovations that would require these firms' participation.

The most over-represented sectors were the metal-using industries; as Table 6.4 shows, SIC's 22 and 31–37 accounted for an average of 52.20 per cent of plants across the twelve London electrical engineering boroughs, compared to only 25.18 per cent for all new plants in the London region. These shared both important input-output linkages and common ancillary services. Smith noted the development of an interrelated industrial complex in West Middlesex, based around motor vehicles but including a variety of component, accessory, and ancillary firms classified under other sectors – such as electrical or mechanical engineering.[68] In Enfield the establishment of Enfield Rolling Mills (which operated one of only two British plants for fire-refining copper), led to the development of a substantial local electric cable industry, while the demands of these, and other, large local firms encouraged the growth of a contract engineering base.[69] A 1951 study of the Slough Estate indicated that most firms had extensive local linkages (the main exception being large plants of over 500 workers). Quite a number were found to trade with 20 or more local firms, linkages being particularly prevalent in engineering-related sectors.[70] Ford attracted many suppliers to the Ford Estate and other areas of Dagenham – though the type of 'hub-and-spoke' development that this represented, based around a single dominant firm, was not evident in the other boroughs.[71]

Rosenberg externalities thus appear to have been significant. Yet complementarities regarding production methods and labour requirements appear to have been of still greater importance. Some of the key innovations influencing costs, productivity, and profitability concerned factors common not only to metal-using sectors, but to these boroughs' other over-represented industries. These had important functional complementarities in terms of the organisation and layout of production and

67 Smith, *Industries of Greater London*, pp. 80–84.

68 Ibid., p. 88.

69 NCSRS, C1/137, report on Enfield by J. Forrester, May 1941.

70 W. Davies, 'The nature and significance of trading estates with special reference to the Treforest and Slough Estates', unpublished MA dissertation, University of Wales, 1951.

71 Peter Scott, 'Industrial estates and British industrial development: 1897–1939', *Business History*, 43, 2 (2001), 73–98, p. 83; A. Markusen, 'Sticky places in slippery space: a typology of industrial districts', *Economic Geography*, 72 (1996), 293–313.

associated issues concerning the labour process, such as the recruitment and efficient deployment of cheap labour. Despite their sectoral diversity, many plants shared key product characteristics. Analysis of the GLRDC register (which, unlike the SID's, includes firms' names) reveals a high proportion of nationally-known branded consumer goods manufacturers, encompassing all the major over-represented sectors.[72] Production of standardised goods contributed to common process characteristics that were the major source of functional commonalities.

Unlike post-war functional specialisation, based around the geographical division of functions within particular firms via branch plant formation, interwar manufacturing plants generally undertook the broad range of activities associated with the firm's production. Yet in these clusters the dominant activity of most firms (in terms of employment and value added) involved assembly or other simplified, repetitive, tasks, entailing broadly similar skills. Consumer product manufacturers in the engineering and metal trades, chemicals, and food & drink processing, were shown by industry-studies in the *New Survey* to have experienced a marked convergence towards common process characteristics involving the growth of un/semi-skilled 'repetition work', accompanied by increased employment of women and juveniles and the spread of piece rate remuneration systems.[73] These findings are corroborated by Smith's survey, which found that the bulk of West Middlesex firms manufactured branded consumer products in which assembly operations by unskilled, mainly female, workers played an important part.[74] Even textile plants in these areas were dominated by branded consumer goods manufacturers – mainly in hosiery and knitwear – who located outside traditional centres for these trades in order to employ new production methods that required less skilled labour and would have been subject to union restrictions in traditional centres.[75] Thus, while traditional industrial districts were product-based clusters composed of process-specialised firms, these new industrial areas were dominated by product-based firms with common process characteristics.

Firms in these boroughs demonstrated a preference for cheap workers with the necessary 'flexibility' to accept new systems for machine pacing, remuneration, and the simplification of tasks into narrow, repetitive operations – as discussed in Chapter 9. Common labour requirements in turn raised substantial possibilities for knowledge spillovers regarding the organisation of production, and the pacing, monitoring, and payment of workers. Techniques aimed at intensifying worker effort, such as the Bedaux system, were introduced by a number of prominent firms in these areas, particularly American and other overseas-based multinationals.[76] While there are no London-based studies of the local diffusion of such practices, E.D. Smithies' study of

72 London Metropolitan Archives, MCC/MIN/65/3.

73 LSE, *New Survey... Volume II*, p. 7; *Volume V*, pp. 26–27 and 200.

74 Smith, *Industries of Greater London*, p. 104.

75 S. D. Chapman, *Hosiery and Knitwear. Four Centuries of Small-Scale Industry in Britain, c. 1589-2000* (Oxford, 2002), pp. 174–8; Richard Gurnham, *A History of the Trade Union Movement in the Hosiery and Knitwear Industry, 1776–1976* (Leicester, 1976).

76 Miriam Glucksmann, *Women Assemble: Women Workers and the New Industries in Inter-war Britain* (London, 1990), p. 175.

Luton emphasised the demonstration effect on local manufacturers of Vauxhall's plant layout and production line techniques, as well as the plant organisation and personnel management systems of Electrolux and Skefco.[77]

Conclusions

During the interwar period Greater London constituted the main centre for new consumer-goods manufacturers, with even the West Midlands losing ground to London's new industrial suburbs and satellite communities. Its inter-regional advantages included unparalleled marketing and business and financial services facilities, based on the growing concentration of control over these activities by national companies headquartered in the capital. Meanwhile its major industrial clusters offered strong locational externalities. These clusters were of two broad types: traditional, centrally-located, industrial districts of craft-based, consumer-goods industries, providing Marshallian externalities, and new industrial communities in less central areas, encompassing a broader range of complementary sectors and providing strong inter-sectoral, as well as intra-sectoral, externalities. Statistical analysis of plant location patterns in London's 33 densely-industrialised boroughs, using correlation and factor analysis, corroborates these findings. Location patterns for clothing and printing are found to be weakly related to those in other sectors, while the clustering of electrical engineering plants is shown to be strongly related to plants in metal-using and assembly industries, but weakly related to sectors with which it had no significant production or functional linkages.[78]

London's electrical engineering boroughs and the outer-London furniture boroughs – both in areas of war-time industrial development and post-war arterial road construction – attracted most of the firms decentralising from inner-London, their locational externalities out-weighing the attractions of cheaper sites beyond London's outer-rim. As the *New Survey* noted, while during the nineteenth century the transition of a London industry from craft to mechanised production had often been accompanied by plant migration from London to the provinces, this pattern had now been largely superseded by a centrifugal movement within London.[79] This chapter has highlighted two key factors behind the rapid growth of new industrial areas in outer-London – the spread of industrial estates and the development of a new un/semi-skilled manufacturing workforce. These are further explored in the following chapters.

77 E. D. Smithies, 'The contrast between north and south in England 1918–1939: a study of economic, social and political problems with particular reference to the experience of Burnley, Halifax, Ipswich, and Luton', unpublished Ph.D. thesis, University of Leeds, 1974, p. 65.

78 Peter Scott and Peter Walsh, 'Patterns and determinants of manufacturing plant location in interwar London', *Economic History Review*, LVII, 1 (2004), 109–41, pp. 135–7.

79 LSE, *New Survey... Volume II*, p. 24.

Chapter Nine

Industrial estates and new industrial communities

Introduction

One of the key features of economic growth in the South East between the wars was the emergence of a broad area of new industrial development, spreading northwards and westwards from the outer-London suburbs to the market towns of Hertfordshire, Berkshire, Bedfordshire, Oxfordshire, and even those parts of Surrey and Essex that the new arterial roads brought close to London. Many had no significant manufacturing tradition prior to the First World War, yet proved very attractive to firms in the new assembly and branded goods sectors. This chapter examines both the factors drawing industry to new industrial centres beyond London's borders and the attractions of industrial estates – which constituted the main foci of industrialisation in the rapidly expanding areas of outer-London.

New industrial communities beyond Greater London

Table 9.1 provides information on seven of the most rapidly growing industrial centres outside Greater London. These include five London 'satellite towns' – Letchworth, Welwyn, Slough, Watford, and Luton, together with Coventry – the most rapidly growing centre of the West Midlands, and Oxford, which had important industrial links with both London and the West Midlands. The seven centres were all dominated by engineering-related and assembly industries, together with printing (generally involving activities such as books and standardised commercial stationery, where frequent face-to-face contact with customers and rapid turn-around times were not important).

The centres around London have a number of important common features. The attraction of firms decentralising from inner-London and/or overseas multinationals proved key to their growth,[1] while in each centre a promoting authority had played a leading role in attracting these firms. At Luton and Watford the role of promoter

---

1 Nuffield College Library, Oxford, Nuffield College Social Reconstruction Survey papers [hereafter NCSRS], CI/58 (Part 1), Hertfordshire Local Survey Report, January 1943; W. G. Holford, 'The location and design of trading estates', *Journal of the Town Planning Institute* (March 1939), p. 154; NA: HLG90/440, Ministry of Town and Country Planning, New Towns Research Section, 'Welwyn Garden City: some aspects of its economic history', June 1950 [hereafter Welwyn report]; Royal Commission on The Distribution of The Industrial Population, *Minutes of Evidence* (London, 1940), p. 342.

had been taken by 'new industry committees' formed by their local councils and business communities prior to the First World War;[2] in Letchworth and Welwyn it was played by the garden city companies that developed these towns; while in Slough it was filled by Slough Estates Ltd, developers of the Slough Trading Estate. These promoting agencies provided factories and/or sites for in-coming firms, or assistance with acquiring sites (sometimes in combination with other inducements). They also engaged in extensive advertising and other publicity to attract manufacturers.

Table 9.1: Examples of seven rapidly-growing industrial centres outside Greater London

Centre	Population 1921	Population 1939	Main industries
Letchworth	10,313	17,400[a]	Engineering, clothing, vehicles, printing, metal industries, furniture, scientific instruments
Welwyn	430[b]	14,100	Metal industries, chemicals, electrical engineering
Watford	45,910	66,520	Printing & paper, food & drink, electrical engineering, motor vehicles
Slough	16,000	60,000[e]	Motor vehicles, food and drink, electrical engineering, chemicals, musical instruments
Luton	57,075	94,110	Motor vehicles, engineering, hats
Oxford	67,290[c]	96,350[d]	Motor vehicles, printing
Coventry	128,152	224,267	Motor vehicles and cycles, metal goods, electrical engineering, mechanical engineering, rayon

Source: Peter Scott, 'Women, other "fresh" workers, and the new manufacturing workforce of interwar Britain', International Review of Social History, *45 (2000), 449–74, p. 457.*

Notes: a – end of 1938; b – 1920; c – includes area covered by a 1929 boundary extension; d – 1937; e – 1938. N.B.: late 1930s population figures are estimates.

2 Stephen Bunker, '"A small town outside Vauxhall": Luton in the twentieth century', unpublished paper, presented at ESRC Colloquium on Industry and Urbanisation, University College London, 8 May 1993; W. Francis Goodrich, *Watford: Its Advantages as an Industrial and Residential centre* (Watford, c. 1908), pp. 10 and 12.

Rapidly expanding London satellite towns were generally situated close to major long-distance roads leading north or west from London, such as the Great North Road (A1: Welwyn, Letchworth), Bath Road (A4: Slough), and Manchester Road (A6: Luton) while also having good rail links to London and the Midlands. They combined good transport links with lower land prices than those of the outer-London suburbs; for example in 1932 sites at Welwyn were estimated to cost around £800 per acre, compared to £2,500 per acre in Acton, Willesden and Cricklewood; £1,500 in Merton, Micham and Croydon; and £1,000 in Hayes, Southall, Purfleet, and Barking.[3] The 'new' character of these areas (as centres for their principal interwar industries) also appears to have been an important attraction for industrialists. There is strong evidence that manufacturers deliberately located outside their industries' established centres, partly to escape union restrictions on production methods. Contemporary evidence suggests that firms avoided both areas with a general reputation for union militancy and those with a strong union presence in their particular industry.[4] Meanwhile the availability of a large pool of cheap, un-unionised workers from outside the established manufacturing workforce constituted a strong positive attraction to industrialists. Innovations in production and labour management methods proved easier in the less regulated labour markets of London's 'outer ring' than, for example, in inner-London, a factor highlighted by the *New Survey* as having contributed to substantial outward plant migration.[5]

The remaining centres, Coventry and Oxford, developed their new industries along more evolutionary lines. As noted in Chapter Three, Coventry had made a successful transition from a ribbon and watch-making industrial base of artisan workshops to cycle and, later, motor vehicle manufacture, initially using the same artisan producers. Small scale was initially compensated for by extensive sub-contracting and components purchases from Birmingham and the Black Country, before the more successful firms moved to factory production.[6] Oxford's motor industry similarly developed from much smaller-scale enterprises in the cycle trade, initially relying on extensive components purchases from West Midlands' suppliers.[7]

While Britain had very low rates of inter-regional manufacturing plant migration or branch plant formation during this period, new industrial centres in areas of the South East outside London appear to have attracted higher proportions of such plants than was the case for the major outer-London industrial areas. Of the first 50 firms established in Letchworth, 12 per cent had migrated from areas of England outside London; similarly 12.5 per cent of the 128 firms established on the Welwyn trading estate during the interwar period (for which information on their origins is available) were transfers or

3 D.H. Smith, *The Industries of Greater London* (London, 1933), p. 163.

4 NA, BT56/40/CIA1800/71; S. R. Dennison, *The Location of Industry and the Depressed Areas* (London, 1939), p. 80.

5 LSE, *The New Survey of London Life and Labour. Volume II: London Industries I* (London, 1931), pp. 5–6.

6 P. W. Carr, 'Engineering workers and the rise of labour in Coventry, 1914–1939', unpublished Ph.D. thesis, University of Warwick, 1978, Chapter One.

7 P. W. S. Andrews and Elizabeth Brunner, *The Life of Lord Nuffield* (Oxford, 1955).

branches of firms from areas of Britain other than London (almost three quarters of which were branches).[8] Meanwhile the garden cities also attracted substantial numbers of London plants (transfers and branches accounting for 22 per cent of Letchworth, and 14.1 per cent of Welwyn, plants); and overseas enterprises (comprising 18 per cent and 22.7 per cent of plants respectively). However new firms made the largest contribution to their plant numbers, comprising 48 per cent of firms at Letchworth and 50.8 per cent at Welwyn. Watford was more dependent on firms decentralising from London, it being estimated that around half its firms had migrated from the capital (particularly Islington, Bermondsey, and Soho). This was strongly linked to its high representation of printing firms: London-based printers found Watford an attractive location as it was just outside the London Wage Scale area and thus allowed them to pay Provincial Area wages.[9]

With the exception of Slough, none of the seven centres received sufficient firms with 25 or more employees during 1932–38 to be included in the national analysis of 'substantial' clusters (with 25 or more new plants). Coventry, Oxford, and Luton were dominated by large firms, many of which had been established before 1918. However, the centres nearer London mainly attracted what were initially small-scale enterprises. For example, Welwyn hosted 113 manufacturing firms over the interwar period; yet the combined GLRDC/SID dataset records only 13 plants with an initial employment of 25 or more. Furthermore most of these were of modest size, the GLRDC/SIDs recording only three plants at Welwyn and four at Watford with an initial employment of over 100.

The London satellite centres also generally had relatively few manufacturing plants that had been established there before 1918. The expansion of what were initially small firms thus appears to have been key to their industrial growth. For example, the five biggest firms at Welwyn in 1948 had experienced an increase in their combined workforce of well over ten-fold since their establishment there (between 1926 and 1936).[10] The largest, Murphy Radio Co., commenced operations at Welwyn in 1929 in a 1,700 sq. ft 'nest' factory (designed for very small start-up enterprises), employing six people; by the end of 1937 it employed around 700–800.[11] Similarly, some of the most successful companies on the Slough Estate, such as Mars and High Duty Alloys, were initially very small firms, established in nest factories.[12] The experience of these centres thus illustrates the importance of what were initially very small enterprises to industrial growth in, at least, some new industrial areas.

8 Holford, 'The location and design of Trading Estates'; NA, HLG90/440, Welwyn report. Firms of foreign origin included plant transfers and firms launched by refugee industrialists during the 1930s, in addition to multinational enterprises.

9 NCSRS, CI/58 (Part 1), Hertfordshire Local Survey report, January 1943.

10 NA, HLG90/440, Welwyn report.

11 Modern Records Centre, University of Warwick [hereafter MRC], MSS 200/F/3/S2/19/1, 'Location of Industry', paper presented by S.A. Sadler Forster to the Federation of British Industries' committee on the geographical distribution of the industrial population, 3rd December 1937; R. D. Kaunitz, 'The British trading estate, a study in commercial, local, and central government enterprise', unpublished Ph.D. thesis, Harvard University, 1950, p. 48.

12 L. Nevard, 'The industrial estate – an instrument of social policy', unpublished M. Phil thesis, University of Southampton, 1972, p. 40.

Industrial estates as new industrial centres

All of the outer-London areas with 'substantial' new plant clusters hosted industrial estates, while these also dominated industrial development in some of the most rapidly growing London satellite towns – such as Slough, Letchworth, and Welwyn. Industrial estates accounted for a substantial proportion of new interwar plants in London and the South East, especially with respect to firms producing branded consumer goods (or their components). It is therefore worthwhile reviewing this form of industrial development, and the advantages it offered manufacturing enterprises, in some detail.

Industrial estates were of four basic types. The first, pioneered at Trafford Park in Manchester, was the dock estate. These were established alongside dock facilities, usually covered several hundred acres, and were primarily designed for relatively heavy industry, Other major dock estates included the Bromborough Port Estate at Merseyside, developed by Unilever in the early 1930s (partly to encourage fuller use of the dock, power station, and other infrastructure developed at Port Sunlight) and a similar project launched by Ford at Dagenham from 1931, again partly to support extensive infrastructure development.[13] Less successful dock estate developments were launched at Colwick, on the river Trent near Nottingham, and at Southampton Docks.

The second type was the large free-standing estate. These also covered several hundred acres, but catered for lighter industry, relying on good road and rail transport links. The best examples are Slough and Park Royal, employing 28,500 and 30,000 workers respectively by 1939.[14] The large free-standing estate also formed the model for the government's three major industrial estates developed under its Special Areas initiative. With the exception of Park Royal,[15] most of these estates engaged in extensive provision of on-site utilities and transport infrastructure.

The third type of estate, the factory estate, was similar to the free-standing estate but was smaller in size and offered fewer on-site utilities. Factory estates were generally under 100 acres in size and were almost all located within broader zones of new industrial development in outer-London. Their growth mushroomed during the 1930s, new developments being dominated by four companies – Allnatt, Commercial Structures, John Laing & Son, and Percy Bilton – who collectively developed around 26 estates on the fringes of the London conurbation. These were mainly small estates of around 20 acres, but included one or two more substantial projects of over 100 acres. Figure 9.1 shows Bilton's largest factory estate, developed on a 60-acre site at Perivale from 1931. This was fronted by the Hoover building and accommodated firms producing a range of branded and assembly products – such

13 Quoted in Mira Wilkins and Frank Ernest Hill, *American Business Abroad: Ford on Six Continents* (Detroit, 1964), p. 204.

14 Royal Commission on the Industrial Population, *Report* (London, 1940), p. 285; NA, HLG 52/746, Report by London Passenger Transport Board and main line rail companies to the Technical Committee of the Standing Conference on London Regional Planning, 18 November 1938.

15 Park Royal was unusual in that it was developed by several different promoters rather than constituting a single unified estate.

Figure 9.1: Percy Bilton's Perivale Industrial Centre, Ealing, c. 1936

Source: Percy Bilton Ltd, 'Twixt Green Fields and the City': Percy Bilton Model Factory Estates *(London, c. 1937).*

as radios, clocks, cosmetics, paint, condensers, and cider. Laing, Allnatt, and Bilton combined at least some industrial estate developments with adjacent house building. Laing was the most ambitious in this respect, developing estates as part of integrated projects combining residential, industrial, and commercial districts.[16] Their largest development was the Elstree estate, launched in the late 1930s, which included a 130 acre industrial estate and 1,800 houses.[17]

The final type was the garden city estate, developed as part of an integrated programme of new residential community development. The best examples are the two garden cities launched by the Garden City and Town Planning Association as model communities – Letchworth (1903) and Welwyn Garden City (1920). During the interwar years garden city ideas also influenced the development of purely commercial developments that combined industrial estates and housing, such as Laing's Elstree estate, the Thames Land Company's West Thurrock estate, and Lever Brothers' Bromborough Port estate.[18]

They also influenced council housing programmes – several major local authorities developed municipal housing in the form of integrated satellite communities, complete with their own industrial estates. The best examples are Wythenshawe, developed by Manchester City Council, and Liverpool Corporation's Speke development. Less ambitiously, the Doncaster County Borough launched the Wheatley Hall estate in around 1928 in an attempt to zone new industrial development and combine it with new municipal housing.[19] Meanwhile the Bilston and Bristol corporations developed estates purely as local employment-creation measures. From 1936 national government also instigated industrial development in Britain's regionally-assisted Special Areas, as discussed in Chapter 13.

The industrial estate had emerged following the advent of smoke-free electric power, which enabled large numbers of plants using powered machinery to cluster together while still maintaining a relatively 'clean' environment. The world's first industrial estate had been founded at Trafford Park in 1897, though the development of further estates was initially slow, as shown in Table 9.2. Although the number of estates and their employment experienced rapid and accelerating growth during the first quarter of the century, as late as 1927 there were still only 13 estates, employing around 55,000 people. Their number and employment more than doubled during the next five years and had more than doubled again, to 65 estates accommodating around 285,000 employees, by 1939. The garden city and central and local government estates were of relatively minor importance compared to purely commercial estates, collectively accounting for only around 12.3 per cent of estate employment in 1939.

---

16 Roy Coad, *Laing: the Biography of Sir John W.Laing, C.B.E. (1879–1978)* (London, 1979), pp. 102–103.

17 John Laing & Son Ltd., *Laings Factory Sites: on Barnet Bypass Road* (undated leaflet, c. 1938).

18 Peter Scott, 'Planning for profit: the garden city concept and private sector industrial estate development during the inter-war years', *Planning History*, Vol. 16 (1994), 9–15.

19 W. Davies, 'The nature and significance of trading estates with special reference to the Treforest and Slough estates', unpublished MA dissertation, University of Wales, 1951, p. 269.

Table 9.2: The growth of British industrial estates and their employment, 1900–1939

Year	1900		1910		1920		1927		1932		1939	
Estates	No.	Employment	No.	Employment	No.	Employment	No.	Employment	No.	Employment	No.	Employment
Commercial	2	5,080	3	11,700	6	35,000	10	49,587	25	112,565	48	250,416
Garden city	0	0	1	2,470	2	3,800	2	5,739	2	7,500	2	15,250
Local govt.	0	0	0	0	0	0	1	N/A	2	N/A	5	10,118
National govt.	0	0	0	0	0	0	0	0	0	0	10	9,870
Total	2	5,080	4	14,170	8	38,800	13	55,326	29	120,065	65	285,654

Sources: UK Data Archive, AHDS History, SN 5191, Peter Scott, 'Growth of British industrial estates, 1900–1939', deposited 2005; Peter Scott, 'Industrial estates and British industrial development: 1897–1939', Business History*, 43, 2 (2001), 73–98.*

While estate employment only represented a small proportion of the UK manufacturing workforce in 1939, estate plants accounted for a significant proportion of its interwar growth. Between 1920 and 1939 industrial estates gained an estimated 247,000 workers, while the UK's employed insured manufacturing workforce rose by roughly 564,300 between 1923 and 1938.[20] Interwar estate employment growth was also substantial compared to that of Britain's other rapidly-expanding manufacturing centres, out-stripping the collective *total population* growth of Coventry, Luton, Oxford, and Watford – of about 183,000 people.

Table 9.3: The regional distribution of employment on British industrial estates in 1932 and 1939

	1932		1939	
Region	**Employment**	**%**	**Employment**	**%**
Greater London	52,465	43.70	152,266	53.30
Other South East	19,500	16.24	50,400	17.64
Total South East	71,965	59.94	202,666	70.95
South West	0	0.00	Negligible	Negligible
East Anglia	0	0.00	0.00	0.00
East Midlands	c.1,000	0.83	c.1,000	0.35
West Midlands	c.500	0.42	3,588	1.26
North West	46,600	38.81	68,430	23.96
Yorkshire & Humberside	0	0.00	100	0.04
North	0	0.00	4,880	1.71
Scotland	0	0.00	2,000	0.70
Wales	0	0.00	2,990	1.05
Total	120,065	100.00	285,654	100.00

Sources: As for Table 9.2.

Note: The employment figures for the East Midlands, and for the West Midlands in 1932, are based on indirect employment estimates for the only estate in each region, which are accurate only to a rough order of magnitude.

20 Department of Employment, *British Labour Statistics: Historical Abstract 1868–1968* (London, 1971), Table 114. Data refers to workers aged 16 and over in 1923 and 16–64 in 1938.

Estate employment was strongly concentrated in the South East, as is shown in Table 9.3. In 1932 an estimated 43.7 per cent of national industrial estate employment was in Greater London, while the South East as a whole contained around 60 per cent. The only substantial provincial estates were in the North West: at Trafford Park and Bromborough Port. Despite central and local government estate development in less prosperous regions, the concentration of estate employment in the South East increased substantially during the 1930s, Britain's provincial regions accounting for only around 29 per cent of national estate employment by 1939. Figure 9.2 shows the locations of estates outside the Greater London area. Private sector estates (including the garden cities) were restricted to the South East, the Midlands, and the North West. Government estates were developed in Britain's depressed industrial periphery, while local authority estates were based in less peripheral areas, which were experiencing some employment problems but which had sufficient economic vitality to undertake estate development using municipal funds.[21]

During the 1930s estate development became increasingly concentrated in Greater London, which accounted for 39 of Britain's 65 industrial estates and 53.3 per cent of national estate employment by 1939. Figure 9.3 shows the approximate locations of estates in the Greater London area, demonstrating their clustering along the new arterial road network – often on the sites of war-time munitions factories. Those boroughs in West Middlesex and the Lea Valley, identified in the previous chapter as constituting the main clusters of new manufacturing plants in outer-London, also represented the main concentrations of estates.

It is possible to examine the contribution of industrial estates to industrial development in the South East over the period 1932–38, using data from the SID's.[22] While in many cases the SID localities were not sufficiently specific to isolate individual estates, this proved possible for six major estates, which collectively accounted for 43.0 per cent of estate employment growth in this region from 1932–39.[23] The SID's record 204 new factories or extensions on these estates. The data were grossed-up to provide aggregate estimates for all estates in the South East using a multiple (2.3236) based on total estate employment growth in the region from 1932–39 divided by employment growth on the six estates. As new firms and extensions involving less than 25 employees are omitted, such a procedure substantially underestimates the number of factories established on estates (and omits the type of firms that occupied nest factories).

Estate plants are estimated to have accounted for 21.8 per cent of new factories in the South East (including transfers) and 22.66 per cent of initial employment in new and extended factories. Their relative importance was greatest in outer-London – the London Passenger Transport Board estimated that 'Of the 470 factories opened or extended in the outer [London] areas during the years 1933 to 1936, some two fifths were established on such factory estates.'[24] Transfers of production from other districts accounted for 30.1 per cent of new estate plants, compared to 25.3 per cent for all new plants in London and 11.9 per cent for plants in the rest of the South East. Meanwhile branches accounted for only 6.9 per cent of estate plants, compared to 9.0 per cent for Greater London and 12.9 per cent for the rest of the South East. Industrial estates thus appear to have been important reception centres for plants decentralising from inner-London, but not for firms expanding via branch plant formation. Estates also appear to have attracted a high proportion of new plants established by overseas multinationals. Analysis of 132 overseas-based enterprises which established production in Britain from November 1931 to the early months of 1933 indicated that at least 29.5 per cent (or 38.2 per cent of those which located in the South East) obtained factories on industrial estates.[25] Overseas multinationals proved important to the development of a number of estates, including Hayes, Park Royal, Slough, Letchworth, Welwyn, and Perivale.[26]

Table 9.4 provides estimates of the industrial composition of new plants and extensions on industrial estates in the South East, compared to all new/extended plants in the region (again using grossed-up data from the six estates) together with location quotients (calculated so as to compare each sector's contribution to total new estate firms/extensions with the proportion of all South East firms and extensions in that sector). The Table reveals that for some sectors industrial estates were of considerable importance. Around 72.9 per cent of the region's new chemicals plants and extensions are estimated to have been located on estates. Other strongly over-represented industries include metal manufacturing, attracting 63.4 per cent of plants and extensions, motor vehicles (53.6 per cent),[27] electrical engineering (42.2 per cent), rubber and plastics (33.2 per cent), food, drink and tobacco (32.9 per cent), other metal goods (28.5 per cent) and instrument engineering (27.9 per cent). These sectors, which broadly correspond to those identified by Chandler as the 'new industries' of the 'second industrial revolution',[28] accounted for 64.2 per cent of estate plants and extensions, compared to only 33.7 per cent for the South East as a whole.

One over-represented industry which does not fit this definition is textiles. Yet estate plants operated in sections of the textile industry such as hosiery, knitwear, and ribbon manufacture, which involved a high proportion of branded consumer goods. They had also witnessed a substantial conversion to continental production methods during the 1930s – involving machinery not hitherto generally used in Britain – accompanied by a switch in the location of new plants to areas outside established textile centres in order to avoid union restrictions on production methods.[29] Other traditional industries, such as non-metallic mineral products, leather goods, and clothing and footwear, are shown to be significantly under-represented.

The advantages of industrial estates as manufacturing locations

Industrial estates offered a number of advantages to manufacturers. One important benefit was a reduction in start-up costs, by converting the fixed cost of the factory into a rental stream. One of the major factors which made the financing of small manufacturing businesses more costly than similarly-sized tertiary sector enterprises was the need to find the full purchase cost of premises. While shop and office property could be easily rented, or mortgaged, to reduce its immediate cost, such facilities were not available for factories, as they had a low re-sale value. Factory buildings had traditionally been too specific in design to be easily sold or let to alternative tenants should the business in question fail, while suitable locations were sufficiently diffused for there to be less of a premium value associated with factory sites than

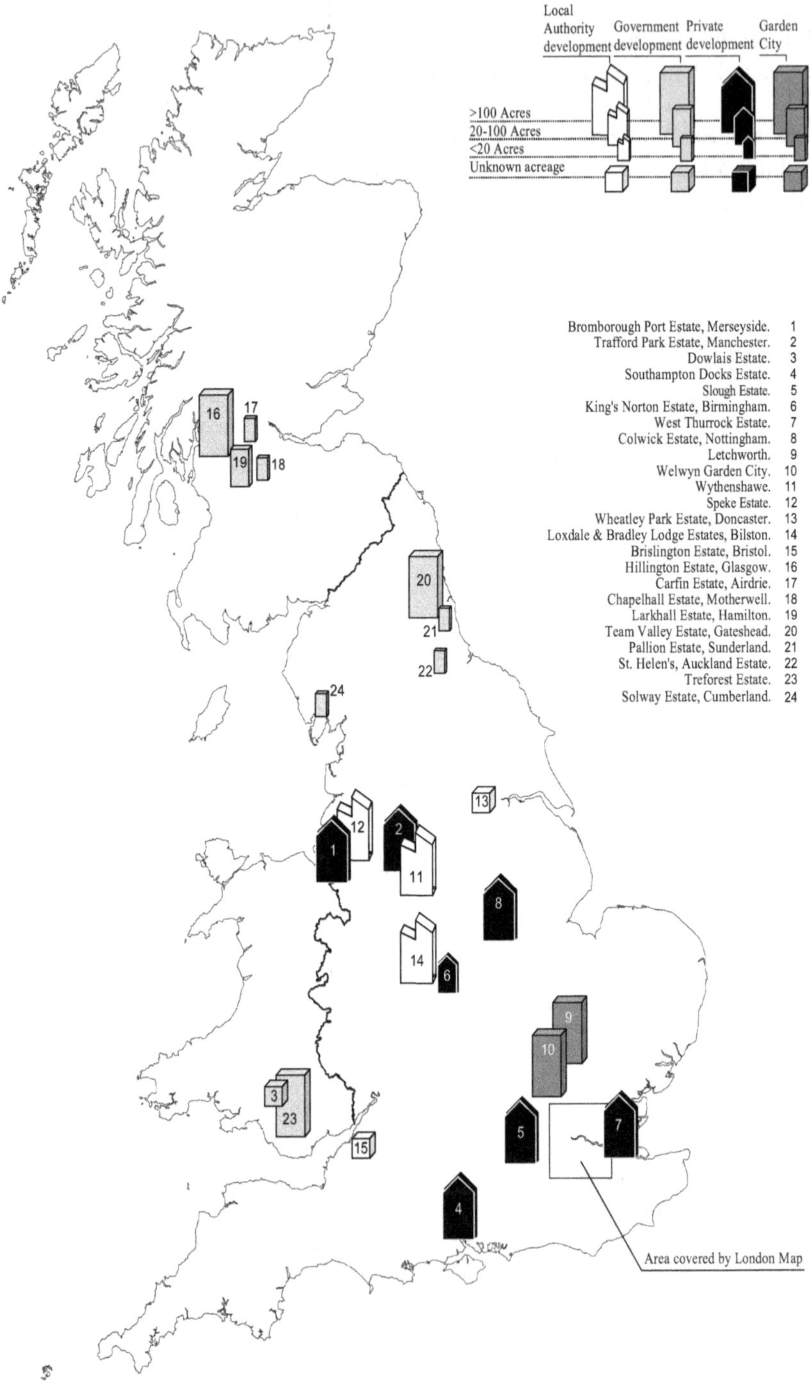

Figure 9.2: Industrial estates established outside the Greater London area by 1939

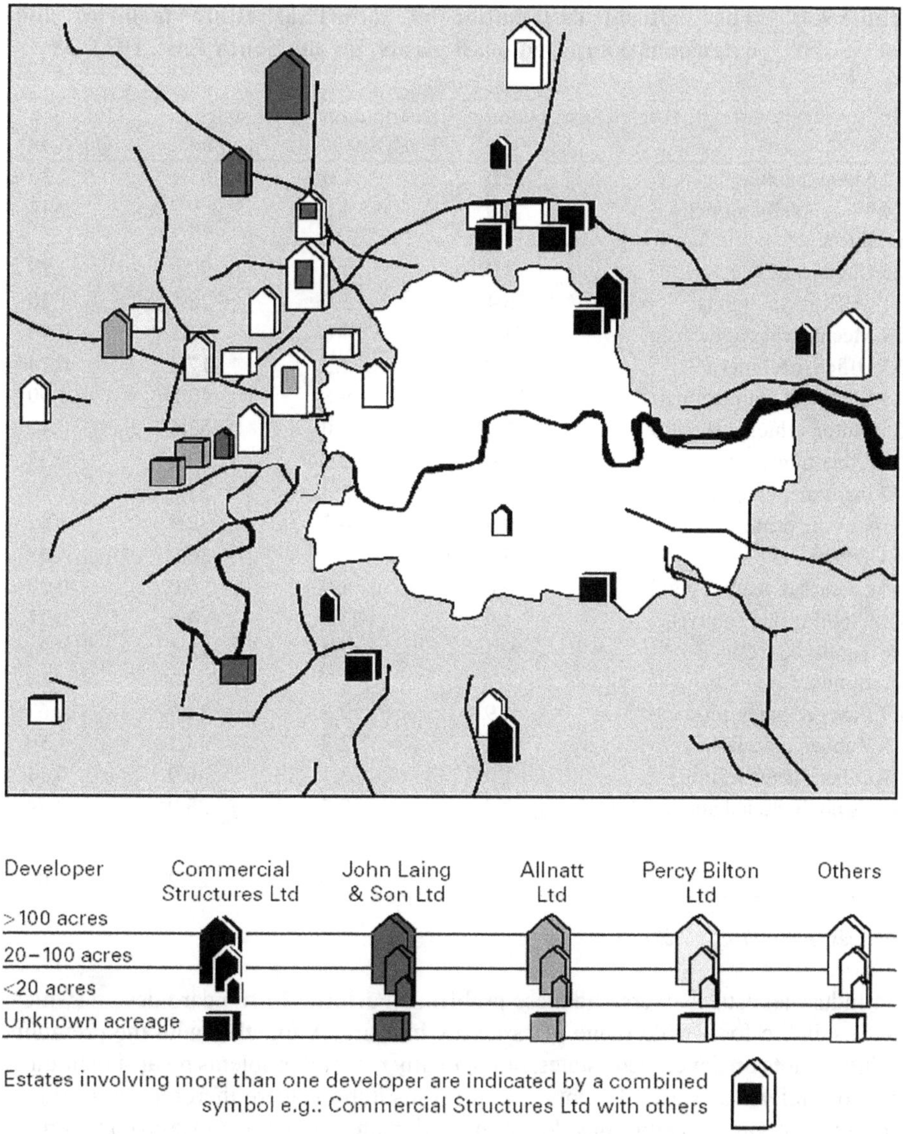

Figure 9.3: Industrial estates established within Greater London by 1939

Source: As for Table 9.2

was the case with land in shop or office districts (though as factories required much larger plots relative to their turnover, this was not necessarily reflected in lower land costs).[21]

21 Peter Scott, *The Property Masters: A History of the British Commercial Property Sector* (London, 1996), pp. 85–6.

Table 9.4: The sectoral distribution of industrial estate factories and extensions compared to all plants, for the South East, 1932–38

SIC	Distribution estates %	Distribution South East %	Estates as % of total	Location Quotient
22 Metal manufacturing	2.9	1.0	63.4	2.86
24 Non-metallic mineral products	2.0	4.5	9.7	0.44
25 Chemicals	13.2	4.0	72.9	3.29
31 Other metal goods	6.4	5.0	28.5	1.28
32 Mechanical engineering	4.4	4.6	21.3	0.96
33 Office machinery	1.0	1.3	17.2	0.78
34 Electrical engineering	18.6	9.8	42.2	1.90
35 Motor vehicles & parts	7.4	3.0	53.6	2.42
36 Other transport	1.0	2.9	7.4	0.33
37 Instrument engineering	2.9	2.3	27.9	1.26
41/2 Food, drink, & tobacco	9.3	6.3	32.9	1.49
43 Textiles	5.4	3.3	36.0	1.62
44 Leather & leather goods	0.0	1.9	0.0	0.00
45 Clothing and footwear	4.9	23.5	4.6	0.21
46 Timber & wooden furniture	9.3	11.1	18.5	0.84
47 Paper & paper products	4.9	7.3	14.9	0.67
48 Rubber and plastics	3.4	2.3	33.2	1.50
49 Other manufacturing	1.0	3.1	6.9	0.31
SIC's not included above	2.0	2.7	23.9	0.74
Total	100	100	22.2	1.00

Sources: As for Table 9.2.

Industrial estates overcame these problems. Factories of standard design (which were suitable for a wide range of assembly industries), together with the premium value of plots on developed estates, dramatically reduced problems regarding finding new occupiers for vacated plants. Financial institutions were therefore prepared to provide mortgages to estate developers at similar interest rates to those on commercial property. For example, over the 1930s the insurance company National Provident Institution provided over £1 million of mortgage finance to the estate developer Allnatt.[22] Estate companies were thus able to provide factories for renting, or sale via mortgage. Slough Estates adopted a policy of providing factories for rental only, while a few developers only sold sites and/or buildings. However it was most common for developers to offer industrialists a choice of options, including renting (sometimes with an option to purchase), hire-purchase, or sale (usually with the

22 National Provident Institution papers, 'Loans to the Allnatt group of companies', 30 July 1954.

developer offering mortgage finance).[23] Bilton's publicity claimed that, 'A factory can be purchased... as easily as a man buys a house on the repayment system with the aid of a building society...'[24] Mortgage interest rates were similar to those for residential or commercial property; for example in around 1938 Laing quoted a rate of 4.5 per cent.[25]

Given that land and buildings often accounted for more than half the cost of establishing a manufacturing business, removing the need to provide this cost 'up front' had a major impact on the financial barriers facing new or expanding firms.[26] This mirrored the practice found in traditional industrial districts, both in London and the provinces, of renting 'room and power' to manufacturers. However, this had generally involved space in multi-storey buildings, whereas industrial estate developers pioneered the renting of modern single storey sheds, designed to serve a wide range of assembly industries. A. T. K. Grant's 1936 study of the British capital market noted the importance of industrial estates and instalment finance for machinery in reducing the costs of corporate start-ups and expansion.[27] In a 1935 *Business* survey of 648 executives regarding the most important factors influencing plant location, the possibility of renting factories received the second highest proportion of first place votes, 23.0 per cent (the most important, proximity to markets, receiving 26.6 per cent). Meanwhile 75.0 per cent of executives stated that the availability of rented premises was an important factor (some of the remaining firms may have required specialised premises, for which renting would not have been an option).[28]

The provision of rented factories contributed to high rates of company failures, as it both lowered the cost of business entry and exit. For example, a 1931 Ministry of Labour study of the Slough Estate indicated that Slough attracted a substantial number of firms which were in an experimental or under-capitalised state and did not desire, or could not afford, to erect premises for themselves.[29] G.R. Allen estimated that the proportion of firms established at Slough before 1935 which 'failed' was as high as 56 per cent, while that for firms renting factories in Welwyn, established between January 1929 and December 1935, was 57 per cent.[30] Yet, despite relatively

---

23 C. Day, 'Need a factory', *Business* (July 1938), p. 33.

24 D. G. Wolton (ed.), *Trading Estates: a Review of the Development of Planned Factory Units Throughout Great Britain* (London, 1938), p. 95.

25 John Laing & Son Ltd., *Laings Factory Sites.*

26 William Bredo, *Industrial Estates: Tools for Industrialisation* (Glencoe, 1960) p. 47.

27 A. T. K. Grant, *A Study of the Capital Market in Britain from 1919–1936*, 2nd edn (London, 1967), pp. 276–7.

28 '"Business" country-wide survey of 3 years' industrial development', *Business* (December 1935), 9–34.

29 NA, BT56/38/CIA18002, memorandum by W. Eady, 23 February 1931.

30 G. R. Allen, 'The growth of industry on trading estates, 1920–39, with special reference to Slough Trading Estate', *Oxford Economic Papers*, new. ser., l, 3 (1951), 272–300, p. 286. It is unclear whether these all represented corporate failures. According to an official study of the 55 firms which left Welwyn prior to 1948, 56.4 per cent involved the closure of the business, 12.7 per cent involved its sale, and 30.9 per cent represented transfers to another area (NA: HLG90/440, Welwyn report).

high failure rates, the number of firms and employees at Slough and Welwyn experienced rapid growth. As in traditional industrial districts, the ease with which physical and human capital could be transferred from failing to new firms allowed estates to prosper in the aggregate despite numerous failures.

Financial losses associated with tenant/mortgagee failure were small as it was usually possible to rapidly dispose of the factory concerned at its market value. A study of Allnatt's mortgage finance by John Armstrong found that they were able to recoup all money owed by defaulters from the subsequent sale of their premises.[31] Thus, while rented or mortgaged premises reduced the entrepreneur's costs of business failure, the costs to estate developers of such failures were not usually substantial. Industrialists sometimes derived further financial benefit from the estate developer, via reduced rents at the start of the lease – as an inducement to locate on the estate – and, sometimes, from financial assistance to tenants experiencing difficulties. Both Slough Estates and Brixton Estate Ltd. (which developed a small estate in South West London) assisted some tenants, largely via postponing rental payments. In 1930 Slough also implemented a scheme under which tenants could arrange loans of up to £3,000 to help them survive the depression.[32]

Such facilities were of particular benefit to new and/or small firms. Some developers offered reduced rents at the start of a lease, while several provided 'nest' factories, specifically targeted at small companies requiring a very low floorspace. These were pioneered at Trafford Park prior to the First World War, premises of around 2,500 sq. ft. being built for rental, and were also developed at Slough, Kings Norton, Letchworth, Welwyn, and on government-financed estates in the Special Areas.[33] Evidence provided by Trafford Park Estates Ltd in the late 1930s stated that while the rent charged for its nest factories, 10d per square foot, did not make them directly profitable, they were maintained since the small enterprises established in them often rapidly grew to require larger factories.[34] The importance of estate facilities to new firm growth in the South East appears to have been considerable. A survey conducted in the mid-1960s, of 38 firms that had begun life as new enterprises in north-west London during the interwar years, indicated that 17 had been established on industrial estates: 'there is clearly a case for arguing that North West London, with its extensive industrial estates and rapidly growing numbers of cheap, rentable premises, offered a peculiarly attractive environment for early growth...'[35]

Industrial estates also facilitated corporate expansion. The ease with which firms can move premises is important as movement is closely associated with expansion, modernisation, and reorganisation. Analysis by S.R. Dennison of firm moves from inner London to expanding 'trading estate' areas in outer-London during the 1930s revealed that in all cases examined movement was accompanied by other measures of reorganisation involving new machinery, extended output, or industrial

31 Armstrong, 'The development of Park Royal', p. 72.

32 Cassell, *Long Lease*, pp. 65–71.

33 Kaunitz, 'The British trading estate', p. 158.

34 H. G. Huckle, 'Trading estates for light industry', p. 31.

35 D. E. Keeble, 'Industrial growth in North West London: a geographical analysis', unpublished Ph.D. thesis, University of Cambridge, 1967, p. 172.

concentration.[36] Companies that had developed their own premises might get only a fraction of the construction cost from their subsequent disposal. Furthermore, finding suitable land and arranging the construction of a new plant was often a long and sometimes difficult process, involving costs that could not be accurately estimated in advance. Such problems remain substantial; for example, a study conducted during the mid-1980s found that unsuitable sites and buildings pose a major obstacle to growth and efficiency for a large proportion of manufacturers.[37]

Estate developers greatly simplified the process of factory acquisition, offering a range of rented standard factories of different sizes, often built in advance of demand.[38] If a firm wished to expand it could surrender the lease to the estate company, usually at no cost, and simultaneously take out a lease on a larger factory. Estate developers also facilitated the process of acquiring custom-made factories. Several advertised a 'comprehensive' service, including architectural design, liaising with planning authorities, factory construction, the provision of access roads and utilities, and arranging development finance.[39] Estate promoters simplified the assessment of the comparative costs of various locations, by providing manufacturers with a range of information regarding rents, lease terms, local wage rates, and transport and utility charges.[40] Constructing standard factories in bulk also reduced costs and decreased construction times to around 10–15 weeks.[41] Estate developers also often maximised potential extension space by laying out plants so as to allow a certain amount of pooled expansion space for each group of factories.

The extent of turnover in factory premises is illustrated by data from the Welwyn estate, shown in Table 9.5. This covers the period 1921–38, though as only 32 firms had established production on the estate prior to 1930 the age of most of the factories covered in the Table was considerably shorter. The average number of occupiers per plant at Welwyn was 2.1 for rented factories and 1.2 for factories purchased by their occupiers. Turnover rates were particularly high for nest factories of under 2,000 square feet.

Estate developers also provided factories of a significantly more efficient design than those which firms transferring to estates typically vacated. The characteristic estate plant was a single-storey north-light or single span factory, usually fronted by an office block. These were claimed to produce substantial productivity improvements. Steel frame and reinforced concrete 'shed' factories required minimium internal supports (that might encumber production lines), provided natural daylight

---

36 Dennison, *The Location of Industry*, p. 144.

37 Stephen Forthergill, Sarah Monk, and Martin Perry, *Property and Industrial Development* (Triptree, 1987), p. 84.

38 Wolton, *Trading Estates*, p. 145; Percy Bilton Ltd., *Twixt Green Fields & the City: Percy Bilton Model Factory Estates* (London, c. 1937); Armstrong, 'Development of Park Royal'.

39 Wolton, *Trading Estates*, p. 95.

40 NA, HLG27/32, memorandum for the Royal Commission on the Distribution of the Industrial Population by Sir Noel Mobbs, Chairman, Slough Estates, 3 February 1938.

41 *Times Trade and Engineering Supplement* (October 1935), p. 24; Percy Bilton Ltd., *Twixt green fields*, p. 26; Armstrong, 'Development of Park Royal', p. 76.

throughout, and reduced temperature variations.[42] A *Business* review of estate development by Commercial Structures noted that firms occupying such factories experienced average productivity increases of about 10 per cent.[43] Similarly, Smith's 1933 study of the industrial development of north-west London noted that the type of factories being developed on industrial estates both cost less to build and entailed much lower working costs than many older factory buildings.[44]

Estate developers also emphasised the importance of landscaping, together with their estates' semi-rural locations, in creating a healthy, 'garden city' working environment.[45] Laing claimed that, 'as compared with city conditions, this type of "garden" estate factory gets from 5 to 10 per cent more production per person.'[46]

Table 9.5: The turnover in premises on the Welwyn trading estate, 1921–48

Factory size (sq. ft).	Rented factories		Purchased factories		Total	
	Number	Occupiers per plant	Number	Occupiers per plant	Number	Occupiers per plant
Under 2,000	15	3.2	4	1.5	19	2.8
2-3,000	20	2.0	3	1.3	23	1.9
3-4,000	31	1.7	0	n.a.	31	1.7
4-6,000	33	2.0	4	1.0	37	1.9
6-10,000	9	2.7	5	1.0	14	2.1
Over 10,000	4	1.5	19	1.2	23	1.3
Total	112	2.1	35	1.2	147	1.9

Source: NA, HLG90/440, Ministry of Town and Country Planning, New Towns Research Section, 'Welwyn Garden City: some aspects of its economic history', June 1950.

Such benefits were corroborated by the government's Chief Inspector of Factories and Workshops, whose 1937 report noted the superiority of, 'light and airy modern single-storey factories, scientifically planned to economise labour, and situated in open and healthy surroundings', compared to 'old many-storeyed buildings with their restricted supply of fresh air and daylight. Work is consequently carried on under far more advantageous conditions both as regards the health of the workers and economy of labour and overhead charges'.[47]

42 James Marshall, *The History of the Great West Road: Its Social and Economic Significance on the Surrounding Area* (Hounslow, 1995), p. 56.

43 Day, 'Need a factory', p. 40.

44 Smith, *Industries of Greater London*, p. 162.

45 Slough Estates Ltd., *Slough, London's Industrial Centre* (Slough, c. 1934), p. 4; Nottingham Colwick Estate Ltd., *Britain's Best Industrial Sites* (Nottinham, c. 1924), p. 43; Bromboro [name later changed to Bromborough] Port Estate Ltd., *Bromboro Port Estate* (Port Sunlight, c. 1929), p. 13.

46 *Business* (May 1938), p. 31.

47 H. M. Factory Inspectorate, *Annual Report of the Chief Inspector of Factories and Workshops, 1937* (London, 1938), p. 13.

The modern, clean, image of industrial estates was cited by Welwyn's industrial development manager, in private evidence to the Federation of British Industries, as a major attraction for firms.[48] He also emphasised the publicity advantages of a prominent location on an attractive estate facing an arterial road. These comments were echoed by consultant engineers Alexander Gibb & Co., 'many businesses set considerable store from an advertising point of view on amenities and country-like nature of their surroundings'.[49] They claimed that a site on a main road was worth at least double one on a by-road for many classes of industry, particularly consumer goods. This was stated to be as true for estates as for individual factories, an estate on an arterial road benefiting all its occupants. This advertising value was capitalised on most notably by companies such as Hoover, whose factory was fronted by an architecturally-designed 'jazz-style' office facade that remains among the most impressive examples of interwar British architecture.

Industrial estates as agents for promoting locational externalities

The most important benefits accrued by firms on industrial estates involved locational externalities. As noted in the previous chapter, the tight clustering of firms on compact campus sites produced similar plant densities to those found in traditional inner-urban industrial districts. Such proximity enables firms to form a 'local integration' – exchanging goods without much packaging or the use of expensive fast vehicles, and fosters knowledge spillovers – which rapidly dissipate with distance.[50] Industrial estates' promotional literature sometimes alluded to 'inter-trading' among estate firms[51] and some estate developers tried to facilitate such links. Both Slough and Trafford Park published directories of estate firms, while the products of firms at Slough were also advertised to other tenants in the *Slough Estate Journal*, which included a list of tenants, plus details of new arrivals and the services they offered.[52] While the available evidence is not particularly rich, contemporary and near-contemporary surveys of major British industrial estates do indicate substantial input-output links between firms, especially in the metal-working sectors.[53] Sometimes such links were based around certain very large firms, which drew their suppliers to the estate on which they located, examples including Ford at Dagenham; British Westinghouse at Trafford Park, and Unilever at Bromborough

48 MRC, MSS 200/F/3/52/19/1, 'Location of industry: notes made by S.A.Sadler Forster', 3 December 1937.

49 NA: BT104/31, report on sites for trading estates prepared by Sir Alexander Gibb & Partners for North Eastern Trading Estates, March 1936.

50 P. S. Florence, *Investment, Location, and Size of Plant* (Cambridge, 1948), p. 68; S. A. Rosenthal and W. C. Strange, 'The determinants of agglomeration', *Journal of Urban Economics*, 50, (2001), 191–229.

51 Trafford Park Estates Ltd., *Trafford Park, Sites for Works* (Manchester, 1915), p. 28; Slough Estates Ltd., *London's New Industrial Centre* (Slough, c. 1926).

52 Slough Estates Ltd., *The Slough Estates Journal*, Vol. 2, 16 (1930), p. 449.

53 Peter Scott, 'Industrial estates and British industrial development: 1897–1939', *Business History*, 43, 2 (2001), 73–98, pp. 83–5.

Port.[54] However, strong input-output links were also found on the Slough Estate (which was less dominated by very large firms) and were particularly extensive among the estate's smaller enterprises.[55]

However, externalities regarding the organisation of production appear to have been of greater importance. These were closely associated with the type of workers employed and systems for their recruitment, pacing, monitoring, and remuneration. Estate firms typically sought cheap, 'flexible', workers with general production-line skills rather than sector-specific training. Yet this 'flexibility' was very different to that of traditional industrial districts (the skills necessary to produce a range of goods using simple machinery). Instead, employers sought flexibility with respect to accepting new systems for machine pacing, payment systems, and the simplification of tasks into narrow, repetitive operations. Common labour requirements in turn raised substantial possibilities for knowledge spillovers regarding the organisation of production. For example, techniques aimed at intensifying worker effort, such as the Bedaux system, were introduced by a number of prominent firms on estates in outer-London and the South East, particularly American and other overseas-based multinationals.[56]

Such innovations were facilitated by the labour market conditions that estates fostered. They were viewed by contemporaries as unregulated, 'union-free', environments, in which firms could experiment with new systems for organising work, simplifying and standardising processes, and employing cheaper un/semi-skilled workers.[57] Armstrong's study of the Park Royal estate found it to have been characterised by a high proportion of female and juvenile labour, the absence of any trade union tradition, and substantial barriers to union organisation.[58] The TUC similarly perceived areas such as Acton, Willesden, and Dagenham to be in the vanguard of a trend towards unregulated labour markets.[59] Location on private estates itself acted as a significant barrier to unionisation, as many union recruitment practices, such as factory gate meetings, were strictly illegal.[60]

The prevalence of such methods, and the extent to which they transcended sectoral boundaries, is illustrated by the example of Slough. Photographs in a 1934 promotional brochure for the Slough Estate show broadly similar arrangements of women workers undertaking repetitive, standardised, operations at Aspro (pharmaceuticals); Be-Ze-Be Honey and St. Martin's Preserving Co. (food processing); and O'Cedar (furniture and metal polish).[61] More broadly-based information regarding production methods

54 D. A. Farnie, *The Manchester Ship Canal and the Rise of the Port of Manchester 1894–1975* (Manchester, 1980), p. 131; Kaunitz, 'The British trading estate', p. 29.

55 Davies, 'The nature and significance of trading estates'.

56 Miriam Glucksmann, *Women Assemble: Women Workers and the New Industries in Inter-war Britain* (London, 1990), p. 175.

57 Dennison, *The Location of Industry*, p. 80; NA, BT56/40/CIA1800/71.

58 John Armstrong, 'International influences on the development of London business: the case of the Park Royal industrial estate between the wars', unpublished paper.

59 Peter Scott, 'The wolf at the door: the trade union movement and overseas multinationals in Britain during the 1930s', *Social History,* 23, 2 (1998), 195–210.

60 Mike Savage, 'Trade unionism, sex segregation, and the state: women's employment in "new industries" in inter-war Britain', *Social History*, 13 (1988), 209–30, p. 221.

61 Slough Estates Ltd, *Slough: London's Industrial Centre* (Slough, 1934).

and employment practices on the Slough Esates is provided by surveys of Slough's large manufacturers, prepared for the TUC in 1936 and 1938; extracts from these are reproduced in Table 9.6, covering firms in a variety of sectors. With the exception of a few companies such as Intertype Ltd (which ran an apprenticeship system and had low labour turnover) the surveys revealed low wage rates, extensive employment of females and juveniles (some on jobs usually undertaken by adult males), and the use of the Bedaux system and other 'speed-up' methods. Levels of unionisation were found to be typically low and the use of piece-rates common, especially for female and juvenile workers.[62]

Estate factory workers were generally drawn from outside the core manufacturing workforce and included women, juveniles, former-agricultural labourers, and long-distance migrants from Britain's depressed areas. Yet frequent large-scale lay-off's by individual firms potentially threatened to undermine the inflow of workers and the loyalty of long-distance commuters and in-migrants to the local labour market. The clustering of large numbers of firms requiring similar labour solved this problem, stabilising aggregate labour demand despite substantial variations in employment levels for individual firms. A large labour pool with the necessary speed, discipline, and flexibility to efficiently undertake assembly production was particularly important for firms of this type, as variations in direct employment constituted their main means of dealing with volatile market demand. Many experienced great variations in demand and, as they typically produced standardised, often branded, goods using quantity production methods, there was much less scope to deal with demand variations by sub-contracting than was the case in, for example, clothing. Instead firms reacted by making large and frequent variations in the size of their workforces, often hiring and firing large numbers of workers to cope with even seasonal demand fluctuations.[63]

The extent of such fluctuations is illustrated by firms on the Slough Estate. A 1930 Ministry of Labour survey noted that while Slough's industrial growth maintained high aggregate labour demand, employment at its larger firms varied greatly over time, examples including Gillette (established with 12 employees and peaked at 250, but fell back to 80); D. M. Davies (employment fluctuating according to contracts, from 324 or less, to 600); St. Martins Preserving Co. (varying from about 500 to nearly 800); Graham Amplion (fluctuations of over 50 per cent); O-Cedar (peak employment of 500, fell to118); and Citroen (decline from 888 in 1926 to 225 in 1929). The 1936 TUC survey of the Slough Estate similarly emphasised heavy employment fluctuations, together with very frequent changes in pay rates, especially for female workers, apparently in line with labour demand.[64]

By clustering alongside other firms with similar labour requirements – for inexpensive workers with general assembly skills and a willingness to accept new working practices – estate firms effectively collectivised the problems of labour recruitment, training, and retention. Thus, like the inner-London quarters, the new

62 See also Savage, 'Trade unionism, sex segregation, and the state', pp. 221–2.

63 See, for example, Glucksmann, *Women Assemble*, pp. 32, 115.

64 MRC, Mss. 292/57.1/5, TUC General Council report on industrial survey of Slough, 11 March 1936.

Table 9.6: Some examples from Slough and District Trades Council surveys of large* firms at Slough, 1936 and 1938

Firm	Products	Employees	Extracts from comments
1936 Survey			
Mc Michael's Ltd	Wireless	300	'Workers discontented owing to speed-up.' 'Boys of 15 at riveting machine at 5d per hour. Was man's job at 1/- hour'
G. D. Peters & Co. + subsidiaries**	General engineers	00-1,000	'Very few get local rate.' 'Few members of A.E.U.' '…piece work system very bad.'
D. M. Davies Ltd	Cabinet makers (mass production)	800-1,200	'Grossly under-paid. Large number of boys & girls at 4d-6d…' 'Unorganised. Considerable unrest among workers.' 'Accidents, minor, frequent.'
British Technical Cork Co.	Gaskets, etc.		Large proportion semi-skilled female labourers at 1/- per hour. 'Appears to be tendency to substitute piece-rate for hourly rate.'
O'Cedar Ltd	Polishes etc.	50 girls	'7.5 d an hour, but general piece-work'
Aspro	Medicinal tablets	95% females	'Single women preferred. Conditions very good.'
1938 Survey			
Cygnet Rings	Piston Rings	60	'Girls working machines.'
Rheostatic Co.	Electrical apparatus	400	'Large number of boys.'
High Duty Alloys Ltd ***	Hiduminium & bronze castings	1,200-1,400	'Many paid on bonus system.' 'Bedaux system recently introduced.'
International Alloys Ltd	Alloys	300	'Men have been sacked for union activities.'
Zwicky Ltd	Engineering	80	'Abnormal number of boys [paid] from 4.5d to 10d [per hour].'

Sources: Modern Records Centre, University of Warwick, Mss. 292/57.1/5, TUC Organisation Committee, reports on industrial surveys of Slough, 11 March 1936 and 21 July 1938.

Notes: * Employing 50 workers or more. ** Not named. *** Plus subsidiaries – Magnesium Castings & Products Ltd and High Duty Bronze Ltd.

outer-London industrial estates developed a 'floating workforce' with loyalty to the area, rather than the individual factory. Relying on varying direct throughput to cope with variations in market demand may at least partially explain another characteristic feature of most of these firms – the use of labour-intensive methods rather than moving production lines or other capital-intensive techniques that would have incurred heavy fixed cost penalties if operated substantially below capacity.[65] This emphasis on labour-intensive production methods suitable for cheap labour, rather than the use of expensive American-style production-line machinery, may also at least partially explain the larger *labour* productivity gap between British and American factories in the assembly industries than in the old staples – where Britain came closer to American labour productivity levels.[66]

Conclusion

Industrial estates played an important role in fostering location externalities for the new and, initially, often small firms that characterised many of the dynamic growth industries of the 'second industrial revolution'. They also offered important benefits with regard to reducing start-up and expansion costs and easing the physical problems associated with factory expansion. Their concentration in the South East constituted a major factor attracting, and retaining, firms in that region, reinforcing its other major locational advantages of good market access and transport links. The above analysis has highlighted the importance of pools of cheap, flexible, labour to the new production methods pioneered both on industrial estates and other areas of rapid industrial growth such as Watford, Luton, and Oxford. However, this raises the question as to how firms in these areas managed to keep wages low and workers pliable despite the very rapid growth in their working populations, which might have been expected to have exhausted local supplies of cheap workers. The sources and nature of the new workforce for Britain's rapidly expanding manufacturing centres are discussed in the following two chapters.

65 See Peter Scott, 'Women, other "fresh" workers, and the new manufacturing workforce of interwar Britain', *International Review of Social History*, 45 (2000), 449–74.

66 Nicholas Crafts, 'Long-run growth', 1–24 in Roderick Floud and Paul Johnson (eds), *The Cambridge Economic History of Modern Britain. Volume II: Economic Maturity 1860–1939* (Cambridge, 2004) p. 21.

Chapter Ten

The new industrial workforce

Introduction

During the interwar years structural, organisational, and technological changes had far-reaching effects on the nature of manufacturing work in Britain, in common with other industrialised nations.[1] Skilled and physically demanding work became less prevalent, while there was a dramatic expansion in unskilled and semi-skilled employment.[2] These trends were particularly evident in the consumer and branded goods sectors, while most of the staple industries experienced much more gradual, evolutionary, change. This and the following chapter examine the composition of the new manufacturing workforce in the rapidly expanding industrial communities of the South East and West Midlands. Employers in the 'new' industries are shown to have generally recruited their workers not from the established manufacturing workforce but from a 'reserve army of labour', whose characteristics were determined by the multiple dimensions of gender, age, previous employment, and location.

Workers 'fresh' to manufacturing employment, such as women, juveniles, and former-agricultural labourers, constituted preferred sources of labour on account of their cheapness, flexibility, and lack of any union tradition. However, the labour requirements of Britain's most rapidly expanding centres eventually exhausted such sources and employers increasingly turned to long-distance migrants, who provided a seemingly endless supply of new workers at prevailing (relatively low) wages. As a result by the late 1930s a substantial proportion of the populations of new industrial centres such as Slough, Coventry, and Welwyn were from South Wales and other depressed areas.

New workers and new industrial communities

As Doreen Massey has noted, major changes in the labour process have important implications for the location of industry. Even if these involve no 'real' deskilling, they may enable jobs to be formally downgraded, often through the employment of a new workforce with a weaker negotiating position. Historical episodes of deskilling

1 For examples from the Netherlands and USA, see Gertjan de Groot and Marlou Schrover, 'Between men and machines: women workers in new industries, 1870–1940', *Social History*, XX (1995), 279–96; Ruth Milkman, 'Female factory labor and industrial structure: control and conflict over "woman's place" in auto and electrical manufacturing', *Politics and Society*, XII (1983), 159–203.

2 Kevin Whitston, 'Worker resistance and Taylorism in Britain', *International Review of Social History*, XLII (1997), 1–24.

have typically involved the employment of women, juveniles, or other groups outside the established manufacturing workforce, on jobs traditionally undertaken by men. She argues that the locations for such de-skilled production are determined by the interaction between these labour requirements and the geography of an area's previous industrial inheritance, in conjunction with other factors such as proximity to markets, power and materials supplies, and the organisational structure of capital.[3]

Employing such 'fresh' workers both decreases labour costs and erodes the power of organised labour. Karl Marx, who argued that the substitution of adult male labour by females and juveniles was a key feature of mechanisation,[4] also noted that their employment constituted a means of reducing the opposition of organised labour to mechanisation. 'By the excessive addition of women and children to the ranks of the workers, machinery at last breaks down the resistance which the male operatives in the manufacturing period continued to oppose to the despotism of capital'.[5] These processes were evident during the interwar years, as a result of changes in manufacturing technology and the organisation of production which greatly increased the proportion of jobs involving relatively simple, repetitive, tasks.

'New' industries such as electrical engineering and motor vehicles involved a high proportion of assembly and other un/semi-skilled operations. Meanwhile some traditional industries, such as footwear and hosiery, also witnessed the introduction of new production methods, leading to a substantial growth in female and juvenile employment and the establishment of new production centres in areas lacking any strong union presence.[6] New, standardised, production technology thus offered an incentive to employ female, juvenile, and other weakly unionised labour, in order to prevent unions resisting its introduction or opposing restrictions on its use, while simultaneously reducing the value of skills possessed by workers trained in older techniques. Both effects made new industrial centres preferable to their long-established counterparts from the viewpoint of manufacturers.

In order to examine the extent and impact of these changes it is necessary to establish both the age and gender composition of the manufacturing workforce and their wage differentials. A 1935 official survey provides the best available data, summarised (for manufacturing sectors) in Table 10.1. For all industries covered (including some non-manufacturing trades) average weekly earnings were 64.5 shillings for men aged over 21, 31.3 shillings for women over 18, 23.0 shillings for males under 21 and 16.3 shillings for females under 18.[7] More disaggregated evidence regarding wage differentials for younger workers can be gained from social surveys of Welwyn Garden City and Watford. The Welwyn survey, conducted in 1939, indicated that average weekly wages for workers aged 16–21 were 33 shillings

3 Doreen Massey, *Spatial Divisions of Labour. Social Structures and the Geography of Production* (London, 1984), pp. 22–6 and 42.

4 Karl Marx, *Capital*, Vol. 1 (London, 1954), p. 372.

5 Marx, *Capital*, Vol. 1, p. 379.

6 Alan Fox, *The History of the National Union of Boot and Shoe Operatives 1874–1957* (Oxford, 1958), pp. 484–5; Richard Gurnham, *A History of the Trade Union Movement in the Hosiery and Knitwear Industry, 1776–1976* (Leicester, 1976), pp. 105–6.

7 *Ministry of Labour Gazette* (July 1937), 257–8.

Table 10.1: Average weekly wages and employment distribution by age and gender for various industries in October 1935

	Men's wages (shillings)	Relative wages (% of men)			Employment distribution (%)			
		Women	Boys	Girls	Men	Women	Boys	Girls
Textiles	55.9	54.20	41.32	30.77	33.63	47.41	7.17	11.79
Woodworking industries	65.1	51.92	33.64	23.96	67.06	7.61	22.23	3.10
Clothing	64.5	50.70	34.73	23.26	20.29	54.86	6.37	18.48
Food, drink, & tobacco	63.7	50.39	39.09	26.69	49.73	29.00	8.87	12.40
Non-metallic mineral products	60.7	47.94	46.62	28.50	87.78	1.10	10.60	0.52
Leather	61.8	47.73	36.89	24.76	58.69	18.45	14.93	7.92
Chemicals, bricks, pottery, glass	63.0	46.67	38.73	24.29	67.16	13.75	12.83	6.27
Other manufacturing	64.9	46.38	38.67	25.12	49.07	26.98	12.38	11.57
Metal & engineering industries	67.6	46.01	32.99	25.59	67.79	10.39	17.99	3.83
Paper & printing	83.7	39.90	27.36	18.52	52.51	25.00	10.78	11.72
Average of sectors	65.1	48.18	37.01	25.14	55.37	23.45	12.41	8.76

Source: Ministry of Labour Gazette *(February 1937), pp. 46–8; (March 1937), pp. 88–9; (April 1937), pp. 133–5; (May 1937), pp. 174–6; (July 1937), pp. 257–8.*

Notes: 'Women' refers to females aged 18 years and over and 'Girls' to those under 18; 'Men' refers to males aged 21 years and over and 'Boys' to those under 21.

for boys and 28 shillings for girls, while both boys and girls aged 14–16 averaged only 16.75 shillings. In addition to gender differentials narrowing for younger workers, these also had lower sectoral wage differentials.[8] Similarly, the Watford survey, conducted in around 1933, showed narrower gender wage differentials for younger juveniles, together with strong age differentials for boys – their wages rising from 12.5–15 shillings at ages 14–15 to 15–17.5 shillings at 15–16 and 20–30 shillings at 16–18.[9]

Table 10.1 also reveals considerable differences between industries regarding age and gender wage differentials and employment distributions. Dual Labour Market [DLM] theory provides a useful starting-point for the analysis of variations in workforce composition. This argues that the labour market is segmented into 'primary' and 'secondary' sectors. The primary sector is characterised by high wages and fringe benefits, skilled jobs, training and promotion opportunities, and employment stability. Conversely the secondary market is distinguished by low wages and fringe benefits, lack of skill or opportunities for promotion or training, labour-intensive production, and unstable employment. The primary market is dominated by white adult males, while in the secondary market females, young workers, and ethnic minorities are over-represented.[10]

Primary labour markets are created by employers in order to minimise the turnover of workers on whom a premium is placed as they embody enterprise-specific skills (skills specific to the particular firm, rather than being more generally available) and associated on-the-job training. 'Technological specificity' is one important type of enterprise-specific skill. This involves the entire set of tasks which comprise a work process and imparts specificity to skill mainly through the speed and accuracy with which these are executed.[11] Technological specificity is likely to be of particular importance for capital-intensive industries, where maximising the throughput of expensive machinery will have the greatest impact on overall costs. Workers in such industries are often paid above market rates in order to secure a workforce who can keep pace with this capacity throughput. High-wage policies consistent with such production strategies were adopted by some firms using highly mechanised production techniques, most notably the UK branches of some American multinationals, such as Shredded Wheat, Kodak, and Ford (together with its associated Dagenham companies Briggs Bodies Ltd and Kelsey-Hayes Wheel Co).[12]

---

8 Welwyn Garden City Library, Sir Frederic Osborn Archive, K256, Jacqueline Tyrewhitt, 'Life and Labour in Welwyn Garden City', typescript, 1939 [hereafter, Tyrewhitt, Welwyn Survey].

9 Watford Reference Library, Civic Survey Council, 'Watford Civic Survey 1933' [hereafter, Watford Civic Survey], volumes 2 and 3, manuscript, c. 1933.

10 Peter B. Doeringer and Michael J. Piore, *Internal Labour Markets and Manpower Analysis* (Lexington, Mass., 1971); Peter Sloane, 'The structure of labour markets and low pay for women', 127–64 in Peter Sloane (ed.), *Women and Low Pay* (London, 1980).

11 Doeringer and Piore, *Internal Labour Markets*, p. 16.

12 John H. Dunning, *American Investment in British Manufacturing Industry* (London, 1958), p. 255.

Ford and its associated companies provide good instances of technological specificity, employing 'new types of skilled men' who were characteristic of the new high-wage mass production workers:

> Unskilled men could be trained within a month or two to do a good deal of the work of the machinists and assemblers, but the [Ford] Company pays a high rate of wage and is able to secure men ... who have had previous experience. Such men very quickly become efficient at the particular job for which they are required and there is the advantage that their skill and knowledge does not apply to one operation alone and they can be transferred ... In ... Briggs Bodies Ltd., there is a higher proportion of the work which could be given to men who have had less previous experience of the motor industry, but the work in the main is only suitable for those who are experienced and fairly intelligent and quick. Metal finishing, paint spraying, part of the assembly work, part of the work in the upholstery department is being done by unskilled workers who have been trained. If these ... reach the required standard, they are often in possession of skill which is marketable elsewhere.[13]

Conversely, secondary sector jobs 'are, above all, jobs in which there is a low investment in human capital'.[14] Barron and Norris identify five main attributes that make a particular social group a likely source of secondary workers: dispensability; clearly visible social difference; little interest in acquiring training; low economism;[15] and lack of solidarity.[16] Dispensability is defined as the ease with which an employee can be removed from a redundant job. An important component is high voluntary turnover – characteristic of women, 'mavericks' (chronic job changers), and youths. As women and youths were perceived as a barrier to unionisation during this period, high employment of such workers also facilitated dispensability through involuntary redundancies.[17]

Ruth Milkman has offered an explanation of sex-typing in interwar American industry with strong similarities to DLM theory. Taking the examples of the motor vehicle and electrical goods industries, she argues that the much higher proportion of female employees in electrical goods was due to the labour-intensive and de-skilled nature of production and the consequent reliance on elaborate piecework systems, facilitating female and juvenile employment. In motor vehicles, by contrast, production was very capital-intensive and employers used high wages to retain a workforce sufficiently reliable to maintain production at the pace determined by the

13 Terence Young, *Becontree and Dagenham* (London, 1934), p. 126.

14 R. D. Barron and G. M. Norris, 'Sexual divisions and the dual labour market", in Diana L. Barker and Sheila Allen (eds), *Dependence and Exploitation in Work and Marriage* (London, 1976), p. 60.

15 Defined as the relative importance a worker places on monetary rewards.

16 Barron and Norris, 'Sexual divisions', p. 53.

17 See, for example, Sheila Lewenhak, *Women and Trade Unions* (London, 1977), pp. 186–210; Glucksmann, *Women Assemble*, p. 193; Sylvia Walby, 'Spatial and historical variations in women's unemployment and employment', 161–76 in Lancaster Regionalism Group, *Localities, Class, and Gender* (London, 1985); Gail Braybon, *Women Workers in the First World War: The British Experience* (London, 1981).

moving assembly line.[18] Mike Savage has argued that British employment practices mirrored those found by Milkman in America.[19] If this is correct there should be a strong relationship between the percentage of adult male workers employed in each industry and its fixed capital per worker.

While there are no published data on fixed capital per worker, analysis of the available proxies by P. S. Florence concluded that horse-power per worker – despite being an imperfect measure of capital – is the best available, agreeing tolerably with other less easily obtainable measures.[20] Figure 10.1 examines the relationship between the proportion of adult men employed in 29 industrial sub-divisions covered in the 1935 survey, and their average horsepower per worker according to Florence's (1930) data.[21] This shows a strong correlation between capital-intensity and the proportion of men employed, as is confirmed by regression analysis.[22] Thus it appears that, at sectoral level, there was a clear relationship between capital-intensity and the allocation of jobs between adult male and cheaper workers.

Flexibility and low industrial militancy were desired characteristics common to both primary and secondary sectors of the new manufacturing workforce. Some manufacturers, in industries such as motor vehicles – where capital-intensive production required high throughput to keep costs down – also placed a considerable premium on a reliable, stable, highly-productive workforce, evolving employment strategies characteristic of primary labour markets. These typically used machine-pacing and tight worker supervision, and were prepared to pay high time wages to retain reliable staff. Their ideal workforce consisted of adult male workers – on account of their low voluntary labour turnover – drawn from sectors such as agriculture that were perceived to be relatively free of industrial militancy or entrenched attitudes regarding working practices. Meanwhile other manufacturers, in labour-intensive sectors such as electrical engineering, faced much lower fixed costs and thus aimed to minimise their greatest costs – wages – by drawing on cheaper workers. These evolved strategies characteristic of secondary labour markets, employing a large proportion of women, juveniles and – when such workers were in short supply – internal migrants, and often using piece-rate systems to motivate output and link wages directly to productivity. The new industrial workforce in both capital and labour intensive sectors was thus drawn from a 'reserve army' of workers, whose composition was determined by the multiple dimensions of age, gender, occupational background, and geographical mobility, as outlined below.

---

18 Milkman, 'Female factory labor'.

19 Savage, 'Trade Unionism', pp. 217–18.

20 P. S. Florence, *Investment, Location, and Size of Plant* (Cambridge, 1948), pp. 90–100.

21 The sample excluded particularly heavy industries, in which the heavy nature of the work was an important factor excluding women and juveniles from many jobs.

22 % Men = 22.922 + 13.080 Horsepower per worker

(6.234)* (7.768)*

$R2 = 0.691$ $N = 29$ F-statistic = 60.338

t-values are in parentheses.

* Significant at the 1 per cent confidence interval.

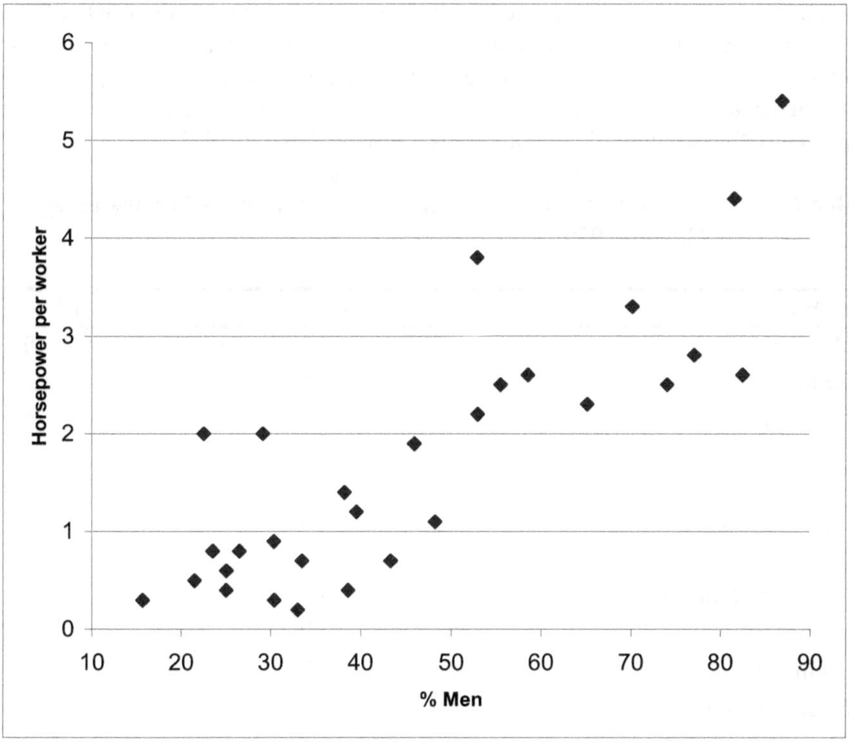

Figure 10.1: The relationship between adult male employment (1935) and horsepower per worker (1930) for 29 British industrial sub-divisions

Sources: employment – as for Table 10.1; horsepower per worker – P. S. Florence, Investment, Location, and Size of Plant *(Cambridge, 1948), Appendix IV.*

The Gender Dimension

The proportion of women aged over 16 in the insured workforce rose slightly, from 26.1 to 26.6 per cent from 1923–27, while the proportion aged 16–64 experienced a further slight rise, from 27.2 to 27.7 per cent, from 1927–39.[23] This relative stability was largely due to the decline of the textile industry (traditionally by far the largest industrial employer of women), which cancelled out much of the growth of female employment in other sectors. From 1923–37 the number of female insured workers (employed and unemployed)[24] rose by 68.7 per cent in vehicle construction and repair, 64.2 per cent in the metal industries, and 62.5 per cent in engineering.[25] However,

23 C. E. V. Leser, 'Men and women in industry', *Economic Journal*, LXII (1952), 326–44, p. 327.

24 Aged 16 and over in 1923 and 16–64 in 1937.

25 Glucksmann, *Women Assemble*, pp. 48–9.

much of this increase was accounted for by the general employment growth of these sectors, the proportion of women employed in vehicles and metal industries showing only modest increases. As Table 10.2 demonstrates, the only industries with over 50 per cent female employment in 1939 were those traditional sectors where women had already formed more than half the insured workforce in 1923.

Table 10.2: Women as a proportion of insured employees in various sectors, 1923 and 1939

Sector	1923*	1939**
Clothing	65.0	70.2
Textiles	60.3	61.3
Pottery, earthenware, etc.	50.5	56.3
Food, drink, tobacco	40.5	42.3
Paper, printing	38.8	38.7
Miscellaneous	31.7	38.9
Misc. metal industries	30.1	32.0
Leather	29.9	37.7
Chemicals	25.2	26.7
Woodworking	15.6	15.6
Glass	15.1	19.7
Bricks, tiles, etc.	12.2	6.3
Vehicles	8.6	8.9
Engineering	6.5	10.3
Metal manufacture	5.1	5.6
Non-metallic mineral products	3.6	5.1
Shipbuilding	1.5	1.8

Source: C. E. V. Leser, 'Men and Women in Industry', Economic Journal, *LXII (1952), 326–44, p. 330.*

Notes: * Aged 16 and over. ** Aged 16–64.

Data from the 1931 Census shows that the proportion of females in the occupied population was highest in the textile-dominated North West (41.9 per cent) and in London and the South East (39.9 per cent). The Midlands, Scotland, and Yorkshire followed, with the more agricultural regions below them, and finally the coal-based Northern region and Wales with rates of less than 25 per cent.[26] The case-study 'new

26 For workers aged 14 and over, including those unemployed. Leser, 'Men and Women', p. 339.

industrial communities' (discussed in the previous chapter) had female employment ratios below the average for their regions.[27] Female employment in these centres may be underestimated by the Census, as it appears that women and girls formed a relatively high proportion of workers commuting from surrounding villages. Yet estimates of the composition of the workforce, rather than working population, at Slough and Welwyn indicate that, while such under-estimation did occur, women workers were still under-represented.[28] This was probably largely due to these centres' industrial composition, dominated by those industries which achieved the largest national employment growth – motor vehicles, electrical engineering, mechanical engineering and metal goods. These were sectors in which female employment rose significantly over the interwar period but was still generally below the average for all industries. The lower geographical mobility of women may also have been an important influence, as these towns experienced considerable long-distance in-migration.

Female workers tended to be employed on repetitive, labour-intensive, un/semi-skilled processes. Within particular factories there were usually very strong demarcation lines between men's and women's work – men and women rarely working side by side, as shown in the examples from the Slough Estate in Figure 10.2. However, segregation was sometimes less clear-cut between factories. As a 1929 official study noted, in a diverse group of industries certain processes were conducted by men in one factory and women, or in some cases boys, in another.[29] The demarcation of particular jobs as 'women's work' accords well with DLM theory, which highlights women's high 'voluntary' labour turnover as a key feature of their concentration in secondary labour markets. As the 1929 study argued, the expected termination of work on marriage encouraged women's employment in un/semi-skilled jobs:

> The industrial life of women is, in general, a short one. This makes them unwilling to spend much time on [...] training and disposes them to seek occupations where they can earn a good wage as quickly as possible. For the same reason, managers are unwilling to train up workers for skilled occupations if they are likely to lose them when they have become really useful.[30]

---

27 Great Britain, General Register Office, *Census of England and Wales, 1931, Occupation Tables* (London, 1934), Tables 16 and 17; A. Shenfield and P. S. Florence, 'Labour for the war industries: the experience of Coventry', *Review of Economic Studies*, XII (1) (1944–45), 31–49, p. 34.

28 Savage, 'Trade Unionism'; W. Davies, 'The nature and significance of trading estates with special reference to the Treforest and Slough Estates', unpublished MA thesis, University Of Wales, 1951, p. 138; Tyrewhitt, Welwyn survey; NA: HLG90/440, Ministry of Town and Country Planning, New Towns Research Section, 'Welwyn Garden City: some aspects of its economic history', June 1950 [hereafter Welwyn report].

29 UK, Parliament, *A Study of the Factors Which Have Operated in the Past and Those Which are Operating Now to Determine the Distribution of Women in Industry*, Cmd 3508 of 1930 [presented to Parliament in 1929].

30 UK, Parliament, A *Study of the Factors*, p. 29.

In 1921 and 1931 69 per cent of working women were under 35, as women *generally* left full-time paid work on marriage – though this varied greatly according to location and industry.[31] The proportion of working women who were married varied from 28 per cent for weavers to only 5 per cent in electrical apparatus manufacture and 7 per cent for sugar confectionary, scientific instruments, printing, and photography.[32] Tradition played a pivotal role regarding geographical patterns; some centres such as the Lancashire cotton textile districts, or Luton, had a tradition of married women's employment which became reflected in the new industries that settled there.[33] In many other areas women rarely continued in work after marriage, social pressure being reinforced by employers' formal or informal marriage bars.

Many employers justified marriage bars on moral grounds, though even at Rowntrees, where the owners' Quaker values moulded labour policy, the firm's rigid marriage bar was temporarily relaxed when shortages of suitable labour made this necessary.[34] Marriage bars in fact had an important economic rationale. At firms like Courtaulds, which recruited girls at 14, they were part of a wider policy of fostering a 'respectable' atmosphere which made it more socially acceptable for families to send girls into factory work. More importantly, marriage bars fostered dispensability, providing a relatively uncontroversial means of dismissing older females, and thus keeping the average age of women workers, and their strongly age-related wages, low.[35] In 1931 the labour force participation rate for women aged 14–24 was 69 per cent; for those aged 25–34 it fell to only 36 per cent on account of marriage (single women's participation rates were 76 and 81 per cent respectively).[36] By taking older women out of the workforce as they married (typically during their early twenties), the marriage bar allowed Courtaulds to maintain the proportion of juveniles in their female workforce at a constant one third over the interwar period.[37]

As Veronica Beechey has noted, Marx's argument that employers use female and juvenile workers to weaken the resistance of organised labour to mechanisation implies that such tactics will produce union opposition to their employment.[38] Women's employment was seen as a threat by unions, as many processes offered

31 Catherine Hakim, *Occupational Segregation. A Comparative Study of the Degree and Pattern of the Differentiation Between Men and Women's Work in Britain, the United States and Other Countries*, Dept. of Employment Research Paper No. 9. (London, 1979), p. 10.

32 UK, Parliament, *A Study of the Factors*, p. 33.

33 Stephen Bunker, '"A small town outside Vauxhall": Luton in the twentieth century', unpublished paper, presented at ESRC Colloquium on Industry and Urbanisation, University College London, 8 May 1993.

34 Robert Fitzgerald, *Rowntree and the Marketing Revolution, 1862–1969* (Cambridge, 1995), p. 238.

35 UK, Parliament, *A Study of the Factors*, p. 24.

36 Hakim, *Occupational Segregation*, pp. 6–7.

37 Josie Castle, 'Factory work for women: Courtaulds and G.E.C. between the wars', 133–71 in Bill Lancaster and Tony Mason (eds), *Life and Labour in a Twentieth Century City: The Experience of Coventry* (Coventry, 1986), pp. 144–7.

38 Veronica Beechey, 'Some notes on female wage labour in capitalist production', *Capital and Class*, III (1977), 45–66, p. 55.

Figure 10.2: Men's and women's work on the Slough Estate – Parfumerie Fabrik and Intertype Ltd

Source: Slough Estates Ltd, Slough. London's Industrial Centre of 600 Acres *(Slough, c. 1938).*

considerable scope for the replacement of male by female labour, especially when changes in technology or the organisation of production allowed reclassification in terms of skill and gender. The *New Survey* noted that in industries where male and female labour 'is largely employed side by side' male unemployment was substantially higher than that for women (almost twice as high in the engineering trades and even greater in footwear and tailoring).[39] Such competition also had a generational component; adults of both sexes experienced higher unemployment than juveniles.[40]

Unions vigorously resisted the extension of female employment into sectors where women might compete with adult males. Their success varied geographically according to local union strength and labour market conditions, producing the phenomenon of certain processes being done almost exclusively by men in one area and women in another.[41] Variations over time in labour market conditions could also influence the gender allocation of jobs. For example at Rowntrees the onset of depression from 1929 enabled the firm to gain union compliance for a policy of substituting female or juvenile workers for men on some processes.[42]

The Age Dimension

The division of labour, and employment competition, between men and women was overlaid by the relationship between adult and juvenile employment. Juveniles formed a significant sector of the interwar labour market, most children leaving school at 14. As noted above, both boys and girls were paid wages well below those for adult women, and thus constituted a preferred source of labour for processes where there was little productivity loss from their employment or where labour-intensive production and piece rates made their employment more profitable despite their lower productivity. While recorded unemployment in Britain averaged almost 14 per cent from 1920–38, juvenile unemployment averaged only 5 per cent. There may be some under-recording of juvenile unemployment, particularly with regard to those under 16, for whom registration was voluntary prior to 1934.[43] However, comparison of the Insurance Office data with the Census estimate for 1931 indicates no significant underestimation.[44]

As Table 10.1 shows, in 1935 the employment of 'juveniles' in manufacturing was almost as great as that of women (though applying age cut-offs at 18 for girls and 21 for boys distorts the comparison). Juveniles constituted a particularly important segment of the female workforce; girls aged 14–17 comprised only 9.1 per cent of the British female population aged 14–64 in 1931, but made up over a quarter of the female workforce in 1935 for every sector in Table 10.1 (with the exception of textiles). An investigation of particular firms, conducted by S. R. Dennison in the

---

39 London School of Economics *The New Survey of London Life and Labour. Volume II: London Industries I* (London, 1931), pp. 20–21.

40 Ibid, p. 36.

41 UK, Parliament, *A Study of the Factors*, pp. 9–10.

42 Fitzgerald, *Rowntree*, pp. 274–91.

43 W. R. Garside, 'Juvenile unemployment between the wars: a rejoinder', *Economic History Review*, 2nd ser. XXXII (1979), 529–32.

44 Daniel K. Benjamin, and Levis A. Kochin, 'What went right with juvenile unemployment policy between the wars: a comment', *Economic History Review*, 2nd ser. XXXII (1979), 523–8.

late 1930s, revealed a preference for engaging juveniles. Employers believed that they could be more easily trained; indeed the specialised skills of older workers were often regarded as a disadvantage. Dennison also found, using aggregate statistical evidence, that the proportion of juveniles was considerably higher in expanding than in declining sectors.[45]

Evidence from the case-study centres examined in the last chapter indicates that juvenile workers were under-represented, as in-migrants made up a large proportion of their working populations and younger juveniles had low geographical mobility. This produced local shortages of juvenile labour, girls and younger boys having very low unemployment rates. For example, in the Watford area men aged over 21 and 18–20 had unemployment rates of 6.4 and 7.0 per cent in September 1933, while boys under 18 had recorded unemployment of only 0.6 per cent. Meanwhile unemployment rates for females aged over 21, 18–20, and under 18 were 1.9 per cent, 0.4 per cent and 0.3 per cent respectively.[46] The Welwyn survey reported very low unemployment rates for juvenile females and males under 16. While male unemployment increased sharply after age 16, female unemployment remained very low until age 21, but then rose from an average of 0.8 per cent for ages 18–21 to 4.8 per cent for women over 21. Some Welwyn firms laid great stress on difficulties in obtaining sufficient young (14–16-year-old) girls – a sector of the population with particularly low geographical mobility.[47]

Similar results were obtained in Hatton and Bailey's analysis of the *New Survey* juvenile unemployment data. They found that unemployment for males aged 16–21 rose sharply and continuously with age, the unemployment rate for 21 year olds being almost three times that for those aged 16.[48] Meanwhile there was no similar increase for juvenile females. The absence of increased unemployment for older female juveniles was probably largely due to the fact that girls' wages rose much less sharply with age than was the case for boys, culminating in wide gender wage differentials for adults.

The demand for juvenile labour was partly for juveniles *per se*. The Ministry of Labour noted that there was little demand for juvenile (especially boy) 'transferees' – government-assisted internal migrants – aged 17–18 (relative to younger juveniles), despite these often having more years of school education, as few juvenile jobs were available that would enable them to become self-supporting on reaching 18 (i.e. jobs leading to adult employment).[49] Many juveniles were employed in 'blind alley' jobs and dismissal at ages 18–21 was said to be common for boys.[50] Such

45 S. R. Dennison, *The Location of Industry and the Depressed Areas* (London, 1939), p. 78.

46 Watford Civic Survey, Vol. 2. Unemployment data for August 1932 reveal similar age/gender differentials.

47 Tyrewhitt, Welwyn Survey.

48 Timothy J. Hatton and Roy E. Bailey, 'Unemployment incidence in interwar London', *Economica*, 69 (2002), 631–54.

49 Ministry of Labour, *Report for the Year 1936* (P.P. 1936–37, XII), p. 42; *Report for the Year 1938* (P.P. 1938–39, XII), p. 43.

50 John Gollan, *Youth in British Industry* (London, 1937); G. Mikoleit, 'Industrial restructuring and women's employment: the case of the food industry in inter-war Britain',

workers, having learned no skill of sufficient value to compensate for their age, were largely relegated to 'dead-end' secondary labour market jobs.[51] In some expanding industrial centres with significant unionisation, such as Coventry, juvenile males were particularly valued by employers, as they fell outside the scope of local collective wage negotiations and their employment, followed by dismissal at age 21, constituted an important means of counteracting union wage pressure.[52] This job competition led unions to oppose juvenile employment on many processes (especially outside regulated apprenticeships). According to a 1937 study by John Gollan, a growing number of small-scale strikes were occurring in the engineering trades against piecemeal attempts to introduce boys on machines previously operated by skilled men.[53]

The Local Dimension

While it is generally true that employers in the new industries rejected established industrial workers in favour of those drawn from outside manufacturing, in some areas workers made redundant from declining local industries did constitute a significant source of labour for new firms. For example rayon plants became concentrated in areas such as Coventry and Lancashire, where (in addition to other factors) appropriate labour was available from declining textile industries.[54] In Luton the straw hat trade provided an important source of labour for its new industries,[55] while Birmingham's electrical components industry drew large numbers of workers from its declining jewellery quarter.[56] These cases all involve supplies of predominantly female workers, suggesting that these were much easier to redeploy to new industries than their male counterparts (probably largely due to their lower wages and weaker unionisation). Another local source of workers were domestic servants (especially important in affluent areas with large servant communities). In Oxford many younger college servants turned to better-paid work in the local motor vehicle industry.[57] Similarly, many domestic servants in London and the South East turned

---

unpublished M.Phil thesis, Polytechnic of the South Bank, 1986, pp. 100–101.

51 Gollan, *Youth in British Industry*, pp. 184–90; P. W. Carr, 'Engineering workers and the rise of labour in Coventry, 1914–1939', unpublished Ph.D. thesis, University of Warwick, 1978, p. 438.

52 Carr, 'Engineering workers', p. 438.

53 Gollan, *Youth in British Industry*, p. 67.

54 J. Harrap, 'Rayon', 276–302 in Neil K. Buxton and Derek H. Aldcroft (eds), *British Industry Between the Wars* (London, 1979).

55 Fred Grundy and Richard Morris Titmuss, *Report on Luton* (Luton, 1945), p. 25.

56 Michael Beesley, 'Changing industrial advantages in the British motor car industry', *Journal of Industrial Economics*, VI (1957), 47–57.

57 D. Ian Scargill, 'Responses to growth in modern Oxford', 110–30 in R. C. Whiting (ed.), *Oxford: Studies in the History of a University Town since 1800* (Manchester, 1993), p. 111.

to manufacturing, domestic service being regarded as a residual occupation which most women would only consider when factory employment was unavailable.[58]

A further local source of workers were agricultural labourers, together with their female and juvenile relatives. National employment in agriculture and forestry declined from an average of 1,004,000 in 1920–22 to 735,000 in 1937–38. The heaviest falls were for males under 21, whose numbers declined by 44 per cent between 1921–24 and 1938.[59] Workers were drawn from agriculture by higher manufacturing wages; for example wages for adult male agricultural workers in the Watford area were around two thirds, or less, of those for factory workers.[60] These proved a considerable incentive; the migration of farm labourers to Ipswich and other East Anglian towns was so substantial during the 1930s that it eventually produced a shortage of agricultural workers in the region.[61] Male farm workers were particularly sought-after by manufacturers in capital-intensive 'primary' labour markets, such as motor vehicles, as they were viewed as being flexible, reliable, and non-unionised. For example, Oxford's motor industry relied heavily (especially during its early development) on workers from surrounding rural districts. According to an estimate by R. C. Whiting, by 1936 there were around 3,000 ex-agricultural workers in the Cowley motor industry (compared to 1,266 long-distance migrants from Wales, the North, and Scotland).[62]

Locally-recruited adult male workers, such as former agricultural labourers and Oxford's college servants, shared the characteristics of low previous wages, weak (if any) unionisation, and non-industrial backgrounds. As such they formed part of what Marx termed the latent reserve army of labour – workers attracted from non-industrial sectors offering inferior pay and conditions. While more expensive than women or juveniles, such workers were of particular attraction to employers in primary labour market sectors such as motor vehicles, as they were seen as being reliable, disciplined, and willing to accept the working conditions set by employers.

Meanwhile women and juveniles in neighbouring agricultural areas were particularly attractive to employers in secondary labour markets, on account of their low transfer wages from rural work. In Letchworth 30–40 per cent of factory workers in 1935 were said to be young people who commuted in daily from surrounding villages.[63] Welwyn's factories relied extensively on rural commuters, especially girls – some 28 per cent of its workforce living 2–20 miles away, while the Slough

58 LSE, *New Survey... Volume II*, p. 429; Glucksmann, *Women Assemble*, pp. 247–48.

59 Sidney Pollard, *The Development of the British Economy 1914–1990* (London, 1992), p. 66.

60 Watford Civic Survey, Volumes 2 and 3.

61 E. D. Smithies, 'The contrast between North and South in England 1918–1939: a study of economic, social and political problems with particular reference to the experience of Burnley, Halifax, Ipswich, and Luton', unpublished Ph.D. thesis, University of Leeds, 1974, p. 115.

62 R. C. Whiting, *The View from Cowley: The Impact of Industrialisation upon Oxford, 1918–1939* (Oxford, 1983), pp. 39–66.

63 Letchworth Museum, 'Letchworth – Some Economic and Industrial Aspects', typescript, 1935, author not known.

Estate also recruited a large number of such workers.[64] As houses in Welwyn and Letchworth were expensive, the recruitment of cheap labour was heavily dependent on rural workers with lower accommodation costs.[65] Many adult male ex-agricultural workers in Oxford and Coventry also continued to commute from their villages of origin. This assisted car manufacturers in retaining such workers despite occasional temporary lay-offs during the summer slack season, as they were able to switch to harvest work rather than seek new permanent employment.[66]

Industrial areas on the fringes of major cities such as London and Birmingham also employed considerable numbers of un/semi-skilled commuters from the central areas of these cities. For example around 50 per cent of workers in West Middlesex commuted in, mainly from central London.[67] Central London had a higher proportion of cheaper housing that was affordable for workers in the low-wage assembly industries, while the outer-boroughs had a high proportion of modern semi-detached owner-occupied and council housing, which only relatively well-paid workers could usually afford. This spatial mis-match between employment and housing producing heavy daily commuter flows both from inner-London to the outer factory areas and in the reverse direction.[68] The physical separation of workplace and home acted as a further barrier to unionisation, as workers faced with long travel times (and poorer transport services after the early evening) were less willing to attend union meetings after work.

The migrant dimension

In addition to commuting from inner-city and agricultural areas to new industrial centres, the interwar years witnessed considerable migration to these centres.[69] One important migration stream was from the County of London (which experienced a net loss of 339,000 people from 1921–35) to outer-London, or beyond, sometimes led by the decentralisation of industry.[70] Many firms moving from London to areas such as Letchworth, Watford and Welwyn brought at least part of their workforce (especially skilled workers) with them. Other major cities, such as Birmingham, also

64 Tyrewhitt, Welwyn Survey; Savage, 'Trade unionism', p. 220.

65 MTCP, Welwyn Report.

66 Jonathan Zeitlin, 'The Emergence of shop steward organization and job control in the British car industry: a review essay', *History Workshop Journal*, X (1980), 121–37, p. 126.

67 Nuffield College Library Oxford, Nuffield College Social Reconstruction Survey papers [hereafter NCSRS], C1/108, report on Middlesex industry by P. J. Self, January 1943.

68 Noreen Branson and Margot Heinemann, *Britain in the Nineteen Thirties* (St Albans, 1973), p. 82.

69 E. H. Hunt, *Regional Wage Variations in Britain: 1850–1914* (Oxford, 1973), pp. 257–62.

70 Dov Friedlander, 'London's urban transition 1851–1951', *Urban Studies*, XI (1974), 127–41; London Passenger Transport Board, *Report for Year Ended 30 June 1936* (London, 1936), p. 9.

witnessed significant population decentralisation of firms and their workers to new suburban and satellite industrial areas.

New suburban municipal housing estates constituted another important mechanism of population decentralisaton. The London County Council established a number of major housing estates outside the County of London; the largest, such as Becontree, at Dagenham (population 112,500) and St. Helier, at Morden (population almost 40,000) had a considerable local impact on labour supply.[71] A 1941 survey indicated that 30.5 per cent of residents at Becontree and 20.1 per cent at St. Helier worked within a two mile radius of their estates. The proportions working within five miles were 58.1 and 36.4 per cent respectively.[72] Housing allocation policies favoured large families, providing an ample supply of juvenile workers; half the residents of Becontree, and almost half those of the Watling estate at Hendon, were under 18.[73]

Ruth Durant's survey of Watling, a cottage estate of 19,000 people designed for the 'elite' of the working class, indicated that while only 26.3 per cent of household heads worked in Hendon, 54.3 per cent of other employed family members worked locally. This was due to the fact that Hendon's recently-established (and rapidly expanding) factory sector sought unskilled labour, rejecting 'family fathers' in favour of 'their wives ... sons and daughters'.[74] Durant divided the estate's juvenile employment geographically between the majority employed in dead-end local factory jobs and a minority whose family connections had helped them secure jobs with 'prospects' in old established firms. Such jobs entailed commuting towards London's centre: 'for Watling youngsters Hendon is a place where one can earn money, provided one is young enough, and London is a place which harbours prospects, provided one is rich enough to aspire to them'.[75]

Short distance migration, via population decentralisation from inner-urban areas, or through former agricultural workers leaving their villages for better-paid factory employment, made an important contribution to the workforces of expanding industrial centres in the South East and West Midlands. Yet, particularly during the 1930s, long-distance migrants from Britain's depressed areas formed a large and growing proportion of in-migrants. Large inflows of such workers had both major economic and social impacts on reception areas, as is explored in the following Chapter.

71 Andrzej Olechnowicz, *Working-class Housing in England Between the Wars: the Becontree Estate* (Oxford, 1997), p. 2.

72 NCSRS, C1/105, G. R. Mitchison, 'Greater London supplementary report no. 2 – journeys to work', November 1941.

73 Olechnowicz, *Working-class Housing*, p. 72; Ruth Durant, *Watling: A Survey of Social Life on a New Housing Estate* (London, 1939), pp. 12–13.

74 Durant, *Watling*, pp. 12–13.

75 Ibid, p. 14.

Chapter Eleven

Long-distance migrants in the new industrial workforce

Introduction

The 1930s witnessed unprecedented long-distance internal migration to the South and Midlands from depressed industrial areas in northern England, Wales, and Scotland. The most rapidly-expanding areas came to rely extensively on migrant workers and by the late 1930s a substantial proportion of the populations of centres such as Slough, Welwyn, Coventry, Watford, Hendon, and Willesden originated from the depressed areas. Government encouraged and assisted migration, under its 'industrial transference' programme of taking workers to the work. So great was the inflow of labour into some rapidly-expanding centres that despite their prosperity employment competition from in-migrants kept wages below the national average for their industries. This often provoked a hostile response from local residents – accentuated by the perceived 'foreignness' of the in-migrants.

Patterns and drivers of migration

Interwar internal migration has been somewhat neglected compared to the substantial volume of research on the pre-1914 decades,[1] partly due to serious deficiencies in the census data. The 1921 and 1931 censuses provide no birthplace data, while no census was taken in 1941. Yet long-distance internal migration probably played a greater role in economic and social change in interwar Britain than at any time since the industrial revolution. E.H. Hunt has compared regional migration over 1921–31 with that from 1861–1911. Although he concludes that migration was at least as great between 1861–1911 as in the 1920s, his figures indicate that net inter-regional migration during 1921–31 was higher than for some pre-1914 decades.[2] Moreover, estimates by D.E. Pitfield (using net migration residuals derived from the population

1 For example, George R. Boyer and Timothy J. Hatton, 'Migration and labour market integration in late nineteenth-century England and Wales', *Economic History Review*, L, 4 (1997), 697–734; Dov Friedlander, 'Occupational structure, wages, and migration in late nineteenth-century England and Wales', *Economic Development and Cultural Change*, XL (1992), 295–318; E. H. Hunt, 'Industrialization and regional inequality: wages in Britain, 1760–1914', *Journal of Economic History* XLVI, 4 (1986), 935–66; D. E. Baines, *Migration in a Mature Economy* (Cambridge, 1985).

2 E. H. Hunt, *Regional Wage Variations in Britain: 1850–1914* (Oxford, 1973), pp. 257–62.

and vital statistics data of the Registrar-General for England and Wales) indicate that net internal migration was much higher in the 1930s than during the 1920s. The number of net inter-county moves in Great Britain were estimated to have risen from 686,958 over 1920–29 to 1,481,327 during 1929–39. Longer-distance migration experienced a much greater increase, net inter-regional moves over these periods rising from 282,994 to 772,292.[3]

The available statistical evidence thus indicates that over the interwar period as a whole the volume of long-distance internal migration was greater than before 1914, despite evidence that higher post-war housing costs, stronger unions, and unemployment benefit acted to impede the geographical mobility of labour.[4] While such pressures may have significantly reduced labour mobility *per se*, chronic unemployment in many peripheral areas, together with large regional unemployment disparities, proved sufficient to outweigh such impediments, while government assistance also boosted migration rates.

The volume of migration varied over time inversely with national unemployment and positively *vis-à-vis* regional unemployment disparities. Very high nationwide unemployment during the 1929–32 depression produced a substantial decline in migration,[5] while over one-third of in-migrants living in the South East in 1936 were attributed to moves during the 1932–36 boom (during which regional unemployment differentials widened markedly). These also included a substantially higher proportion (relative to earlier migrants) of long-distance moves from Wales, the North East, and Scotland.[6] Despite countervailing fertility trends, the volume of long-distance migration was sufficient to change the balance of population between 'inner' and 'outer' Britain. In 1923 the area covered by the Ministry of Labour's London and South East, South West, and Midlands divisions accounted for a minority of Britain's population, 46.5 per cent. However, by 1937 their populations had risen to 53.4 per cent of the British total.[7] According to Pitfield's estimates the London and South East division experienced net in-migration from outside the region of 1,221,000 people over 1920–39, while its South West and Midlands divisions had net receipts of 222,000 and 36,000 people respectively.[8] London and the Home Counties, together with the Midlands counties of Staffordshire, Warwickshire, Worcestershire, Leicestershire, and Northamptonshire, contained about 35 per cent

3 D. E. Pitfield, 'Labour migration and the regional problem in Britain, 1920–1939', unpublished Ph.D. thesis, University of Sterling, 1973, p. 48.

4 D. E. Baines, 'Population migration and regional development, 1870–1939', 29–61, in R. Floud and D. McCloskey (eds), *The Economic History of Britain since 1700*, 2nd Edn, Volume 2 (Cambridge, 1994), pp. 60–61.

5 G. H. Daniel, 'Some factors affecting the movement of labour', *Oxford Economic Papers*, III (1940), 144–79.

6 Brinley Thomas, 'The influx of labour into London and the South East 1920–36', *Economica*, IV (1937), 323–36, p. 330.

7 Brinley Thomas, 'The influx of labour into the Midlands 1920–37', *Economica*, V (1938), 410–34.

8 Pitfield, 'Labour migration', pp. 120–22.

of Britain's population in 1937, but accounted for almost 70 per cent of the net national increase in population from 1921–37.[9]

Studies of internal migration prior to the First World War have tended to emphasise wage differentials and the presence of earlier migrants from the same source area as the main positive determinants of regional migration rates, while distance between origin and destination is seen to constitute the main negative factor.[10] Conversely, during the interwar period migration was driven primarily by unemployment rather than wage differentials. Dov Friedlander has argued that even before 1914 'redundancy' arising from technical change in agriculture and other declining sectors constituted a major stimulus to migration, though this was demonstrated primarily through wage disparities rather than unemployment.[11] Regional wage variations within particular sectors were greatly eroded by the First World War and postwar inflation (due to flat rate increases to compensate for rising living costs) and, of longer-term importance, the growth of national wage bargaining and unemployment insurance.[12] Meanwhile chronic depression, high unemployment, and downwards wage rigidity in Britain's peripheral regions led workers to travel long distances and accept wages no better than those prevailing for fully-employed workers in the declining staple industries.

The regional incidence of out-migration was strongly influenced by unemployment differentials and industrial structure. Particularly depressed mining regions such as South Wales and the North East experienced substantially higher out-migration than textile-dominated regions such as the North West.[13] The extent of migration from Wales was such that only in 1961 did its population return to its 1921 level.[14] Lower out-migration from depressed textile areas than those mining areas with similar unemployment rates was probably largely due to their higher female participation ratios (which made it more likely for at least one household member to remain in work), together with the greater incidence of short-time and under-employment in textiles compared to coal.[15] Out-migration was also strongly influenced by the proximity of the area in question to that of relatively prosperous localities. South Wales, in addition to experiencing chronic unemployment, was also relatively close to major reception areas such as Coventry, Oxford and Slough, a return journey to which could be made during a day. 'Distance' had both a physical and psychological component. East South Wales had witnessed heavy in-migration between 1880–1914;

9 Royal Commission on the Distribution of the Industrial Population, *Report* (London, 1940), pp. 36–7.

10 See Boyer and Hatton, 'Migration and labour market integration'.

11 Friedlander, 'Occupational structure'.

12 Hunt, 'Industrialization and regional inequality', p. 959; Baines, 'Population, migration and regional development', p. 58.

13 Thomas, 'Influx of labour into London', p. 328; idem, 'Influx of labour into the Midlands', p. 416.

14 G. W. Williams, 'From grand slam to great slump: economy, society and rugby football in Wales during the depression', *Welsh History Review*, XI (1983), 338–57.

15 Thomas, 'Influx of labour into the Midlands', p. 417. This was confirmed by a contemporary Ministry of Labour investigation – NA, LAB8/218, 'Report of enquiry into the industrial transference scheme (adults), part I', May 1938.

depression therefore confronted a population of whom a substantial proportion did not have particularly long roots in Wales.[16]

Further factors influencing migration included information and assistance from previous migrants – the 'friends and relatives effect'.[17] These can have direct economic effects on the decision to migrate – through lowering the costs of travel, adjustment, job search, and general uncertainty.[18] Uncertainty regarding conditions in potential reception areas constituted a formidable deterrent to migration. As the Oldham textile worker Jane Walsh (who had spent most of the 1930s in crushing poverty, raising a family on the dole) recalled, she was originally hostile to her husband's suggestion that he should seek work in Coventry (following the example of one of his friends):

> Why should we leave the town in which we had been born and bred to settle among strangers? It would be almost like admitting defeat. Besides, my old enemy – fear- raised its ugly head. I knew the worst in Oldham, but if Charlie lost his job – assuming he had one – in Coventry, I would be sunk. I did not know the cheapest shops there. And how could we move our furniture. I was still paying a shilling a week off the money we had borrowed for the last move ... We had a [rented] home of our own, a precious thing in these days of housing shortage. We could shut our door and semi-starve in privacy.[19]

Contemporary evidence indicates that links with earlier migrants helped both to reduce the psychological distance of particular reception areas and provide specific information and assistance regarding such things as job vacancies, accommodation, maintenance while seeking work, and (for migrating families) child-care.[20] Such information flows explain the chain migration evident in several areas; of the 1,195 Welsh 'foreigners' in Oxford in July 1936, 534 came from six Exchange districts (150 of whom came from a single mining village – Pontycymmer). Interview evidence supported the view that this concentration arose due to the friends and relatives effect,[21] as did analysis of letters from 'transferees' (assisted migrants) to relatives and friends in Whitehaven and Cleaton Moor.[22] One family which had migrated from Cwmamman was said to have been responsible for 36 others following them. Similarly, a migrant from Heywood, Lancashire, to Birmingham had, on having

---

16 Williams, 'From grand slam to great slump'; A. Shenfield and P. S. Florence, 'Labour for the war industries: the experience of Coventry', *Review of Economic Studies*, xii (1) (1944–45), 31–49, p. 43.

17 Pitfield, 'Labour migration', pp. 145–7.

18 Boyer and Hatton, 'Migration and labour market integration', p. 699.

19 Jane Walsh, *Not Like This* (London, 1953), p. 88. Yet eventually she agreed to let her husband go to the Midlands in search of work.

20 G. H. Daniel, 'Labour migration and age-composition', *Sociological Review*, xxxi (1939), 281–308, p. 295; London Metropolitan Archives [hereafter LMA], Acc. 2720/01/07/01, 'Migration to London from South Wales', unsigned memorandum for National Council of Social Service, 1936.

21 Barnett House Survey Committee, *A Survey of the Social Services in the Oxford District* (Oxford, 1938), p. 59.

22 NA: LAB8/218, 'Report of enquiry into the industrial transference scheme (adults), part I', May 1938.

been promoted to foreman, been instrumental in securing the transfer of 80–100 Heywood men to that plant in a year. As a result certain rapidly expanding centres had concentrations of people from particular depressed areas: the Welsh in Birmingham, Luton, Slough and Oxford; workers from the Oldham area in the Washwood Heath district of Birmingham; and pockets from Scotland and/or Durham in other reception areas.[23]

Government industrial transference policy

During the interwar period the state came to play a significant role in the internal migration process. While the advent of 'industrial transference' is generally dated from 1927, government-assisted internal migration had been in operation since the end of the First World War.[24] The Labour Exchange system had been established shortly before the War with the aim of increasing labour mobility and it was appreciated that the cost of seeking distant employment constituted an important barrier to mobility. Powers were consequently provided for Exchanges to loan applicants the travel costs incurred in taking employment more than five miles from their home Exchange.[25] Once the Exchange service had developed its system of inter-regional clearing houses it became an organisation for promoting migration, the later launching of a formal transference scheme being merely an extension of this placing system.[26]

During the early 1920s government had looked principally to empire, rather than internal, migration as a means of simultaneously easing the unemployment problem and strengthening empire connections. In 1922 the Overseas Settlement Committee entertained visions of an annual emigration of 500,000–700,000 people; instead total emigration for the whole 1922–32 period amounted to only 1.07 million, including 404,329 assisted migrants.[27] The onset of world depression in 1929 closed the door to mass emigration for the rest of the interwar period and government was forced to look to relocating the unemployed to more prosperous areas within Britain's own borders.

By the late 1920s the scale and geographical concentration of unemployment had already led government to initiate an internal migration policy. As early as 1926

23 Ibid.

24 Pitfield, 'Labour migration', p. 268.

25 T. S. Chegwidden and G. Myrddin-Evans, *The Employment Exchange Service of Great Britain* (London, 1934), p. 120. This was originally limited to workers placed through the Exchange system, but later extended to men over 18 who obtained employment independently.

26 A. D. K. Owen, 'The social consequences of industrial transference', *Sociological Review*, XXIX (1937), 331–54, p. 336; M. M. Attlee, *Mobility of Labour. A Consideration of the Question of Industrial Transference, with some Examples from the Inter-war Period and Suggestions for a Post-war Policy* (Oxford, 1944), p. 8.

27 Roger Middleton, *Government Versus the Market. The Growth of the Public Sector, Economic Management and British Economic Performance, c. 1890–1979* (Cheltenham, 1996), p. 395.

the Ministry of Labour had advocated in its annual report that the transference of miners should be encouraged in order to restore the 'fluidity' of the labour market.[28] A formal transference initiative was first discussed in Cabinet in November 1927, though by this time the Ministry had already commenced small, experimental schemes.[29] Transference received a high government profile – including the issue of a letter in 1928 by the Prime Minister, Stanley Baldwin, to employers – asking for their cooperation – followed up by visits from Exchange officials.[30]

Industrial transference was supported both by the 'carrot' of government assistance for migrants and the 'stick' of reduced assistance for those unwilling to migrate. Government cut back relief schemes in depressed areas.[31] In addition, Alan Booth found that, while the evidence is circumstantial, it appears to have tightened up the administration of the Poor Law in depressed coalfield districts from 1927 to encourage migration.[32] Such a policy was hinted at in a memorandum circulated by the Ministry of Health in January 1928: 'The only hope for the South Wales area is the redistribution of population which can be effected only by the economic pressure. Unemployment Benefit and poor relief have … tended to postpone the operation of this pressure, and it would be fatal … to introduce special measures to the relief of distress in the area.'[33]

In 1929 the Ministry of Labour widened the coverage of transference to include the iron and steel and shipbuilding industries.[34] The Exchanges also gave higher priority to transferees. They already positively discriminated in their favour in that, while vacancies were first advertised locally, they were then circulated to Exchanges in depressed areas before being advertised nationally.[35] Now Exchanges were given a target number of depressed area men to place. Some asked local employers to provide jobs, or earmark vacancies, for transferees. However, it was more common for them to meet targets by taking transferees to the front of the queue for general vacancies. While Exchanges were officially required to give first preference to local applicants, and then those at neighbouring offices, before considering transferees (with the exception of earmarked jobs), a Ministry of Labour enquiry indicated that,

---

28 M. E. Daly, 'Government policy and the depressed areas in the inter-war years', unpublished D.Phil thesis, University of Oxford, 1978, pp. 84–5.

29 A. E. Booth, 'The timing and content of government policies to assist the depressed areas, 1920–1939', unpublished D. Phil thesis, University of Kent, 1975, p. 90.

30 NA, LAB8/218, 'Report of enquiry into the industrial transference scheme (adults), part I', May 1938.

31 B. Staines, 'The movement of population from South Wales with specific reference to the effects of the industrial transference scheme, 1928–37', 237–50 in C. Baber and L. J. Williams (eds), *Modern South Wales: Essays In Economic History* (Cardiff, 1986).

32 Booth, 'Timing and content', p. 97.

33 NA: HLG30/47, memorandum by Ministry of Health, 23 January 1928.

34 In October 1930 it was further extended, to incorporate depressed cotton districts.

35 Royal Commission on The Distribution of The Industrial Population, *Minutes of Evidence* (London, 1940), p. 256.

'in their desire to further ... transference ... some [Exchange] Managers have obtained depressed area labour when local or nearby labour was available.'[36]

Benefits offered to transferees were of three types. The first, 'transfer relief payments', provided a varied package of benefits, including: free fares; lodging allowances and pocket money while seeking work in a new area; loans in advance of the first week's wages; expenses connected with household and family removals; and special financial assistance for juvenile (14–18-year-old) transferees (including grants towards maintenance, where wages did not cover living expenses).[37] The second category involved 'transfer relief works': from November 1928 local authorities in prosperous areas were offered 'transfer grants' towards relief works, on a more favourable basis than those for areas of exceptional unemployment. It was originally stipulated that 50 per cent of labour had to be recruited from depressed areas, but from July 1929 this was not rigidly enforced, due to local antipathy, and was waived altogether from July 1930.[38] This, together with the decision to discontinue (from March 1931) the payment of a higher rate of grant to 'transfer schemes' made such assistance of minor long-term importance.[39]

The final type of inducement, of particular importance in targeting transferees at certain reception areas, was training. The government's transferee training schemes were built on experience the Ministry of Labour had gained from training disabled ex-servicemen.[40] In autumn 1925 it was decided to extend training to young men who, owing to the War and/or the post-war depression, had had little or no opportunity to train for a skilled trade. The centres used rapidly developed into Government Training Centres [GTC's] – reception training centres for transferees.

By 1929 about 90 per cent of GTC places were reserved for depressed area men.[41] From 1925–36 57,149 men completed GTC courses, 50,717 of whom then found work.[42] By the beginning of 1938 the GTC's were capable of training 17,000 men per year.[43] The great majority were aged under 35, preference being given to younger workers (but not juveniles, for whom the Ministry had no powers to directly provide training).[44] GTC's offered six-month courses, generally aimed at producing

36 NA, LAB8/218, 'Report of enquiry into the industrial transference scheme (adults), part II', June 1938.

37 Owen, 'Social consequences', p. 337.

38 Pitfield, 'Labour migration', p. 158.

39 Pitfield, 'Labour migration', pp. 158–69; NA: LAB8/218, 'Report of enquiry into the industrial transference scheme (adults), part I', May 1938.

40 J. Sheldrake and S. Vickerstaff, *The History of Industrial Training in Britain* (Aldershot, 1987), p. 13.

41 Chegwidden and Myrddin-Evans, *Employment Exchange Service*, p. 148.

42 Royal Commission on The Distribution of The Industrial Population, *Minutes of Evidence*, p. 333.

43 Ibid, p. 260.

44 Ibid., pp. 259–60 and 332.

'handymen' or 'improvers'[45] rather than skilled craftsmen.[46] Training was provided in skills for which the Ministry of Labour detected unsatisfied demand, such as engineering, building, and motor vehicle trades, together with some service-sector occupations such as hairdressing.[47] The Centres were also intended to play a role in rehabilitation and preparation for employment via their regular hours, workshop practice, and discipline.[48] Mike Savage argues that they also played an important role in lowering trainees' wage expectations (compared to the high wages in some staple industries) and 'deunionising' them.[49] The cost of GTC training was almost £50 per man.[50] This was expensive compared to the costs of industrial transference per se. Dennison estimated that family removals under the transference scheme cost about £12, while individuals cost around £10.[51] Meanwhile the Ministry of Labour estimated the cost of transference in 1937 at only £3.65 per person.[52]

Some 33.1 per cent of GTC trainees from depressed areas, placed in employment outside their home areas from October 1936 to October 1937, found employment in the Ministry of Labour's London division. Other significant reception areas were the South East (28.1 per cent), South West (16.5 per cent) and Midlands (16.4 per cent), the remaining divisions attracting only 6.0 per cent of trainees.[53] New GTC's were mainly located in rapidly expanding industrial centres, in turn facilitating their expansion by acting as ports of entry into their labour markets. Five GTC's in centres of exceptionally rapid industrial growth (Park Royal, Watford, Letchworth, Waddon (Croydon) and Slough) accounted for 59.6 per cent of workers admitted to GTC's during 1936.[54] By 1938 the Park Royal GTC alone was said to have trained over 12,000 men, of whom over 8,000 were placed in employment.[55] Its presence acted as a magnet for firms seeking cheap labour. In 1930 Allnatt, the main developers of the Park Royal estate, wrote to the Ministry of Works, noting the large number of

45 Improvers were workers who had recently finished apprenticeships and were not yet fully qualified as craftsmen.

46 Modern Records Centre, Warwick [hereafter MRC], Mss. 292/103/1, report submitted to Parliamentary Building Trade Group and TUC General Council by National Federation of Building Trades Operatives, February 1930.

47 Booth, 'Timing and content', p. 100.

48 Sheldrake and Vickerstaff, *History of Industrial Training*, p. 14.

49 Mike Savage, 'Trade unionism, sex segregation, and the state: women's employment in "new industries" in inter-war Britain', *Social History*, 13, 2 (1988), 209–30, p. 223.

50 R. C. Davison, *British Unemployment Policy. The Modern Phase since 1930* (London, 1938), p. 116.

51 S. R. Dennison, *The Location of Industry and the Depressed Areas* (London, 1939), pp. 117–18.

52 NA, LAB8/218, 'Report of enquiry into the industrial transference scheme (adults), Part I', May 1938.

53 Royal Commission on The Distribution of The Industrial Population, *Minutes of Evidence*, p. 333.

54 Ministry of Labour, *Report for the year 1936* (PP, 1936–37, XII), p. 110.

55 Acton Town Council, *Acton: Official Guide* (Cheltenham, 1939), p. 28.

firms which had been attracted by the GTC's presence and offering to build a second centre there.[56]

The government's other main training initiative for men, Transfer Instructional Centres (TIC's) – which provided much more basic training for the long-term unemployed – was less important as an instrument of transference, accounting for only 19.5 per cent of men transferred through training from October 1936 to October 1937.[57] Training for women and juveniles played only a minor role in their government-assisted migration. While 26.5 per cent of adult men transferred up to the end of 1936 were placed after GTC or TIC courses, non-residential training schemes for women (orientated towards domestic service and other non-industrial occupations) and juvenile males – both not directly organised by the Ministry of Labour – accounted for only 6.6 per cent of women transferred to this date and 7.9 per cent of boys transferred during 1936.[58]

Despite the introduction of a limited, experimental, policy of 'taking work to the workers' in several particularly depressed areas during the mid-late 1930s, transference continued as the main geographically-orientated employment policy (in terms of job placements) throughout the interwar period.[59] Table 11.1 shows official data on the number of transferees during 1928–38, recording 339,843 assisted moves. However, these figures underestimate the role played by Exchanges and the transference initiative; as officials noted, a considerable volume of assisted transference was not reflected in the official records.[60] Exchanges played a vital role as an employment agency, finding work for the unemployed in distant areas about which they often had little first-hand knowledge. While Table 11.1 indicates that over 1932–36 an average of 28,267 workers migrated via the transference initiative, other Ministry of Labour data indicate that during this period an average of 420,496 vacancies were filled by Exchanges with applicants from other Exchange districts.[61] Although many of these would be within workers' normal travel to work areas, the figure nevertheless appears large in relation to the volume of officially-recorded transference.

Official transference figures are mainly based on workers placed in employment prior to transference. However, a large majority of undirected transferees were unskilled workers, who migrated independently of the Exchange system – primarily

56 NA, LAB 18/167, A. Endicott, Minister of Works, to R. J. Passmore, Director of Training, Ministry of Labour, 22 March 1930.

57 Royal Commission on The Distribution of The Industrial Population, *Minutes of Evidence*, p. 334.

58 Ministry of Labour, *Report for the year 1936*, p. 113; Royal Commission on The Distribution of The Industrial Population, *Minutes of Evidence*, p. 256.

59 For a discussion of the tensions between these two strands of policy see D. E. Pitfield, 'The quest for an effective regional policy, 1934–37', *Regional Studies*, XII (1978), 429–43.

60 NA, LAB8/218, 'Report of enquiry into the industrial transference scheme (adults), part II', June 1938; Chegwidden and Myrddin-Evans, *Employment Exchange Service*, pp. 152–4.

61 Royal Commission on The Distribution of The Industrial Population, *Minutes of Evidence*, p. 255.

Table 11.1: Officially-recorded industrial transference, 1928–38

Year	Labour transferred to employment through Exchanges						Other assisted transfers @	
	Men	**Women**	**Boys**	**Girls**	**Total individuals**	**Household & family removals**	**(1)**	**(2)**
1928	3,600*	360**	1,840	n.a.	c. 8,500	0	1,500*	0
1929	36,843	2,239	2,622	1,994*	43,698	2,850	0	0
1930	28,258	1,752	1,313	1,708	33,031	2,100	0	0
1931	17,889	2,631	868	1,986	23,374	1,680	0	0
1932	8,359	2,651	628	2,502	14,140	990	0	0
1933	5,333	4,038	1,117	2,955	13,443	605	0	0
1934	6,828	4,420	1,661	3,512	16,421	1,308	0	0
1935	13,379	6,350	5,376	4,648	29,753	3,718	1,016	n.a.
1936	20,091	8,008	9,449	5,958	43,506	10,025	2,039	4,000
1937	24,000***		7,675	6,450	38,125	7,673	2,052	3,000
1938	18,000***		4,131	5,496	27,627	4,000	n.a.	2,000

Source: D. E. Pitfield, 'Labour migration and the regional problem in Britain, 1920–1939', unpublished Ph.D thesis, University of Sterling, 1973, p. 248; A. E. Booth, 'The timing and content of government policies to assist the depressed areas, 1920–1939', unpublished D. Phil thesis, University of Kent, 1975, p. 204; NA, LAB8/218, 'Report of enquiry into the industrial transference scheme (adults), part I', May 1938.

Notes: (1) Transference to areas where vacancies were expected in the near future. (2) Transference to employment found other than through the Exchanges and assisted by the Ministry of Labour (free fares). @ An additional subsidiary scheme assisted 354 household removals to Stewart and Lloyds steelworks, Corby, in 1935 and a further 15 in 1936. * Part of year only. ** Represents only women and girls transferred after training. No records available for other female transfers. *** No disaggregated figures available for adult transfers.

since many unskilled vacancies were filled by employers 'at the gate' or from personal recommendation.[62] Both local and reception area Exchanges nevertheless played a major role in advising such workers where they might have the best chance of finding work, while some were subsequently placed in employment by reception area Exchanges.[63] Of the 105,050 men who migrated from depressed areas during 1936 and 1937, 72 per cent (75,794) moved on their own account. Only 35 per cent of these 'undirected transferees' moved to jobs they had already secured.[64] Of the 48,912 undirected male transferees who moved without first finding employment, 18.4 per cent were placed in their first reception area job by its local Exchange.

Furthermore, most financial benefits offered to official transferees were also available to workers who migrated on their own accord. The Ministry of Labour believed that, 'there can be little doubt that the [financial] provisions... have played a very important part in securing the satisfactory settlement in the non-depressed areas of large numbers of workers from the depressed areas.'[65] 25 per cent of those who had found work on their own account prior to transference in 1936 and 1937 had been given free fares (and, possibly, other assistance).[66]

While free fares had only been introduced in around 1935, loans covering fares for non-directed transferees had been provided throughout the interwar period, but their recipients were not included in the official transference data.[67] In the case of female migrants the degree of underestimation is greater as, in addition to industrial workers not pre-placed by Exchanges, the statistics did not include the substantial numbers of women transferred to private domestic service (though girls transferred to such work were included).[68] Given that 39.8 per cent of girls transferred during 1936 were placed in domestic service (and a larger percentage in previous years), the omission of adult women transferred to such employment may impart a significant downwards bias to the transference data.

Return migration was higher for transferees than other migrants (excluding family removals, which had low wastage rates).[69] The Ministry estimated that the 'coefficient of wastage' for juvenile transferees was about 35 per cent and for adults about 27 per cent.[70] Pitfield estimated the overall wastage rate for transferees at

---

62 NA, LAB8/218, 'Report of enquiry into the industrial transference scheme (adults), part I', May 1938.

63 Royal Commission on The Distribution of The Industrial Population, *Minutes of Evidence*, p. 257; NA, LAB8/218, 'Report of enquiry into the industrial transference scheme (adults), part I', May 1938.

64 NA, LAB8/218, 'Report of enquiry into the industrial transference scheme (adults), part I', May 1938. Based on data collected by the Ministry of Labour from 1936.

65 Ibid.

66 Ibid.

67 Ministry of Labour, *Report for the Year 1935* (P.P. 1935–36, XIII), pp. 21–2.

68 NA, LAB8/218, 'Report of enquiry into the industrial transference scheme (adults), part I', May 1938; Royal Commission on The Distribution of The Industrial Population, *Minutes of Evidence*, p. 259.

69 Owen, 'Social consequences', p. 339.

70 Ibid., p. 338.

around 30 per cent.[71] Return migration appears to have diminished during the more prosperous mid-late 1930s. Higher wastage rates during the early 1930s may have been due to significant unemployment in reception areas, as it was much cheaper to live on the dole in depressed areas than in the South (a factor accentuated by the support available from family networks in source areas).[72] A further major factor influencing return migration was the isolation many transferees felt, reinforced by the hostility they experienced from local people.

The contribution of long-distance migrants to the new industrial workforce

Early analyses of the contribution of migrants to population growth in reception areas used data from insured workers' 'employment books'. These documents, introduced in 1920, recorded workers for the Unemployment Insurance scheme, showing the office at which workers were first registered, together with subsequent changes (recorded annually) following a move to another area. Employment book data underestimate in-migration, mainly because they only record workers who migrated after entering insured employment. For example, a 1939 social survey of Welwyn compared the origins of workers according to employment books with that revealed by a direct survey of 602 working class families. The employment book data indicated that 30.1 per cent of Welwyn's working class population originated locally, while the household survey revealed no inhabitants born in Welwyn (as would be expected given that it had a negligible population prior to 1920). Meanwhile the survey indicated that 33.3 per cent of working families came from the North, Wales, and Scotland, compared to only 20.5 per cent according to the employment book data.[73] Similarly, the proportion of migrants in Coventry's 1935 population was estimated at 40 per cent,[74] while a 1937 analysis of employment books (which cover insured workers, a sector of the population in which migrants are usually over-represented) indicated that only 13.3 per cent were 'foreign' to the local Exchange division.[75]

Although employment books omit a large proportion of migrants, they are still useful as a means of ranking those areas receiving the highest in-migration (in the absence of superior data). Brinley Thomas examined the proportion of 'foreign' books for each district in the Ministry's South East division, which originated from

71 Pitfield, 'Labour migration', p. 263.

72 Daniel, 'Some factors', p. 174.

73 Welwyn Garden City Library, Sir Frederic Osborn Archive, K256, J. Tyrewhitt, 'Life and labour in Welwyn Garden City', unpublished typescript, 1939 [hereafter Tyrwhitt, Welwyn Survey]. Sample size = 4,985 for employment book data and 602 for survey data. Employment book data referred to individuals whereas survey data referred to working-class families living in Welwyn (including those who worked elsewhere).

74 Bill Lancaster, 'Who's a real Coventry kid? Migration into twentieth century Coventry', 57–80 in Bill Lancaster and Tony Mason (eds), *Life and Labour in a Twentieth Century City: The Experience of Coventry* (Coventry, 1986), p. 70.

75 NA, LAB8/218, 'Report of enquiry into the industrial transference scheme (adults), part I', May 1938.

outside the region, in 1932 and 1936,[76] and conducted a similar exercise for the Midlands division in 1937.[77] The area with the highest proportion of 'foreign' books (49.2 per cent) was Corby in the East Mildands.[78] Two thirds were Scots migrants, mainly representing planned migration from Motherwell associated with the new Stewart and Lloyds iron and steel plant.[79]

Similarly, the South East district with the largest proportion of foreign books in 1932 was Dagenham, with 28.7 per cent; many represented Ford workers who had moved with the firm from its previous Manchester factory. There were also special factors regarding the area with the second highest proportion, the Kent coalfield – one of the few examples of the rapid interwar expansion of a heavy staple industry in the South East. Other major reception areas were concentrated around London, on its western periphery (Slough, Staines, Southall, Hayes, Uxbridge, and Hounslow); on its north-western periphery (Welwyn, Watford, Harrow, St. Albans, Hendon, and Willesden) and in other areas on the fringes of the conurbation (Tilbury and Caterham).[80] Rugby and Coventry had the highest proportions of foreign books for the West Midlands.[81]

There are few published contemporary studies examining the influence of transference on reception areas, other than those concerning Oxford, a city which was significantly closer to a major source area (South Wales) than most of the above centres and received a smaller proportion of migrants than some more rapidly growing communities. The impact of migrants was obviously directly related to their representation in the populations of reception areas. Many industrial areas experiencing moderate expansion could draw sufficient workers from the local labour market or its surrounding agricultural hinterland and, as noted above, local females and juveniles were generally preferred by employers (where they were available in sufficient numbers) while adult male ex-agricultural workers were also viewed as more flexible and less militant than migrants from declining industrial regions.[82]

Even in Oxford, whose employed population grew by 41.8 per cent over the interwar period, local agricultural workers out-numbered migrants from the depressed areas in the Cowley motor industry in 1936 by more than two to one.[83] However, supplies of local workers and short-distance migrants proved insufficient to meet the labour requirements of the most rapidly expanding industrial areas, such as West Middlesex, Slough, Dagenham, Watford, Welwyn, Letchworth, Luton, and Coventry. For example, according to contemporary estimates by the late 1930s some 40 per cent of workers on the Slough Estate had migrated from the depressed

76 Brinley Thomas, 'The movement of labour into South-East England 1920–32', *Economica*, I (May 1934), 220–41; idem, 'The influx of labour into London and the South East'.

77 Thomas, 'The influx of labour into the Midlands'.

78 Ibid., p. 421.

79 Ibid., p. 420.

80 Thomas, 'The movement of labour into South-East England', p. 234.

81 Thomas, 'The influx of labour into the Midlands', p. 421.

82 Dennison, *Location of Industry*, p. 78.

83 R. C. Whiting, *The View from Cowley: The Impact of Industrialisation upon Oxford, 1918–1939* (Oxford, 1983), pp. 39–66.

areas; while migrants from Wales alone were said to make up at least 20 per cent of Slough's total population.[84] As the *New Survey* noted, in contrast to the late Victorian period, 'the type of migrant whom London now attracts is not so much the low-paid agricultural labourer... as the unemployed townsman of the "depressed areas"'.[85]

Government policy proved important both in concentrating migrants in the most rapidly-growing centres and in providing the type of cheap un/semi-skilled migrant workers sought by employers. Migrants were dominated by relatively young (and therefore relatively cheap) workers. A study of Welsh migration to Oxford between 1928–37 showed that 19.1 per cent of the sample had first left Wales between the ages of 16–19, and a further 39.4 per cent at 20–24, while around 80 per cent had left when aged below 35.[86] Young workers had also dominated internal migration before 1914. This can be explained in terms of migration being a forward-looking decision driven by economic criteria and therefore appearing more attractive to young people with a longer future working life over which to enjoy its benefits and lower costs of occupational and lifestyle readjustments.[87]

The classic groups of 'cheap' workers during this period, women and juveniles, made up only a small proportion of official transferees in the early years of the initiative, but their representation increased substantially during the 1930s. Over 1933–38 boys and girls accounted for 17.4 per cent and 17.2 per cent of official transferees respectively, the total proportion of juveniles being almost four and a half times their proportion of the national insured population. An additional 22.1 per cent of official transferees over the period 1933–36 were adult women.[88]

During the late 1920s the government had become concerned that the low birth rate during the War years, together with a prospective increase in the school leaving age, might produce shortages of juvenile workers in some areas and had taken steps to assess the potential of transference to remove such shortages.[89] By the mid-1930s the Ministry of Labour perceived that juvenile unemployment in the South East and most of the Midlands was largely 'frictional' – arising from juveniles switching between jobs or waiting for better job opportunities.[90] Meanwhile the depressed areas contained over three quarters of unemployed juveniles (aged 14–18) and had a serious problem of long-term juvenile unemployment. The Exchange system provided the means of redressing geographical imbalances in juvenile labour; together with the Juvenile Employment Bureaux it was responsible for placing 38.7

84 NA: HLG27/32, memorandum presented to the Royal Commission on the Distribution of the Industrial Population by Sir Noel Mobbs, Chairman, Slough Estates, 3 Feb. 1938; LMA, Acc. 2720/1/71/1, memorandum by South Wales & Monmouthshire Council of Social Service, n.d., c. 1939.

85 London School of Economics, *New Survey of London Life & Labour. Volume VI: Survey of Social Conditions (2) The Western Area* (London, 1934), p. 260.

86 Daniel, 'Labour migration'.

87 See Boyer and Hatton, 'Migration'.

88 Source: Table 11.1.

89 Ministry of Labour, *Memorandum on the Shortage, Surplus and Redistribution of Juvenile Labour in England and Wales During the Years 1930–1938* (London, 1931).

90 MRC, Mss. 292/132.2/12, Ministry of Labour report for National Advisory Council for Juvenile Employment (England and Wales), July 1936.

per cent of insured juveniles engaged in insurable work during 1932 and could thus direct large numbers to areas where demand outstripped supply.[91]

Employers in rapidly growing industrial centres actively lobbied their local authorities to recruit juveniles (of which there was usually a local shortage) via the transference initiative. Following persistent lobbying by local employers, Coventry's Director of Education launched an initiative to recruit boys from the depressed areas.[92] Other Local Education Authorities (LEA's) stated to be particularly active in placing transferred juveniles included Birmingham, Leicester, and Smethwick.[93] 25 per cent of juveniles transferred during 1937 were sent to areas in which the LEA actively encouraged their in-migration and placing.[94] Individual firms also lobbied the Ministry of Labour for juvenile workers. For example, the Swedish multinational Skefko (following advice from the local branch of the Engineering Employers Association) approached the Ministry of Labour with a view to securing transferees for its Luton factory, as it faced serious recruitment problems owing to local labour scarcity and the higher wages offered by non-federated firms.[95]

Juvenile transferees' earnings were directly subsidised by the Ministry of Labour, via grants where wages (traditionally set at a level only intended to augment family income) fell below subsistence levels. 61.9 per cent of boys and 20.4 per cent of girls transferred to industrial employment during 1933–38 were subsidised in this way.[96] A.D.K. Owen claimed that, without this indirect wage subsidy to employers in reception areas, 'Many firms would certainly not have been able to develop in quite the same way...'[97] Some employers, such as the Raleigh cycle works, were said to rely extensively on subsidised juvenile transferees, who were automatically given six months' notice on reaching 18.[98] A Ministry of Labour official at Slough recalled that during the 1930s some boys transferred there received up to 15 shillings a week from The Lord Mayor's Fund and other sources, to bring their income to a level where they could afford lodgings.[99]

Transference thus aimed to serve the twin purposes of reducing unemployment in depressed areas and removing labour supply bottlenecks in rapid growth centres. Owen cited the case of a firm which decided to locate in West London rather than Lancashire on the basis of an assurance that an adequate supply of transferees would

91 Chegwidden and Myrddin-Evans, *Employment Exchange Service*, p. 178. Until 1935 juveniles aged under 16 were excluded from unemployment insurance.

92 Ibid, p. 441.

93 Ministry of Labour, *Annual Report for the Year 1937* (P.P. 1937–38, XII), p. 44.

94 Ibid., p. 42.

95 L. T. Holden, 'The history of Vauxhall Motors to 1950', unpublished M.Phil thesis, Open University, 1983, pp. 266–7.

96 Ministry of Labour, *Annual Reports for the Years 1933–38* (PP, 1934–39). Excludes boys transferred through vocational training schemes and girls transferred to domestic employment.

97 Owen, 'Social consequences', p. 346.

98 John Gollan, *Youth in British Industry* (London, 1937), pp. 72–3.

99 Slough Museum, transcript of 'The Story of Slough', BBC Home Service broadcast, 2 December 1952.

be provided.[100] The Nuffield College Social Reconstruction survey noted that during the 1930s there had been a particular shortage of semi-skilled, female, and juvenile labour in Hertfordshire, which had been addressed using transference. During the late 1930s over 1,500 juveniles were transferred to St. Albans alone.[101] In Letchworth, one contemporary noted, with the arrival of each new firm:

> ...the problem of adequate labour re-emerges in piquant form... this labour hunger appears to be well on the road to being satisfied owing to the tragedy of the depressed areas... Men with their families are being drafted from these Northern districts by the Ministry of Labour... Over 3,000 youths from the mining districts have also been transferred... [to] a Government Centre in Letchworth...[102]

Female juveniles were largely transferred to domestic service rather than industry. They were in high demand, as factory employment provided a powerful lure for girls in the South East, many of whom considered domestic service an occupation of last resort.[103] By 1929 over 70 per cent of females entering domestic service in the County of London were born outside Greater London.[104] However, rather than acting as an alternative to factory work, domestic service usually constituted a transitional phase towards industrial employment. By providing accommodation it allowed girls to establish themselves in reception areas and accumulate funds until they could afford their own accommodation and enter factory work.[105] As unemployment fell and the industrial demand for girls increased, more were able to move immediately to factory employment. While around 85 per cent of girls transferred during 1934 were placed in domestic service, by 1936, despite a substantial increase in the number transferred, this had fallen to 41 per cent.[106]

However, the bulk of transferees were young (but not juvenile) men. These were particularly important in reception areas with GTC's, as these did not train females, or males under 18. The impact of transference in depressing reception area wages was greatest for adult males, for whom the balance between labour supply and demand was generally less favourable than for females and juveniles. This is demonstrated by analysis of local wage data for three rapidly-growing industrial centres. The 1939 survey of Welwyn indicated that men over 21 earned 65s a week (compared to 64.5s in the October 1935 national survey, since when national wages for manual workers had risen by 8.8 per cent). Wage data for other workers are not

100 A. D. K. Owen, 'The social consequences of industrial transference: a rejoinder to Mr Michael Daly', *Sociological Review*, XXX (1938), 414–20, p. 416.

101 Nuffield College, Oxford, Nuffield College Social Reconstruction Survey Archive, CI/58 (Part 2), P. Power, Hertfordshire local survey report, January 1943.

102 Letchworth Museum, author unknown, 'Letchworth – some economic and industrial aspects', typescript (1935), p. 6.

103 LSE, *New Survey of London Life and Labour. Volume II: London Industries I* (London, 1931), p. 429; Miriam Glucksmann, *Women Assemble: Women Workers and the New Industries in Interwar Britain* (London, 1990), pp. 247–8.

104 LSE, *New Survey of London Life and Labour. Volume II*, pp. 449, 467.

105 Glucksmann, *Women Assemble*, pp. 249–50.

106 Royal Commission on The Distribution of The Industrial Population, *Minutes of Evidence*, p. 259.

directly comparable with the national survey, as women's wages covered those 21 and over, while boys and girls were disaggregated into the age groups 14–16 and 16–21. However, given that the survey indicated that women (over 21) earned around 66 per cent of men's wages, while boys and girls over 16 earned around 51 per cent and 43 per cent respectively (juveniles of both sexes aged 14–16 earning 25.8 per cent), comparison with the October 1935 Ministry of Labour survey suggests that age and gender wage differentials in Welwyn were substantially narrower than was the case nationally.[107] This cannot be explained as being due to Welwyn's industrial structure, which was dominated by industries that nationally had relatively wide age/gender wage differentials.

Similarly, according to a (very limited) sample of wage data in a 1936 TUC industrial survey of Slough, *hourly* wages for women and juveniles (over 16) were about 73 and 62 per cent of those for men. Meanwhile, typical wage rates for adult males, at around 11.25d per hour, were substantially below the national average (even allowing for bonus payments, etc.).[108] Data for Watford in 1933 also indicate relatively low wages, adult male un/semi-skilled factory workers receiving 45 – 55s per week and skilled factory workers typically receiving 70s. The differential between male and female earnings in Watford was roughly in line with the national data, though as figures are given in broad earnings bands, precise comparison is difficult.[109] The data thus indicate that, despite their rapidly growing demand for labour (which might otherwise have been expected to have forced up wage rates) prevailing wages for adult men in these new industrial centres were below the national average. However, age and gender differentials were narrower in at least two centres, reflecting the lower geographical mobility of juvenile and female workers, even after the countervailing influence of government intervention.

How green was Thames Valley?

The use of transferred labour to reduce upwards wage pressures inevitably produced a hostile local reaction. This was strongest with respect to Welsh migrants, whose high perceived social difference produced an antipathy in many areas of high in-migration bordering, at times, on overt racism.[110] Contemporaries reported 'acute social friction' between Welsh and, to a lesser extent, other transferees and their host populations in Oxford, Watford, Welwyn, Willesden, Slough, and Dagenham.[111] Similar problems were even evident in the Kent coalfield, despite the fact that,

107 Tyrewhitt, Welwyn Survey, pp. 257–8.

108 MRC, Mss 292/S7.1/5, TUC General Council report on industrial survey of Slough, 11 March 1936. See also Savage, 'Trade unionism', p. 221.

109 Watford Reference Library, Civic Survey Council, 'Watford civic survey 1933' three-volume manuscript, c. 1933, volumes 2 and 3.

110 Overseas immigrants to Britain experienced markedly stronger hostility during this period; see James Walvin, *Passage to Britain: Immigration in British History and Politics* (Harmondsworth, 1984), Chapter 5.

111 Owen, 'Social consequences', p. 348. Tyrewhitt, Welwyn Survey; Attlee, *Mobility of Labour*, p. 36; Andrzej Olechnowicz, *Working-Class Housing in England Between the*

unlike the manufacturing centres, locals generally had no interest in the jobs miners took.[112]

Women appear to have found the adjustment process at least as difficult as men. For example, the wives of migrants to the Kent coalfield reported hostility from local women and shopkeepers and, according to a study by Gina Harkell, were more strongly affected by hostile local reactions, as the men were in a community of migrants when at work, while they had to spend more time mixing with the local population. They also missed the local support networks that had existed in their old communities.[113] Similarly, a Welsh-speaking family in Oxford told an interviewer:

> When they came to Oxford they found it very lonely. They expected a minister from one of the local chapels to visit them and give them a welcome, but no one came. Oxford people were antagonistic. On her way home in the bus one day an Oxford woman began to say that the Welsh were stealing jobs in Oxford by working for low wages, and that they were uneducated and could not speak English properly... The two younger boys for a long time were afraid to leave the house because 'one night a gang of English boys met them, called them Taffies and tried to make them swear and sing "God Save the King."'[114]

Such tensions were exacerbated by perceived differences in temperament between migrants and host populations. As a contemporary study of migrants to the Kent coalfield noted:

> The differences between the miners and the Kentish people were marked. The solid, mild, tradition-loving and conservative southerners found the newcomers... too violently independent and lacking in respect for authority or property, too flagrant in their disregard for moral codes, too thriftless and pleasure-seeking. The miners, in turn, despised the Kentish folk for their smugness and 'servility.'[115]

As in most migrant populations, 'mavericks' demonstrated a higher propensity to migrate and were therefore over-represented. In-migrants to the Kent coalfield recalled that the migrant community included a substantial proportion of 'rough' types and that the new mining villages were plagued by petty theft, fighting, and other low-level criminality.[116] However, perceived social differences between migrant and host communities probably also reflected the general unease felt by communities experiencing high in-migration (typically dominated by young, single, men). The perceived 'foreignness' of migrants added to local antipathy towards them. In Banbury, an area of heavy in-migration during the 1930s, a social survey conducted during 1948–51 indicated that 1930s migrants were still regarded as 'foreign'. They still refer to them as "Scots, Irish, and Welsh" with "Those northerners" added as a

Wars: The Beacontree Estate (Oxford, 1997), p. 122; Wal Hannington, *The Problem of the Distressed Areas* (London, 1937), p. 162.

112 Gina Harkell, 'The migration of mining families to the Kent coalfield between the wars', *Oral History*, 6, 1 (1978), 98–113, p. 104.

113 Ibid, pp. 105–8.

114 Daniel, 'Some factors', p. 175.

115 Attlee, *Mobility of Labour*, pp. 30–31.

116 Harkell, 'The migration of mining families'.

concession to the possible Englishness of some', despite the fact that only 32.4 per cent of in-migrants and immigrants in Banbury at the time of the survey had come from Scotland, Wales, the North east, Yorkshire, Lancashire and Cheshire, Northern Ireland, or Eire.[117]

Migrants from depressed industrial areas often left communities characterised by residential proximity to the workplace, employment focused around a single mine, shipyard, or foundry, and close community relations cemented by a uniformity of education and upbringing, life experiences, and employment. Typical reception areas, were, by comparison, anonymous communities, often composed of recently-arrived families employed in a variety of trades and establishments. There was thus no uniformity of interests, based on commonalities of skill, employment, or outlook, to bind them to their new communities. Viewed as foreigners, and used to much stronger traditions of neighbourliness and community, many migrants experienced acute isolation and loneliness. One Lancashire woman described how, during the first months after her arrival in Banbury, she used to sit down and cry, 'I thought I'd never get to know anyone; they're so much more friendly at home.'[118] Welsh migrants to London, interviewed in 1936, emphasised their sense of isolation, together with the absence of any feeling of community and neighbourliness, 'Here a body can be ill, dead and buried before the next door neighbour knows.'[119] However, a minority welcomed the absence of 'scandalmongering and gossip' which they saw as characteristic of life in their home towns and villages.[120]

Antipathy between migrants and their host communities could easily become translated into open hostility, or even violence, in situations where there was significant competition for jobs or accommodation. Such friction found its most extreme form in conflicts between transferees and young unemployed local men. In 1929 the 'Dagenham Unemployed Workers' Committee' kept watch day and night at the Ford site following rumours that 400–500 unemployed Welsh miners were on their way.[121] Street fights between local youths and in-migrants were reported in several London localities which had received large numbers of migrants from South Wales, such as Willesden.[122] Watford experienced similar problems; the *West Herts. Post* reported in January 1930 that:

> A feud... between parties of Watford youths and Welshmen who are at the Ministry of Labour's Training Centre... has caused a great deal of excitement... Last night, there was a wild scene in the High-street. Razors and lengths of lead piping were flourished, and there were several free fights... One of the leaders of the Watford youths told a "Post" reporter... that the trouble started on Saturday evening, when the Welshmen set upon a Watford

117 Margaret Stacey, *Tradition and Change: a Study of Banbury* (Oxford, 1960), p. 13.

118 Ibid.

119 LMA, Acc. 2720/01/07/01, 'Migration to London from South Wales', unsigned memorandum for National Council of Social Service, 1936.

120 Ibid.

121 Olechnowicz, *Working-Class Housing*, p. 122.

122 Hannington, *Problem of the Distressed Areas*, p. 162.

youth... A remark of another youth suggested that employment questions were connected with the trouble, for he said: "When the Welshmen go we shall get work."[123]

Such conflict was fuelled by perceptions that Welsh migrants under-cut local wage rates. Aneurin Bevan (M.P. for Ebbw Vale), speaking at a conference on transference organised by the South Wales and Monmouthshire Council of Social Service in 1936, argued that transference should not be encouraged, as, 'considerable resentment and hostility was shown in the South East of England, and Welshmen had acquired a bad reputation for offering their services at below the standard Trade Union rates. The position was comparable with that which existed in the 19th century when large numbers of Irishmen settled in Wales.'[124]

Transferees were also strongly associated by workers and unions with deskilling and a deterioration in working conditions.[125] Concerns regarding the use of transferees to erode wage differentials and weaken the power of organised labour led to considerable union hostility. From 1928 a number of unions and trades councils in reception areas voiced protests and passed resolutions opposing the undercutting of local wage rates by transferees. In December 1928 the TUC decided to circulate all affiliated unions and trades councils for information on the impact of transference. This produced complaints regarding workers being employed at below standard rates; the displacement of local labour; preference for vacancies being given to transferees; promises made to transferees not being honoured and their being refused Unemployment Benefit on their return. However, only a minority of respondents reported problems and some concerning wages were not substantiated when subsequently investigated.[126] Union complaints persisted during the 1930s. GTC trainees were particularly resented, due to fears that they would be used to erode apprenticeships and skill differentials. Some union members placed embargoes on trainees and engaged in industrial action to get them dismissed.[127]

Opposition to migrants sometimes received local political support; for example at Slough a campaign, led by the local Conservative MP, was successful in bringing about the temporary closure of the GTC in 1932.[128] Some firms discriminated against transferees; in 1938 several adverts in the Slough Exchange stated 'no Welsh need apply'.[129] However, some local workers perceived themselves to be discriminated

123 *West Herts. Post*, January 1930, reproduced in T. Paish et al., *The Book of Watford* (Watford, 1987), p. 177.

124 LMA, Acc. 2720/01/07/01, minutes of conference on transference convened by South Wales and Monmouthshire Council of Social Service, 15–16 May 1936.

125 P. W. Carr, 'Engineering workers and the rise of labour in Coventry, 1914–1939', unpublished Ph.D. thesis, University of Warwick, 1978, p. 434.

126 MRC, Mss. 292/103/1, TUC General Council memorandum on industrial transference, 21 February 1929; memorandum providing supplementary information, n.d., c. 1929.

127 Ibid, letter from Felt Hatters and Trimmers Unions to TUC, 4 March 1939 and report submitted to Parliamentary Building Trade Group and TUC General Council by National Federation of Building Trades Operatives, February 1930.

128 Savage, 'Trade unionism'.

129 Ibid., p. 223.

against. There is anecdotal evidence that transferees were explicitly used by local employers to force down prevailing wages. In March 1932 the *Slough Observer* reported one man's claim that on several occasions he had been asked 'Are you a local man?' and on replying 'Yes', being told that they could get plenty of men from the Exchange for two-thirds of the local pay rate.[130] There were also persistent reports in Slough that transferees were given preference by the local Exchange[131] – such discrimination by some Exchanges was also noted by the Ministry of Labour, as discussed above. Thus, rather than being placed at the back of the queue for jobs, as a result of weaker local contacts and discrimination,[132] labour markets in reception areas acted, at least in some instances, to take transferees to the front of the queue.

In addition to job competition, transferees placed considerable pressure on the housing stock of reception areas, forcing up rents and providing a further source of social friction. For example in Luton a letter to the local paper stated, 'if some of these people would go back to the North, locals might have a hope of getting a house at a reasonable rent'.[133] Migrants often became concentrated in new housing developments, such as Banbury's 'little Rochdale', which provided a vivid illustration to locals of the demands that in-migrants were making on the housing stock.[134] However in some areas in-migrants appear to have faced discrimination regarding council housing – during a period when municipal authorities enjoyed considerable discretion over housing allocation. As a miner who migrated to Deal in Kent recalled:

> I remember coming out of a Council meeting having failed … to get anything out of them about the housing there, and I was almost in tears and the … Chaplain for the Council, I went to him and I said, "what's wrong, why can't we make any progress here?" "Well", he said… "I can understand it to some extent… they've now moved into Swans Road and that used to be one of our best roads."'[135]

Migrants also faced discrimination in the market for private lodgings. As a migrant to the Kent coalfield recalled, 'You used to see it in the paper as regular as clockwork: "House to Let, or Rooms to Let – no miners, no dogs, no children"'.[136] Again the Welsh appear to have been particularly targeted.[137] As one Welsh migrant recalled, regarding the boycott by many Oxford landladies and general hostility from locals, 'The Oxford people didn't want the Welsh, because the Welsh were

130 *Slough Observer*, 18 March 1932, cited in ibid.

131 Savage, 'Trade unionism', p. 223.

132 Timothy J. Hatton, 'Unemployment and the labour market in inter-war Britain', 359–85 in Floud and McCloskey (eds), *Economic History of Britain*, p. 376.

133 *Luton News*, 17 March 1938, p. 9.

134 Stacey, *Tradition and Change*, p. 109.

135 Harkell, 'The migration of mining families, p. 103.

136 Ibid.

137 Daniel, 'Some factors', p. 177.

undercutting the English ... When I went to live on the [Florence Park] estate the hatred there against the Welsh was terrible.'[138]

Yet, despite these problems, evidence suggests a reasonable level of satisfaction among in-migrants. A 1936 survey of 45 South Wales migrants to London (dominated by young men and women under 30 who had been in London for over a year but less than five years) indicated that 25 would return to South Wales gladly if a reasonable job were offered, 5 were doubtful, and 15 said that they would prefer to stay in London.[139] However, even among those who wished to return home, most stated that, '*on no account would they return to work underground.*'[140] A 1938 *Listener* article on Rhondda in-migrants to London similarly reported a split between those who preferred their new lives and (in this case generally older) in-migrants who would return 'if there was work'.[141]

The presence of local colonies of in-migrants in many major reception areas acted to reduce feelings of isolation and loneliness. Migrants, particularly the Welsh, were also active in creating or adapting social and religious institutions (which played a particularly important role in the social life of South Wales mining villages) in their new communities. By the late 1930s Welsh clubs or centres had been established in a number of areas of high in-migration in and around London, including Luton, Dagenham, Kingston, Wimbledon, Clapham, Wood Green, Ealing, Harrow, and Croydon.[142] Of 45 Welsh in-migrants surveyed in 1936, 18 were members of Welsh social or religious organisations (those in the sample having also joined a variety of non-Welsh institutions).[143]

Similar Welsh institutions existed in large provincial in-migration centres, such as Birmingham, together with more broadly-based associations such as the Birmingham Association for Relief of Distressed Areas (B.A.R.D.A.), formed in 1924 by a group of young men from the depressed areas to support in-migrants.[144] The Ministry of Labour tried to establish similar organisations to assist transferees in London and other major centres, in association with voluntary organisations such as

138 A. Excell, 'Morris Motors in the 1930s: Part II', *History Workshop Journal*, VII (1979), 45–65, p. 46.

139 LMA, Acc. 2720/01/07/01, 'Migration to London from South Wales', unsigned memorandum for National Council of Social Service, 1936.

140 Ibid.; emphasis in original.

141 M. Davies, 'Exiled in London', *The Listener* (20 April 1938), 854–5.

142 LMA, Acc. 2720/01/07/01, preliminary report on social provision at the 'reception end' for workers transferred from South Wales, by South Wales & Monmouthshire Council of Social Service, Committee on Transference, n.d., c. 1939; minutes of conference on transference convened by South Wales and Monmouthshire Council of Social Service, 15–16 May 1936.

143 LMA, Acc. 2720/01/07/01, 'Migration to London from South Wales', unsigned memorandum for National Council of Social Service, 1936.

144 LMA, Acc. 2720/01/07/01, preliminary report on social provision at the 'reception end' for workers transferred from South Wales, by South Wales & Monmouthshire Council of Social Service, Committee on Transference, n.d., c. 1939.

the Welsh churches.[145] The Welsh churches also played a major direct role as social institutions for Welsh in-migrants. It was reported that a number of Welsh migrants to London switched denominations in order to find a Welsh church within reasonable distance, one girl interviewed in 1936 having learnt Welsh while in London in order to join in the Welsh services.[146]

One set of non-Welsh institutions in which in-migrants came to play a central role were those connected with trade unions and working-class politics. The relative importance of migrants to the growth of union activity in sectors such as motor vehicles is controversial.[147] However, the evidence examined for this study indicates that, despite initial union hostility to transferees, some in-migrants from areas with strong union traditions came to be ranked among the most ardent union activists in the new factories. Contemporaries generally perceived that migration attracted potential leaders, 'those who were most ready to leave were the leaders in the social life of their district, the most virile part of the population who possessed courage and a spirit of adventure'.[148] Evidence from Banbury suggests that in-migrants played a leading role in the development of working-class politics, dominating Banbury's Labour Party and trade union membership.[149] Similarly George Hodgkinson, who had worked in Coventry's engineering industry since 1914, acting as a shop steward for a number of years, recalled that it was the 'injection of the class-conscious injured workman from the "Distressed Areas" which fermented the political change in Birmingham and Coventry', during the years following the General Strike.[150] This was corroborated by former Coventry car workers, interviewed during the 1980s for an oral history project.[151]

The 1936 survey of South Wales migrants to London indicated that, while many former union members had not joined unions after gaining employment in London, Welshmen were generally no more reluctant to join unions than their London counterparts, while several key union positions were held by recent migrants from the

145 LMA, Acc. 2720/01/07/01, minutes of conference on transference convened by South Wales and Monmouthshire Council of Social Service, 15–16 May 1936.

146 LMA, Acc. 2720/01/07/01, 'Migration to London from South Wales', unsigned memorandum for National Council of Social Service, 1936.

147 See Jonathan Zeitlin, 'The emergence of shop steward organization and job control in the British car industry: a review essay', *History Workshop Jounal*, X (1980), 121–37; D. Lyddon, 'Workplace organization in the British car industry. A critique of Johnathan Zeitlin', *History Workshop Journal*, XV (1983), 131–40; Jonathan Zeitlin, 'Workplace militancy: a rejoinder', *History Workshop Journal*, XVI (1983), 131–6.

148 LMA, Acc. 2720/01/07/01, minutes of conference on transference convened by South Wales and Monmouthshire Council of Social Service, 15–16 May 1936, summary of 'the general feeling of the conference'.

149 Stacey, *Tradition and Change*, pp. 48–9 & 83–4.

150 George Hodgkinson, *Sent to Coventry* (Bletchley, 1970), p. 100.

151 Coventry Record Office, Acc. 1647, interviews recorded for a project on the social history of car workers and deposited with the Record Office by Paul Thompson, University of Essex, in 1986; for example 1647/1/56.

mining valleys.[152] Thus, while many migrants for whom union membership had been 'a tradition to which they subscribed without exercising much thought',[153] left the movement following moves to weakly-unionised industrial centres, migrant union activists played a significant role in extending unionisation to such communities.

Conclusions

Just as the industrial revolution had witnessed a switch in the focus of new industrial development to new areas, drawing on a 'reserve army' of labour from outside the core industrial workforce, similar processes influenced industrial location patterns in interwar Britain.[154] Marx classified the reserve army into three main forms: the floating (workers in insecure industrial employment), the latent (workers attracted from non-industrial sectors offering inferior pay and conditions), and the stagnant (marginal and underemployed industrial workers such as outworkers).[155] Employers in secondary labour markets generally preferred juvenile workers, and then women, on account of their low wages and flexibility, while their counterparts in primary labour markets preferred reliable workers with low labour turnover but without industrial experience or unionisation, such as former agricultural workers. These groups were drawn mainly from the latent reserve. Only when industrial growth was sufficient to exhaust the local supply of such workers was the floating reserve – in the shape of long-distance migrants formerly employed in the staple industries – called upon in substantial numbers by employers in either primary or secondary labour markets. Moreover, preferred migrants were again women, juveniles, and young men without significant industrial experience.

The composition of the new industrial workforce casts further doubt on the 'old optimist' thesis, based around the work of Aldcroft and Richardson, that market-based transfers of resources from old to new sectors offered a long-term solution to Britain's interwar economic problems (though the employment transfer was viewed as having been delayed by the new industries being more capital intensive than the declining staples – a claim which has been challenged by subsequent research).[156] In fact, despite an increase in manufacturing employment of around 565,000 from 1923–38, relatively few of the jobs created went to displaced staple industry workers. Not only were the new jobs in different regions from those of the declining industries,

152 LMA, Acc. 2720/01/07/01, 'Migration to London from South Wales', unsigned memorandum for National Council of Social Service, 1936.

153 Ibid.

154 Maxine Berg and Pat Hudson, 'Rehabilitating the Industrial Revolution', *Economic History Review*, 2nd ser. XLV (1992), 24–50, pp. 36–7.

155 Karl Marx, *Capital*, Vol. 1 (London, 1954), pp. 600–602.

156 Derek. H. Aldcroft and H. W. Richardson, *The British Economy 1870–1939* (London, 1969); G. N. Von Tunzelmann, 'Structural change and leading sectors in British manufacturing 1907–68', 1–49 in Charles P. Kindleberger and Guido di Tella (eds), *Economics in the Long View: Essays in Honor of W. W. Rostow* (London, 1982); Stephen N. Broadberry, 'Unemployment in interwar Britain: a disequilibrium approach', *Oxford Economic Papers*, XXXV (1983), 463–85.

the very nature of the jobs themselves placed adult male workers with significant industrial experience at a considerable disadvantage compared to cheaper workers or those perceived to be more flexible. Only in the most rapidly expanding centres was employment growth sufficient to outstrip the supply from the latent reserve of labour and force employers to recruit substantially from the floating reserve.

Migration played an important role in the expansion of the most rapidly-growing industrial centres during this period, by removing the upward pressure on wages that would have otherwise been inevitable as industrial growth outstripped the capacity of their local labour markets. Thus centres such as Slough, Watford, and Welwyn were able to combine extremely rapid industrial growth with wages below the national average for manufacturing workers. While the bulk of long-distance migration was not state-assisted, a significant proportion of migrants are shown to have received official help, either financially or through the advisory and placement activities of the Exchange system. The concentration of government activity (particularly the GTC's) on the most rapidly-growing centres suggests that the role of state assistance in encouraging migration was substantially greater in these areas than was the case generally. This accords with the findings of Owen,[157] and, more recently, Mike Savage,[158] regarding the central role of state intervention in migration to such communities.

Like Commonwealth immigration after the Second World War, government encouragement of internal migration during the interwar period was motivated by the aim of providing cheap labour for areas in which it was in short supply (in addition to transference's principal objective of reducing high unemployment in depressed regions). As such, the policy had a negative impact on the host populations of reception areas, who experienced considerable upward pressure on housing costs together with downward pressure on local wages and an increased threat (especially for adult males) of displacement by cheaper labour. This, together with the perceived social difference of migrants, especially the Welsh, produced considerable hostility from host populations, paralleling (though in much milder form) the reception of post-war overseas migrants. Yet despite initial hostility, in-migrants soon came to play an active role in the social, religious, and political life of their new communities and made a substantial contribution to the long-term development of the principal centres in which they settled.

157 Owen, 'Social consequences', p. 350.

158 Savage, 'Trade unionism', p. 211.

Chapter Twelve

Rural and coastal Britain

Introduction

J. B. Priestley famously summed up his *English Journey* by dividing the nation into three Englands – 'Old England ... the country of cathedrals and minsters and manor houses and innes, of Parson and Squire; guide-books and quaint highways and byeways'; nineteenth century industrial England; and modern post-1918 England.[1] Priestley's second England faced divergent development paths after 1918, with stagnation and decay in the north and rapid modernisation in the South. Yet just as the prosperous, southern part of his second England had been transformed into the urban core of his third England, so rural areas accessible from the South East and West Midlands experienced a similarly dramatic transformation into the third England's suburban hinterland and leisure/tourism periphery. Meanwhile many rural areas in northern Britain underwent a decline that was, in some respects, as severe as that of their urban areas.

Depression and decline in British agriculture

Depression in Britain's staple industries, and the areas they dominated, was mirrored by that of British agriculture and most rural areas. National employment in agriculture and forestry declined from an average of 1,004,000 in 1920–22 to only 735,000 in 1937–38. As with the staple industries, war-conditions had led to heavy increases in world output, raising capacity to levels that substantially exceeded peace-time demand. Following the brief post-war boom agricultural produce experienced severe price declines – wheat and oat prices, which had reached 80s 10d and 63s per quarter respectively in 1920, had fallen to 42s 2d and 42s by 1923.[2] Government offered little help to farmers; despite guarantees enshrined in legislation, such as the Corn Production Act, 1917, and the Agricultural Act, 1920, these were quickly repealed once the slump set in – via the 'Great Betrayal' of the 1921 Corn Production Acts (Repeal) Bill. The repeals also extended to the minimum wage protection for farm workers under the 1917 legislation.

Perversely, most farmers initially welcomed repeal, as the abolition of the Wages Board would allow them to cut wages – a major cost for farming – and remove an unwelcome source of government intervention in their labour relations. Furthermore, farmers were offered a further 18 months of short-term subsidies to protect cereal prices. The most obvious losers were the farm workers; indeed it was George

1 J. B. Priestley, *English Journey* (London, 1934), pp. 397–405.

2 C. L. Mowat, *Britain Between the Wars 1918–1940* (London, 1955), p. 251.

Edwards, founder to the Farm Workers' Union and Labour MP for South Norfolk, who branded the episode a great betrayal.[3] Following the removal of minimum wage protection, farm wages experienced a steep decline from their immediate post-war level of 42s for a 48 hour week; for example in Norfolk, following a strike in 1923, farm workers agreed to accept 25s for a 50 hour week.[4] Despite the re-institution of agricultural wage-fixing machinery by the Labour government in 1924, wages did not generally reach levels of above around 30s a week (though subject to significant regional variations) for the rest of the decade. The second half of the 1930s saw some improvement in farm wages, yet ordinary farm workers' earnings still averaged only 35s 3d per week in 1937, while B.S. Rowntree calculated that, in order to achieve minimum nutritional standards set by the British Medical Association, a rural family with three children would require a wage of 41s.[5]

Farm workers' families also suffered from very poor housing. Few agricultural workers' cottages had indoor plumbing, while as late as 1939 some 25 per cent of English parishes lacked any mains water supply and a higher proportion lacked mains sewerage.[6] Typically cold, damp, farm cottages made agricultural labourers' families particularly vulnerable to diseases such as rheumatism, tuberculosis, and bronchitis. The growing popularity of the countryside with town-dwellers further reduced the stock of better-quality rural housing, which began to be purchased by the middle classes as weekend retreats.

At the other end of the social scale, the aristocracy and gentry were experiencing their own crisis, hit both by the fall in prices for agricultural produce and war-time hikes in death-duties, which were further increased during the years following the Armistice. Their traditional guardians, the Conservative Party, prioritised urban votes and City interests over rural and agricultural concerns and offered them little support until after the final demise of the gold standard in 1931. Faced with higher taxes, lower agricultural incomes, and little short-term prospect of political salvation, the great landowners began to sell off parts of their estates, often to their former tenants, as did the much larger number of lesser landowners. On the eve of the First World War only 11 per cent of the acreage of England and Wales had been owner-occupied; by 1927 this had risen to 37 per cent.[7]

Land sales appear to have been concentrated in the industrial counties of Northern Britain and the North Midlands, landed families abandoning their traditional estates in favour of the glamorous and prosperous south. For example in Nottinghamshire, where all the major landowners had forsaken their estates by 1939, the landed elite were describing the county as 'uninhabitable' by the 1930s. Counties such as Lancashire, Cheshire, and Staffordshire were regarded as too polluted, urbanised, and depressed for landed society; who migrated to the environs of London. Conversely

---

3 Alun Howkins, *The Death of Rural England. A Social History of the Countryside since 1900* (London, 2003), p. 45.

4 Ibid, p. 252.

5 Howkins, *The Death of Rural England*, p. 86.

6 Peter Dewey, 'Agriculture, agrarian society, and the countryside', 270–85 in Chris Wrigley (ed.), *A Companion to Early Twentieth Century Britain* (Oxford, 2003), p. 281.

7 Peter Mandler, *The Fall and Rise of the Stately Home* (New Haven, 1997), p. 228.

land sales in the South East usually occurred on a smaller scale and for positive reasons, such as cashing in on the demand for suburban housing.[8] This regional pattern provides support for the thesis that the demise of great estates was often a matter of cold calculation by landed families seeking to rebalance their portfolios under new economic and social conditions, rather than a process of forced sales brought on by depression and death duties.[9]

Nationally, land sales were concentrated in the 1919–21 post-war boom period, major landowners shrewdly scaling down their estates while prices were still relatively favourable. Conversely, most farmers who purchased land did so via loans and at inflated prices, saddling them with debts that were often to prove onerous during the following lean years. By 1923, when the full impact of the unfettered free market on agricultural prices and land values had become fully apparent, many farmers (especially in arable areas) who had initially supported the repeal of protection, were also talking of it as a great betrayal.[10]

Falling interwar world food prices led to a resumption of the pre-war trend away from arable farming in favour of dairy produce, meat, poultry, eggs, fruit, and market gardening – products which maximised the value of proximity to a large, affluent, market and were more suited to Britain's high land costs and small fields.[11] Dairy output experienced particularly vigorous growth; by 1939 milk and milk products accounted for 31 per cent of the value of gross output for agricultural holdings in England and Wales, while all grain crops comprised a mere 4.5 per cent.[12] The sector benefited from both favourable demand shifts and lower input costs – as lower grain prices meant cheaper animal feed. Yet despite the growing domestic market for such produce (due to rising living standards), low-cost overseas producers were able to encroach even on some of these markets on account of advances in food preserving and packing technologies. Meanwhile the switch away from arable farming necessarily added to unemployment in the sector, as pastural farming required between seven and nine fewer men per thousand acres than arable land.

There was a pronounced regional divide in the expansion of dairy production, even in pastoral areas. Traditional dairy counties in areas such as the South West experienced a rise in output by 1930 of 20–40 per cent above the pre-war level, while areas close to prosperous centres, such as parts of the South Midlands, also made significant gains. Yet dairy farmers in the northern industrial counties saw only a marginal expansion, as industrial depression limited local demand.[13]

While agriculture had been given only very limited government support during the 1920s, in the changed environment of the 1930s it received substantially more help. Following the government's belated abandonment of free trade in 1931, and in the wake of the collapse in farm prices during the 1929–32 depression, the Wheat

8 Howkins, *The Death of Rural England*, p. 56.

9 See, for example, Mandler, *The Rise and Fall of the Stately Home*, pp. 242–5.

10 Ibid., pp. 39 and 46.

11 Sidney Pollard, *The Development of the British Economy 1914–1990* (London, 1992), p. 63.

12 Howkins, *The Death of Rural England*, p. 54.

13 Ibid., p. 47.

Act (1932), Import Duties Act (1932), and Agricultural Marketing Acts of 1931 and 1933 transformed British agriculture in to a highly protected and subsidised industry. The Wheat Act provided direct price subsidies, while protectionism (under both the Import Duties Act and subsequent legislation) gave farmers privileged access to the prosperous home market. Meanwhile the Marketing Acts introduced the various marketing boards for domestic foodstuffs which became a long-term feature of British agricultural support. Further support was provided in the late 1930s, as part of Britain's preparations for war, under the 1937 Agriculture Act and the 1939 Agricultural Development Act.

The annual cost of agricultural subsidies and protection during the 1930s has been estimated at between £32–41 million, while the additional costs of growing food in Britain that could have been purchased more cheaply overseas might raise this sum to, perhaps, around £100 million.[14] Some of this cost inevitably fell on urban consumers, who were forced to indirectly subsidise their agricultural counterparts by paying higher prices for food. Yet farming was still a barely profitable industry and continued its decline. In 1920–22 the sector had accounted for 6.3 per cent of total employment and 6.1 per cent of national income; by 1937–38 these had fallen to only 3.9 per cent and 3.5 per cent respectively.[15] Agriculture nevertheless experienced substantial productivity growth – partly as a result of its considerable labour shedding.

Meanwhile wages and working conditions for farm labourers continued to be among the worst of any British industry. A major Ministry of Labour survey found that during 1937/38 employed agricultural workers' families had an average household income of 57s 4d, compared to 85s for employed non-agricultural working-class households. [16] Poor wages and labour conditions were matched by semi-feudal relations with farmers and landowners and limited provision of public services. Yet there had been some decline in deference since the late nineteenth century, together with improvements in rural social amenities. Developments originating, or gathering momentum, during the First World War – including women's institutes, village halls, and agricultural trades unionism – both reduced the isolation of rural workers and weakened the hegemonic role of the gentry and clergy over the social institutions of rural life. Meanwhile the radio, improved public transport, and the growth of film shows in village halls increased rural workers' access to urban and metropolitan culture.[17]

However, standards of state education remained particularly poor in agricultural areas, with many smaller schools having only one or two teachers who struggled to teach children aged between five and fourteen. In 1936 around two thirds of rural

14 Sidney Pollard, *The Development of the British Economy*, p. 65.

15 Ibid., p. 66.

16 NA: LAB17/7, 'Weekly expenditure of working-class households in the United Kingdom in 1937–38', unpublished report, Ministry of Labour and National Service, July 1949.

17 Jeremy Burchardt, 'Reconstructing the rural community: village halls and the National Council of Social Service, 1919 to 1939', *Rural History*, 10 (1999), 193–216; Howkins, *The Death of Rural England*, pp. 33–6.

children attended such 'all age' schools, while only about a third of rural teachers had teachers' certificates. For such children, prospects of obtaining qualifications and, following school, achieving anything beyond a labourer's job, were limited indeed – in the mid-1920s it was estimated that only around five per cent of rural entrants to secondary schools were the children of agricultural labourers. Barriers included both the poor quality of village schools and, perhaps more importantly, their parents' need to put them into work as soon as possible to supplement their meagre household incomes.[18]

For most rural landowners, farmers, and agricultural workers, the interwar period was an era for prolonged depression and decline. However, those fortunate enough to be located on the fringes of expanding urban centres, or in areas that had both scenic beauty and reasonable transport links to the South East and Midlands, often fared substantially better – as the rest of this chapter will demonstrate.

The town invades the countryside: suburbanistion and ribbon development

> The country towns dream no more. The rattle of the motor bus has roused them. The char-a-banc are parked in their market places. The multiple shops have invaded them... The roads between the towns are thick with traffic; the entrance to the towns is through a barrage of unsightly advertisements and the sides of the roads are fringed with villas and bungalows.[19]

The interwar years witnessed a transformation of the British countryside, especially for areas within easy cycling or bus distance of prosperous metropolitan centres. For those who could afford them, expanded mains electricity and the radio brought a new level of comfort and modernity into rural life, while new forms of transport, on superior roads, greatly extended the distance of daily and weekly commutes. The result was a major population exodus from inner-urban areas to new suburban housing estates. Rising living standards and changes in families' housing preferences in favour of suburban lifestyles and modern suburban housing boosted demand for the new houses, while low agricultural land prices and a virtual absence of effective planning controls allowed property developers to meet this demand. During the interwar period the urban area of England and Wales increased by around 26 per cent, well in advance of the 15 per cent increase in the urban population. Some 862,500 new houses were built in rural districts, together with further developments in greenfield areas on the fringes of towns[20] Between 1927–28 and 1933–34 housing development took an average of 38,000 acres of land each year; while over 1934–35 to 1938–39 this rose to 50,000 acres.[21]

18 Steve Humphries and Beverley Hopwood, *Green and Pleasant Land* (London, 1999), pp. 16–19.

19 H. A. Mess, Director, Tyneside Council of Social Service, 1929. Cited in Howkins, *The Death of Rural England*, p. 94.

20 John Lowerson, 'Battles for the countryside', 258–80 in Frank Gloversmith (ed.), *Class, Culture and Social Change. A New View of the 1930s* (Brighton, 1980), p. 258; John Sheail, *Rural Conservation in Inter-War Britain* (Oxford, 1981), pp. 24–7.

21 David Matless, *Landscape and Englishness* (London, 1998), p. 34.

Local government was a major instigator of new suburban housing development. Council housing expanded from less than one per cent of Britain's 1914 housing stock to around 10 per cent in 1938, with over 90 per cent of the 1.1 million new interwar council houses located on suburban estates. Councils took advantage of cheap land beyond urban boundaries, developing estates which often imposed long commutes on their occupants. However, privately developed housing for sale to owner-occupiers proved the major driver of the suburban housing boom. Owner-occupation expanded from around 10 per cent of Britain's 1914 housing stock to around 32 per cent in 1938, mainly due to new developments (an estimated 1.8 million new houses were built for owner-occupiers during this period, compared to 1.1 million existing houses transferred from the privately-rented to owner-occupied sector). As with council houses, the vast majority of new owner-occupied housing was located on suburban estates. Around 900,000 houses were also developed for private renting, again concentrated in the suburbs.[22]

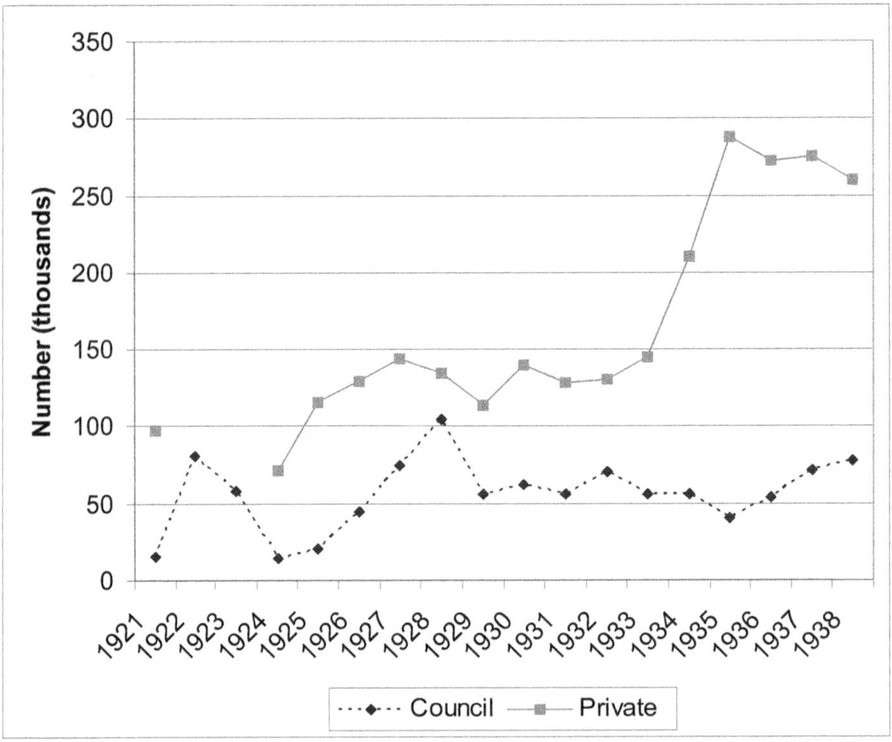

Figure 12.1: Annual number of houses built by local government and private enterprise, 1921–38

Source: Marion Bowley, Housing and the State 1919–1944 *(London, 1945), p. 271.*

22 Stephen Merrett, *Owner-occupation in Britain* (London, 1982), pp. 1 and 16; Andrzej Olechnowicz, *Working-class Housing in England Between the Wars: the Becontree Estate* (Oxford, 1997), p. 1.

Middle-class families led the exodus to suburbia. Some council estates developed during the 1920s initially attracted a significant proportion of lower-middle class tenants, though by 1930s falling house prices and the extension of council housing to successively lower income groups had led most of these to migrate to more 'select' owner-occupied estates. As Figure 12.1 shows, the 1930s witnessed a major boom in private sector house-building, annual development reaching an all-time peak during the middle years of the decade. A survey of 1,360 middle-class households in 1938–39 indicated that some 46.5 per cent were buying their house on mortgage and a further 18.2 per cent owned their house outright.[23]

Most of the new middle-class owner-occupiers lived in suburban properties developed after 1920. Houses designed for the Victorian middle classes had fallen out of favour, partly on account of the decline in domestic service – the ratio of domestic servants to households having fallen from 1 in 5 to 1 in 12.[24] Lower-middle class housewives were faced with having to do a greater share of their own housework, and found houses designed to be maintained by servants too much of a burden. Instead they sought housing with labour-saving features, which would reduce their workload and allow them to make the most efficient use of the new labour-saving consumer durables such as the electric iron, carpet sweeper, and vacuum cleaner (the latter still restricted to only 25 per cent of English homes by 1939). Developers of new suburban homes stressed the attractions of labour-saving kitchens and modern utilities. These were also promulgated in women's magazines and women's sections in newspapers, which idealised the 'professional housewife', providing a happy, clean, home environment for her family via labour saving devices and efficient household management practices.[25]

Meanwhile 'green-field' suburban locations, offering what the developers described as 'garden city' living conditions and 'exclusive' neighbourhoods, proved much more attractive than inner-urban living – which entailed closer proximity to people of different classes and greater dangers (especially to children) from traffic and pollution. Developers both emphasized suburbia's advantages of clean air, space, and healthy living and tapped in to the contemporary upsurge in popular enthusiasm for the countryside.[26] For example, in 1933 one of London's most prolific developers,

23 Philip Massey, 'The expenditure of 1,360 British middle-class households in 1938–39', *Journal of the Royal Statistical Society*, 105, 3 (1942), 159–96.

24 A. Howkins and J. Lowerson, *Trends in Leisure, 1919–1939* (London, 1979), p. 14.

25 Diana Gittins, *Fair Sex: Family Size and Structure, 1900–39* (London, 1982), pp. 182–3; Margaret Judith Giles, 'Something that bit better. working-class women, domesticity, and "respectability", 1919–1939', unpublished D. Phil thesis, University of York, 1989, pp. 108–9.

26 Pyrs Gruffudd, 'Selling the countryside: representations of rural Britain', 247–63, in John R. Gold and Steven V. Ward (eds), *Place Promotion. The Use of Publicity and Marketing to Sell Towns and Regions* (Chichester, 1994); John R. Gold and M. M. Gold, '"A Place of Delightful Prospects": Promotional Imagery and the Selling of Suburbia', 159–82, in L. Zonn (ed.), *Place Images in Media. Portrayal, Experience, and Meaning* (Savage, Maryland, 1990), pp. 167–8.

New Ideal Homesteads, advertised houses from £395 on an estate in Barnehurst, offering:

> beautiful unspoiled country in the very heart of Kent … it is intended that this charming countryside shall permanently maintain its rural character and not suffer disfigurement in any way … Barnehurst enjoys all that the countryside has to offer, commanding entrancing views, while away to the North-east stretches the Thames, a silvery ribbon, winding seawards bringing fresh breezes which sweep across the countryside at every change of the tide...[27]

There thus developed a pronounced 'suburban aspiration' – defined by Mark Clapson as comprising three main elements: a wish to escape from inner-city living; a desire for a suburban-style house and garden; and 'social tone' – the appeal of a high-quality residential environment, both in terms of its material qualities and type of people.[28] These aspirations were tapped into, and in the process reinforced, by building industry and building society advertising. For example, a poster for the Planet Building Society showed a bridge spanning the chasm between a dark, dense, group of terraced streets, with small rear courts and narrow windows, and a brilliantly-lit suburban neighbourhood of bungalows with large windows and generous gardens (in which a small girl rides a bicycle, out of danger of the traffic), alongside the slogan 'Bridging the gap between tenancy and ownership'.[29]

Meanwhile, around 25 per cent of urban working-class families also moved to suburban council, owner-occupied, or privately-rented accommodation over the interwar period.[30] While council housing was initially dominated by the upper strata of the working class (and, in many cases, the lower middle class), by 1938 reductions in rents, slum clearance programmes, and the migration of middle-class council tenants to owner-occupied estates had transformed it into an overwhelmingly working-class tenure, encompassing a broad range of working-class incomes. Meanwhile during the 1930s falling interest rates under the government's new cheap money policy, together with liberalised mortgage terms, reductions in building costs, and rising real incomes (for those in work) substantially widened access to owner-occupation. Between 1931 and 1933 alone average mortgage payments on new homes fell by nine per cent, following a more gradual decline over the previous decade.[31] Lower prices and easier mortgage terms opened the door for large numbers of working-class families to purchase their own homes. Several developers offered houses priced from around £395 in London, or £350 in the provinces, which could

27 Bexley Local Studies and Archive Centre, New Ideal Homesteads brochure, *Super 1933 Homes. Barnehurst Estate, Barnehurst, Kent* (1933).

28 Mark Clapson, *Suburban Century. Social Change and Urban Growth in England and the United States* (Oxford, 2003), pp. 51–2 and 69.

29 Gold and Gold, '"A Place of Delightful Prospects"', pp. 169–71.

30 Peter Scott, 'Visible and invisible walls: suburbanisation and the social filtering of working-class communities in interwar Britain', University of Reading Economics and Management Discussion Paper O2404 (2004).

31 Barry Eichengreen, 'The British economy between the wars', 314–43 in Roderick Floud and Paul Johnson (eds), *The Cambridge Economic History of Modern Britain. Volume II: Economic Maturity 1860–1939* (Cambridge, 2004), pp. 334–5.

be purchased with a five per cent deposit and weekly payments of 12s or less. Some higher-income working-class families could afford better-quality houses, priced at around £550–600.[32]

A major national survey of working-class household expenditure, conducted by the Ministry of Labour during October 1937–July 1938, indicated that some 17.8 per cent of non-agricultural working-class families were owner-occupiers; at least double the proportion at the start of the decade.[33] Working-class owner-occupation spanned a broad income range, being as high as 12.3 per cent even for families with a weekly expenditure of 50–60 shillings (compared to the urban working-class household average, for those in employment, of 85 shillings).[34] Owner-occupation rates varied substantially by region, being as low as 5.9 per cent in Scotland and 5.3 per cent in Northern Ireland (with only a third of Scottish, and a sixth of Northern Irish, owner-occupiers making mortgage payments), compared to rates of around 20 per cent in the South, Midlands, North West, and Wales. The proportion of households buying their house on mortgage appears to have been particularly weighted towards the South and Midlands; for example five sixths of London's owner-occupiers were making mortgage payments.

Regional variations in owner-occupation and, in particular, the proportion of families buying new houses on mortgage, were reflected in variations in house-building and suburbanisation. Despite the particularly low quality of Scotland's pre-1914 housing stock, and its serious overcrowding problem, interwar house-building was much lower than was the case south of the border; being equivalent to only 28 per cent of Scotland's 1911 housing stock, compared to 52 per cent for England and Wales.[35] Depressed industrial areas in northern England and Wales also had markedly lower levels of house-building and suburbanisation than the South and the West Midlands. Most workers in these areas lacked the stability of employment necessary to purchase houses on mortgage, depression eroded the local rates-base available to fund municipal housing, and migration to more prosperous areas eased pressures on the existing housing stock.

---

32 Peter Scott, 'Selling owner-occupation to the working-classes in 1930s' Britain', University of Reading Economics and Management Discussion Paper 02304 (2004).

33 NA, LAB17/7, 'Weekly expenditure of working-class households in the United Kingdom in 1937–38', Ministry of Labour, July 1949. This is probably an over-estimate, as it excludes families experiencing long-term unemployment. It also includes some families with heads of household in middle-class occupations but earning less than £250 a year. However, given that annual earnings below £250 were generally restricted to young white-collar workers, men in this group generally married relatively late, and owner-occupation almost always occurred on or after marriage, their inclusion is unlikely to substantially distort the results. For an estimate of the rate of owner-occupation in around 1931, see George Speight, 'Who bought the inter-war semi? the socio-economic characteristics of new-house buyers in the 1930s', University of Oxford Discussion Paper in Economic and Social History No. 38 (2000), p. 14.

34 NA, LAB 17/7, 'Weekly expenditure of working-class households in the United Kingdom in 1937–38', Ministry of Labour, July 1949. The average number of wage/salary earners per family was 1.75.

35 Marian Bowley, *Housing and the State 1919–1944* (London, 1945), p. 266.

Interwar suburban working-class housing estates were distinguished from their urban counterparts both by their location and the character of their housing. Prior to the First World War new working-class neighbourhoods on the edges of towns were typically developed in long terraces, at densities of thirty or more per acre, and were of similar design to inner-urban housing.[36] The 1918 Tudor Walters Report on the standards of post-war local authority housing set out a new blueprint, drawing on contemporary planning ideas (pioneered in garden city and model workers' village projects), that sought to improve economic and social conditions by creating healthier and better-designed housing and communities.[37] Proposed specifications were well in advance of current standards, including a minimum of three ground floor rooms (living-room, parlour and scullery with larder), three bedrooms (at least two of which could take two beds), plus a bathroom. Houses were to be built at a density of no more than 12 per acre, semi-detached or in short terraces, with wide frontages to increase natural daylight and a cottage appearance enhanced by front and rear gardens.[38] Low plot densities (often only 8 or 10 houses per acre for owner-occupied estates) meant that even medium-sized estates, such as John Laing & Son's Golders Green Estate of around 1,000 houses, consumed significant amounts of previously agricultural land.

Tudor Walters standards embodied the basic features of both the council house and its owner-occupied working-class and lower-middle class counterpart (private developers following them mainly on account of their popularity with purchasers). Yet within these broad parameters a spectrum of housing designs emerged, providing a physical reflection of gradations in status both between estates and different areas of the same estates. Developers of owner-occupied estates aimed at providing houses of variegated design, drawing heavily on the English venacular tradition and producing the 'Tudorbethan' semi that remains, for many people, the ideal house. Meanwhile councils rapidly developed a preference for a 'neo-Georgian' style of plainer houses in near-identical rows, both as a means of economising on costs and emphasising their municipal identity. As Dorothy Barton, who moved with her parents from Charlton to the London County Council's (LCC's) St. Helier Estate in 1934 recalled, 'When we arrived at 10 Rewley Road, we found it was one of a short road of square red brick boxes, all exactly alike.'[39]

There was also substantial variation in house design within each tenure. The ambitious standards of the first council houses were gradually relaxed during the interwar years in order to reduce costs and widen access to lower income groups. The proportion of houses with parlours fell, the bathroom was sometimes sacrificed for a bath in the kitchen (with a removable top so that it could serve as a table

---

36 Alison Ravetz, *Council Housing and Culture. The History of a Social Experiment* (London, 2001), p. 62.

37 This Committee was established by the Local Government Board, which was also responsible for implementing its recommendations.

38 John Burnett, *A Social History of Housing 1815–1985*, 2nd edn (London, 1986), pp. 222–6.

39 Age Concern Reminiscence Center, autobiographical exert provided for Age Concern, 'Just Like the Country' project, by D. Barton, c. 1987.

Figure 12.2: John Laing & Son's Golders Green housing estate, London, developed during the early 1930s

when not in use) and the dimensions of rooms became less generous. Developers for owner-occupation also sought to build down to lower income groups, particularly from the mid-1930s. For example, New Ideal Homesteads – one of London's most prolific housebuilders – offered a range of house designs on each estate, sometimes including a low-cost design based on a three bedroom non-parlour terrace with a bath in the kitchen – very similar to the cheaper type of non-parlour council house.[40]

Yet virtually all new suburban houses shared the minimum characteristics of modern plumbing and utilities, fitted baths, front and rear gardens, and Tudor Walters (or better) building standards. The chasm that separated pre-1914 middle and (even better quality) working class houses thus narrowed considerably. This had major socio-economic implications; as Orwell noted:

> The modern Council house, with its bathroom and electric light, is smaller than the stockbroker's villa, but is recognizably the same kind of house, which the farm labourer's cottage is not. A person who has grown up in a Council housing estate is likely to be – indeed, visibly *is* – more middle class in outlook than a person who has grown up in a slum.[41]

The housebuilding boom had a major direct macroeconomic impact, the increase in house building accounting for around 17 per cent of the growth in GNP between 1932 and 1934. When the expansion of construction materials is added, it is estimated to have accounted for 30 per cent of the increase in employment during the first three years of the recovery.[42] Indeed its overall (direct and indirect) impact was even greater, as family moves to larger, more modern, homes were accompanied by a substantial increase in demand for consumer durables, furniture, and status-related goods required to 'keep up with the Jones's' in the new, aspirational, suburban neighbourhoods.[43] Housebuilding also accentuated the switch from coal to newer household power sources, as new housing generally had mains electricity and gas or electric cookers (and, often, fires). This contributed to an increase in average domestic electricity consumption of some 10 per cent per annum during the 1930s.

Beyond the suburban rings, in what remained true countryside, another tier of seasonal and weekend commuter homes sprang up, including both second homes for the middle classes (though these often preferred to purchase 'picturesque' existing houses) and the 'plotlands' of converted railway carriages, self-builds, beach huts, bungalows, and other low-cost structures that provided weekend and summer retreats for the working and lower middle classes and others seeking a bohemian escape from the city. Another variant of the interwar plotland phenomenon involved the sale of plots for permanent occupation, including plots for smallholdings – in locations

---

40 Bexley Local Studies and Archive Centre, New Ideal Homesteads brochure, *Super 1933 Homes. Barnehurst Estate, Barnehurst, Kent* (1933).

41 George Orwell, *The Lion and the Unicorn: Socialism and the English Genius* (London, 1941), p. 52.

42 Eichengreen, 'The British economy between the wars', pp. 322–3.

43 Peter Scott, 'Did owner-occupation lead to smaller families for interwar working-class households', University of Reading Economics and Management Discussion Paper 025-04 (2004).

such as Granmere on the Isle of Wight – or for commuting, such as Laindon Pitsea in South Essex.[44] Their rise was closely bound up with the collapse in agricultural land values; typically involving areas of poor land beyond the main commuter belt that were unattractive to either farmers or mainstream developers and could therefore be purchased for very low prices by speculative developers who sub-divided them into affordable small plots. The resulting communities were reviled as rural slums, but offered their occupants an escape from the real slums from which many of them travelled, together with much greater access to the countryside or seaside than they could have otherwise afforded. The largest grew into significant communities, such as Canvey Island on the Thames Estuary, which drew people from London's East End seeking cheap holidays and had a permanent population of around 5,000 by the eve of the Second World War.[45]

Along with suburbanised housing came suburbanised services, developed alongside major arterial roads and capturing both local and passing traffic. These included 'road-houses' – night clubs aimed at the affluent (originally the rich) and, in their grandest form, offering facilities for dancing, drinking, swimming, and so forth.[46] More common and (after the initial rush of popularity) successful were the parades of shops developed along arterial roads, often with a branch of a multiple such as Woolworths or Sainsbury's at their centre and including the six 'essential trades' – butcher, baker, grocer, greengrocer, dairyman and newsagent/ tobacconist/ confectioner.[47] These and a range of other service facilities, such as petrol stations and garages, brought new employment into what had formerly been countryside areas. Their importance as employers of former agricultural workers was dwarfed, however, by the building industry. During the interwar years the building trade drew in large numbers of such workers – as developers sought to cut cost by the increased use of un-unionised, non-apprenticed labour and, like manufacturing employers, valued agricultural labourers for their flexibility, low unionisation, and low wage expectations. The extension of bus services and better roads into the new residential areas also increased the accessibility of urban centres to surrounding villages and thus made it easier for former agricultural labourers to commute to urban employment.

The rural leisure industry

Urban prosperity spilled over into the countryside beyond the suburban rings principally via the growing popularity of rural Britain as a leisure venue. Prior to 1914 the countryside had been relatively inaccessible to the mass of Britain's urban citizens, compared, for example, to their German and American counterparts, mainly on account of the high concentration of rural land-holdings, which had limited its

44 Dennis Hardy and Colin Ward, *Arcadia for All. The Legacy of a Makeshift Landscape* (London, 1984), p. 7.

45 John K. Walton, *The British Seaside. Holidays and Resorts in the Twentieth Century* (Manchester, 2000), p. 37.

46 Howkins and Lowerson, *Trends in Leisure*, p. 14.

47 Alan A. Jackson, *Semi-Detached London: Suburban Development, Life and Transport, 1900–39*, 2nd edn. (Didcot, 1991), p. 91.

commercial exploitation for mass leisure.[48] Perversely the crises in British agriculture and land-holding opened up new opportunities for the development of a rural tourism and leisure industry. The small farmers who purchased land in the 1920s had greater enthusiasm for urban visitors than an aristocracy and gentry who regarded providing entertainment for white-collar (let alone blue collar) urban dwellers as beneath them. Even where great estates were preserved, they were often too poorly staffed for their borders to act as an effective barrier to the hoards of tourists who flocked from the cities and failed to appreciate why they should be denied access to open land.

Britain's urbanites enjoyed increased leisure time, the length of the working week having been reduced from 54 hours prior to the First World War, to an average of 48.5 hours for male workers in 1938 (the main gains occurring in around 1919 and subsequently being partially reversed for some groups, such as miners and farm workers). Lower working hours produced an increase in both leisure time and available energy for using that time in active pursuits.[49] For many workers, however, long commutes to new council or private suburban estates at least partially consumed these extra hours.

Meanwhile the same developments in transport that opened up the suburbs to mass commuting also facilitated the mass exodus of townsfolk into the countryside each weekend. While prior to 1914 destinations had been largely confined to areas around rural railway stations, the growth of the motor car, motor cycle, bicycle, and motor coach opened up vast new swathes of the British countryside to the town-dweller. By 1931 there were a million private cars on Britain's roads, at least as many motor cycles, and ten times as many bicycles; together with a large fleet of coaches on both excursions and regular routes. It was estimated that by 1936–37 annual passenger numbers on 'pleasure coaches' – undertaking excursions, tours, and contract services, numbered 82,400,000. [50] Meanwhile the virtues of rural motoring and touring were promulgated to the public via a plethora of guidebooks, topographies, 'countryside companions', motorists' maps, and associated literature, in a publishing boom which itself stands as an important testament to the scale of the interwar rural leisure industry.[51]

During the Edwardian era Scotland, the Lake District, and North Wales had been Britain's only important inland tourist areas; by the eve of the Second World War any village enjoying reasonable transport links to a major urban centre and a modest amount of scenic beauty could attract its share of visitors: 'Derelict hotels and inns were rejuvenated, cottage parlours blossomed forth as tearooms, the village blacksmith became a motor mechanic and a petrol station sprang up where once the village smithy stood.'[52] What was, in many areas of Britain, a virtually new industry

48 Mandler, *The Fall and Rise of the Stately Home*, p. 231.

49 Harvey Taylor, *A Claim on the Countryside. A History of the British Outdoor Movement* (Edinburgh, 1997), p. 233.

50 Elizabeth Brunner, *Holiday Making and the Holiday Trades* (London, 1945), p. 38.

51 Lowerson, 'Battles for the countryside', pp. 262–3.

52 J. A. R. Pimlott, *The Englishman's Holiday. A Social History* (London, 1947), p. 257.

of tea shops; tourist pubs; hotel, bed & breakfast, and hostel accommodation; garages and petrol stations; caravans and camping sites; and advertising hoardings sprang up alongside the improved roads to service the weekend and summer urban visitors. Attendance figures at popular rural tourist events mushroomed; numbers at Stratford's Shakespeare Festival increased from 14,000 in 1904 to some 200,000 by 1938; while those paying admission to Stonehenge rose from less than 4,000 in 1901 to 100,000 by 1930.[53]

There was also a considerable boom in outdoor pursuits such as cycling, camping, and mountaineering, the most important of which was the huge craze for 'hiking' (particularly during the 1930s). The formation of the Youth Hostels Association in 1930 and Scottish Youth Hostels Association in 1931, led to the rapid development of a network of hostels offering simple, cheap, bunk-bed dormitory accommodation for hikers. By 1939 there were 397 hostels in the British Isles, run by four associations with 106,524 members.[54] Many were based in country houses that had been abandoned by the rural gentry. The total number of hikers was estimated at over 500,000 by the late 1930s, the Derbyshire Peak alone attracting 10,000 on a summer weekend.[55] Platoons of hikers in distinctive continental-style khaki uniforms, open-necked shirts, berets, and ankle socks, journeying from one night's youth hostel to the next, became a familiar sight in the British countryside.

It was in the hiking movement that the meeting of town and country (or, more accurately, town and rural land-owners) took on a political dimension. Access to open land displayed a distinct regional profile, which in turn had strong class overtones. Many southern areas favoured by hikers, such as the Chilterns and North and South Downs, had a network of tracks and footpaths often dating from ancient times; while walkers did not threaten their established commercial uses, such as sheep pasture and similar low value agricultural activities. Furthermore, hikers in these areas were generally more middle-class than their northern counterparts and, therefore, more acceptable to rural landowners.[56] Similarly, in remote rural areas of 'outer-Britain' such as North Wales and the Lake District, where distance deterred most hikers who could not afford substantial transport costs, access was less restricted and did not provoke conflict.[57]

Conversely, in more highly populated areas of northern England such as Yorkshire, southern Lancashire, and Derbyshire, many workers entered the beautiful moorland that surrounded their towns only to find that they were not welcome. Since the early nineteenth century landowners in these areas had imposed a *cordon sanitaire* to keep the public out of the grouse moors. For example, only 764 of the Peak District's 84,000 acres were publicly accessible. A public access campaign gathered widespread support and powerful momentum during the 1930s, including a series of famous mass trespasses and other demonstrations. The campaign had an important political

53 Mandler, *The Fall and Rise of the Stately Home*, p. 231.

54 Taylor, *A Claim on the Countryside*, p. 252.

55 Howkins and Lowerson, *Trends in Leisure*, p. 49.

56 Lowerson, 'Battles for the countryside', p. 269.

57 Mike Parsons and Mary B. Rose, *Invisible on Everest. Innovation and the Gear Makers* (Philadelphia, 2003), p. 120.

strand; the Left capitalising on an issue which so clearly demonstrated the excesses of unconstrained private property. Yet the magnitude of its support reflected a much wider popular revulsion against the cutting off of huge swathes of moorland to the public, often even involving the closing of long-established footpaths. The problem was exacerbated by the fact that major landowners had begun to take much greater interest in the monetary side of their grouse shooting interests – another aspect of the commercialisation of countryside leisure – and were in no mood for compromise.

The most celebrated battlefield for the access movement was the Peak District's Kinder Scout in Derbyshire. This high plateau was largely owned by the Duke of Devonshire and used for grouse shooting; though one area was in the possession of the Sheffield Corporation, which took a similarly hostile stance to those who might disturb its profitable grouse shooting interests. Campaigns to gain public access to Kinder Scout had been waged for several decades, but gathered renewed momentum during the hiking boom, culminating in the famous April 1932 Kinder Scout mass trespass – which stands as the enduring monument to the rural access movement.

Despite the relatively small numbers involved – the best estimates suggest that 100 or fewer protesters actually left the footpath to trespass on the moor, and the very limited violence – a series of minor scuffles in which one keeper was unintentionally injured, this episode, like that of the Tolpuddle martyrs, was given great symbolic importance by the unjust nature of the following trial and the draconian punishments meted out to those arrested. Six Manchester trespassers were charged with illegal assembly and assault and the five who were found guilty received sentences of between two and six months by a grand jury consisting of two brigadier-generals, three colonels, two majors, three captains, and two aldermen.[58] Such protests did lead to some voluntary access agreements between land-owners and local walking groups. However, the only significant piece of legislation, the 1939 Access to Mountains Act (which had been repeatedly, but unsuccessfully, proposed since 1888) was so watered down during its passage through Parliament that it had little real impact. An effective 'right to roam' over open land was not to reach the statute books for another 61 years.

Meanwhile concern regarding urbanisation of the countryside and the accompanying road hoardings, petrol stations, tea rooms, camping sites, plotland settlements, and litter, led to the development of an influential rural preservation lobby. This included both pre-existing and new groups, such as the National Trust (founded in 1894) the Council for the Preservation of Rural England (established in 1926); the Society for Checking the Abuses of Public Advertising (SCAPA, founded in 1893), the Society for the Preservation of Ancient Buildings (1877), and local bodies – such as the Surrey Anti-Litter League. Yet interwar town and country planning acts generally proved so weak as to be ineffective; like contemporary proposals for national parks, or access to open land, planning restrictions were seen as a threat to private property rights, that might set dangerous precedents for further intervention.

By the 1930s a new commercial landscape had emerged in the British countryside, composed of sprawling suburban and ribbon development, advertising

58 Harvey Taylor, *A Claim on the Countryside*, p. 260.

hoardings, petrol stations, mock-Tudor tea shops and holiday homes. Yet, away from the suburbs, villages, and roads, the essential heart of the rural landscape remained little changed. Chemical fertilisers, insecticides, and herbicides had not yet made a significant impact; many areas retained their small fields and long-established land boundaries; and a broad range of wild animals and wild flowers were common throughout rural Britain. It was to be the post-1945 economic and political alliance of newly-prosperous British farmers and agro-chemical combines, rather than the interwar town dweller, who was to be the real culprit behind the murder of the British countryside.

Coastal and holiday Britain

Urban spending power in the South and Midlands travelled beyond the area covered by commuting and short trips to the countryside via the growth of British holiday making. This period saw a substantial increase in the availability of paid holidays, culminating in the 1938 Holidays with Pay Act. The Ministry of Labour estimated that in March 1925 around 1.5 million manual workers were entitled to holidays with pay under collective agreements – a considerable increase over 1914 levels. For the next decade the growth of collective agreements was slow; in April 1937 they were still only estimated to cover some 1.5–1.75 million workers. Yet when workers who were otherwise entitled to paid holidays were added, a total of around 4 million of Britain's 18.5 million workers earning under £250 a year were covered (together with perhaps a million workers on higher incomes). During the late 1930s paid holidays witnessed rapid expansion, especially following the passing of the Holidays with Pay Act, 1938 (some years after most other industrialised countries had introduced similar legislation). By June 1939 the number of employees earning under £250 entitled to paid holidays had reached over 11 million.[59]

Most received a week's holiday, though many workers in public utilities and administration got a fortnight, while some distributive trades' workers had as much as three weeks. Middle-class salaried workers also generally received two or three weeks. In 1937 Political and Economic Planning estimated that the number of people in Britain taking a holiday of a week or more away from home was around 15 million, roughly a third of the population.[60] The proportion was greatest in prosperous centres such as London (*The New Survey of London Life and Labour* estimated that about half London's workers took holidays in 1934) and in industrial towns in parts of northern England (such as the Lancashire and West Yorkshire textile belt) where the wakes week holiday system had become firmly entrenched in popular culture and employment patterns even prior to the First World War.[61]

Coastal areas were particularly important beneficiaries of this increase in holiday-making. Between 1911 and 1951 the population of the 145 seaside resorts in England and Wales increased from just over 1.6 million (just under 4.5 per cent of the population) to 2.5 million (5.7 per cent); by 1931 they already comprised 5

59 Pimlott, *The Englishman's Holiday*, pp. 214–19.

60 Brunner, *Holiday Making and the Holiday Trades*, p. 3.

61 Pimlott, *The Englishman's Holiday*, p. 215.

per cent of the population.[62] The fastest-growing resorts featured among Britain's most rapidly expanding communities. Resort growth did not demonstrate as strong a North/South divide as industrial development. While Sussex resorts achieved an impressive 43.6 per cent population growth between 1911 and 1951, Lancashire's resorts recorded an astounding 86.6 per cent growth over the same period and the much smaller resort economy of North Wales managed 88.4 per cent (both drawing large numbers of tourists from the prosperous West Midlands as well as more northerly regions).[63] Resort growth was boosted by entrepreneurial councils who invested heavily in piers, gardens, promenades, concert halls, lidos, indoor swimming pools and other improvements designed to attract tourist income, together with promotional marketing to bring the new facilities to the attention of the tourist public.

Evidence regarding the sources of the holiday-makers is poor, but it appears that the chief areas of growth were the expanding industrial districts of the South East and Midlands.[64] For example, good rail links to the Midlands was an important factor behind the success of resorts in Lancashire and North Wales (despite the growth in road transport, a near-contemporary study found that rail links were still the chief determinant of tourist flows).[65] On other northern coastlines less accessible from the Midlands growth was slower. Similarly, Scotland's holiday resorts experienced relative stagnation, the population of its southern industrial belt turning to the warmer English resorts and the livelier atmosphere of major centres such as Blackpool. Meanwhile Scotland's considerable potential for rural tourism was not exploited during this period, the Highlands remaining 'beautiful but impoverished and inaccessible'.[66]

As with other aspects of the interwar economy, the emphasis of the expanding tourist industry was on the mass market rather than the more expensive and socially exclusive holidays that had characterised pre-1914 tourism. Middle class Edwardian resorts lost out to the vigorous democracy of fleshpots such as Blackpool and Brighton.[67] According to contemporary estimates, Blackpool had 7 million visitors per year (including excursionists); and had the capacity to accommodate as many as half a million at any one time. Southend had 5.5 million visitors (including excursionists), Hastings nearly 3 million, Bournemouth and Southport 2 million, Eastbourne over 1 million, and Ramsgate 1 million.[68] Such figures are of questionable accuracy and the methods by which they were calculated are unknown, but they

62 Walton, *The British Seaside*, pp. 31–2.

63 Ibid, p. 33.

64 Ibid, p. 58.

65 Brunner, *Holiday Making and the Holiday Trades*, p. 38.

66 Ibid, p. 3.

67 Walton, *The British Seaside*, p. 35; Clifford O'Neil, '"The most magical corner in England": tourism, preservation and the development of the lake district, 1919–1939', Chapter 13 in John K. Walton (ed.), *Histories of Tourism: Representation, Identity and Conflict* (Clevedon, forthcoming 2005).

68 Brunner, *Holiday Making and the Holiday Trades*, p. 8; Pimlott, *The Englishman's Holiday*, p. 240.

Figure 12.3: The first Butlins holiday camp, opened in Skegness in 1936

are not unreasonable, given that the railways carried 20 million more passengers in August than in May or October.

A major area of expansion for the tourism industry involved extending access to lower income groups, who had often not previously been able to afford holidays. New, less formal, low-cost forms of holiday were developed, such as self-catering chalets, bungalow towns, and holiday camps. By the late 1930s there may have been as many as 200 holiday camps in Britain, capable of accommodation around 30,000 people each week. These pioneered modern 'all-in' mass package tourism, providing accommodation, 'free' facilities and entertainment, together with 'community' activities led by specialist staff, from around £3 a week.[69] These were sometimes located alongside funfairs and amusement parks, often developed by the same impresarios who launched the holiday camps.[70] For example Billy Butlin developed a chain of amusement parks from 1927, choosing two of their locations for his first two holiday camps – Skegness (1936) and Clacton (1938).[71]

Camping offered even cheaper holidays for those with the necessary resources to make the initial investment in equipment. The Camping Club of Great Britain and Ireland offered weekly camping sites for 3/- for pedestrians, 3s 9d for motorists, and 4s 6d for caravanners.[72] The numbers taking holidays under canvas or in camps of all kinds (presumably including holiday camps) was estimated at 1.5 million in 1939.[73]

Some seaside resorts, especially in the warmer climes around England's south coast, also began to attract substantial numbers of retired people, during an era which witnessed a substantial increase in the proportion of the population over 65. These were generally middle class people with significant savings. Their consumption patterns were skewed towards personal services, further accentuating the services bias of resort areas. Their presence both raised the general income levels of towns in which they congregated and helped to even out seasonal imbalances in economic activity.

Holiday trade also boosted the rural economy in some areas. Many farmers in scenic areas such as Devon, Cornwall, and parts of Wales, came to earn a substantial part of their income from taking in tourists during the summer months on farmhouse holidays. Others set up camping and caravan sites, provided 'farmhouse teas', or sold farmhouse produce to tourists. It was estimated that on the Devon moors the tourist trade accounted for 50–75 per cent of some farmers' total income.[74] Rural Britain derived particular benefit from the trend towards more short break holidays and weekend excursions, as most countryside areas and historic towns were more suitable for short break visits or coach tours covering several centres than for longer, single-destination, holidays. The car and motor coach led to an increase in the proportion of visitors on day-trips or short-stay holidays in areas

69 Howkins and Lowerson, *Trends in Leisure*, p. 12.

70 Brunner, *Holiday Making and the Holiday Trades*, p. 5.

71 Butlins Memories website, http://www.butlinsmemories.com/21/id3.htm.

72 Brunner, *Holiday Making and the Holiday Trades*, p. 5.

73 Ibid., p. 8.

74 Ibid., p. 61.

such as the Lake District, where long travel times had hitherto been reflected in relatively long stays.[75] This was, in turn, reflected in a shift in tourist spending from established hotels to day-time leisure and catering facilities. Resorts within a short train journey of major population centres, such as Brighton, were also major beneficiaries.

The boom in holiday-making provided well-situated coastal communities and some rural areas with a valuable source of additional employment at a time when major traditional trades, such as fishing, shipbuilding, and agriculture, were in serious decline. Indeed available indicators point to seaside resorts having relatively high levels of prosperity compared to other British towns.[76] Resort employment also had a wider geographical impact, drawing in large numbers of (mainly female) seasonal workers, often from considerable distances. Yet many resorts experienced substantial seasonal unemployment. While those around the south coast could draw some visitors even in winter, their northern counterparts had no such off-season business, while the prospects of workers laid off during the winter finding other employment were also much bleaker. Whereas unemployment in Bournemouth rose from 6.1 per cent in the summer months to 8.8 per cent in winter, in Blackpool the rates were 11.6 and 24.9 per cent respectively.[77]

Table 12.1 shows the regional distribution of employment in what Elizabeth Brunner identified as the best Census proxies for the 'holiday trades' (including some very rough proxies, such as private domestic service), relative to the national average in 1931. The South East maintained its long-established lead in personal and leisure services employment. Other areas with employment in activities such as holiday accommodation and catering substantially above the national average were the 'rest of Wales' (excluding Brecknock, Camarthan, Glamorgan, and Monmouth) and the South West – both regions with good transport links to prosperous industrial regions, extensive coastlines, and low population densities. Conversely the densely-populated and almost land-locked West Midlands (the Census definition included Gloucester) and East Midlands (defined to exclude Lincolnshire) had low employment ratios in these trades despite their relative prosperity.

The figures corroborate local evidence that regional prosperity spilled over to other (mainly adjacent) regions via tourist spending and that rural regions with extensive coastlines and good long-distance transport links to prosperous urban areas derived the greatest relative benefit from the leisure and tourism boom. Conversely depressed industrial areas such as Northumberland, Durham, South Wales, and west-central Scotland failed to share in this inter-regional redistribution of consumer spending despite their extensive coastlines.

75 O'Neil, '"The most magical corner in England"'.

76 Walton, *The British Seaside*, pp. 149–50.

77 Brunner, *Holiday Making and the Holiday Trades*, p. 43.

Table 12.1: Regional distribution of holiday trades in 1931 (per head of population, Great Britain = 100)

Region	Lodging & boarding houses, hotels, restaurants	Entertainment & sport	Personal service	Private domestic service	Laundries, dyeing, cleaning	Manicure, hair, etc.	All other personal services
South East	144	138	137	131	165	120	145
Rest of Wales*	140	66	128	141	55	77	48
South West	128	77	148	171	92	100	68
North & East Riding of Yorkshire, Cumberland, Westmorland	108	85	113	123	67	98	86
Eastern England**	91	87	118	140	66	95	68
Northern Scotland	84	61	108	123	115	75	41
Lancashire & Cheshire	82	99	70	60	80	98	102
East-central Scotland	73	94	80	82	86	91	71
West Midlands	70	73	82	88	73	86	80
Northumberland & Durham	69	88	78	83	59	91	86
West-central Scotland	68	89	66	61	93	98	59
Southern Scotland	65	45	117	151	87	73	29
West Riding of Yorkshire***	63	81	65	63	61	93	91
South Wales	60	78	71	78	40	89	77
East Midlands	57	62	70	75	55	86	77

Source: Adapted from Elizabeth Brunner, Holiday Making and the Holiday Trades *(London, 1945), p. 33.*

Notes: Based on 1931 Census regions. * Welsh counties, excluding Brecknock, Camarthen, Glamorgan, and Monmouth. ** Cambridgeshire, Huntingdonshire, Lincolnshire, Norfolk, Rutland, and Suffolk. *** Also includes York County Borough.

Conclusion

Rural and coastal Britain demonstrated a more complex geographical pattern of prosperity than their urban counterpart. Yet the same broad contours of uneven development was still evident. Regions with depressed industrial areas generally had a markedly less prosperous agricultural sector than the Midlands and south (even when specialised in types of production that were expanding nationally – such as dairy farming). They necessarily experienced more limited suburbanistion and (with the exception of coastlines or scenic areas accessible to more prosperous regions) did not fully participate in the interwar rural leisure and holiday-making boom. The disadvantages of northern rural Britain, stemming from its colder climate and generally poorer land, were reinforced by the those of its depressed industrial centres – via reduced urban purchasing power, pollution, and, perhaps not least, a negative image of stagnation and decay. The landed families who abandoned their northern estates were not the only section of society to see southern England as Britain's prime rural playground.

Chapter Thirteen

The genesis of British regional policy

Introduction

The most enduring feature of the interwar years in the popular memory is the mass long-term unemployment of 'outer Britain'. Britain witnessed both high nationwide unemployment and staggeringly high rates in its traditional industrial areas, peaking at over a quarter of the insured population. The initial post-war slump produced substantial unemployment throughout the country and it was only during the mid–late 1920s that a clear pattern of high long-term unemployment in Scotland, Wales, and northern England became evident. Unemployment rates in these regions soared during the 1929–32 depression, reaching 36.5 per cent in Wales, 27.7 per cent in Scotland, and 28.5 and 25.8 per cent in the Ministry of Labour's North East and North West divisions in 1932 (for insured workers). While unemployment rates declined during the following years, differentials between these regions and the prosperous South widened further. At the peak of the recovery, in 1937, unemployment in the regions of outer-Britain[1] averaged 17.3 per cent, more than ten percentage points in excess of Britain's other regions.[2]

Meanwhile within these regions there were pockets of much higher unemployment, reaching levels of 50–60 per cent during 1930–32 in the worst-affected areas – typically dominated by a single staple industry, or even a single firm.[3] Unemployment was strongly concentrated in densely-populated industrial areas outside the factory belt, together with south Lancashire. During most of the interwar period around 45–50 per cent of national unemployment was found in five areas – South-east Scotland, the North-east coast, Lancashire, Merseyside, and South Wales (these accounted for less than a third of the insured population and just over a quarter of the total British population).[4] It was these areas that formed the main focus of Britain's embryonic regional policy initiative.

After initially treating unemployment as a transitory problem that could be solved by the re-establishment of the gold standard and a return to normal international trading relations, government sought to reduce unemployment in particularly depressed areas by encouraging workers to migrate under the industrial transference initiative. Indeed transference remained the most importance strand of policy (in

1 Comprising the North, North West, and North East Ministry of Labour regional divisions of England, plus Scotland and Wales.

2 D. E. Pitfield, 'Labour migration and the regional problem in Britain, 1920–1939', unpublished Ph.D thesis, University of Sterling, 1973, p. 23.

3 Peter Mathias, *The First Industrial Nation. An Economic History of Britain 1700–1914* (London, 1969), p. 437.

4 Derek H. Aldcroft, *The British Economy. Volume 1 The Years of Turmoil 1920–1951* (Brighton, 1986), p. 119.

terms of placing the unemployed in jobs) throughout the 1930s. However, it became increasingly unpopular – critics noted that it deprived the depressed areas of their most able people; was successful in attracting mainly young, single men, rather than families; was inefficient in that a substantial proportion of assisted migrants subsequently returned to their home communities; and it produced considerable popular resentment in reception areas. Largely in response to popular pressure, from 1934 the government embarked on an experimental and – from its perspective – largely cosmetic initiative to investigate what steps might be taken to reinvigorate the depressed regions.

The economic and political context of the new policy framework

Britain's experimental, 'regional' or, rather, 'depressed areas' policy was to mark a watershed in popular conceptions of the State's role in regional development. Yet the government's intention, in taking the steps which led to the introduction of the initiative, had been to implement a policy of minimal action aimed at appeasing public opinion while avoiding precedents for further government intervention or substantial costs to the Exchequer. Its hand was forced by rising popular awareness, and concern, regarding the depth and intractability of depression, unemployment, and poverty in Britain's peripheral industrial areas. By the 1930s prolonged economic depression had produced divisions in attitudes, outlook, and aspirations between the northern and western industrial areas of Britain and the metropolitan South that were larger than at any time since at least the advent of the railways. As Charles Loch Mowat noted, the staple industry areas had become:

> a land apart; much written of, but seldom visited by outsiders, save for the devoted social workers and the thoughtful undergraduates who played the Good Samaritan in the community centres and club houses. The Welsh mining valleys were numb with distress. Industrial Lancashire was at a standstill… In Wigan one man in three was on the dole. The mining villages of county Durham, the steel works and shipyards of Tyne and Tees were derelict: Gateshead, Hebburn, Jarrow, Wallsend, Crook … So it was in west Cumberland. So it was in Scotland: in Glasgow perhaps half the population was unemployed.[5]

By 1932 some 62 per cent of Britain's shipbuilding workers were unemployed, together with 48 per cent of iron and steel workers and over a third of coal-miners. Meanwhile the misery of the long-term unemployed had been further deepened by government cut-backs in relief expenditure, particularly the introduction of the household means test in 1931. 'Dole' claimants had hitherto received their full benefit entitlement regardless of their financial resources. The means test forced those who had exhausted their right to unemployment benefit to submit to what amounted to a Poor Law evaluation of their circumstances, something which both evoked bitter resentment and led to wide local and regional variations in the assessment of claims and the level of benefits (on account of differences in interpretation regarding the yardsticks that should be applied). Local and regional disparities were exacerbated

5 C. L. Mowat, *Britain Between the Wars 1918–1940* (London, 1955), p. 481.

by the fact that, following the creation of the Unemployment Assistance Board, the long-term unemployed could claim local public assistance in cases where this would leave them financially better off. An official survey of 80 county boroughs in 1933, involving nine 'specimen' cases, revealed the extent of these variations. The most parsimonious council, Blackpool, was found to pay only 28.9 per cent of the benefit levels allocated by the most generous, West Ham.[6]

Britain's recovery from the 1929–32 depression was one of the strongest for any major industrial nation; yet unemployment in the staple industries, and in the areas that relied on them, remained stubbornly high. In 1936 some 205,000 people had been unemployed for two years or more, while almost 53,000 had been out of work for at least five years. The proportion of unemployed workers in long-term unemployment had actually grown over the recovery period, from 16.4 per cent in 1932 to 24.3 per cent by August 1937. Long-term unemployment among redundant staple industry workers proved particularly intractable. In Northern England, Wales, and Scotland 29.6 per cent of unemployed insured workers had been out of work for more than 12 months in June 1937, compared to only 12.5 per cent in the south and Midlands.[7]

Long-term unemployment was strongly concentrated among older, male, workers. Market forces, even when assisted by government transference measures, proved incapable of moving such workers to the work – given that the demand for older male workers, with the skills and outlook typical of the heavy staple industries, was extremely limited and that older workers were inherently less mobile. Nor was there any real prospect of a substantial revival in the fortunes of these areas' dominant industries, in the face of rising overseas tariff walls, their excess capacity of obsolete plant, and the formidable barriers to their structural and technological modernisation – discussed in Chapter Four.

Unemployment benefits usually provided sufficient income to maintain at least a minimum acceptable standard of life (by contemporary working-class standards); cases were occasionally even found where, particularly for large families, they exceeded some of the lowest wages on offer. Yet evidence suggests that despite this long spells of unemployment led to physical and mental deterioration, on account of both malnutrition and the psychological impact of inactivity –including neurosis, depression, and other mental illnesses. Such effects were particularly severe for the very long-term unemployed, as clothing and other durable goods which wore out could not easily be replaced, while satisfying the means test often required the sale of any furniture or other possessions with a second hand value. The nature of the deprivations that life on the dole inflicted on such families are neatly summed up by the account of one Oldham textile worker's thoughts when she heard that her husband had finally found work after migrating to Coventry:

6 Noel Whiteside, 'The social consequences of interwar unemployment', 17–30 in Sean Glynn and Alan Booth, *The Road to Full Employment* (London, 1987), pp. 19–20.

7 Roger Middleton, *Government Versus the Market. The Growth of the Public Sector, Economic Management and British Economic Performance, c. 1890–1979* (Cheltenham, 1996), p. 281.

> It was in the quietness of the night that I realised fully what it meant. No more dodging the Means Test to earn an extra shilling. No more fasting a full day on the sly, to save the price of a loaf of bread so that I could buy Charlie half an ounce of twist tobacco, or give him sixpence to go to a whist drive. No more going to bed in winter to save putting coal on the fire, so that we could have Margaret's shoes repaired instead of buying a bag of coal. I would be able to buy a jam sponge sandwich – one of those silly little things I had always wanted to buy.[8]

The physical impact of long-term or frequent unemployment was evident even in the mortality statistics – particularly for infants.[9] In Wigan, Liverpool, and St. Helens, infant mortality rates stood at 103, 94, and 88 per thousand live births respectively in 1931, compared to an average of 62 for England and Wales. Meanwhile data on death rates (standardised for age structure) suggest that by the late 1930s high unemployment was associated with a mortality rate some 25–50 per cent above the national average.[10] In Jarrow, which faced one of Britain's highest unemployment rates, the tuberculosis death rate stood at twice the national average during the 1930s, while infant mortality (112 per thousand live births) was almost double the national rate.[11] Increased morbidity and mortality appear to have been strongly linked to problems of malnutrition; for example, in 1934 the provision of free food by a voluntary agency for pregnant women in part of the Rhondda led to a dramatic decline in maternal mortality.[12]

Despite these hardships, mass unemployment provoked remarkably little political protest in the depressed areas. Parties and candidates of the radical left, or the embryonic nationalist movements in Wales and Scotland, were completely marginalized by the established Labour and Conservative parties in even the worst blackspots. In Merthyr Tydfil, which was both severely depressed and one of the most radical boroughs in South Wales, an intense 1934 by-election campaign by the Communist Party, with the popular Wal Hannington as their candidate, failed to lift him above last place in the poll.[13] Similarly nationalist parties were confined to a mere 1 per cent of the Scottish popular vote during the 1930s.[14] Depression and apathy, rather than anger and revolt, proved the usual psychological fruits of long-term unemployment, as found by contemporary studies in both Britain and other industrialised nations. The fact that long-term unemployment was concentrated in geographically peripheral blackspot areas accentuated this trend, as people measured

8 Jane Walsh, *Not Like This* (London, 1953), p. 91.

9 While the relationship between unemployment and mortality is complex, as high unemployment is often concentrated in areas experiencing other forms of economic disadvantage, a clear link is nevertheless evident.

10 Stephen V. Ward, *The Geography of Interwar Britain: The State and Uneven Development* (London, 1988), pp. 28–9.

11 Noreen Branson and Margot Heinemann, *Britain in the Nineteen Thirties* (St. Albans, 1973), p. 65.

12 Whiteside, 'The social consequences of interwar unemployment', p. 22.

13 Wayne Parsons, *The Political Economy of British Regional Policy* (London, 1988), p. 33.

14 Clive Lee, *Scotland and the United Kingdom. The Economy and the Union in the Twentieth Century* (Manchester, 1995), p. 6.

their poverty relative to that of their neighbours and friends rather than the population of the distant south.

Britain stood alone among the stable democracies in pursuing a policy of minimal direct intervention in the face of mass unemployment. Policy remained constrained by the government's macroeconomic stance, which still followed the traditional Treasury orthodoxy of balanced budgets, low public expenditure, and a belief that increased public spending would be futile, as it would crowd-out an equal amount of private investment. Instead, government continued to seek a market-based solution – through transference and similar initiatives – while direct job creation measures remained largely token political gestures.

Taking work to the workers

By 1934, with recovery evident in the South but outer-Britain still severely depressed, there was a dramatic increase in popular support for government intervention to assist the depressed areas, reflected in Labour Party election gains and press comment in *The Times* and elsewhere.[15] In April 1934 government responded by appointing 'special investigators' to report on conditions in four particularly depressed areas: Clydeside, Durham and Tyneside, part of South Wales, and West Cumberland (excluding the cities of Cardiff, Newcastle, and Glasgow) and make policy recommendations. Given that most of these areas had been surveyed in detail for the Board of Trade by university economists only four years earlier, the Surveys were not justified in terms of gathering information. Yet commissioning them offered government a breathing-space, allowing them to claim that they were taking action while delaying any real policy changes.[16]

The Cabinet's instructions to the investigators militated against any new policy initiatives, focussing on industrial transference and the possibilities of limited assistance by private individuals and organisations. Three of the reports broadly supported current government policy, though the fourth, Euan Wallace's report on the North East, advocated much greater intervention, including national action on the location of industry, raising the school leaving age, earlier retirement pensions, and a variety of local and regional initiatives.[17] It also proposed the appointment of a Commissioner to coordinate government schemes for the rehabilitation of the Durham and Tyneside area, recommending that the Commissioner should not be under the necessity of referring any but major questions to London.[18]

Meanwhile the public mood was moving strongly in favour of intervention, partly on account of an influential series of articles in The Times, that graphically illustrated the extent of poverty in County Durham. In October 1934 a Cabinet committee noted

15 F. M. Miller, 'The unemployment policy of the National Government, 1931–1936', *Historical Journal*, 19 (1976), 453–76, p. 465.

16 Alan E. Booth, 'An administrative experiment in unemployment policy in the thirties', *Public Administration*, 56 (1978), 139–57, p. 143.

17 Ward, *The Geography of Interwar Britain*, p. 212.

18 D. E. Pitfield, 'The quest for an effective regional policy 1934–37', *Regional Studies*, XII (1978), 429–43, p. 435.

Figure 13.1: The Special Areas, 1934

Source: Depressed Areas (Development and Improvement) Act, 1934, First Schedule (B.P.P., 1934–35, X).

that implementing the recommendations of the three investigators' reports which advocated no major policy changes would be unlikely to satisfy public expectations raised by their appointment. It was therefore decided to appoint two 'Special Areas Commissioners' (one for Scotland and one for England and Wales), to oversee the four depressed regions, a course of action which 'would have an important psychological effect in persuading the persons in the Depressed Areas that the Government had their plight very much at heart'.[19]

This new policy was given statutory authority via the 1934 Special Areas Act. In the Commons debate on the Act, the Chancellor of the Exchequer, Neville Chamberlain, stated, 'We are going to give the Commissioners a very wide discretion. They must not be afraid of trying experiments even if those experiments fail.'[20] This emphasis on the Special Areas as fields for experiment helped justify their restricted and arbitrary boundaries, which were limited to those areas surveyed by the investigators. These excluded major cities, with the exception of Newcastle (as shown in Figure 13.1), despite the fact that these might have acted as potential growth centres. Meanwhile encouraging the Commissioners to experiment, free from close government supervision, distanced the initiative from government, thus reducing the danger of creating unwelcome precedents for further intervention.[21]

This experimental emphasis also provided a useful justification for the Treasury when it sought to constrain expenditure, in that experimental measures need not be of sufficient scale to seriously address the unemployment problem. In practice government sought to constrain the Commissioners' activities, desiring the minimum activity sufficient to appease public opinion. The powers given to the Commissioners by the 1934 Act were limited, precluding activities under the normal jurisdiction of local or central government, assistance to profit-making organisations, or the provision of direct employment. Furthermore, the Commissioners' initial funds were set at only £2 million, with vague promises that any commitments entered into by them would be honoured. Yet in practice government proved reluctant to provide further funds; as a January 1935 Treasury note to the Chancellor stated:

> ...if Mr Stewart [Malcolm Stewart, the Special Areas Commissioner for England and Wales] is carefully handled, it should not be difficult to keep him both contented and reasonably straight. It seems very desirable that you should tell him in confidence the general budget situation so that he may see 'that there are not countless millions available...'. He should then be asked to recognise that schemes costing great sums of money can only be financed by him and told that government have ... the proposals made by Mr Lloyd George under consideration and that they need a little time to decide what they can do. It should be quite sufficient to calm Mr Stewart for the time being.[22]

---

19 Ibid.

20 Commissioner for the Special Areas (England and Wales), *First Report* [7 July 1935] (Cmnd 4957 of 1935), p. 2.

21 Ward, *The Geography of Interwar Britain*, p. 214.

22 Quoted in Parsons, *The Political Economy of British Regional Policy*, pp. 16–17.

As Stewart noted in his first report, the limitations of the act made the Commissioner, 'as much subject to orthodox financial control as any government department'.[23] A number of legal opinions and administrative decisions further constrained the Commissioners' powers, while the term of their appointment, initially only two and a half years, limited any long-term initiatives. Government even failed to show commitment to the experimental value of the initiative, as illustrated by its initial support for a Treasury proposal to wind-up the initiative in June 1938 (though by November this had been deemed politically impossible given rising unemployment).[24] Yet Special Areas policy did result in a number of measures that were to greatly influence post-war regional policy. This was largely due to the actions of Stewart, who pushed his powers to the limit, advocating an interventionist strategy in the face of considerable Treasury opposition. As the Chancellor, Neville Chamberlain, commented, 'I am afraid we have made a mistake with our Commissioner and I anticipate more trouble'.[25]

The first years of the Commissioners' activities were dominated by social welfare and land settlement schemes rather than measures primarily designed to attract industry. Of £5.5 million spent by the Commissioner for England and Wales by the end of 1936, only £180,000, devoted to site clearance, development councils and trading estates, could be viewed as directly promoting industrial development The remainder went on agricultural schemes and health and social service projects.[26] Meanwhile, by the end of 1935 75 per cent of expenditure by the Scottish Commissioner had been granted for sewerage schemes, reflecting his greater willingness to conform to the government's view of Special Areas policy as one of limited action, aimed primarily at public health programmes.[27] However, Stewart succeeded in launching two major policy strands directly aimed at attracting industry to the Special Areas. These were based on contemporary perceptions that outer-Britain lacked facilities to support new enterprises in two key areas: industrial estates and corporate finance.[28] Developments in these areas during 1936–39 were to provide the blueprints for the much more ambitious post-war regional policy programme.

23 Commissioner for the Special Areas (England and Wales), *First Report*, p. 6.

24 See, for example, G. C. Peden, *The Treasury and Public Policy, 1906–1959* (Oxford, 2000) pp. 273–4.

25 Booth, 'An administrative experiment', p.149.

26 NA: CAB 27/577, 6 November 1934, cited in M. E. Daly, 'Government policy and the depressed areas in the inter-war years', unpublished D. Phil thesis, University of Oxford, 1978, pp. 214–15.

27 S. R. Dennison, *The Location of Industry and the Depressed Areas* (London, 1939), pp. 160–61.

28 These initiatives were facilitated by the 1937 Special Areas (Amendment) Act, which gave the Commissioners powers to erect factories for renting and to offer inducements to industrialists via contributions towards rents, rates and taxes. The Act also empowered the Treasury to provide loans to new undertakings in assisted areas.

Government-financed factory development

The lack of industrial estate facilities and suitable factories was highlighted by contemporaries as a major impediment to attracting new manufacturing enterprises to Britain's peripheral regions. A typical article, published in a 1928 issue of Glasgow's *Evening Citizen*, contrasted the rapid growth of the Slough Estate with the lack of similar developments in Glasgow; the example being quoted of British Safety Glass, which had considered Glasgow but had gone instead to Slough, being offered a new factory within 36 hours of opening negotiations.[29] Stewart's first report discussed the need to clear derelict industrial sites to facilitate industrial development, while his second report proposed the development of government-financed trading estates:

> ...an outstanding difficulty [in attracting new industry] is the lack of vacant sites ... with adequate facilities readily available. The small industrialist seeking a site for a new factory is attracted by the admirable facilities ... on estates like those at Trafford Park and Slough, where among other advantages, he is able to obtain suitable factory premises on lease, and is repelled from the Special Areas by the lack of such facilities and the expense of the preliminary work ... necessary in their absence ... Such development would be encouraged by the creation of well situated trading estates where new businesses can be established on a small scale without a heavy capital outlay on purchase of land and buildings.[30]

In August 1935 he proposed that he be empowered to establish one or more trading estates in the Special Areas; meanwhile a number of other bodies, such as the North East Development Board, were also lobbying for government-funded estate development.[31] Government was originally hostile to Stewart's proposal, but official policy changed when the 1935 election called for a more active employment policy to counter the interventionist programmes of the opposition parties. Trading estate development even featured in the 1935 National Government manifesto. The importance of electoral considerations is revealed by a Ministry of Labour document which recalled that, 'When the government came to draw up their election programme ... they wanted some novel proposal in regard to the Special Areas; official opposition to Sir Malcolm's proposal was withdrawn.'[32]

The acceptance of this departure from orthodoxy was also influenced by the fact that trading estate development did not conflict with established vested interests to anything like the same extent as most Opposition proposals for regional assistance, as there were no private sector estates in any of the assisted regions. As a Board of Trade note stated, given the need for a government initiative, trading estates were, 'as unobjectionable a way as possible'.[33] Non-profit trading estate companies were

---

29 'Attracting Industry', *Evening Citizen* (6 August 1928).

30 Commissioner for the Special Areas (England and Wales), *Second Report* [6 Feb. 1936], (Cmnd 5090 of 1936), p. 13.

31 Ibid.; Herbert Loebl, *Government Factories and the Origins of British Regional Policy, 1934–1948* (Aldershot, 1988), p. 62.

32 Ibid., p. 75.

33 NA, BT64/11, 'Trading Companies', memorandum by the Board of Trade, 9 September 1935, and note, 29 August 1935, cited in C. E . Heim, 'Uneven regional development in interwar Britain', unpublished Ph.D. thesis, Yale University, 1982, p. 540.

established in each of the Special Areas, funded by the Special Areas Commissioners. Their aim was to break-even financially, after an initial development period of about five years.[34] Rents were set at around 6 per cent of factory development costs, to recoup the government finance (with interest), plus administrative costs and depreciation.[35] The government intended that the estates would eventually be privatised, the proceeds repaying their costs.[36]

Development initially focused on one major estate in each of the main Special Areas. This was partly due to the government's desire for a few large, high profile, estates to show the public that action was being taken.[37] The strategy was also influenced by the success of the giant estates at Slough and Trafford Park, which were often cited as evidence that estates acted as magnets for new manufacturing enterprises. The first and largest government-financed estate was developed from August 1936 on a 706.5-acre site at Team Valley, on the outskirts of Gateshead, close to the Great North Road (A1). Figure 13.2 shows the layout of the estate in the late 1940s.

By the end of 1936 development of a 170-acre estate had commenced at Treforest in South Wales – between Cardiff and Pontypridd – and in 1937 a third major estate was launched on a 325-acre site at Hillington, near Glasgow. The final Special Area, West Cumberland, had a much lower population (and population density) than the others and hosted a small (17-acre) estate at Maryport, developed from 1938.

Sites for the large states were chosen so as to maximise their attraction to industry, with good road and rail links and proximity to major local industrial centres. The attractions of the estates were also promoted via the incorporation the best planning features of private sector estates, with regard to estate layouts, factory designs, services, and landscaping. Factories were provided for renting, built to both standard designs and to the special requirements of manufacturers, including 'nest' factories for small firms. Like Slough and Trafford Park, the estates offered extensive on-site utilities. For example factories at Team Valley were equipped with electrical, gas, and water mains, two-storey office accommodation, lavatories, hot water, central heating, and, if desired, private sidings to the estate's internal railway system. Each group of factories was also provided with its own canteens, kiosks, cycle sheds, etc.[38] Treforest even provided a mains supply of high temperature and pressure steam for processing and heating purposes from the estate's power station – following the example of the Slough Estate. Estate plans also included extensive provisions of business services. For example a large administration building was placed at the centre of the Team Valley estate, around which were grouped banks, a post office, accountants, and other services – including a research and sales staff to advise tenants on raw materials,

34 Royal Commission on the Distribution of the Industrial Population, *Report* (London, 1940), p. 286.

35 Ibid.

36 H. J. Bush, 'Local, intellectual, and policy responses to localised unemployment in the inter-war period: the genesis of regional policy', unpublished D. Phil thesis, University of Oxford, 1980, p. 191.

37 Ward, *The Geography of Interwar Britain*, p. 216.

38 'The Industrial North East' *Business*, (Supplement, June 1937), p. 12.

markets, and sales methods.[39] The other government-financed estates also provided 'business-consultancy' services, which were of particular value to small firms that lacked expertise in these areas.[40]

Figure 13.2: The Team Valley trading estate in around 1949

The estates succeeded in attracting a diverse range of light industries. It had been intended that they would create employment primarily for men. Yet employers sought cheaper workers and, given abundant local supplies of women and juveniles, had little interest in more expensive adult males. Most firms at Team Valley employed mainly women and juveniles.[41] Similarly some 48 per cent of employees on the Treforest estate in 1939 were female (over half of whom were juveniles), while a further 12 per cent were males aged under 18.[42] Their impact in reducing adult male unemployment was, consequently, very limited.

39 NA, HLG90/144, Ministry of Town and Country Planning, New Towns Research Section, Social and Economic Research, 'Trading estates first paper', 7 February 1949.

40 Royal Commission on the Geographical Distribution of the Industrial Population, *Report* (London, 1940), p. 285.

41 Loebl, *Government Factories and the Origins of British Regional Policy*, p. 166.

42 W. Davies, 'The nature and significance of trading estates with special reference to the Treforest and Slough Estates', unpublished MA dissertation, University of Wales, 1951,

The concept of concentrating resources on one large estate in each Special Area, to act as a focus for the area's wider long-term industrial regeneration, had important similarities to the growth-pole concept – developed by regional economists after the Second World War.[43] As a 1943 report by the Nuffield College Social Reconstruction Survey [NCSRS] noted, '...once light industries had begun to develop on the estates, and had shown that location in the Special Areas was no disadvantage, the way was opened for other firms to follow and to begin to develop in other parts of the Areas... once you have the nucleus, development is enormously speeded up...'[44] Such clustering was particularly important in the Special Areas, as these had no significant existing base of light industries and the concentration of firms in large estates was thus central to fostering the development of local input-output linkages and knowledge spillovers regarding production and labour management methods.

Yet this policy soon began to be undermined by objections from interests in other parts of the Special Areas, who perceived themselves to be neglected. Such concerns found a political voice in the interim report of the Labour Party's Commission of Enquiry into the Distressed Areas, published in 1937. This attacked the idea of a few, large, trading estates designed to act as growth points:

> if new industries are concentrated in one part of a Special Area, the industrial and social position of other parts may become worse than before… There should be several such estates in different parts of each Area and, apart altogether from such estates, steps should be taken to disperse suitable new industries as widely as possible throughout each Area.[45]

All the trading estate companies felt obliged to respond to local pressure for wider development by building small estates, 'group sites', and individual factories. Such a policy, which removed the advantages of firm clustering on sites with highly developed infrastructure and specialist business service facilities, formed only a small part of the Special Areas factory programme prior to the Second World War. Yet the move away from giant estates to scattered factories, often in locations chosen for short-term employment alleviation objectives rather than long-term area development considerations, foreshadowed the post-war expansion of the trading estate initiative. The 1945–51 Labour governments, which massively expanded the use of government-sponsored factory building as a regional policy instrument, rejected large estates in favour of spreading factories throughout the assisted areas on small sites. This had the effect of both preventing the emergence of locational externalities and imposing

p. 138.

43 A. E. Booth, 'The timing and content of government policies to assist the depressed areas, 1920–1939', unpublished D. Phil thesis, University of Kent, 1975, p. 226; Pitfield, 'Labour migration and the regional problem', p. 281.

44 NA, CAB 87/56, IEP (42)36, Nuffield College Social Reconstruction Survey report on methods of influencing the location of industry, 26 August 1942.

45 Labour Party, *Commission of Enquiry into the Distressed Areas, Labour and the Distressed Areas: A Programme of Immediate Action: Interim Report of the Labour Party's Commission of Enquiry into the Distressed Areas* (London, 1937), pp. 8–9.

increased problems of poor transport links and utilities for many factories, to the long-term detriment of the assisted regions.[46]

The Commissioners' commitments with respect to industrial development projects amounted to about £7,250,000 by the end of April 1939, of which nearly £6,000,000 was for trading estates and individual factories, £600,000 for harbour works, etc., and smaller sums for site clearance and improvements and local publicity. At the end of March around £4,500,000 had been disbursed.[47] Estimates of employment in government-financed factories on the eve of the Second World War vary from 12,000–15,000.[48]Government-financed trading estate and factory development proved a strong inducement to enterprises considering establishing production in the Special Areas. Of the 292 firms in receipt of some form of assistance that located in the Special Areas to September 1938, 144 benefited from factory or site provision alone, while an additional 93 had been offered such assistance in conjunction with the provision of capital (20), contributions towards rents or taxes (25), or both these inducements (48). However, the Commissioner for England and Wales considered that financial assistance acted as a more powerful inducement in the case of larger firms in the heavy industries.[49]

Special Areas finance initiatives

The concentration and centralisation of British banking among the London-based 'big five' clearing banks was widely perceived by contemporaries as having reduced access of small firms, and particularly those remote from London, to bank finance. Meanwhile local sources of non-bank finance for new and expanding enterprises – wealthy individuals and locally-based firms – were substantially weakened in Britain's peripheral industrial areas by the interwar depression.[50] For example, Scotland's per capita GDP had fallen from 96 per cent of the UK average in 1920 to less than 88 per cent during 1932–35.[51] These concerns were highlighted by the 1931 report of the Macmillan Committee on Finance and Industry, which identified a gap in the provision of finance to small and medium-sized enterprises, who found the costs of a public share flotation prohibitive but did not always receive a positive reception from the banks.[52] Individuals and organisations concerned with

46 Peter Scott, 'British regional policy 1945–51: a lost opportunity', *Twentieth Century British History*, 8 (1997), 358–82.

47 Bank of England Archive [BEA], EID4/159, 'The Special Areas', note, 26 July 1939.

48 Alix Meynell, 'Location of industry', *Public Administration*, 7 (1959), 9–20, p. 12; EFTA, *Regional Policy in EFTA: Industrial Estates* (Geneva, 1970), p. 30; Second Report from the Select Committee on Estimates, 1946–47, *The Administration of the Development Areas* (London, 1947), p. 4.

49 Pitfield, 'Labour migration and the regional problem', p. 282.

50 NA, CAB 87/56, IEP (42)36, Nuffield College Social Reconstruction Survey report on methods of influencing the location of industry, 26 August 1942; Dennison, *The Location of Industry*, p. 86.

51 Lee, *Scotland and the United Kingdom*, p. 53.

52 Committee on Finance and Industry, *Report*, (P.P., 1930–31, XIII), para. 404.

industrial development in the depressed regions perceived them to be particularly disadvantaged and pressed for special financial facilities for new and smaller firms. Stewart's first report called for a 'Special Fund' to assist entrepreneurs wishing to establish production in the Special Areas, who were unable to raise the necessary capital via normal commercial means. This led to the establishment of three bodies.

The first – the Special Areas Reconstruction Association (SARA) – was launched by the Bank of England in June 1936, following government pressure. SARA had a specified lifetime of ten years. Funds were provided by the City and the financial institutions, the Bank of England perceiving their assistance as a political gesture (indeed it believed that there would be no demand for the funds).[53] SARA also received funding from the Treasury, for its preliminary and winding-up expenses, up to £100,000 towards reserves, up to £20,000 per annum for administrative expenses, and a guarantee against losses amounting to roughly 25 per cent of the sum loaned.[54] SARA was designed to provide loans only on normal commercial lines. Loans were not to exceed £10,000, or be granted for periods of over five years, without written permission from the Treasury.[55] Assistance was designed to breach initial financial difficulties, for concerns that, '...whilst having reasonable expectation of ultimate success on an economic basis... are not for the time being in a position to obtain financial facilities from banks or financial institutions primarily engaged in providing financial facilities for long or medium periods'.[56]

SARA represented a much more radical departure from official orthodoxy than the trading estate initiative, involving competition with existing banking institutions and implying that they did not meet the needs of all industrialists. Its introduction at arms length, via the Bank of England, and its presentation as a temporary, charitable gesture, served to minimise these implications, though it still engendered considerable official disquiet. It was regarded as an undesirable, but politically unavoidable, minimum response to public pressure for action, as indicated in a 1935 Treasury note which described SARA as 'pretty horrible, tho [sic] it may be unavoidable'.[57] In order to obtain the benefit of local knowledge, three Area Boards were formed for SARA, covering South Wales, Scotland, and the two English Special Areas.[58] These undertook the initial review of proposals. Up to 18th June 1939 SARA had received 2,080 enquiries for information, from which 831 definite applications resulted. 622 had been rejected or withdrawn, while 190 had been approved, at least in principle. These totalled £908,750 and were estimated to produce 14,061 new jobs.[59]

---

53 Heim, 'Uneven regional development', p. 538.

54 R. O. Roberts, 'Special finance facilities for industry in the depressed areas with particular reference to the experience of South Wales', *The Manchester School*, 21 (1953), 39–61, p. 47.

55 BEA, SMT2/20, notes for SARA Chairman's speech, 30 June 1938.

56 *Hansard*, Vol. 318, 1936–37, Col. 1392, 2 December 1936, cited in Heim, 'Uneven regional development', p. 424.

57 Heim, 'Uneven regional development', p. 538.

58 BEA, SMT2/20, 'A review of the work of the Association [SARA] from 18th June 1936 to 30th June 1937', n.d., c. 1937.

59 BEA, SMT2/20, notes for SARA Chairman's speech, 29 June 1939.

In December 1936 a second Special Areas finance organisation, the Nuffield Trust, was launched, with funds of £2 million provided as a gift by Lord Nuffield. The Nuffield Trust was more successful in job creation than SARA; in addition to having twice the funds it was also more relaxed in its lending criteria.[60] Unlike SARA and the Treasury Fund (discussed below), the Nuffield Trust was prepared to provide capital in the form of 5 per cent redeemable preference shares, or, in some cases, even ordinary shares, rather than solely as loans. It also imposed no limits regarding the size or duration of assistance. According to its first report, the Trust's main criteria for granting finance were, 'primarily... the extent to which speedy and direct employment of labour was likely to ensue and the probability of permanence of such employment'.[61] Its funds were consciously regarded as part of the government's Special Areas weaponry, the Ministry of Labour being responsible for the choice of trustees.

In March 1937 the government launched a third organisation, the Treasury Fund. £2 million was made available, to the Special Areas and the more widely defined 'certified' depressed areas. The Treasury Fund was designed to meet the perceived inadequacies of SARA and was aimed at larger firms, employing ten or more people. It could only consider applications for projects which had been refused facilities elsewhere.[62] The Treasury Fund charged 3.5–4 per cent interest, compared to 4 per cent and 4.5 per cent respectively for Nuffield Trust and SARA loans (while contemporary bank overdraft rates were around 4–5 per cent).[63] Treasury Fund loans policy was dominated by maximising employment creation. Both it and the Nuffield Trust rejected some applications on account of the small amount of employment anticipated in relation to the capital required.[64] The Treasury Fund also imposed a general (but not absolute) rule that at least half a firm's capital should be British-owned, which prevented them assisting a number of foreign ventures.

SARA, the Nuffield Trust, and the Special etc. Areas Loans Advisory Committee (SALAC – which advised on Treasury Fund loans) enjoyed a strong measure of cooperation; they shared a number of key staff and jointly financed a substantial proportion of projects, as shown in Table 13.1. This was particularly true for the Treasury Fund and Nuffield Trust, while SARA's lending criteria were less influenced by employment considerations. Meetings of the Nuffield Fund and SALAC were mainly held jointly and many projects were jointly-funded.[65] A number of other, smaller and purely commercial, sources of capital for firms in Britain's peripheral regions were also established during this period, included Credit for Industry Ltd (a special finance company, which established a Scottish advisory committee in collaboration with the Scottish Development Council in 1934), the Scottish

60 Ward, *The Geography of Interwar Britain*, p. 219.

61 Nuffield Trust, *First Report*, 19 July 1937, cited in Daly, 'Government policy and the depressed areas', p. 263.

62 Heim, 'Uneven regional development', p. 457.

63 Select Committee on Estimates, *Second Report. Development Areas* (London, 1955–56), p. 430; Heim, 'Uneven regional development', p. 458.

64 NA, T187/1, notes for SALAC meeting of 27 April 1939; Heim, 'Uneven regional development', p. 447.

65 Heim, 'Uneven regional development', pp. 447–8.

Development Financial Trust Ltd, formed at the end of 1938 to assist small firms in Scotland, and the Create More Work Trust, an associate of Hambros Bank, which assisted a number of firms in South Wales. [66]

The three Special Areas finance organisations (hereafter SAO's), and particularly SARA, attracted a great deal of contemporary criticism regarding their restrictive lending criteria.[67] SARA aimed to apply normal banking practices – a policy which appears self-defeating in view of the fact that its establishment was aimed at correcting perceived deficiencies in the provision of industrial finance by the banking system. In practice it rapidly developed a preference for established firms, which set up branches in the depressed areas.[68] As such, its policies ran counter to its stated aim of breaching the Macmillan gap by helping small industrialists with ideas but not capital. Furthermore, both SARA and the Treasury Fund required at least half a project's capital to be supplied from sources other than the SAO's, so that assistance was effectively limited to 'topping-up' finance.[69]

The NCSRS investigator for South Wales criticised this restriction, arguing that, 'to say to the entrepreneur: "if you can find the first £5,000 we will provide another £5,000" is about as useful as to say "You find the first million pounds and we will find the second". The firm that can get £5,000 can usually equally well get £10,000 from private sources'. He noted that there had been remarkably few failures among SARA's clients and that, in view of the special need to encourage enterprise in the depressed areas, somewhat greater risks might well have been taken.[70] The Nuffield Fund was less stringent than SARA, but did reject at least one application on the grounds that the promoters were investing insufficient capital.[71] It also rejected some proposals for assistance to establish new firms on account of opposition from large competing enterprises outside the Special Areas.[72] However, such cases sometimes led some objecting firms to agree to establish Special Area branches in order to prevent potential new competitors receiving finance, examples including Turner & Newall, Welsh Metal Industries, and Pilkingtons.[73]

66 NA, CAB 87/56, Nuffield College Social Reconstruction Survey, Memorandum 24, Methods of Influencing the Location of Industry, July 1942.

67 Dennison, *The Location of Industry*, p. 90.

68 C. E. Heim, 'Limits to intervention: the Bank of England and industrial diversification in the depressed areas', *Economic History Review*, 2nd Ser., 37, (1984), 533–50, p. 547.

69 NA, T187/1, 'Special etc. Areas Loans Advisory Committee, statement of position at 24 March 1938', n.d., c. 1938.

70 NA, CAB 87/56, Nuffield College Social Reconstruction Survey, Memorandum 24, 'Methods of influencing the location of industry', July 1942.

71 Heim, 'Uneven regional development', p. 447.

72 Daly, 'Government policy and the depressed areas', p. 242.

73 Heim, 'Uneven regional development', p. 559.

Table 13.1: Financial assistance offered to new firms in the Special Areas by the Special Areas finance organisations, to 30th September 1938

	No. of firms assisted	Value of assistance (£)	Estimated number employed
Nuffield Trust alone	17	276,400	2,365
SARA alone	68	333,550	3,804
Treasury Fund alone	3	300,000	925
Nuffield and SARA	21	425,000	3,279
Nuffield and Treasury	10	1,472,000	4,155
SARA and Treasury	1	27,000	250
All three bodies	1	40,000	126
Total	121	2,874,000	14,904

Source: NA, CAB 87/56, IEP (42)36, Nuffield College Social Reconstruction Survey report on methods of influencing the location of industry, 26 August 1942.

Companies receiving financial assistance from the SAO's were characteristically small, single-product firms operating with relative autonomy (even in the case of subsidiaries). Their sectoral composition spanned a wide range of light manufactured goods, including many industries previously poorly-represented in the Special Areas. Analysis by Carol Heim of those firms receiving assistance which subsequently failed indicated that managerial problems, rather than distance from their main markets or other directly location-specific factors, was the main cause (though some firms did emphasise the lack of appropriately-trained local labour).[74]

One interesting aspect of the SAO initiative was the provision of financial and managerial advice. SARA's staff contained trained accountants and other technical experts, who vetted applications to both it and the other SAO's. They also made inspection visits to both SARA's and the Treasury Fund's smaller clients.[75] In March 1937 the Special Areas Commissioners' Industrial Officers proposed that firms receiving finance should be given assistance with managerial problems. Similarly, the third report of the Nuffield Trust, covering January – June 1938, noted that:

> some of the smaller undertakings which have been assisted need guidance upon the various problems which have arisen regarding the methods of operating and more particularly of keeping accurate records… In suitable cases the Trustees therefore propose to offer to provide the Undertakings in question with the assistance of experts to advise upon the avoidance of errors of judgement and practice in the hope thereby of improving the prospects of the businesses becoming permanently and successfully established.[76]

74 Ibid., pp. 565–9.

75 Ibid., p. 458.

76 Nuffield Trust, *Third Report*, 1 January–30 June 1938, paragraph 10, cited in Daly, 'Government policy and the depressed areas', p. 250.

Progress in developing such assistance proved slow, partly due to concerns that it might lead the SAOs to be perceived as being partly responsible for any failures. Nevertheless in the aftermath of some failures the Nuffield Trust employed one of the Industrial Officers, Cecil D. Morrison, to visit companies in receipt of assistance from any of the SAO's and make recommendations concerning management or accountancy practices.[77] Morrison subsequently became a director of a number of companies where the Trust held investments. The provision of expert staff to correct deficiencies in applicants' managerial or administrative structures, an approach which bore stronger similarities to that taken by continental banks than to traditional British banking practice, was developed more fully, with some success, in the government's post-war regionally-assisted areas industrial finance machinery.[78]

According to a Bank of England memorandum, the finance provided by the SAO's to the end of January 1939 amounted to £3,825,000, for some 207 enterprises, of which 109 were new to the Special Areas. About a third were located on the trading estates.[79] The NCSRS estimated that total employment created by the SAO and factory development initiatives by the Spring of 1939 would be about 20,000–25,000 when the firms were in full production. By 1941 this figure had risen to roughly 50,000.[80]

Other regional policy measures

Another policy of considerable importance to the attraction of new enterprises to the Special Areas was the steering of refugee industrialists there. Following the rise of the Hitler government in February 1933 Britain had received a growing stream of Jewish refugee industrialists. Their numbers rose substantially during the late 1930s, Germans being joined by Austrians and Czechs. In February 1936 Stewart stated in his Second Report that he had been attempting to persuade some firms entering Britain as a result of 'unsettled conditions in certain countries', to locate in the Special Areas.[81] The Ministry of Labour, Board of Trade, and Home Office later considered making admission of refugee industrialists conditional on their agreeing to locate in one of the Special Areas, or at least an area of high unemployment. A more moderate policy was eventually adopted. In May 1937 a new aliens' admission procedure was introduced, involving the two Special Areas Commissioners for the first time. While refugee industrialists were not officially compelled to locate in the Special Areas, the Home Office informed them that, 'the question of the locality in which it is proposed to establish the enterprise will be considered, among other

77 Daly, 'Government policy and the depressed areas', pp. 249–51.

78 Francesca Carnevali and Peter Scott, 'The Treasury as venture capitalist: DATAC industrial finance and the Macmillan Gap 1945–60', *Financial History Review*, 6 (1999), 47–65.

79 BEA, EID4/159, 'The Special Areas', 26 July 1939.

80 NA, CAB 87/56, Nuffield College Social Reconstruction Survey, Memorandum 24, 'Methods of influencing the location of industry', July 1942. This excludes employment created via expenditure on improving amenities or information and publicity services.

81 Commissioner for the special areas of England and Wales, *Second report* [6 Feb. 1936], (Cmd. 5090 of 1936), para. 59.

matters', and let it be known that admission would be granted more quickly to industrialists seeking to locate in high unemployment areas.[82]

From the early months of 1937 government began to actively seek out foreign manufacturers who might be willing to establish plants in the Special Areas, using the commercial counsellors at British embassies and consulates in Europe, in cooperation with local and regional development organisations and the government's trading estate companies.[83] By August 1939 refugee firms in Britain numbered about 500, sixty per cent of which were based in the Special Areas.[84] These formed a substantial proportion of tenants on the government-financed trading estates; it has been estimated that half the firms at Treforest by September 1939 were refugee enterprises and these accounted for 27 per cent of manufacturing tenants at Team Valley at the end of 1939.[85] While they were, to a very considerable extent, directed to the Areas by government, they also derived important benefits from the trading estate and corporate finance initiatives.[86] The long-term survival rate of these enterprises appears to have been high; a study by Herbert Loebl indicated that two-thirds of refugee firms established in the Northern region of England prior to 1940 (mainly on government trading estates) were still in existence in the region by 1974.[87]

A further aspect of regional policy that was explored, but not resolved, during the 1930s was the desirability of government action to control factory development in low unemployment areas, particularly Greater London. In his final, October 1936, report, just prior to his resignation, Stewart called for the restriction of industrial development around London, unless firms could show strong reasons for locating there.[88] In July 1937 government responded by establishing a 'Royal Commission on the Geographical Distribution of the Industrial Population', under the chairmanship of Sir Montague Barlow. The Barlow Committee completed its report in August 1939 though the onset of War delayed its presentation to Parliament until January 1940. After assessing a considerable amount of evidence, the Report concluded that uneven regional development represented a national problem – of depression in Britain's peripheral regions and congestion in London and other rapidly growing centres. This was to be solved by controls on new factory development in the South East, exercised by a central authority with regulatory, advisory, and research powers. These recommendations foreshadowed the much more interventionist industrial location policy that emerged following the Second World War.

---

82 Cited in Herbert Loebl, *Government Factories and the Origins of British Regional Policy 1934–1948* (Aldershot, 1988), p. 170.

83 Herbert Loebl, 'Refugees from the Third Reich and industry in the depressed areas of Britain', in W. E. Mosse (ed.), *Second Chance: Two Centuries of German-speaking Jews in the United Kingdom* (Tubingen, 1991), p. 387.

84 C. Holmes, 'Immigrants and refugees in Britain', in Mosse, *Second Chance*, p. 22.

85 Davies, 'The nature and significance of trading estates', p. 58; Loebl, *Government Factories*, p. 172.

86 Heim, 'Limits to intervention', pp. 533–50.

87 Loebl, 'Refugees', p. 396.

88 Commissioner for the Special Areas (England and Wales), *Third Report* [27 Oct. 1936], (Cmnd 5303 of 1936), p. 7.

The cost-effectiveness of Special Areas assistance

Assessing the cost effectiveness of regional assistance measures is subject to a number of methodological problems. Policy expenditure will produce a deadweight effect – some assistance merely funding investment and job creation that would have occurred (at least partially) even in its absence. Measures may also produce some displacement effect, creating jobs in assisted firms by displacing jobs that would have been provided to other local businesses. Multiplier effects, arising from sales by local enterprises to new/expanded firms in receipt of assistance, and their workers, must also be taken into account. Even after allowing for these effects, job creation will not be matched by an equivalent reduction in unemployment, as it will reduce migration out of the region and increase labour force participation.

Assessment of the cost-effectiveness of regional policy during the 1930s is further complicated by the short interval between the commencement of the main initiatives and their effective termination following the onset of war in 1939. The trading estates did not have factories available for renting until 1937 and even the first of the SAO's only commenced operations in June 1936, while the Treasury Fund was not launched until March 1937. Assisted firms were thus still in their initial growth phase when war intervened. This is a particular problem with trading estate development, as land and infrastructure costs produce relatively high costs per job created until a substantial proportion of the estate is occupied (private sector estates of similar size to the main government estates generally took well over ten years to become fully occupied). Furthermore, as noted earlier, the estates had a long-term 'growth point' role, that could only be expected to yield substantial results after several years of development. However, even when applying the restrictive yardstick of the cost per job created during their brief window of active policy, the trading estate and SAO initiatives proved very cost-effective.

Table 13.2 provides estimates of the costs per job created under the Special Areas factory development and industrial finance initiatives (net of receipts and interest on the funds committed).[89] The factory development programme is estimated to have cost around £81 per job created prior to the Second World War (using the lowest employment estimate). The cost per job of SAO finance is more difficult to determine, as there are no suitable figures covering all three organisations. However data for SARA indicate a cost per job of around £17, while the Nuffield Trust (which approved some higher-risk investments on political -mainly employment creation – grounds) produced one job for every £85 of expenditure. Insufficient financial information is available regarding the Treasury Fund, though as the composition of its clients and its loans policy were broadly similar to that of the Nuffield Trust, its cost per job can also be expected to be roughly similar. Assuming that Nuffield Trust and Treasury Fund costs per job were of similar magnitude, and weighting all three funds by the value of the finance provided over their lifetime, gives an aggregate cost per job figure for the SAO's of around £73.

89 For details regarding the assumptions on which these estimates are based, see Peter Scott, 'The audit of British regional policy: 1934–39', *Regional Studies*, 34, No.1 (2000), 55–65.

Table 13.2: A summary of the cost-effectiveness of the main Special Areas policy instruments

Initiative	Gross Expenditure (£)	Employment*	Estimated net cost per job created (£)**
Factory development ***	4,500,000	12,000-15,000	81
SARA ****	754,000	12,500	17
Nuffield Trust*****	1,914,301	12,803-14,752	85
Treasury Fund******	1,160,500	N.A.	N.A.

Source: Peter Scott, 'The audit of British regional policy: 1934–9', Regional Studies, *34, No.1 (2000), 55–65.*

Notes:
* There is some overlap between employment created under these different initiatives.
** Net of receipts, but not taking into account savings in welfare payments, or tax generation, arising from the expenditure.
*** Expenditure – to end of March 1939; employment – at around September 1939.
**** To June 1943.
***** To end of June 1939; expenditure figure also includes commitments.
****** Refers to the total amount loaned over its lifetime.
N.A. = not available.

The total estimated costs per job for the factory development and corporate finance initiatives were well below the per annum cost of employment creation via government public works schemes, estimated by the Unemployment Grants Committee at around £400 per job.[90] In calculating the net social cost to the exchequer, savings in unemployment benefit and other welfare payments must be taken into account, together with the corporate and individual taxation accruing from the new factories. There is no universally accepted means of calculating average benefits to the unemployed during this period. Estimates by Metcalf, Nickell, and Floros, and by Ormerod and Worswick, provide figures of £64.98 and £45.67 per annum respectively.[91] Even taking the lower figure gives an annual return on government factory development expenditure and on SAO finance of around 56 and 63 per cent

90 William R. Garside, *British Unemployment 1919–1939. A Study in Public Policy* (Cambridge, 1990), pp. 313–14. If indirect employment was added, contemporaries expected the cost per job to fall to about £250.

91 D. Metcalf, S. J. Nickell and N. Floros, 'Still searching for an explanation of unemployment in interwar Britain', *Journal of Political Economy*, 90 (1982), 386–99, Table 1, Col. 5; P. A. Ormerod and G. D. N. Worswick, 'Unemployment in interwar Britain', *Journal*

respectively. The employment created by these initiatives would have included some workers not entitled to benefit, though the effect of their inclusion would be more than counter-balanced by the additional government saving in the administrative costs of benefit provision, together with receipts of individual and employers' national insurance and taxation payments.

Even when the significant margins of error inherent in the above estimates are taken into account, the policy initiatives clearly offered attractive rates of return. Furthermore, these initiatives also offered longer-term benefits to the assisted areas. While no comprehensive data are available, the 348 firms receiving assistance from either the SAO's and/or the Commissioners by the eve of the Second World War appear to have experienced significant employment growth during the following years. For example, R.O. Roberts' study of a sample of 22 firms in South Wales that received SAO assistance indicates that their total employment rose from 2,485 at the middle of 1939 to 3,929 by 1945 and 4,926 by 1949.[92] Furthermore, assisted firms made an important contribution to war production, in parts of Britain where munitions workers were in relatively plentiful supply.[93]

Government rearmament expenditure in Britain's peripheral regions

Special Areas trading estate and corporate finance initiatives were important chiefly as successful experiments in regional intervention, rather than in the employment they created. Confined to an experimental scale, their aggregate economic impact was minimal. Yet during the late 1930s the Special Areas, and other parts of 'outer-Britain' did receive a considerable government-induced economic boost, from rearmament. According to evidence assembled by the NCSRS, rearmament constituted the chief single factor in the revival of employment in the depressed areas from 1935. For example, some 56 per cent of employment provided in new plants in South Wales from 1936–41 concerned wartime industries, while existing plants also benefited from preferences given to high unemployment areas in the allocation of government contracts.[94]

After the First World War defence expenditure had been rapidly reduced to a very low, stable, level, following the logic of the 'ten year rule' that no war was expected for (what proved to be a rolling period of) ten years. Given the absence of any credible aggressor, higher defence spending was viewed as unjustified, while keeping expenditure low supported the policy of a minimal state that was thought essential to the restoration, and then maintenance, of the gold-standard. From the early 1930s, however, the Japanese invasion of Manchuria raised the spectre of military aggression against Britain's Far East interests, while a possible future threat

---

of Political Economy, 90 (1982), 400–409, Tables 1 and 5. These refer to the periods 1935–38 and 1936–37 respectively.

92 Roberts, 'Special finance facilities for industry', p. 55.

93 BEA, SMT2/20, note by SARA's managing director, Maurice Gibb, regarding its operations to June 1943.

94 NA, CAB 87/56, Nuffield College Social Reconstruction Survey, Memorandum 24, 'Methods of influencing the location of industry', July 1942.

from Germany and Italy was also recognised.[95] Thus the 10 year rule was cancelled in March 1932, though the Geneva disarmament conference and the government's continued low-expenditure fiscal stance delayed any real change in policy until after 1934.

The collapse of the disarmament conference, together with the growing threat from Germany and Japan, strengthened the case for rearmament. Yet government still pinned its hopes on a policy of appeasement, partly due to the expenditure implications of large-scale rearmament. As Mark Thomas noted, the 'Treasury spirit was only gradually exorcised from the administration of the rearmament programme'.[96] Treasury opposition reflected fears regarding the threat to investors' confidence in sterling, and to City interests, of increased spending, implicitly putting the City's financial interests ahead of defence considerations. This contributed to a delay in rearmament which very nearly led an ill-prepared Britain into military defeat or political capitulation to Germany during 1940. Even as late as 1938 Britain had increased defence expenditure to less than 7 per cent of national income, compared to Germany's allocation of more than 23 per cent of 1938 GNP to its military sector.[97]

Locations for new armament factories were crucially influenced by the threat of enemy bombing. In November 1934 the Air Council had produced an air safety classification of Britain into safe, unsafe, and dangerous zones, which remained operative until 1940. This placed much of southern and eastern England into the dangerous zone, and much of the West Midlands into the unsafe zone. With the exception of Durham and Northumberland, all Britain's severely-depressed areas fell within the safe zone.[98] Conversely, as Figure 13.3 shows, with the exception of Clydeside almost all Britain's existing strategic manufacturing capacity was in either the unsafe or dangerous zones. As a result efforts were made to relocate the most exposed aircraft factories and London's three historic Royal Ordnance Factories, and to duplicate the explosives capacity of ICI's vulnerable Billingham-on-Tees plant.[99]

Local unemployment also had some influence on the location of new defence capacity. Meanwhile certain types of production were subject to local infrastructure and skill endowment considerations – for example warship construction could be most conveniently located in existing shipyards, while aircraft factories required skilled metal-working and engineering labour. The result of these various pressures was a northward and westward shift of strategic manufacturing capacity, mainly to the West Midlands, the North West, Scotland, and Wales, and a virtual absence of new developments in the South East. Many locations were compromises between air-safety and other considerations, For example, some 'shadow' aircraft factories were located around Birmingham and Coventry, which had both the necessary engineering skills and volume car-producers – who could assist with the shift to mass-production techniques that were alien to aircraft manufacturers.

95 Ward, *The Geography of Interwar Britain*, p. 76.

96 Mark Thomas, 'Rearmament and economic recovery in the late 1930s', *Economic History Review*, XXXVI (1983), 552–79, p. 554.

97 Ibid.

98 William Hornby, *Factories and Plant* (London, 1958), p. 286.

99 Ward, *The Geography of Interwar Britain*, p. 93.

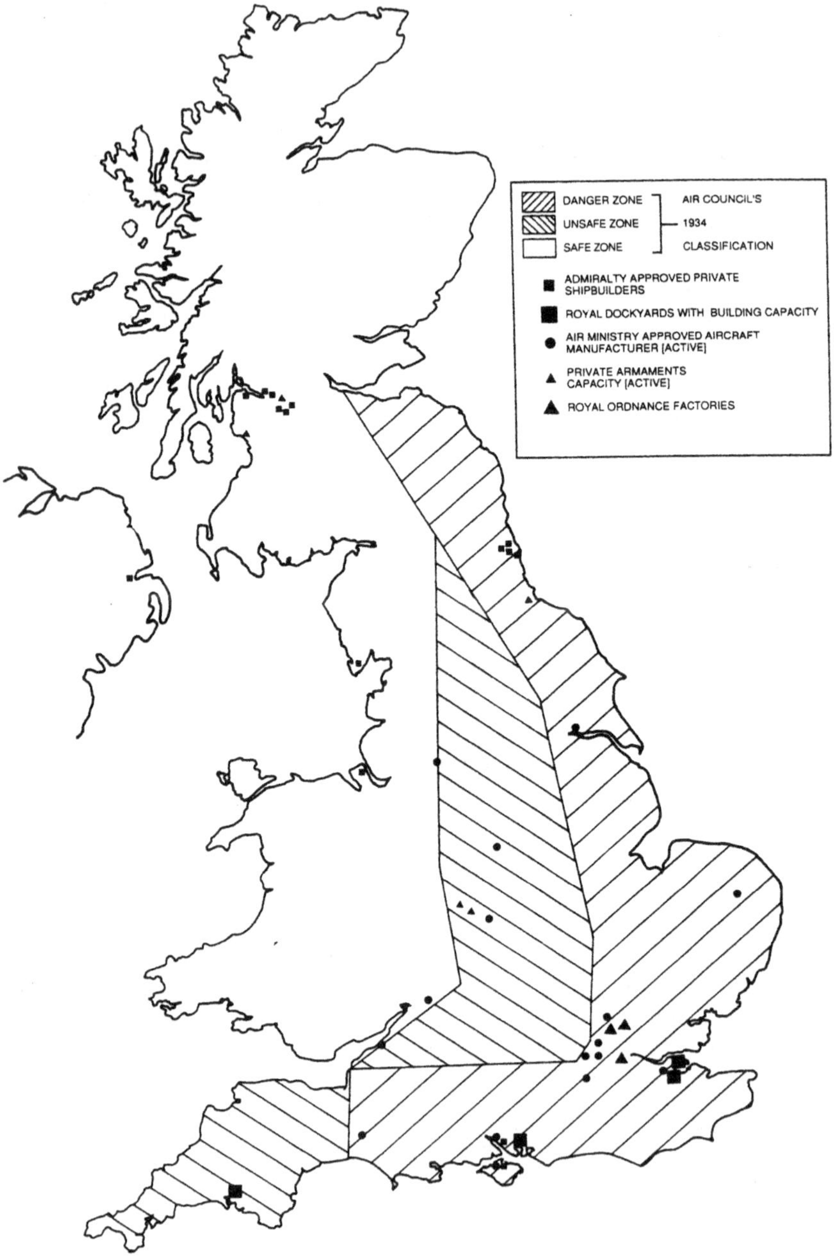

Figure 13.3: The Air Council's safety zonal classification of Britain and strategic manufacturing capacity in 1935

Source: Stephen V. Ward, The Geography of Interwar Britain: The State and Uneven Development *(London, 1988), p. 78.*

From 1937, as the threat of War increased, there was a further shift northwards and westwards. Meanwhile depressed areas' considerations played an increasingly important role in the choice of locations. For example, in January 1937 it was announced in Parliament that the Rootes airframe shadow factory would be located at White Waltham near Reading. Questions regarding vulnerability to enemy air attack were rebutted by the Secretary of State for Air, who stated that an isolated location behind the defences of London was acceptable. Furthermore, he argued, proximity of management was a key factor and shadow factories were essentially satellites that should be located close to their managing firms. Yet depressed areas' considerations proved harder to rebut, and within a few days the Prime Minister announced that a site was being sought in Lancashire (despite the 'parent' firm being based in Coventry). Similarly, later in 1937 two more shadow factories were located in Lancashire, despite their parent companies being based in London and Wolverhampton.[100]

From the summer of 1938 the importance of proximity to the shadow plant's parent was also being undermined by the need to secure sufficient labour and subcontracting capacity. For example, a major Rolls Royce shadow aero-engine factory was located near Glasgow, far from the firm's other activities, following failures to identify sufficient labour and subcontracting capacity near its Crewe and Derby plants. Yet even on the eve of War the militant reputation of the depressed areas raised problems; Rolls Royce had some qualms regarding whether even a military project involving a firm whose name was so synonymous with luxury might provoke labour hostility in 'Red Clydeside'. [101]

Stephen Ward has argued that the development of rearmament factories played a significant role in the evolution of multi-plant, multi-location, firms in Britain, with more spatially divided production than was evident in previous British moves towards large-scale multi-plant enterprise. This included the emergence of the characteristic post-war functional distinction between the main site, where higher managerial, R&D, and similar activities were concentrated, and the branch factory undertaking large-scale production of standardised goods. Similarly, state-organised production involved a split between R&D and strategic management in the South and mass production in the outer regions.[102] Shadow factory projects such as Rolls-Royce at Glasgow, Ford at Trafford Park, and Bristol Aeroplane Co. at Accrington demonstrated how plants could be efficiently managed by distant head offices.[103]

According to estimates by Thomas, additional defence expenditure between 1935 and 1938 produced over a million jobs, or around 81 per cent of the total increase in civilian employment over this period, while producing no significant crowding-out of private sector investment or supply bottlenecks for skilled labour.[104] It also played an important macroeconomic role in shielding Britain from the full impact of the 1937–38 recession. Engineering trades were the main beneficiaries, while the

100 Hornby, *Factories and Plant*, pp. 289–90.

101 Ibid., p. 290.

102 Ward, *The Geography of Interwar Britain*, p. 97.

103 Hornby, *Factories and Plant*, p. 291.

104 Thomas, 'Rearmament and economic recovery'.

aircraft, construction, and shipbuilding sectors each received between 20 and 25 per cent of total job creation. The coal industry also received considerable benefit, on account of induced demand from other sectors (particularly iron and steel).

Thomas has estimated the regional impact of the programme, using inter-regional input-output analysis. His results, shown in Table 13.3, indicate that the largest beneficiaries were Wales and the South West, the North East, and eastern England. Central Scotland also benefited significantly, while London and the South East received employment growth below (but not greatly below) that which would be expected on the basis of their share of non-agricultural insured employment. Meanwhile the north & north west and the rest of Scotland & Northern Ireland were strongly under-represented.

Table 13.3: The regional distribution of rearmament employment relative to Britain's non-agricultural insured population (%)

Region*	(1) Insured population (16–64), July 1938**	(2) Employment created by rearmament, 1935-38	Ratio of (2) to (1)
London & South East	35.74	33.09	92.6
North & North West	22.37	13.14	58.7
North East	4.13	6.55	158.6
Midlands	16.41	21.06	128.3
East	3.22	4.98	154.7
Wales & South West	6.80	11.47	168.7
Central Scotland	7.50	8.26	110.1
Rest of Scotland & Northern Ireland	3.82	1.37	35.9

Source: Mark Thomas, 'Rearmament and economic recovery in the late 1930s', Economic History Review, *XXXVI (1983), 552–79, p. 569.*

Notes:

* Based on 1935 Census of Production regions.

** General scheme only; excludes agricultural scheme.

Conclusions: the impact of regional policy

Regional policy during the 1930s is best characterised as a series of experimental activities that, while successful relative to the resources committed, made a negligible impact on Britain's regional problem. Government trading estates and Special Areas finance facilities nevertheless had an important demonstration effect in showing that light manufacturing industries could be successfully conducted in Britain's peripheral regions. Rearmament expenditure had a much greater impact, both augmenting and modernising the factory infrastructure of these areas and training workers in general 'production line' skills of the type the expanding manufacturing sectors sought. Perhaps more importantly (in the long-term) they gave major firms experience of dividing production geographically in order to take advantage of cheap factor inputs in less prosperous regions for those activities that did not require proximity to markets or strong locational externalities. Thus the period from 1935–39 was one of industrial development and modernisation for Britain's peripheral areas (compared to the previous 15 years). Yet some fundamental weaknesses in their infrastructure remained virtually untouched. By far the most important were their poorly-developed road transport networks.

As noted in Chapter Four, following the First World War road haulage rapidly became a major competitor to the railways and good road links constituted a key determinant of industrial location, particularly for relatively 'light' industries, producing goods with a high value relative to their bulk. Yet the development of Britain's long-distance road network lagged considerably behind that of most other major industrial nations, reflecting a wider reluctance by British governments to play a major role in infrastructure development, as this might threaten Britain's long-term macroeconomic stance of minimal balanced budgets.[105] Thus while motorway networks were pioneered by Italy, Germany, and the U.S. during the 1920s, and introduced in Belgium, the Netherlands, and Canada during the 1930s, it was not until the late 1950s that Britain reluctantly embarked on a motorway programme.[106] Perversely, despite the very poor state of Britain's road network, Treasury officials resisted the arguments of those who advocated public works on employment creation or macroeconomic grounds by stating that it was difficult to find worthwhile projects.[107] In addition to Treasury opposition on expenditure grounds, legislation for motorway development and other road-related infrastructure projects was repeatedly blocked by vigorous opposition from railway interests, who lobbied aggressively both at parliamentary and local authority levels.[108] This included blocking projects that would have improved the accessibility of Britain's peripheral areas, such as the Severn Bridge.[109]

The Special Areas Commissioners were unable to sponsor road development, even where this was integral to industrial site improvement schemes, as they were prohibited from providing financial assistance to activities eligible for other government grants.[110] Meanwhile, as the proportion of goods carried by road increased markedly over the interwar years, and national road conditions deteriorated (in relation to traffic volumes), under-investment in the roads network increasingly exacerbated the depressed areas' geographical disadvantage and peripherality.[111]

Poor transport links, remoteness from the Greater London marketing and business service hub, and industrial legacies that deterred new enterprises (on account of perceptions of labour militancy and inflexible craft traditions) all militated against

105 P. Anderson, 'The figures of descent', *New Left Review*, 161 (1987), 20–77.

106 James Drake, *Motorways* (London, 1969), pp. 27–61.

107 See, for example, Peden, *The Treasury*, p. 271.

108 Ibid., p. 35.

109 Bush, 'Local, intellectual, and policy responses', p. 162.

110 Ibid., p. 173.

111 D. J. Dyos and D. H. Aldcroft, *British Transport: An Economic Survey from the Seventeenth Century to the Twentieth* (Leicester, 1969), pp. 369–70.

the attraction of new manufacturers to Britain's peripheral areas. Meanwhile obsolete plant, path dependence, an over-valued currency (for much of the period) and formidable barriers to export markets, made any major peacetime revival of their traditional staple industries unlikely. The only light at the end of the tunnel for 'outer-Britain' appeared to be the light of the approaching train – the growing threat of another major war with Germany and the associated rearmament work.

Chapter Fourteen

Conclusions

In 1914 London had been only one of a number of areas of relatively high working-class incomes, stretching as far north as the Clyde and as far west as South Wales. Events during the next decade were to end the prosperity of the coal/iron & steel/shipbuilding regions and the textile regions and plunge them into a long, painful, period of depression. A return to peace-time prosperity was not to occur until after the Second World War, in the context of a branch plant economy undertaking activities considered too peripheral for the core plants of the firms in question.

In some respects this represented a return to the economic geography of medieval and early-modern England, when London had dominated the nation's urban hierarchy and the contours of prosperity had radiated out from the capital. The industrial revolution had marked a break with this trend, creating a more regionally-dispersed pattern of high-income areas. This involved the complementary development of an export-orientated base of non-factory resource-intensive heavy industries in the 'industrial periphery' of Scotland, Wales, and England's most northern counties; an export-orientated factory manufacturing base in the 'industrial heartland' of the Midlands, south Lancashire, and West and South Yorkshire; together with a continuation of London's established role as the 'metropolitan hub' of services and variegated consumer goods industries.

However, from the late nineteenth century the complementary relationship between the metropolitan hub and the industrial provinces began to be undermined, as the 'Dutch disease' effect of London's growing invisibles surplus progressively crowded out the commodity exports of Britain's provincial regions. High overseas investment had the short-term effect of sending the invisibles surplus back overseas, but eventually accentuated the Dutch disease problem, as receipts from overseas assets came to outweigh new foreign investment. Thus London-based, non-wage, incomes formed a progressively larger proportion of Britain's GNP, as its growing comparative advantage as a rentier and services-exporting, rather than industrial, nation began to crowd out its provincial export industries.

The First World War marked a second major break in Britain's long-term spatial pattern of economic development. Britain's international creditor status was weakened by considerable sales of overseas securities to finance its war-time trade deficit and by government war debts. Meanwhile disruptions and dislocations of pre-war international trading and payments relationships led to the suspension of the gold standard and transformed the world from a system of relatively open markets to one of high tariff walls. New York and Paris began to compete with London as international financial centres and the nexus of trading, currency, services, and investment pre-eminence that had underpinned the City's pivotal role in the international financial system was fatally undermined. These developments halted the relative growth of

Britain's services and investment exports; the invisibles surplus, which had been equivalent to 10.73 per cent of GNP during 1900–1913, averaged only 6.27 per cent over 1921-38.[1]

Yet the adverse impact of the War on Britain's invisible exports was dwarfed by that on its staple export industries. War demand had led to considerable increases in their capacity, whilst producing relatively little structural or technological modernisation. Meanwhile euphoric expectations regarding their post-war market position fuelled a post-war speculative mania that transformed war-time profits into massive debts, which were to burden them throughout the interwar period. Their true international market position, faced with rising tariff walls and strong new competitors in markets they had been forced to neglect during the War years, soon became evident. Furthermore, overseas producers employed modern capital-intensive technology – that enabled them to achieve rapid productivity growth – while British firms found themselves 'locked-in' to traditional, labour-intensive, production methods via path dependence effects (which had already become evident in some industries before 1914).

Devaluation offered at least a short-term means of maintaining their price competitiveness; yet this clashed with the interests of the City, which pressed for a restoration of the gold-standard at its pre-war parity – requiring a major effective revaluation of sterling – to help restore the City's pre-war hegemony as the world's leading financial centre. Given the rise of New York and Paris as alternative centres, the unstable world economy, the erosion of sterling's international role and Britain's creditor status during the War years, and the weak state of the staple export industries, the desirability, or even practicability, of such a policy was extremely doubtful. Yet the political strength of City interests in matters of economics and overseas trade and finance proved sufficient to secure government support. Returning to gold involved a policy of deflation, first in an attempt to bring British and international prices into line at sterling's pre-war parity and then to defend the restored parity. This depressed British growth, while leaving sterling sufficiently over-valued to make the price-sensitive export staples uncompetitive in world markets. Eventually, in the autumn of 1931, international confidence in sterling collapsed and the gold standard was finally abandoned, though by this time considerable damage had been done both to the British economy and, especially, its staple industries and the regions that relied on them.

Interwar Britain compensated for the decline in visible and invisible exports through the growth of import-substituting industries serving the expanding domestic market. Whereas imports of goods and services had been equivalent to 30.87 per cent of GDP in 1913, the ratio had fallen to only 17.96 per cent by 1938.[2] The main area of growth involved the production of standardised, branded, consumer goods. Yet it was in precisely these industries that the government had unwittingly made a huge investment in the resource endowments of the Greater London area during the First World War, via initiatives to expand munitions capacity, develop new sources of

1 C. H. Feinstein, *National Income, Expenditure and Output of the United Kingdom, 1855–1965* (Cambridge, 1982), pp. T8 and T82.

2 Ibid, pp. T10–T11.

un/semi-skilled munitions labour, and mechanise the overland transport of military supplies. Total war had entailed a massive expansion of armaments production, much of which was located around the fringes of London. This involved both the development of a large volume of modern factory premises and the diffusion of new assembly production methods, involving standardised machinery and un/semi-skilled, 'cheap' workers drawn from outside the core manufacturing workforce. Goods transport also experienced a decisive change, owing to the rapidly-accelerated development of motorised road haulage for the war-effort, using vehicles which were later sold to civilian hauliers.

During the following years the areas of former munitions production around London experienced rapid industrial development, involving a broad range of consumer and/or branded goods sectors that were moving towards standardised assembly production and, initially, using many of the same factories, production methods, and workers, that had been employed in the war effort. The attraction of these areas for branded goods production was further increased by the rise of motorised road haulage. Road haulage offered both cost and, especially, service advantages over the railways for items of high value in relation to bulk, especially if this involved delivery in small consignments to numerous separate destinations. Yet both the limited technical development of vehicles and the poor state of many roads made it most effective over short-medium distances, thus favouring locations close to market hubs. New arterial roads (developed, in part, to combat high post-war unemployment in outer-London munitions centres) gave these areas good access to both inner-London and to Britain's long-distance road network and many new firms occupying former munitions factories relied extensively on the new motorised road hauliers, especially for distributing their outputs.

Re-deployed war-time infrastructure and labour sparked a process of cumulative development. The old munitions sites formed the nuclei for new industrial estates, while these areas' growing reputations as centres of factory work for people lacking craft skills drew in further supplies of such workers – first mainly via commuting and short-distance migration, but later increasingly involving long-distance migrants from Britain's depressed areas. Government assisted this process through its industrial transference programme, including the establishment of Government Training Centres for transferred workers in several of the former munitions centres. Such was the magnitude of the labour inflow that major new industrial centres around London managed to combine massive population expansion with wages that remained below the national average for their sectors (at least for adult male workers).

London thus gained new outer industrial areas of rapid growth industries, of a similar aggregate acreage to that of its traditional industrial districts, while the South East's only other significant centres for such industries were based on the fringes of the conurbation, in satellite towns such as Letchworth, Luton, Slough, Watford, and Welwyn. The emergence of new outer-London and London satellite industrial areas represented a major break with the capital's industrial inheritance. While London had been an important centre for consumer goods industries, these had traditionally been craft-based sectors and moves to standardised production had hitherto been associated with firm migration to the provinces. Yet after 1918 this pattern was replaced by a centrifugal movement from London's centre to its periphery, in new areas that combined good access to its central marketing facilities, modern premises, cheap labour, and well-developed road transport links. These areas were also free from the traditions of strong unionisation that characterised many provincial industrial centres, thus facilitating the diffusion of new, de-skilling, production methods and systems of worker recruitment, pacing, monitoring, and payment.

London also consolidated its position at Britain's central marketing hub. Control over national retailing, banking, media, and a range of other services activities became markedly more concentrated in nationwide firms, headquartered in London, while the proportion of industrial output represented by very large firms, headquartered in or around the capital, also experienced substantial growth. This further increased London's attractions for firms seeking proximity to markets, as a growing proportion of both corporate purchasers and retail distributors conducted their transactions in London, involving goods destined for locations throughout Britain. The further centralisation of service industries, and particularly media, in London also strengthened the capital's hegemonic influence over the nation's social, cultural, and political life, during an era when radio and cinema newsreels brought the chimes of Big Ben to all corners of the nation for the first time.

Industrial development in the West Midlands had some features in common with both Greater London and the provincial regions. Centres which had already established a reputation in motor vehicle and related sectors by 1914, such as Birmingham and Coventry, witnessed continued prosperity, the War boosting the development of a range of interrelated engineering and metal-working assembly industries. Conversely areas dominated by traditional industries in 1914, such as the Black Country and the Potteries, experienced higher unemployment and slower growth. Yet even in the motor vehicle centres the range of expanding assembly industries was narrower, and the growth of new plants much slower (at least during the 1930s) than was the case in Greater London. Meanwhile the region as a whole received a lower share of new plants during the 1930s than would be expected given its share of national manufacturing employment at the start of the decade, while even during 1911–31 the growth of its manufacturing workforce failed to match that of Greater London.

Britain's other provincial regions did not share in the consumer goods boom. Centres such as Manchester's Trafford Park, or Nottingham, which had attracted major consumer goods manufacturers prior to the First World War, failed to maintain their earlier momentum. The few successful consumer goods centres in northern Britain, such as the clothing districts of Leeds, central Manchester, and Salford, were traditional, sectorally-specialised, industrial districts, in long-established sectors that tied in to expanding domestic consumer demand. The main economic contribution of most provincial regions to the expanding assembly industries was in providing a massive reserve army of cheap labour, that enabled the new industrial 'boom towns' of the South East to undergo massive expansion without having to offer higher wages (as migrants were attracted there by a greater chance of finding employment, rather than a higher wage once in employment). Those new firms that settled in the provinces were few in number and generally reflected long-established local specialisations, mainly in declining sectors. In the new light industries, it was generally only marginal firms seeking very cheap premises and labour who were tempted to consider the vacant textile factories of Lancashire and Yorkshire.

The most positive sign of the potential for a revival in Britain's peripheral regions occurred at the very end of the period under discussion, when a renewed military threat from Germany – this time including massive aerial bombardment for southern and eastern England – led to the development of branch plants by major defence-related firms, in less vulnerable regions with plentiful labour supplies. Meanwhile the 'Special Areas' initiative had established a precedent for government financial assistance for firms who were prepared to bring employment to depressed areas. These developments foreshadowed the post-1945 revival of Britain's industrial periphery, based around branch plants of firms that were typically headquartered around London (or overseas multinationals), that moved their labour-intensive production there due to a combination of low factor costs and government inducements and/or coercion.[3]

Thus the interwar years saw the start of a longer-term trend towards 'outer-Britain' acting as a reserve army of labour for the prosperous south – though after 1945, rather than workers migrating to low value-added assembly jobs, these jobs were more often brought to them – via branch plant development. Meanwhile those seeking managerial, R&D, technical, and other 'white-collar' or skilled employment faced a restricted range of opportunities in northern and Western Britain compared to the South and, especially, Greater London. For example, two studies conducted during the late 1980s revealed that those regions that corresponded to the depressed areas of the 1930s had become characterised by low ratios of white collar business services jobs to manufacturing employment, together with high proportions of manufacturing employment in large firms headquartered more than 100 miles away.[4] Conversely those areas of massive interwar industrial expansion around London, such as West and North Middlesex, Hertfordshire, and Slough, remain major centres of headquarters, R&D, pilot production, and other high value-added activities, contributing to the dominant position of the South East in Britain's manufacturing spatial hierarchy.[5]

A major theme running through this book has been the key role of the British state in pursuing policies conducive to the development of a London-dominated, financial and commercial services-orientated, economy. During the nineteenth century the City came to play a hegemonic role in British economic policy, underpinned by classical political economy and reflected in a policy framework designed to protect its status as the world's premier financial centre – through maintaining confidence in Sterling and avoiding impediments to the free international movement of goods, labour, and capital. These policies reflected Britain's comparative advantage in

3 The main instrument of coercion involved Industrial Development Certificates, which restricted factory development in areas of low unemployment.

4 J. N. Marshall, *Services and Uneven Development* (Oxford, 1988); R. I. D. Harris, 'Market structure and external control in the regional economies of Great Britain', *Scottish Journal of Political Economy*, 35 (1988), 334–60.

5 See Doreen Massey, *Spatial Divisions of Labour. Social Structures and the Geography of Production* (London, 1984); Harvey Armstrong and Jim Taylor, *Regional Economics and Policy*, 3rd edn. (Oxford, 2000), Chapter 8.

financial and commercial services, but – especially during the late Victorian and Edwardian periods – they served to progressively concentrate GNP among London-based non-wage income recipients. Meanwhile mechanisms for redistributing the gains from services exports and investment revenues more widely, and encouraging more broadly-based economic development (such as increased government expenditure on education and training, or on social insurance – which would have boosted demand for consumer goods, by stabilising incomes) were impeded by the City's insistence that minimal balanced budgets were essential to the maintenance of confidence in Sterling.

By the Edwardian period Britain's laissez-faire, free-trade, orthodoxy, and the combination of private wealth and public squalor that it produced, was being challenged on a number of fronts. Yet the City's hegemony in financial and commercial policy proved sufficient to hold the main lines of policy intact. Indeed City interests proved so pivotal to the determination of economic policy that even during the 1920s – when the costs and risks of prioritising Sterling's international status over other policy considerations had become much greater – it still held sway over government policy, under both Conservative and Labour administrations. So central was the belief that 'what is good for the City is good for Britain', to the perceptions of contemporary politicians, officials, and commentators (with the exception of 'mavericks' such as Keynes), that challenging it was considered an act of economic and political heresy.

Even after the events of 1931 forced government to accept that Britain's external economic policy had become untenable, economic management continued to be shaped by the aims of minimising public expenditure and avoiding policies that might set precedents for further intervention, during a period when the other stable democracies were experimenting with much more radical initiatives. Thus opportunities to improve the infrastructure of Britain's provincial regions, for example by developing a system of motorways along the lines pursued by some major industrial countries from the 1920s, were rejected by a Treasury who saw even such seemingly innocuous areas of expenditure as dangerous departures from financial orthodoxy. Even the pace of rearmament expenditure was constrained by Treasury opposition, officials apparently putting fiscal prudence ahead of even national defence (as in the run-up to the First World War).

The 'triumph' (or, rather, hegemony) of the South in British economic development during the early twentieth century was thus a product not just of the problems of Britain's peripheral regions but of the economic and political strength of London. The capital's economic interests (and, particularly, those of its international financial and business services activities) were seen as synonymous with the national interest, enabling government to pursue economic policies that inflicted severe and persistent damage on its provincial regions while provoking remarkably little mainstream political protest. The divergent development paths of provincial and metropolitan interwar Britain serve as a salutary reminder, during a period when the nations of Europe are moving towards closer economic and monetary union, of the dangers that 'peripheral' economies can face if they become tied to government policies designed to meet the needs of 'core' regions.

Appendix A

Interwar data on new manufacturing plants

National data on the opening, extension, and closure of new factory plants (and other plants using powered machinery) was compiled and published by the Board of Trade in a series of annual *Surveys of Industrial Development* [hereafter SID's], covering the years 1932–38.[1] These drew on data from the factory inspectorate, the Ministry of Labour (which had access to data collected through both their local officers and the employment exchange system)[2] and the Travel and Industrial Development Association – which collated information from regional and local industrial development organisations and local authorities. These should have provided comprehensive coverage – for example, H.M. Inspectors of Factories visited most plants of significant size at least annually, while the Ministry of Labour had access to data collected through both their local officers and the employment exchange system.[3] Yet complete accuracy was not achieved, as shown by corrections to the aggregate data for each year, published the following year, which were sometimes substantial.

The data were limited to plants of substantial size, where the opening, extension, or closure involved at least 25 employees.[4] Plant closure data were not used in this study, as no precise geographical information was provided. The SID's included information on each plant's production, location, initial employment (within bands of 100), and whether it arose as the result of a transfer from another locality or through the establishment of a branch plant. Their coverage included a few non-manufacturing plants, such as servicing and repair facilities; these were excluded from the analysis.

Data from the SID's were entered into a database, each plant being coded by UK Standard Economic Region (SER) and 3-digit 1980 Standard Industrial Classification (SIC). SIC coding was based on product/process descriptions; these were usually

1 Board of Trade, 'Survey of industrial development in 1932', *Board of Trade Journal* (29 June 1933), iii-xv; Board of Trade, *Survey of Industrial Development* (London, 1934–39).

2 Board of Trade, 'Survey of industrial development in 1932', iii–xv, p iv; NA, BT 104/20, memorandum, 28 October 1935; Michael Beesley, 'The birth and death of industrial establishments: experience in the West Midlands conurbation', *Journal of Industrial Economics*, 4 (1955), 45–61.

3 Ibid.

4 Board of Trade, 'Survey of industrial development in 1932'; Board of Trade, *Survey of Industrial Development*; NA, HLG71/1330, memorandum, n.d., c. 1943. Government factories established under the rearmament programme were excluded from the Surveys.

sufficiently specific, though ambiguities were encountered in some cases. Where a plant had main and subsidiary production, the coding is based on its main activity. The location information posed further problems. Plants were grouped into a number of 'districts', each then divided into fairly small 'localities' – for example there were separate localities for the central areas of major cities and each 'suburban' industrial zone.[5] Yet for a few districts this practice was not followed, in at least some years. No locality information was provided for the Birmingham district and data for the Manchester district was not disaggregated for 1933 and 1934. When examining plant clustering in central Manchester, it was therefore necessary to discard data for these years. Difficulties were also encountered with the City, Finsbury, and Shoreditch boroughs of London, which were only disaggregated from a collective 'central London' locality from 1935 (and could therefore only be included in the analysis of local clustering from this date). Yet such difficulties were confined to large clusters and (with the exception of Birmingham) do not effect their identification or analysis of their industrial composition.

Further data on new plant formation in Greater London and its hinterland – covering the period from around 1919 to the second quarter of 1936 and assembled from returns provided by the Factory Inspectorate – has been preserved in a register compiled by the Greater London Regional Development Committee (hereafter GLRDC), held at London Metropolitan Archives.[6] This provides information on each establishment's year of opening, activity, and address. Again a few plants in the primary and tertiary sectors were also recorded, though these were excluded from the analysis, as were a few plants with an initial employment of below 25.

The data on new plant formation in London used in Chapter Eight are based on a dataset compiled by splicing together the GLRDC and SID data. The SID data was used for years where the two sources overlap, on account of the wider range of sources the SIDs drew on and the fact that, as published documents, they are likely to have been subject to more thorough checking. The SID's cover 1,416 Greater London plants, an average of 202.3 per year. Meanwhile, during 1919–31 the GLRDC covers 1,360 plants, an annual average of only 104.6.[7] Yet the number of factories derived from the two sources over the period covered by both, 1932–34,[8] was 671 for the GLRDC and 664 for the SID's – a margin of error within the normal year-to-year corrections for the SID's. The lower average plant numbers for the pre-1932 data are partly due to the fact that this was an era of slower employment growth for London. Another significant factor is the deletion from the GLRDC register of some plants that subsequently closed. A further possibility is that the GLRDC might have been less comprehensive during its early years; it records an average of only 82.7 plants per year during 1919–25, compared to 129.0 during 1926–31. There is no evidence

5 For example, the 'Leeds' locality did not include suburban areas such as Armley and Stanningley; 'Sheffield' excluded similar areas such as Intake, Attercliffe, and Ecclesfield; and 'Glasgow' excluded areas such as Pollokshaws and Govan.

6 London Metropolitan Archives, MCC/MIN/65/3.

7 Excluding plants with fewer than 25 employees.

8 The GLRDC also included some data for 1935, though these are incomplete.

that such omissions would bias its geographical coverage, which encompassed an area wider than the London region throughout the period.

Compiling a single dataset from these sources involved some problems. GLRDC data was classified by borough, while the SID's were classified by 'localities' – often involving other, generally smaller, areas, and requiring reclassification into boroughs. Some data could not be so classified; for example, from 1932–34 most plants in the City of London, Finsbury, and Shoreditch were grouped into a 'central London' locality; some in Westminster and parts of neighbouring boroughs were classified as 'West End', while a few localities, such as 'Queensbury' spanned two boroughs. Despite these problems, unclassified plants represented only 7.96 per cent of the 1932–38 total (and concerned densely industrialised boroughs, with sufficient classified plants to examine their industrial structure). Two boroughs, Acton and Willesden, had to be amalgamated into a composite category, as the SID's classified the large Park Royal industrial estate (which spans both) separately. However, as these represented an area of virtually continuous industrial development, this grouping is not problematic.

The databases assembled from this data were compiled in conjunction with Peter Walsh at the University of Portsmouth, with financial assistance from the Nuffield Foundation, whose help is gratefully acknowledged. Our completed databases are available via the UK Data Archive (AHDS History, SN5192, Peter Scott and Peter Walsh, 'National data on new interwar manufacturing plants and extensions, 1919–1938', deposited 2005).

Appendix B

The regional distribution of Britain's employed population by sector in 1911 and 1931

Appendix Table B1: The regional distribution of Britain's employed population by sector, 1911

	London*	Other SE	All SE	EA	SW	WM	EM	NW	YH	Northern	Wales	Scotland	Britain
% of national workforce	14.48	14.35	28.83	2.72	6.61	8.04	6.67	15.11	9.02	6.15	5.58	11.26	100.00
% female workers	34.71	29.39	32.06	26.68	30.38	29.28	27.88	33.63	28.81	20.74	21.06	28.70	29.56
Overall employment distribution													
01-03 Agriculture, forestry, fishing	0.97	11.49	6.27	28.69	16.67	8.03	12.26	3.40	5.00	8.38	12.11	11.76	8.66
11-14, 21 & 23 Mining and quarrying	0.02	0.18	0.10	0.12	3.04	6.33	10.24	4.40	9.28	21.49	25.71	8.05	6.65
16-17 Gas, electricity, water	0.64	0.63	0.64	0.30	0.38	0.46	0.41	0.49	0.54	0.51	0.32	0.43	0.50
22 & 24-49 Manufacturing	30.24	20.26	25.21	20.17	23.28	44.00	36.77	48.26	45.00	26.07	18.02	36.51	33.46
50-99 Construction & Services	68.13	67.44	67.78	50.71	56.62	41.17	40.32	43.45	40.18	43.54	43.84	43.26	50.73
Distribution within manufacturing													
22 Metal Manufacture	0.96	1.61	1.23	2.12	2.07	8.96	5.53	3.92	7.65	15.67	28.13	8.87	6.25
24 Non-metallic mineral products	1.21	4.01	2.34	2.91	3.20	11.89	2.70	1.53	2.53	3.48	4.41	2.20	3.38
25 & 48 Chemicals	2.50	2.66	2.56	2.26	1.85	1.15	0.85	2.56	2.02	3.62	1.99	1.88	2.13
31 Other metal goods	6.63	6.11	6.42	7.18	6.54	28.05	4.21	3.82	10.08	9.08	8.08	6.04	8.59
32 Mechanical engineering	5.60	9.37	7.13	7.50	8.17	7.01	9.13	9.03	8.86	17.24	8.49	11.09	8.96
34 Electrical engineering	3.58	3.18	3.42	1.19	1.01	1.85	1.04	1.47	0.79	1.99	1.61	1.02	1.76
35 & 36 Vehicles (excl. shipbuilding)	3.52	5.63	4.37	4.31	4.74	8.72	3.47	1.56	1.92	1.74	3.02	1.50	3.35
361 Shipbuilding	0.49	3.72	1.80	1.43	2.52	0.09	0.22	1.26	0.64	16.92	3.10	7.24	2.71

37 Instrument engineering	1.56	1.16	1.40	0.71	0.59	0.81	0.42	0.32	0.36	0.48	0.61	0.47	0.67
41/2 Food, drink, tobacco	8.15	9.88	8.85	12.40	11.08	4.22	4.59	3.42	3.30	3.76	5.52	7.28	5.80
43 Textiles	2.24	2.35	2.28	5.96	6.80	4.25	27.88	50.18	40.37	2.88	2.29	24.29	22.54
44 Leather & leather goods**	3.19	1.77	2.61	2.09	1.79	2.71	1.45	0.72	1.19	0.94	1.09	0.85	1.56
45 Clothing & footwear**	32.91	28.98	31.32	34.77	34.76	11.14	30.68	12.06	13.34	14.75	24.55	14.46	19.86
46 Timber & furniture	9.34	7.32	8.52	5.92	6.36	3.39	3.34	2.99	3.26	3.84	3.78	5.05	4.80
47 Paper & printing	14.24	9.81	12.45	6.32	6.93	3.16	3.78	3.57	2.98	3.12	3.03	6.01	5.83
49 Other manufacturing	3.88	2.45	3.30	2.93	1.59	2.59	0.71	1.58	0.70	0.49	0.29	1.75	1.83
Coefficient of specialisation* **	0.35	0.27	0.31	0.26	0.24	0.38	0.16	0.28	0.21	0.34	0.28	0.13	0.00

Source: C. H. Lee, British Regional Employment Statistics 1841-1971 *(Cambridge, 1979), Part III, Series B.*

Notes: Some workers could not be classified by sector.
- * London & Middlesex.
- ** Fur is included under leather & leather goods.
- *** See text.

Appendix Table B2: The regional distribution of Britain's employed population by sector, 1931

	London*	Other SE	All SE	EA	SW	WM	EM	NW	YH	Northern	Wales	Scotland	Britain
% of national workforce	14.98	16.68	31.66	2.49	6.16	8.42	6.81	13.85	8.76	5.46	4.77	11.62	100.00
% female workers	36.48	29.46	32.79	25.98	28.22	31.06	28.38	34.84	30.36	24.30	21.16	30.04	30.62
Overall employment distribution													
01-03 Agriculture, forestry, fishing	0.54	6.67	3.77	23.29	12.69	5.48	9.46	2.88	3.92	7.06	10.52	9.07	6.35
11-14, 21 & 23 Mining and quarrying	0.06	0.40	0.24	0.19	2.29	5.30	10.54	3.38	10.82	19.46	22.86	6.59	5.72
16-17 Gas, electricity, water	1.57	1.57	1.57	0.91	1.11	1.17	0.92	1.15	1.13	1.24	0.78	0.80	1.21
22 & 24-49 Manufacturing	31.43	22.56	26.76	20.76	22.58	46.50	37.09	44.69	41.35	21.80	16.13	33.65	32.50
50-99 Construction & Services	66.40	68.79	67.66	54.84	61.33	41.55	41.99	47.89	42.78	50.44	49.72	49.88	54.23
Distribution within manufacturing													
22 Metal Manufacture	1.32	1.33	1.32	0.54	1.79	11.35	5.49	2.55	8.49	16.52	36.18	9.44	6.25
24 Non-metallic mineral products	1.72	4.65	3.02	4.10	3.88	11.69	3.95	2.28	2.62	3.84	4.57	2.37	3.99
25 & 48 Chemicals	4.24	4.58	4.39	1.82	3.22	1.42	1.87	4.71	3.71	8.42	3.73	2.95	3.69
31 Other metal goods	4.34	3.02	3.75	2.80	2.52	18.02	1.94	2.53	7.91	3.68	4.11	2.56	5.35
32 Mechanical engineering	7.27	7.50	7.37	8.98	6.44	7.29	8.50	6.71	7.28	9.16	3.38	10.02	7.59
34 Electrical engineering	7.25	6.29	6.82	3.36	1.88	5.75	1.87	4.03	1.39	3.37	1.73	1.41	4.01
35 & 36 Vehicles (excl. shipbuilding)	5.14	9.99	7.29	6.58	12.12	14.73	5.70	4.20	3.30	5.77	4.93	3.91	6.71
361 Shipbuilding	0.39	5.37	2.60	1.48	5.41	0.05	0.28	1.84	0.54	13.46	2.76	10.56	3.20
37 Instrument engineering	1.98	1.38	1.71	1.01	0.67	0.56	0.33	0.36	0.50	0.48	0.57	0.55	0.81

41/2 Food, drink, tobacco	12.37	13.84	13.02	22.53	19.82	6.80	7.39	8.47	7.01	11.85	12.99	12.56	10.64
43 Textiles	2.41	2.35	2.39	4.86	5.20	5.86	28.96	40.05	36.16	3.22	3.92	20.69	18.23
44 Leather & leather goods**	2.68	1.32	2.08	1.51	1.50	1.17	1.23	1.09	0.94	0.61	0.64	0.79	1.31
45 Clothing & footwear**	22.53	14.60	19.01	24.08	17.31	6.28	23.37	11.28	12.39	8.19	10.92	6.34	13.50
46 Timber & furniture	7.25	6.78	7.04	6.60	6.85	2.58	3.34	2.45	3.15	4.71	4.46	6.08	4.63
47 Paper & printing	13.06	12.80	12.94	7.43	8.99	3.30	4.63	4.99	3.76	5.52	4.37	6.80	7.13
49 Other manufacturing	6.04	4.22	5.23	2.32	2.41	3.16	1.14	2.45	0.87	1.20	0.74	2.97	2.95
Coefficient of specialisation* **	0.29	0.23	0.24	0.27	0.25	0.35	0.22	0.23	0.23	0.28	0.33	0.19	0.00

Sources & notes: As for Table B1.

Bibliography

Manuscript Sources

Age Concern Reminiscence Center, Blackheath Village, London. Autobiographical excerpt provided for Age Concern, 'Just Like the Country' project, by D. Barton, c. 1987.

Bank of England Archive. EID4/159.

Bexley Local Studies and Archive Centre. New Ideal Homesteads brochure, *Super 1933 Homes. Barnehurst Estate, Barnehurst, Kent* (1933).

British Library of Political and Economic Science Archives. Ward Papers.

Coventry Record Office. Acc. 1647, interviews recorded for a project on the social history of car workers and deposited by Paul Thompson, University of Essex, in 1986.

Croydon Reference Library. *The Waddon Factory Estate* (undated promotional brochure).

Letchworth Museum. 'Letchworth – Some economic and industrial aspects', typescript, 1935, author not known.

London Metropolitan Archives. Middlesex County Council papers and National Council of Social Service Papers.

Modern Records Centre, University of Warwick. Federation of British Industries papers, Mss. 200/F; TUC papers, Mss. 292.

The National Archives, Kew, London. Papers in the BT 56, 104, 106, 177, CAB 87, COAL 22, HLG 17, 27, 52, 71, 90, LAB 8, 17, 18, MT 33, and RAIL 421 classes.

National Provident Institution, London. 'Loans to the Allnatt Group of Companies', memorandum, 30 July 1954.

Nuffield College Library, Oxford. Nuffield College Social Reconstruction Survey Archive.

Slough Museum, transcript of 'The Story of Slough', BBC Home Service broadcast, 2 December 1952.

Watford Reference Library, Civic Survey Council, 'Watford Civic Survey 1933', three volume manuscript, c. 1933.

Welwyn Garden City Library, Sir Frederic Osborn Archive.

Electronic sources

Butlins Memories website, http://www.butlinsmemories.com/21/id3.htm.

UK Data Archive, AHDS History, SN 5191, Peter Scott, 'Growth of British industrial estates, 1900–1939', deposited 2005.

UK Data Archive, AHDS History, SN 5192, Peter Scott and Peter Walsh, 'National data on new interwar manufacturing plants and extensions, 1919–1938', deposited 2005.

British official publications

A Study of the Factors Which Have Operated in the Past and Those Which are Operating Now to Determine the Distribution of Women in Industry (Cmnd 3508 of 1930).

Board of Trade, 'Survey of industrial development in 1932', *Board of Trade Journal* (29 June 1933): iii-xv.

Board of Trade, *Survey of Industrial Development* (London: HMSO, 1934-39).

Board of Trade, *Fifth Census of Production 1935, Final Summary Tables* (London: HMSO, 1944).

Board of Trade, *Jute Working Party Report* (London: HMSO, 1948).

Commissioner for the Special Areas (England and Wales), *First Report* [7 July 1935], (Cmnd 4957 of 1935).

Commissioner for the Special Areas (England and Wales), *Second Report* [6 February 1936], (Cmnd 5090 of 1936).

Commissioner for the Special Areas (England and Wales), *Third Report* [27 October 1936], (Cmnd 5303 of 1936).

Committee on Finance and Industry, *Report* (P.P., 1930–31, XIII).

Department of Employment, *British Labour Statistics. Historical Abstract 1868–1968* (London: HMSO, 1971).

General Register Office, *Census of England and Wales, 1931, Occupation Tables* (London: HMSO, 1934).

H.M. Chief Inspector of Mines, *Annual Report* (London: HMSO, 1922).

H.M. Factory Inspectorate, *Annual Report of the Chief Inspector of Factories and Workshops, 1934-37* (P.P., 1935–38).

Catherine Hakim, *Occupational Segregation. A Comparative Study of the Degree and Pattern of the Differentiation Between Men and Women's Work in Britain, the United States and Other Countries*, Dept. of Employment Research Paper No. 9. (London: HMSO, 1979).

Ministry of Labour, *Memorandum on the Shortage, Surplus and Redistribution of Juvenile Labour in England and Wales during the Years 1930–1938* (London: HMSO, 1931).

Ministry of Labour, *Annual Reports for the Years 1933–38* (P.P., 1934–35 – 1938–39).

Ministry of Labour Gazette (various dates).

Ministry of Munitions, *History of the Ministry of Munitions*, (London: HMSO, 1918–22).

Ministry of Production, *Report of the Cotton Textile Mission to the USA* (London: HMSO, 1944).

Ministry of Transport, *Transport Advisory Council: Report on Services and Rates* (London, 1937).

Royal Commission on Mineral Royalties, *Final Report With Appendices* (P.P., 1893, XLI).

Royal Commission on the Coal Industry (1925), *Report* (P.P., 1926, XIV).

Royal Commission on Transport, *Minutes of Evidence*, Vol. 3 (London: HMSO, 1930).

Royal Commission on the Distribution of the Industrial Population, *Report* (London: HMSO, 1940).

Royal Commission on The Distribution of The Industrial Population, *Minutes of Evidence* (London: HMSO, 1940).

Select Committee on Estimates, 1946–47, *The Administration of the Development Areas* (London: HMSO, 1947).

Other printed sources

Margaret Ackrill and Leslie Hannah, *Barclays. The Business of Banking 1690–1996* (Cambridge: CUP, 2001).

Acton Town Council, *Acton: Official Guide* (Cheltenham: Burrows, 1939).

D. H. Aldcroft, *The British Economy. Volume 1: The Years of Turmoil 1920–1951* (Brighton: Wheatsheaf, 1986).

Derek. H. Aldcroft and H. W. Richardson, *The British Economy 1870–1939* (London: Macmillan, 1969).

B.W.E. Alford, 'Lost opportunities: British business and businessmen during the First World War', 205–27 in N. McKendrick and R.B. Outhwaite, *Business Life and Public Policy: Essays in Honour of D.C. Coleman* (Cambridge: Cambridge University Press, 1986).

G. C. Allen, *The Industrial Development of Birmingham and the Black Country, 1860–1927* (London: Allen & Unwin, 1929).

G. C. Allen, 'Labour transference and the unemployment problem', *Economic Journal*, 40 (1930): 242-8.

G. R. Allen, 'The growth of industry on trading estates, 1920–39, with special reference to Slough Trading Estate', *Oxford Economic Papers*, new. ser., 1, 3 (1951): 272–300.

P. W. S. Andrews and Elizabeth Brunner, *The Life of Lord Nuffield* (Oxford: Blackwell, 1955).

John Armstrong, 'International confluences on the development of London business: the case of the Park Royal industrial estate between the wars', unpublished paper.

John Armstrong, 'The development of the Park Royal industrial estate in the inter-war period: a re-examination of the Aldcroft/Richardson thesis', *London Journal*, 21 (1996): 64–79.

M. M. Attlee, *Mobility of Labour. A Consideration of the Question of Industrial Transference, with some Examples from the Inter-war Period and Suggestions for a Post-war Policy* (Oxford: Catholic Social Guild, 1944).

'Attracting Industry', *The Evening Citizen* (6 August 1928).

David B. Audretsch, 'Agglomeration and the location of innovative activity', *Oxford Review of Economic Policy*, 14 (1988): 18–29.

Philip Bagwell, *The Transport Revolution from 1770* (London: Batsford, 1974).

D. E. Baines, 'Population migration and regional development, 1870–1939', 29–61 in R. Floud and D. McCloskey (eds), *The Economic History of Britain since 1700*, 2nd edn, Vol. 2 (Cambridge: CUP, 1994).

D. E. Baines, *Migration in a Mature Economy* (Cambridge: CUP, 1985).

Paul Bairoch, *Cities and Economic Development* (London: Mansell, 1988).

Michael Ball and David Sunderland, *An Economic History of London 1800–1914* (London: Routledge, 2001).

Barnett House Survey Committee, *A Survey of the Social Services in the Oxford District* (Oxford: Oxford U.P., 1938).

R. D. Barron and G. M. Norris, 'Sexual divisions and the dual labour market', in Diana L. Barker and Sheila Allen (eds), *Dependence and Exploitation in Work and Marriage* (London: Longman, 1976).

Daniel K. Benjamin, and Levis A. Kochin, 'What went right with juvenile unemployment policy between the wars: a comment', *Economic History Review*, 2nd ser. XXXII (1979): 523–8.

Veronica Beechey, 'Some notes on female wage labour in capitalist production', *Capital and Class*, III (1977): 45–66.

Michael Beesley, 'The birth and death of industrial establishments: experience in the West Midlands conurbation', *Journal of Industrial Economics*, 4 (1955): 45–61.

Michael Beesley, 'Changing industrial advantages in the British motor car industry', *Journal of Industrial Economics*, 6 (1957): 47–57.

Walter Bennett, *The History of Burnley from 1850* (Burnley: Burnley Corporation, 1951).

Maxine Berg, *The Age of Manufactures. Industry, Innovation and Work in Britain 1700–1820* (Oxford: Blackwell, 1985).

Maxine Berg and Pat Hudson, 'Rehabilitating the Industrial Revolution', *Economic History Review*, 2nd ser. XLV (1992): 24–50.

John Betjeman, 'Slough', 21-3 in Earl of Birkenhead (ed.), *John Betjeman's Collected Poems* (London: John Murray, 1958).

Mark Billinge, 'Divided by a common language: North and South 1750–1830', 88–111 in Alan R. H. Baker and Mark Billinge (eds), *Geographies of England. The North-South Divide, Material and Imagined* (Cambridge: CUP, 2004).

A. E. Booth, 'The timing and content of government policies to assist the depressed areas, 1920–1939', unpublished D. Phil thesis, University of Kent, 1975.

Alan E. Booth, 'An administrative experiment in unemployment policy in the thirties', *Public Administration*, 56 (1978): 139–57.

Frances Bostock and Geoffrey Jones, 'Foreign multinationals in British manufacturing, 1850–1962', *Business History*, 36, 1 (1994): 89–126.

Marian Bowley, *Housing and the State 1919–1944* (London: Allen & Unwin, 1945).

George R. Boyer, 'Living standards, 1860–1939', 280–313 in Roderick Floud and Paul Johnson (eds), *The Cambridge Economic History of Modern Britain. Volume II: Economic Maturity 1860–1939* (Cambridge: CUP, 2004).

George R. Boyer and Timothy J. Hatton, 'Migration and labour market integration in late nineteenth-century England and Wales', *Economic History Review*, L, 4 (1997): 697–734.

Trevor Boyns, 'Of machines and men in the 1920s', *Llafur*, 5 (1989): 30–39.

Trevor Boyns, 'Jigging and shaking: technical choice in the South Wales coal industry between the wars', *Welsh History Review*, 17, 2 (1994): 230–51.

Noreen Branson and Margot Heinemann, *Britain in the Nineteen Thirties* (St. Albans: Panther, 1973).

Gail Braybon, *Women Workers in the First World War: The British Experience* (London: Croom Helm, 1981).

Stephen N. Broadberry, 'Unemployment in interwar Britain: a disequilibrium approach', *Oxford Economic Papers*, XXXV (1983): 463–85.

William Bredo, *Industrial Estates: Tools for Industrialisation* (Glencoe: Free Press, 1960).

Asa Briggs, *The History of Broadcasting in the United Kingdom. Volume II: The Golden Age of Wireless* (London: Oxford U.P., 1965).

British Road Federation, *Basic Road Statistics, Great Britain, 1950* (London: British Road Federation, 1950).

S. N. Broadberry, 'The emergence of mass unemployment: explaining macroeconomic trends in Britain during the trans-World War I period', *Economic History Review*, XLIII (1990): 271–82.

S. N. Broadberry and Andrew Marrison, 'External economies of scale in the Lancashire cotton industry, 1900–1950', *Economic History Review*, LV, 1 (2002): 51–77.

Bromboro [name later changed to Bromborough] Port Estate Ltd., *Bromboro Port Estate* (Port Sunlight: Bromboro Port Estate Ltd, c. 1929).

C. T. Brunner, *The Problem of Motor Transport: an Economic Analysis* (London: E. Benn, 1928).

Elizabeth Brunner, *Holiday Making and the Holiday Trades* (London: Oxford U.P., 1945).

Stephen Bunker, '"A small town outside Vauxhall": Luton in the twentieth century', unpublished paper, presented at ESRC Colloquium on Industry and Urbanisation, University College London, 8 May 1993.

Jeremy Burchardt, 'Reconstructing the rural community: village halls and the National Council of Social Service, 1919 to 1939', *Rural History*, 10 (1999): 193–216.

Business (May 1938): 31.

D. L. Burn, *The Economic History of Steelmaking 1867–1939. A Study in Competition* (Cambridge: CUP, 1940).

John Burnett, *A Social History of Housing 1815–1985*, 2nd edn. (London: Methuen, 1986).

H. J. Bush 'Local, intellectual, and policy responses to localised unemployment in the inter-war period: the genesis of regional policy', unpublished D. Phil thesis, University of Oxford, 1980.

'"Business" Country-wide Survey of 3 Years' Industrial Development', *Business* (December 1935): 9–34.

N. K. Buxton, 'Entrepreneurial efficiency in the British coal industry between the wars', *Economic History Review*, XXIII (1970): 476–97.

N. K. Buxton, 'Avoiding the pitfalls: entrepreneurial efficiency in the coal industry again', *Economic History Review*, XXV (1972): 669–73.

N. K. Buxton, 'Efficiency and organization in Scotland's iron and steel industry during the interwar period', *Economic History Review*, XXIX (1976): 107–24.

N. K. Buxton, 'Coalmining', 48–78, in N. K. Buxton and D. H. Aldcroft (eds), *British Industry Between the Wars. Instability and Industrial Development, 1919–1939* (London: Scolar, 1979).

P. J. Cain and A. G. Hopkins, *British Imperialism: Innovation and Expansion 1688–1914* (London: Longman, 1993).

Alec Cairncross, 'The economy of Glasgow', in R. Miller and J. Tivy (eds), *The Glasgow Region* (Edinburgh: British Association for the Advancement of Science, 1958).

Alan Campbell, *The Scottish Miners 1874–1939. Volume One: Industry, Work and Community* (Aldershot: Ashgate, 2000).

Bruce M. S. Campbell, 'North-South dichotomies, 1066–1550', 145–74 in Alan R. H. Baker and Mark Billinge (eds), *Geographies of England. The North-South Divide, Material and Imagined* (Cambridge: CUP, 2004).

P. W. Carr, 'Engineering workers and the rise of labour in Coventry, 1914–1939', unpublished Ph.D. thesis, University of Warwick, 1978.

Josie Castle, 'Factory work for women: Courtaulds and G.E.C. between the wars', 133–71 in Bill Lancaster and Tony Mason (eds), *Life and Labour in a Twentieth Century City: The Experience of Coventry* (Coventry: Cryfield, 1986).

Michael Cassell, *Long Lease! The Story of Slough Estates 1920-1991* (London: Pencorp, 1991).

John Cattell, Sheila Ely and Barry Jones, *The Birmingham Jewellery Quarter. An Architectural Survey of the Manufactories* (Swindon: English Heritage, 2002).

W. H. Chaloner, 'The birth of modern Manchester', 131–46 in C. F. Carter (ed.), *Manchester and its Region* (Manchester: Manchester U.P., 1962).

Alfred D. Chandler, *Scale and Scope. The Dynamics of Industrial Capitalism* (Cambridge, Mass.: Belknap, 1990).

S. D. Chapman, 'Economy, industry, and employment', 480–512 in J. Beckett (ed.), *A Centenary History of Nottingham* (Manchester: Manchester U.P., 1997).

S. D. Chapman, *Hosiery and Knitwear. Four Centuries of Small-Scale Industry in Britain, c. 1589–2000* (Oxford: Oxford U.P., 2002).

T. S. Chegwidden and G. Myrddin-Evans, *The Employment Exchange Service of Great Britain* (London: Macmillan, 1934).

Roy Church, *The History of the British Coal Industry, Volume 3, 1830–1913: Victorian Pre-eminence* (Oxford: Clarendon, 1986).

Mark Clapson, *Suburban Century. Social Change and Urban Growth in England and the United States* (Oxford: Berg, 2003).

Peter Cline, 'Winding down the war economy: British plans for peacetime recovery, 1916–19', 157–81 in Kathleen Burk (ed.), *War and the State. The Transformation of British Government, 1914–1919* (London: Allen & Unwin, 1982).

Roy Coad, *Laing: the Biography of Sir John W. Laing, C.B.E. (1879–1978)* (London: Hodder and Stoughton, 1979).

Michael Collins, *Money and Banking in the UK. A History* (London: Routledge, 1988).

R. J. Cootes, *The General Strike 1926*, 2nd edn. (Harlow: Longman, 1983).

Penelope Corfield, 'Urban developments in England and Wales in the Sixteenth and Seventeenth Centuries', 214–47 in D. C. Coleman and A. H. John (eds), *Trade, Government and Economy in Pre-Industrial England: Essays Presented to F. J. Fisher* (London: Weidenfeld and Nicolson, 1976).

J. R. Cotton, 'The changing industrial structure of an east-Lancashire town – Blackburn from 1919–1970', unpublished part II thesis, Geographical Tripos, University of Cambridge, 1970.

W. H. B. Court, 'Problems of the British coal industry between the wars', *Economic History Review*, XV (1945): 1–24.

Nicholas Crafts, 'Regional GDP in Britain, 1871–1911: some estimates', *Scottish Journal of Political Economy*, 52 (2005): 54–64.

Nicholas Crafts, 'Long-run growth', 1–24 in Roderick Floud and Paul Johnson (eds), *The Cambridge Economic History of Modern Britain. Volume II: Economic Maturity 1860–1939* (Cambridge: CUP, 2004).

Nicholas Crafts and Abay Mulatu, 'What explains the location of industry in Britain, 1871–1931?', *Journal of Economic Geography* (forthcoming).

M. E. Daly, 'Government policy and the depressed areas in the inter-war years', unpublished D.Phil thesis, University of Oxford, 1978.

G. H. Daniel, 'Labour migration and age-composition', *Sociological Review*, XXXI (1939): 281–308.

G. H. Daniel, 'Some factors affecting the movement of labour', *Oxford Economic Papers*, III (1940): 144–79.

Lance E. Davis and Robert A. Huttenback, *Mammon and the Pursuit of Empire. The Economics of British Imperialism*, abridged edn (Cambridge: CUP, 1988).

W. Davies, 'The nature and significance of trading estates with special reference to the Treforest and Slough Estates', unpublished MA dissertation, University of Wales, 1951.

C. Day, 'Need a Factory', *Business* (July 1938): 33.

P. Deane and W. A. Cole, *British Economic Growth 1688–1959* (Cambridge: CUP, 1967).

G. Dei Ottati, 'Trust, interlinking transactions and credit in the industrial district', *Cambridge Journal of Economics*, 18 (1994): 529–46.

M. Davies, 'Exiled in London', *The Listener* (20 April 1938): 854–5.

R. C. Davison, *British Unemployment Policy. The Modern Phase since 1930* (London: Longmans, 1938).

S. R. Dennison, *The Location of Industry and the Depressed Areas* (London: Oxford U.P., 1939).

T. M. Devine, *The Scottish Nation 1700–2000* (London: Penguin, 1999).

T. M. Devine, 'Scotland', 388–416 in Roderick Floud and Paul Johnson (eds), *The Cambridge Economic History of Modern Britain. Volume 1: Industrialisation, 1700–1870* (Cambridge: CUP, 2004).

Peter Dewey, 'Agriculture, agrarian society, and the countryside', 270–85 in Chris Wrigley (ed.), *A Companion to Early Twentieth Century* Britain (Oxford: Blackwell, 2003).

Peter B. Doeringer and Michael J. Piore, *Internal Labour Markets and Manpower Analysis* (Lexington, Mass.: Heath, 1971).

J. R. Dowie, '1919–20 is in need of attention', *Economic History Review*, XXVIII (1975): 429–50.

J. H. Dunning, *American Investment in British Manufacturing Industry*, revised edn. (London: Routledge, 1998).

Ruth Durant, *Watling: A Survey of Social Life on a New Housing Estate* (London: King, 1939).

R. S. Edwards and H. Townsend, *Business Enterprise. Its Growth and Organisation* (London: Macmillan, 1958).

EFTA, *Regional Policy in EFTA: Industrial Estates* (Geneva: EFTA, 1970).

Barry Eichengreen, 'The British economy between the wars', 314–43 in Roderick Floud and Paul Johnson (eds), *The Cambridge Economic History of Modern Britain. Volume II: Economic Maturity 1860–1939* (Cambridge: CUP, 2004).

Arthur Excell, 'Morris Motors in the 1930s: Part II', *History Workshop Journal*, VII (1979): 45–65.

D. A. Farnie, *The Manchester Ship Canal and the Rise of the Port of Manchester 1894–1975* (Manchester: Manchester U.P., 1980).

Charles H. Feinstein, 'What really happened to real wages?: trends in wages, prices, and productivity in the United Kingdom, 1880–1913', *Economic History Review*, XLIII, 3 (1990): 329–55.

David Feldman, *Englishmen and Jews. Social Relations and Political Culture 1840–1914* (New Haven: Yale U.P, 1994).

M. P. Feldman and D. B. Audreutsch, 'Innovation in cities: science-based diversity, specialization and localised competition', *European Economic Review*, 43 (1999): 409–29.

K. G. Fenelon, *Railway Economics* (London: Methuen, 1932).

K. G. Fenelon, *British Railways Today* (London: Nelson, 1939).

Robert Fitzgerald, *Rowntree and the Marketing Revolution, 1862–1969* (Cambridge: CUP, 1995).

P. S. Florence, *Investment, Location, and Size of Plant* (Cambridge: CUP, 1948).

James Foreman-Peck, 'Industry and industrial organisation in the inter-war years', 386–414 in R. Floud and D. McCloskey (eds), *The Economic History of Britain Since 1700. Volume 2 1860–1939*, 2nd edn (Cambridge: CUP, 1994).

Stephen Forthergill, Sarah Monk, and Martin Perry, *Property and Industrial Development* (Triptree: Hutchinson, 1987).

Alan Fox, *The History of the National Union of Boot and Shoe Operatives 1874–1957* (Oxford: Blackwell, 1958).

Marvin Frankel, 'Obsolescence and technological change in a maturing economy', *American Economic Review*, 45 (1955): 296–319.

David French, 'The rise and fall of "Business as usual"', 7–31 in Kathleen Burk (ed.), *War and the State. The Transformation of British Government, 1914–1919* (London: Allen & Unwin, 1982).

Dov Friedlander, 'London's urban transition 1851–1951', *Urban Studies*, XI (1974): 127–41.

Dov Friedlander, 'Occupational structure, wages, and migration in late nineteenth-century England and Wales', *Economic Development and Cultural Change*, XL (1992): 295–318.

C. H. Fritzche and E. L. Potts, *Horizon Mining* (London: Allen & Unwin, 1954).

Peter Garrod, 'The Bradford worsted industry and foreign competition, 1870–1939', unpublished M.Phil thesis, University of Leeds, 1981.

William R. Garside, 'Juvenile unemployment between the wars: a rejoinder', *Economic History Review*, 2nd ser. XXXII (1979): 529–32.

William R. Garside, *British Unemployment 1919–1939. A Study in Public Policy* (Cambridge: CUP, 1990).

William R. Garside, 'The economic legacy of conflict: Britain in the aftermath of the First World War', 25–36 in Harmut Berghoff and Robert von Friedeburg (eds), *Change and Inertia. Britain under the Impact of the Great War* (Bodenheim: Philo, 1998).

Margaret Judith Giles, 'Something that bit better. working-class women, domesticity, and "respectability", 1919–1939', unpublished D. Phil thesis, University of York, 1989.

Diana Gittins, *Fair Sex: Family Size and Structure, 1900–39* (London: Hutchinson, 1982).

E. L. Glaeser, H. D. Kallal, J. A. Scheinkman, and A. Shleifer, 'Growth in cities', *Journal of Political Economy*, 100 (1992): 1126–52.

Miriam Glucksmann, *Women Assemble: Women Workers and the New Industries in Inter-war Britain* (London: Routledge, 1990).

Sean Glynn, 'The nature of the problem', 3–16 in Sean Glynn and Alan Booth (eds), *The Road to Full Employment* (London: Allen & Unwin, 1987).

Andrew Godley, 'Immigrant entrepreneurs and the emergence of London's East End as an industrial district', *London Journal*, 21, 1 (1996): 38–45.

Andrew C. Godley, 'Pioneering foreign direct investment in British manufacturing', *Business History Review*, 73 (1999): 394–429.

John R. Gold and M. M. Gold, '"A place of delightful prospects": promotional imagery and the selling of suburbia', 159–82 in L. Zonn (ed.), *Place Images in Media. Portrayal, Experience, and Meaning* (Savage, Maryland: Rowman & Littlefield, 1990).

John Gollan, *Youth in British Industry* (London: Gollancz, 1937).

W. Francis Goodrich, *Watford: Its Advantages as an Industrial and Residential Centre* (Watford: Watford Urban District Council, c. 1908).

A. T. K. Grant, *A Study of the Capital Market in Britain from 1919–1936*, 2nd edn (London: Cass, 1967).

Robert Graves and Alan Hodge, *The Long Week-end. A Social History of Great Britain 1918–1939* (London: Faber & Faber, 1941).

David Greasley, 'The diffusion of a technology: the case of machine cutting in the British coal industry, 1900–38', unpublished Ph.D. thesis, University of Liverpool, 1979.

David Greasley and Les Oxley, 'Discontinuities in competitiveness: the impact of the First World War on British industry', *Economic History Review*, XLIX, 1 (1996): 82–100.

Gertjan de Groot and Marlou Schrover, 'Between men and machines: women workers in new industries, 1870–1940', *Social History*, XX (1995): 279–96.

Pyrs Gruffudd, 'Selling the countryside: representations of rural Britain', 247–63 in John R. Gold and Steven V. Ward (eds), *Place Promotion. The Use of Publicity and Marketing to Sell Towns and Regions* (Chichester: Wiley, 1994).

Fred Grundy and Richard Morris Titmuss, *Report on Luton* (Luton: Gibbs, 1945).

Richard Gurnham, *A History of the Trade Union Movement in the Hosiery and Knitwear Industry, 1776–1976* (Leicester: National Union of Hosiery and Knitwear Workers, 1976).

P. G. Hall, *The Industries of London since 1861* (London: Hutchinson, 1962).

Leslie Hannah, *Electricity before Nationalisation: a Study of the Development of the Electricity Supply Industry in Britain to 1948* (London: Macmillan, 1979).

Leslie Hannah, *The Rise of the Corporate Economy*, 2nd edn. (London: Methuen, 1983).

Wal Hannington, *The Problem of the Distressed Areas* (London: Gollancz, 1937).

Dennis Hardy and Colin Ward, *Arcadia for All. The Legacy of a Makeshift Landscape* (London: Mansell, 1984).

Gina Harkell, 'The migration of mining families to the Kent coalfield between the wars', *Oral History*, 6, 1 (1978): 98–113.

C. N. Harley, 'Trade 1870–1939: from globalisation to fragmentation', 161–89 in Roderick Floud and Paul Johnson (eds), *The Cambridge Economic History of Modern Britain. Volume II: Economic Maturity 1860–1939* (Cambridge: CUP, 2004).

J. Harrap, 'Rayon', 276–302 in Neil K. Buxton and Derek H. Aldcroft (eds), *British Industry Between the Wars* (London: Scolar, 1979).

Timothy. J. Hatton, 'Structural aspects of unemployment in Britain between the World Wars', *Research in Economic History*, 10 (1986): 55–92.

Timothy J. Hatton, 'Unemployment and the labour market in inter-war Britain', 359–85 in R. Floud and D. McCloskey (eds), *The Economic History of Britain since 1700*, 2nd edn, Volume 2 (Cambridge: CUP, 1994).

Timothy J. Hatton and Roy E. Bailey, 'Unemployment incidence in interwar London', *Economica*, 69 (2002): 631–54.

C. E. Heim, 'Uneven regional development in interwar Britain', unpublished Ph.D. thesis, Yale University, 1982.

C. E. Heim, 'Industrial organization and regional development in interwar Britain', *Journal of Economic History*, XLIII (1983): 931–52.

V. Henderson, 'Marshall's scale economies', *Journal of Urban Economics*, 53 (2003): 1–28.

V. Henderson, A. Kuncoro and M. Turner, 'Industrial development in cities', *Journal of Political Economy*, 103 (1995): 1067–90.

Hillier Parker, *Report on the Property Market during 1934* (London: Hillier Parker, 1935).

George Hodgkinson, *Sent to Coventry* (Bletchley: Robert Maxwell, 1970).

L. T. Holden, 'The history of Vauxhall Motors to 1950', unpublished M. Phil thesis, Open University, 1983.

W. G. Holford, 'The Location and Design of Trading Estates', *Journal of the Town Planning Institute* (March 1939): 154.

Katrina Honeyman, *Well Suited. A History of the Leeds Clothing Industry 1850–1990* (Oxford: Oxford U.P., 2000).

Alun Howkins, *The Death of Rural England. A Social History of the Countryside since 1900* (London: Routledge, 2003).

A. Howkins and J. Lowerson, *Trends in Leisure, 1919–1939* (London: Sports Council and Social Science Research Council, 1979).

R. J. Howley, 'Road transport in relation to the general transport problem of the country', *Journal of the Institute of Transport* (March 1924): 192–208.

H. G. Huckle, 'Trading estates for light industry', unpublished RIBA examination thesis, 1939.

Steve Humphries and Beverley Hopwood, *Green and Pleasant Land* (London: Channel 4 Books, 1999).

E. H. Hunt, *Regional Wage Variations in Britain: 1850–1914* (Oxford: Clarendon, 1973).

E. H. Hunt, 'Industrialization and regional inequality: wages in Britain, 1760–1914', *Journal of Economic History* XLVI, 4 (1986), 935–66.

J. M. Hunter, 'Factors affecting the location and growth of industry in Greater Nottinghamshire', *East Midland Geographer*, 3 (1964): 340–41.

'The Industrial North East', *Business* (Supplement, June 1937): 12.

'Industrial site survey', *Business* (March 1937): 32–8.

International Labour Office, *The World Coal-mining Industry, Volume 1: Economic Conditions* (Geneva: ILO, 1938).

Jane Jacobs, *The Economy of Cities* (New York: Random House, 1969).

J. B. Jefferys, *Retail Trading in Britain, 1900–1950* (Cambridge: CUP, 1954).

J. Jewkes, 'The industries of the Manchester province', 81–122 in H. Clay and K. Russell Brady (eds), *Manchester at Work: A Survey* (Manchester: Manchester Civic Week Committee, 1929).

John Laing & Son Ltd., *Laings Factory Sites: on Barnet Bypass Road* (undated leaflet, c. 1938).

Eric L. Jones, 'The constraints on economic growth in southern England 1650–1850', *Third International Conference on Economic History* (Paris, 1965): 423–30.

Eric L. Jones, 'La deindustrializzazione come forma di aggiustamento economico: il case dell'inghilterra sud-occidentale', *Quaderni Storici*, New Ser., 73 (1990): 247–68.

M. E. F. Jones, 'The regional impact of an overvalued pound in the 1920s', *Economic History Review*, XXXVIII (1985): 393–401.

R. D. Kaunitz, 'The British trading estate, a study in commercial, local, and central government enterprise', unpublished Ph.D. thesis, Harvard University, 1950.

D.E. Keeble, 'Industrial growth in north west London: a geographical analysis', unpublished Ph.D. thesis, University of Cambridge, 1967.

J. M. Keynes, 'The economic consequences of Mr Churchill', abbreviated reprinted version, 27-43 in Sidney Pollard (ed), *The Gold Standard and Employment Policies between the Wars* (London: Methuen, 1970).

C. P. Kindleberger, *Economic Growth in France and Britain, 1851–1950* (Cambridge, MA: Harard U.P., 1964).

M. W. Kirby, 'The control of competition in the British coal-mining industry in the thirties', *Economic History Review*, XXVI (1973): 273–84.

M. W. Kirby, 'The Lancashire cotton industry in the inter-war years: a study in organizational change', *Business History*, XVI (1974): 145–59.

Bill Lancaster, 'Who's a real Coventry kid? Migration into twentieth century Coventry', 57–80 in Bill Lancaster and Tony Mason (eds), *Life and Labour in a Twentieth Century City: The Experience of Coventry* (Coventry: Cryfield Press, 1986).

Labour Party Commission of Enquiry into the Distressed Areas, *Labour and the Distressed Areas: A Programme of Immediate Action: Interim Report of the Labour Party's Commission of Enquiry into the Distressed Areas* (London: Labour Party, 1937).

Lancaster Regionalism Group, *Localities, Class, and Gender* (London: Pion, 1985).

John Langton, 'The industrial revolution and the regional geography of England', *Transactions of the Institute of British Geographers*, 9 (1984): 145–67.

John Langton, 'South, North and nation: regional differences and consciousness in an integrating realm, 1550–1750', 112–44 in Alan R. H. Baker and Mark Billinge (eds), *Geographies of England. The North-South Divide, Material and Imagined* (Cambridge: CUP, 2004).

C. M. Law, *British Regional Development Since World War 1* (Newton Abbot: David & Charles, 1980).

William Lazonick, 'Public relations, labor productivity, and the choice of technique: British and U.S. cotton spinning', *Journal of Economic History*, XLI (1981): 491–516.

William Lazonick, 'The Cotton Industry', 18–50 in Bernard Elbaum and William Lazonick (eds), *The Decline of the British Economy* (Oxford: Clarendon, 1986).

Clive H. Lee, *British Regional Employment Statistics 1841–1971* (Cambridge: CUP, 1979).

Clive H. Lee, 'Regional growth and structural change in Victorian Britain', *Economic History Review*, 34 (1981): 438–52.

Clive. H. Lee, 'The service sector, regional specialization, and economic growth in the Victorian economy', *Journal of Historical Geography*, 10 (1984): 139–55.

Clive H. Lee, *The British Economy Since 1700: A Macroeconomic Perspective* (Cambridge: CUP, 1986).

Clive. H. Lee, *Scotland and the United Kingdom. The Economy and the Union in the Twentieth Century* (Manchester: Manchester U.P., 1995).

Clive H. Lee, 'Scotland 1850–1939: growth and poverty', 428–55 in Roderick Floud and Paul Johnson (eds), *The Cambridge Economic History of Britain. Volume 2: Economic Maturity, 1860–1939* (Cambridge: CUP, 2004).

C. E. V. Leser, 'Men and women in industry', *Economic Journal*, 62 (1952): 326–44.

Tim Leunig, 'New answers to old questions: explaining the slow adoption of ring spinning in Lancashire, 1880–1913', *Journal of Economic History*, 61 (2001): 439–66.

Sheila Lewenhak, *Women and Trade Unions* (London: E. Benn, 1977).

M. J. Lewis, 'The growth and development of Sheffield's business structure, 1880–1930', unpublished Ph.D. thesis, Sheffield City Polytechnic, 1989.

Roger Lloyd-Jones and M. J. Lewis, 'Business networks, social habits and the evolution of a regional industrial cluster: Coventry 1880s–1930s', 229–50 in John F. Wilson and Andrew Popp (eds), *Industrial Clusters and Regional Business Networks in England 1750–1970* (Aldershot: Ashgate, 2003).

Herbert Loebl, *Government Factories and the Origins of British Regional Policy, 1934–1948* (Aldershot: Avebury, 1988).

London Passenger Transport Board, *Report for Year Ended 30 June 1936* (London: London Passenger Transport Board, 1936).

London School of Economics *The New Survey of London Life and Labour. Volume II: London Industries I* (London: King, 1931).

London School of Economics, *The New Survey of London Life and Labour. Volume V: London industries II* (London: King, 1933).

London School of Economics, *The New Survey of London Life & Labour. Volume VI: Survey of Social Conditions (2) The Western Area* (London: King, 1934).

E. H. Lorenz, 'An evolutionary explanation for competitive decline: the British shipbuilding industry, 1890-1970', *Journal of Economic History*, 51 (1991): 911–35.

John Lowerson, 'Battles for the countryside', 258-80 in Frank Gloversmith (ed.), *Class, Culture and Social Change. A New View of the 1930s* (Brighton: Harvester, 1980).

W. F. Luttrell, *Factory Location and Industrial Movement. A Study of Recent Experience in Great Britain*, Volume II (London: NIESR, 1962).

D. Lyddon, 'Workplace organization in the British car industry. A critique of Johnathan Zeitlin', *History Workshop Journal*, XV (1983): 131–40.

Roy Macleod and Kay Macleod, 'War and economic development: government and the optical industry in Britain, 1914–18', 165–204 in J. M. Winter (ed.), *War and Economic Development. Essays in Memory of David Joslin* (Cambridge: CUP, 1975).

Ian McIntosh, *Ford at Trafford Park: 'An American Corner of Old Jog-trot England'*, Manchester Sociology Society Occasional Paper No. 30 (January 1991).

Angus Maddison, *Phases in Capitalist Development* (Oxford: Oxford U.P., 1982).

Peter Mandler, *The Fall and Rise of the Stately Home* (New Haven: Yale University Press, 1997).

A. Markusen, 'Sticky places in slippery space: a typology of industrial districts', *Economic Geography*, 72 (1996): 293–313.

Alfred Marshall, *Elements of Economics of Industry*, 4th edn. (London: Macmillan, 1907).

James Marshall, *The History of the Great West Road* (Hounslow: Heritage Publications, 1995).

G. L. Marson, 'Coventry: a study in urban geography', unpublished M.A. thesis, University of Liverpool, 1949.

J. E. Martin, 'Industry in inner London', *Town and Country Planning*, 24 (1957): 125–8.

J.E. Martin, *Greater London: An Industrial Geography* (Chicago: University of Chicago Press, 1966).

Ron Martin, 'The political economy of Britain's north-south divide', *Transactions of the Institute of British Geographers*, New Ser., 13 (1988): 389–418.

David Matless, *Landscape and Englishness* (London: Reaktion Books, 1998).

Karl Marx, *Capital*, Vol. 1 (London: Lawrence & Wishart, 1954).

William Mass and William Lazonick, 'The British cotton industry and international competitive advantage: the state of the debates', *Business History*, 32, 4 (1990): 9–65.

Doreen Massey, *Spatial Divisions of Labour. Social Structures and the Geography of Production* (London: Macmillan, 1984).

Philip Massey, 'The expenditure of 1,360 British middle-class households in 1938-39', *Journal of the Royal Statistical Society*, 105, 3 (1942): 159-96.

Peter Matthias, *Retailing Revolution. A History of Multiple Retailing in the Food Trades based upon the Allied Suppliers Group of Companies* (London: Longmans, 1967).

Peter Mathias, *The First Industrial Nation. An Economic History of Britain 1700–1914* (London: Methuen, 1969).

R.C.O. Matthews, C.H. Feinstein, and J.C. Odling-Smee, *British Economic Growth 1856–1973* (Oxford: Clarendon, 1982).

Stephen Merrett, *Owner-occupation in Britain* (London: Routledge & Kegan Paul, 1982).

Alix Meynell, 'Location of industry', *Public Administration*, 7 (1959): 9–20.

Ranald Michie, 'Options, concessions, syndicates, and the provision of venture capital, 1880–1913', *Business History*, 23 (1981): 147–64.

Ranald Michie, 'The finance of innovation in late Victorian and Edwardian Britain: possibilities and constraints', *Journal of European Economic History*, 17, 3 (1988): 491–530.

Roger Middleton, *Government Versus the Market. The Growth of the Public Sector, Economic Management and British Economic Performance, c. 1890–1979* (Cheltenham: Edward Elgar, 1996).

G. Mikoleit, 'Industrial restructuring and women's employment: the case of the food industry in inter-war Britain', unpublished M.Phil thesis, Polytechnic of the South Bank, 1986.

Ruth Milkman, 'Female factory labor and industrial structure: control and conflict over "woman's place" in auto and electrical manufacturing', *Politics and Society*, XII (1983): 159–203.

F. M. Miller, 'The unemployment policy of the National Government, 1931–1936', *Historical Journal*, 19 (1976): 453–76.

Mervyn Miller, *Letchworth: The First Garden City* (Chichester: Phillimore, 1989).

Alan S. Milward, *The Economic Effects of Two World Wars on Britain*, 2nd edn. (Houndmills: Macmillan, 1984).

C. L. Mowat, *Britain Between the Wars 1918–1940* (London: Methuen, 1955).

Robert Murphy, 'Oscar Deutsch', 89–93 in David Jeremy (ed.), *Dictionary of Business Biography*, Vol. 2 (London: Butterworths, 1984).

Harold Nancollis, *Foden. My Life with the Company* (Glossop: Venture, 1995).

David Nash and David Reeder (eds), *Leicester in the Twentieth Century* (Stroud: Sutton, 1993).

L. Nevard, 'The industrial estate – an instrument of social policy', unpublished M. Phil thesis, University of Southampton, 1972.

T. R. Nevett, *Advertising in Britain. A History* (London: Heinemann, 1982).

Lucy Newton, *The Victorian Economy in Transition: a Regional Perspective* (Aldershot: Ashgate, forthcoming).

Harold Nockolds, *Lucas: The First Hundred Years. Vol. I: The King of the Road* (Newton Abbot: David & Charles, 1976).

Nottingham Colwick Estate Ltd., *Britain's Best Industrial Sites* (Nottingham: Nottingham Colwick Estate Ltd, c. 1924).

Alan O'Day, 'Irish home rule and liberalism', 113–32 in A. O'Day (ed.), *The Edwardian Age: Conflict and Stability 1900–1914* (London: Macmillan, 1979).

Clifford O' Neil, '"The most magical corner in England": tourism, preservation and the development of the lake district, 1919–1939', Chapter 13 in John K. Walton (ed.), *Histories of Tourism: Representation, Identity and Conflict* (Clevedon: Channel View Press, forthcoming, 2005).

Andrzej Olechnowicz, *Working-class Housing in England Between the Wars: the Becontree Estate* (Oxford: Oxford U.P., 1997).

George Orwell, *The Lion and the Unicorn: Socialism and the English Genius* (London: Secker & Warburg, 1941).

George Orwell, *Coming up for Air* (London: Penguin, 2000).

A. D. K. Owen, 'The social consequences of industrial transference', *Sociological Review*, XXIX (1937): 331–54.

A. D. K. Owen, 'The social consequences of industrial transference: a rejoinder to Mr Michael Daly', *Sociological Review*, XXX (1938): 414–20.

T. Paish et. al., *The Book of Watford* (Watford: J. B. Nunn, 1987).

J.R. Parkinson, 'Shipbuilding', 79–102 in N. K. Buxton and D. H. Aldcroft (eds), *British Industry between the Wars: Instability and Industrial Development 1919–1939* (London: Scolar, 1979).

Mike Parsons and Mary B. Rose, *Invisible on Everest. Innovation and the Gear Makers* (Philadelphia: Northern Liberties Press, 2003).

Wayne Parsons, *The Political Economy of British Regional Policy* (London: Routledge, 1988).

E. W. Pasold, *Ladybird Ladybird: A story of Private Enterprise* (Manchester: MUP, 1977).

G. C. Peden, *The Treasury and Public Policy, 1906-1959* (Oxford: Oxford U.P., 2000).

Henry Pelling, *A History of British Trade Unionism*, 4th edn. (Harmondsworth: Penguin, 1987).

Percy Bilton Ltd., '*Twixt Green Fields & the City*': *Percy Bilton Model Factory Estates*, (London: Percy Bilton Ltd, c. 1937).

J. A. R. Pimlott, *The Englishman's Holiday. A Social History* (London: Faber and Faber, 1947).

Michael J. Piore and Charles F. Sabel, *The Second Industrial Divide: Possibilities for Prosperity* (New York: Basic Books, 1984).

D. E. Pitfield, 'Labour migration and the regional problem in Britain, 1920–1939', unpublished Ph.D thesis, University of Sterling, 1973.

D. E. Pitfield, 'The quest for an effective regional policy, 1934–37', *Regional Studies*, XII (1978), 429–43.

Alfred Plummer, *New British Industries in the Twentieth Century* (London: Pitman, 1937).

Political and Economic Planning, *Report on the British Coal Industry* (London: PEP, 1936).

Sidney Pollard, *A History of Labour in Sheffield* (Liverpool: Liverpool U.P., 1959).

Sidney Pollard, *The Development of the British Economy, 1914–1950* (London: Edward Arnold, 1962).

Sidney Pollard, *Britain's Prime and Britain's Decline. The British Economy 1870–1914* (London: Edward Arnold, 1989).

Sidney Pollard, *The Development of the British Economy 1914–1990* (London: Edward Arnold, 1992).

Sidney. Pollard (ed.), *The Gold Standard and Employment Policies between the Wars* (London: Methuen, 1970).

Andrew Popp, *Business Structure, Business Culture and the Industrial District. The Potteries, c. 1850–1914* (Aldershot: Ashgate, 2001).

J. H. Porter, 'Cotton and wool textiles', 25–47 in N. K. Buxton and D. H. Aldcroft (eds), *British Industry between the Wars: Instability and Industrial Development 1919–1939* (London: Scolar, 1979).

A. R. Pred, 'The intrametropolitan location of American manufacturing', *Annals of the Association of American Geographers*, 54, 2 (1964): 165–80.

J. B. Priestley, *English Journey* (London: Heinemann, 1934).

'Railways v. road transport', *The Commercial Motor*, 31 (10 August 1920): 714–15.

Alison Ravetz, *Council Housing and Culture. The History of a Social Experiment* (London: Routledge, 2001).

Goronwy Rees, *St. Michael. A History of Marks and Spencer* (London: Pan, 1969).

A. Renfrew, 'Mechanisation and the miner: work, safety and labour relations in the Scottish coal industry, c. 1890–1939', unpublished Ph.D thesis, University of Strathclyde, 1997.

Mary B. Rose, 'Investment in human capital and British manufacturing industry to 1990', 339–71 in M. W. Kirby and M. B. Rose (eds), *Business Enterprise in Modern Britain from the Eighteenth to the Twentieth Century* (London: Routledge, 1994).

Mary B. Rose, *Firms, Networks, and Business Values. The British and American Cotton Industries since 1750* (Cambridge: CUP, 2000).

Nathan Rosenberg, 'Technological change in the machine tool industry, 1840–1940', *Journal of Economic History*, 23, 4 (1963): 414–43.

S. A. Rosenthal and W. C. Strange, 'The determinants of agglomeration', *Journal of Urban Economics*, 50 (2001): 191–229.

R. E. Rowthorn and S. N. Solomou, 'The macroeconomic effects of overseas investment on the UK balance of trade, 1870–1913', *Economic History Review*, XLIV, 4 (1991): 654–64.

W. D. Rubinstein, *Capitalism, Culture, and Decline in Britain 1750–1990* (London: Routledge, 1993).

Mike Savage, 'Trade unionism, sex segregation, and the state: women's employment in 'new industries' in inter-war Britain', *Social History*, 13, 2 (1988): 209–30.

R. S. Sayers, 'The springs of technical progress in Britain, 1919–39', *Economic Journal*, LX (1950): 275–91.

D. Ian Scargill, 'Responses to Growth in Modern Oxford', 110–30 in R. C. Whiting (ed.) *Oxford: Studies in the History of a University Town since 1800* (Manchester: Manchester U.P., 1993).

A. J. Scott, 'Industrial organization and the logic of intra-metropolitan location: I theoretical considerations', *Economic Geography*, 59, 3 (1983): 233–50.

Peter Scott, 'Planning for profit: the garden city concept and private sector industrial estate development during the inter-war years', *Planning History*, 16 (1994): 9–15.

Peter Scott, *The Property Masters. A History of the British Commercial Property Sector* (London: Spon, 1996).

Peter Scott, 'British regional policy 1945–51: a lost opportunity', *Twentieth Century British History*, 8 (1997): 358–82.

Peter Scott, 'The location of early overseas multinationals in Britain, 1900–1939: patterns and determinants', *Regional Studies*, 32 (1998): 489–501.

Peter Scott, 'The growth of road haulage, 1921–58', *Journal of Transport History*, 19, 2 (1998): 138–55.

Peter Scott, 'The wolf at the door: the trade union movement and overseas multinationals in Britain during the 1930s', *Social History*, 23, 2 (1998): 195–210.

Peter Scott, 'Women, other "fresh" workers, and the new manufacturing workforce of interwar Britain', *International Review of Social History*, 45 (2000): 449-74.

Peter Scott, 'Path dependence and Britain's "coal wagon problem"', *Explorations in Economic History*, 38 (2001): 366–85.

Peter Scott, 'Industrial estates and British industrial development: 1897–1939', *Business History*, 43, 2 (2001): 73–98.

Peter Scott, The twilight world of interwar hire purchase', *Past & Present*, 177 (2002): 195–225.

Peter Scott, 'Selling Owner-occupation to the Working-classes in 1930s' Britain', University of Reading Economics and Management Discussion Paper 02304 (2004).

Peter Scott, 'Visible and invisible walls: suburbanisation and the social filtering of working-class communities in interwar Britain', University of Reading Economics and Management Discussion Paper O2404 (2004).

Peter Scott, 'Did owner-occupation lead to smaller families for interwar working-class households', University of Reading Economics and Management Discussion Paper 02504 (2004).

Peter Scott, 'Path dependence, fragmented property rights, and the slow diffusion of high throughput technologies in interwar British coal mining', *Business History*, 48 (2006), 18–36.

Peter Scott and Tim Rooth, 'Protectionism and the growth of overseas multinational enterprise in interwar Britain', *Journal of Industrial History*, 3, 2 (2000): 31–50.

Peter Scott and Peter Walsh, 'Patterns and determinants of manufacturing plant location in interwar London', *Economic History Review*, LVII, 1 (2004): 109–41.

Peter Scott and Peter Walsh, 'New manufacturing plant formation, clustering, and locational externalities in 1930s' Britain', *Business History*, 47, 2 (2005): 190–218.

Thomas Sharp, *An English Panorama*. Revised edn. (London: Architectural Press, 1950).

John Sheail, *Rural Conservation in Inter-War Britain* (Oxford: Clarendon, 1981).

J. Sheldrake and S. Vickerstaff, *The History of Industrial Training in Britain* (Aldershot: Avebury, 1987).

A. Shenfield and P. S. Florence, 'Labour for the war industries: the experience of Coventry', *Review of Economic Studies*, XII, 1 (1944–45): 31–49.

Peter Sloane, 'The structure of labour markets and low pay for women', 127–64 in Peter Sloane (ed.), *Women and Low Pay* (London: Macmillan, 1980).

Slough Estates Ltd, *London's New Industrial Centre* (Slough: Slough Estates Ltd, c. 1926).

Slough Estates Ltd, *The Slough Estates Journal*, Vol. 2, 16 (1930): 449.

Slough Estates Ltd, *Slough, London's Industrial Centre* (Slough: Slough Estates Ltd, c. 1934).

Slough Estates Ltd, *Slough. London's Industrial Centre of 600 Acres* (Slough: Slough Estates Ltd, c. 1938).

D. H. Smith, *The Industries of Greater London* (London: King, 1933).

E. D. Smithies, 'The contrast between north and south in England 1918–1939: a study of economic, social and political problems with particular reference to the experience of Burnley, Halifax, Ipswich, and Luton', unpublished Ph.D. thesis, University of Leeds, 1974.

Humphrey Southall, 'The origins of the depressed areas: unemployment, growth and regional economic structure in Britain before 1914', *Economic History Review*, XLI (1988): 236–58.

George Speight, 'Who bought the inter-war semi? the socio-economic characteristics of new-house buyers in the 1930s', University of Oxford Discussion Paper in Economic and Social History No. 38 (2000).

Margaret Stacey, *Tradition and Change: a Study of Banbury* (Oxford: Oxford U.P, 1960).

B. Staines, 'The movement of population from South Wales with specific reference to the effects of the industrial transference scheme, 1928–37', 237–50 in C. Baber and L. J. Williams (eds), *Modern South Wales: Essays In Economic History* (Cardiff: University of Wales Press, 1986).

G. W. Sturges, *Edmonton: Past and Present* (London: Montagu School Press, 1941).

Barry Supple, *The History of the British Coal Industry. Volume 4. 1913–1946: The Political Economy of Decline* (Oxford: Clarendon, 1987).

Barry Supple, 'The political economy of demoralization: the state and the coalmining industry in America and Britain between the wars', *Economic History Review*, XLI (1988): 566–91.

A. J. Taylor, 'Labour productivity and technological innovation in the British coal industry, 1850–1914', *Economic History Review*, XIV (1961): 48–67.

E. G. R. Taylor, 'Discussion of the Geographical Distribution of Industry', *Geographical Journal*, 92 (1938): 22–39.

Harvey Taylor, *A Claim on the Countryside. A History of the British Outdoor Movement* (Edinburgh: Keele U.P., 1997).

'The Development of Hayes', *Middlesex and Buckinghamshire Advertiser* (16 February 1907): 5.

Brinley Thomas, 'The movement of labour into South-East England 1920–32', *Economica*, I (May 1934): 220–41.

Brinley Thomas, 'The influx of Labour into London and the South East 1920–36', *Economica*, IV (1937): 323–36.

Brinley Thomas, 'The influx of labour into the Midlands 1920–37', *Economica*, V (1938): 410–34.

Mark Thomas, 'The macro-economics of the interwar years', 320–58 in R. Floud and D. McCloskey (eds), *The Economic History of Britain since 1700. Volume 2: 1860–1939*, 2nd edn (Cambridge: CUP, 1994).

W. A. Thomas, *The Finance of British Industry 1918–1976* (London: Methuen, 1978).

Times Trade and Engineering Supplement (October 1935): 24.

Stephen Tolliday, 'Steel and rationalization policies, 1918–1950', 82–108 in B. Elbaum and W. Lazonick (eds), *The Decline of the British Economy* (Oxford: Clarendon, 1986).

Trafford Park Estates Ltd, *Trafford Park. Past and Present. And Ship Canal Guide* (Manchester: Trafford Park Estates Ltd, 1902).

Trafford Park Estates Ltd., *Trafford Park, Sites for Works* (Manchester: Trafford Park Estates Ltd, 1915).

G. L. Turnbull, *Traffic and Transport: an Economic History of Pickfords* (London: Allen & Unwin, 1979).

Thorstein Veblen, *Imperial Germany and the Industrial Revolution* (London: Macmillan, 1915).

G. N. Von Tunzelmann, 'Structural change and leading sectors in British manufacturing 1907–68', 1–49 in Charles P. Kindleberger and Guido di Tella (eds), *Economics in the Long View: Essays in Honour of W. W. Rostow* (London: Macmillan, 1982).

Jane Walsh, *Not Like This* (London: Lawrence & Wishart, 1953).

John K. Walton, *The British Seaside. Holidays and Resorts in the Twentieth Century* (Manchester: Manchester U.P., 2000).

John K. Walton, *Lancashire. A Social History 1558–1939* (Manchester: Manchester U.P., 2002).

James Walvin, *Passage to Britain: Immigration in British History and Politics* (Harmondsworth: Pelican, 1984).

Stephen V. Ward, *The Geography of Interwar Britain: The State and Uneven Development* (London: Routledge, 1988).

K. Warren, 'Iron and steel', 103–28 in N. K. Buxton and D. H. Aldcroft (eds), *British Industry Between the Wars: Instability and Industrial Development 1919–1939* (London: Scolar, 1979).

Noel Whiteside, 'The social consequences of interwar unemployment', 17–30 in Sean Glynn and Alan Booth, *The Road to Full Employment* (London: Allen & Unwin, 1987).

R. C. Whiting, *The View from Cowley: The Impact of Industrialisation upon Oxford, 1918–1939* (Oxford: Clarendon, 1983).

Kevin Whitston, 'Worker resistance and Taylorism in Britain', *International Review of Social History*, XLII (1997): 1–24.

M. T. Wild, 'The Yorkshire wool textile industry', in J. G. Jenkins (ed.), *The Wool Textile Industry in Great Britain* (London: Routledge and K. Paul, 1972).

Mira Wilkins & Frank Ernest Hill, *American Business Abroad: Ford on Six Continents* (Detroit: Wayne State University Press, 1964).

G. W. Williams, 'From grand slam to great slump: economy, society and rugby football in Wales during the depression', *Welsh History Review* 11 (1983): 338–57.

O. E. Williamson, 'Transactions cost Economics', in R. Schmalensee and R. D. Willig (eds), *Handbook of Industrial Organisation*, Vol. 1 (Amsterdam: North-Holland, 1989).

D. G. Wolton (ed.), *Trading Estates: a Review of the Development of Planned Factory Units Throughout Great Britain* (London: Burrow, 1938).

J. You. and F. Williamson, 'Competition and co-operation: toward understanding industrial districts', *Review of Political Economy*, 6 (1994): 259–78.

Terence Young, *Becontree and Dagenham*. (London: Becontree Social Survey Committee, 1934).

Jonathan Zeitlin, 'The Emergence of shop steward organization and job control in the British car industry: a review essay', *History Workshop Journal*, X (1980): 121–37.

Jonathan Zeitlin, 'Workplace militancy: a rejoinder', *History Workshop Journal*, XVI (1983): 131–6.

Index

www.ingramcontent.com/pod-product-compliance
Lightning Source LLC
LaVergne TN
LVHW011112300926
849160LV00008B/359
* 9 7 8 1 1 3 8 3 5 8 5 1 5 *